The Ordinary Man's Guide to the History of Information Technology
Computing History

By

Lawrence H. Hardy

Lawrence Hardy

Copyright

Another Ordinary Man

DEDICATION

I dedicate this book to the memory of my brother Michael L. Hardy
1953—2007, who was a self-taught computer scientist.

CONTENTS

Copyright	ii
DEDICATION	iv
ACKNOWLEDGMENTS	ix
About the author	xi
Prefaces	xiii
Introduction	1
The Beginnings	9
Early Devices	15
The First Calculators	19
Calculating Engines	33
The Gilded Age	47
Cash Registers, Typewriters, and Tabulators	66
A Brief History of Electricity	85
Twentieth Century Pioneers	119
Kinds of Computers	136
Computer Architecture	165
Operating Systems	183
Programming Languages	192
Memory	204
African American Pioneers	211
Networks	229
Network Cables	264
Network Equipment	268

Wireless Networking   277

Wide area Networks   289

TCP/IP   294

Malware   301

Network Security   317

The Future of Computing   321

Works Cited   339

Index   364

Index of Graphics   370

ACKNOWLEDGMENTS

- John Wolff of the John Wolff's Web Museum (Melbourne Australia) for permission to use photographs of the Burroughs Adding Machine, c. 1910, and the Felt & Tarrant Comptometer Model J, c. 1930

- Peggy A. Kidwell Curator of Technology at Smithsonian Institution for the use of the Baldwin Pinwheel Calculator, Burroughs Registering Accountant, the Standard Model B Adding Machine, 1907; Moon–Hopkins Billing Machine, and the Dalton Adding Machine.

- Stacy L. Fortner at the IBM Archives Reference Desk for emailing photographs of vintage digital calculators

- The IBM Corporation Corporate Archives for allowing access to online archives for access to the IBM 1401, the Hahn and Leupold calculators, the early IBM PC model, the Hill Arithmometer, the Thomas Arithmometer, the Hollerith Tabulator, various displays of printed circuit boards, vacuum tubes, integrated circuit, and microprocessors.

- The National Archives at College Park, Maryland provided access to the images of the Dorr E. Felt Macaroni Box, the Victor Schilt adding machine and the Sholes, Glidden, and Soule typewriter circa 1868

- The United States Patent Office Sketches of Baldwin Pinwheel Calculator

- All photos not included in the above categories were available through the courtesy of Wikimedia, public domain or in government public domain files. The files include Grid Compass, Osborne 1, the Cooke & Wheatstone telegraph, the Step Reckoner, the Thomas Arithmometer, the ENIAC, the Sholes Typewriter Circa 1878, the Calculating Clock, and

Volta Battery, Star, Token Ring, and Bus network architectures. I created all charts of historical data with knowledge of cyber and human history.

- I created all charts of historical data with knowledge of cyber and human history. This is copyrighted material registered with United States Copyright Office October 2010.

About the author

I shall begin by telling you my career as a writer began when Margherita Pagani (Bocconi University, Italy) asked me to write an article for her second edition of her Encyclopedia of Multimedia Technology and Networking published by IGI-Global. Before that, I had considered my writing academic rather than commercial, even though I wrote over 60 graduate essays on information technology and education.

This project taught me how difficult it is to write a book even on such staid and concrete subjects as computer history. When I began this project October 7, 2007, there was an ongoing debate among computer enthusiasts over which was the best operating system Linux, Windows, or Apples IOS. The debate became more complicated when Microsoft introduced Windows 7 sending Windows XP and Windows Vista the way of the dodo bird.

Since September of 2007, Microsoft has introduced a newer version of its Windows operating system, Windows 8 and later 8.1. The advent of Windows 7 signals the end of Windows XP (April 2014). Unlike Windows XP, Microsoft made Windows 8 to takes advantage of cell phone technology. Windows 8 sends Windows 7 to the La Brea Tar Pits. A funny thing happened on the upgrade to Windows 9, Windows 10. By the fall of 2015, Windows 8.1 will follow Windows 7 to the tar pits.

Why this discussion necessary, Linux is does not exploit cell phone technology. Apple IOS is the trailblazer of COS on cell phone. Apple has been so successful with portable devices it dropped the word computers from its name to emphasize its focus on consumer electronics.

Another reason for writing this book is to overcome the grief of my brother's sudden death. Finally, I wrote this book because the computer has always fascinated me ever since I was a child watching the science fiction motion picture The Forbidden Planet. I marveled at the Hollywood interpretation of artificial intelligence in Robbie the Robot and giant the Krell computer that transformed the ideal into reality. Robots and artificial intelligence fascinated me so much, that I read about robots as much as much as I could, however reality has a way of crashing to Earth unexpectedly.

My introduction to a real-world predecessor began with the abacus when I was a third grader at Washington Elementary School in Maywood, Illinois. As it happened, a guest lecturer, a woman, from the Chicago Museum of Natural History displayed a very strange looking contraption she called an abacus. At the special assembly, she commanded she challenged the entire third grade: She said she could add or multiply faster with the abacus than any child could with paper and pencil. No matter what number we decided to use, her abacus moved faster than our number 2 pencils. After about 15 minutes or so, the ninety or so third graders had surrendered. The woman with the strange looking contraption had won.

What are my credentials? I have an undergraduate degree in social sciences from the University of Colorado. I earned my Colorado Teacher credentials from Regis University. I have a degree from Lesley College Graduate School of Education. The focus of my studies, manage and integrate computers and computer networks into the classroom curricula. I have a Master of Science from Capella University emphasis on Information Technology Management of computer networks with either Microsoft or Cisco Systems. I have also taken teaching license renewal classes in educational technology from Loyola University of Los Angeles and the University of Phoenix. Finally, I worked as tier one help desk as part of the USPS call center for five years.

Prefaces

When I first started writing this book, it was intended as a tribute to my late brother Michael. However, as I struggled to understand why African Americans like I cannot find employment in the computer industry. With the anger expressed, the remainder of this book is a response to the initial offering of *The Ordinary Man's Guide to the History of Information Technology*. It has expanded sections on African American history with computers, women, networking, difference engines, kinds of computers, and computer architecture. It is a more robust book than the first. In this book, I have written about several technologies that expand the subject but are not necessarily in historical order.

With a profit in mind and the customer's sense of value, I began again, this time after a thorough search of term papers from both undergraduate studies and as a graduate school; I had enough material to begin anew. The second version of the text was more extensive, covering computing milestones from the Stone Age to the building of the first quantum computer. The second edition was doomed from the start. The word processor I used for the second edition came straight from the twilight zone, Microsoft Word 2010. Both the spell checker and grammar style checker faulted at 25000 words. It corrected needlessly.

Consequently, each edition seems to be filled with errors of all kind from basic grammar to false parallelism. To compensate, I began to look for ancient grammar and style checker once found on shareware sites of Commodore 128 and the old Intel 286 I owned in the 1990s.

To my dismay, the 2010 version was no better than the 2007. So, I spent another six months making corrections. Do not ever bet the fact you are a writer on a typing test. On the typing test, I clocked out at 56 words per minute. The typing test is 5 minutes long. Writing a book can last ten years. No, it is not a fair measure of one's story telling talents.

To add authenticity to my research, I wrote curators at the Smithsonian Institution, the National Archives, and the IBM archives to obtain addition information and license to copyrighted photographs of mechanical adding machines not under public domain. IBM granted privileges to all photographs still under copyright protection without restriction and sent me several high-resolution photographs. Ergo, I did not use any of the material offered by John Wolff of Australia even though he had granted the same with his extensive library.

When it came to the actual writing of the third version, like everyone writing about the history of computers, I started with Charles Babbage the high priest of computing history. The input, output, processing, and control of his Analytical Engine coincided with the computer architecture prescribed by John von Neumann, more than a century later, as the necessary components for the electronic computers. A funny thing, though Babbage is the high priest of modern computing little is known about the pioneers—Wiberg and Grant—who overcame the technical problems that befuddled Babbage.

A close second to Babbage is Herman Hollerith (IBM), the second father of the modern computer. Between the two, more articles about computing history been written about computing than any other person or subject including Bill Gates, Steve Jobs and Thomas J. Watson, the real force behind Hollerith's IBM.

This book is divided into two sections. In the first section, the conversation clearly surrounds the progression of the calculator from pre-historic drawings to the invention of the personal computer by Steve Jobs and Mark Dean. The first discussion examines how mechanical solutions were not sufficient. Then each step in the domestication of electromagnetism demonstrated how information could be transferred, saved, and manipulated. Finally, Atanasoff and Berry combined all the disparate strands into the computer.

Part 2 dwells upon computer networks popularized by the internet researchers like Dr. Philip Emeagwali. Emeagwali envision the first supercomputer by connecting more than 65,000 microprocessors together in one location. Researchers took Emeagwali idea and connected the processors remotely.

To understand how computers and computers relate one must understand, a computer is a standalone miniature network. The microprocessor communicates to all parts of the computer, the screen, the mouse, the printer, the sound card, and so forth. I take you to examine the first 19th century computer, the Hollerith Tabulating Machine. All it could do was read computer tabulating cards the idea of the network become clearer as the technicians add a set of dials and a printer.

No discussion of the rudiments of the Internet is complete without a discussion of the beginning of telegraphy in the 19th century with Samuel Morse and the Morse code. The telegraph demonstrates domestication of electricity makes it possible to communicate over several miles with the aid of a mechanical device such as a locomotive or automobile.

It is safe to say no one has yet to reproduce the Chappe optical telegraph in miniature in the same manner the telegraph was miniaturized. Given the relationship between infrared, microwave, laser and radio—all are forms of electromagnetism. Some have tried to create an optical computer in the late 1980's and early 1990s at the University of Colorado. The closest scientists have come to capturing the power of light is with fiber optics. The United States Navy has made progress in making the laser cannon.

Another variation to the computer network, once limited to the business environment, is the dual core processor. Networking on the small scale instead of linking two distinct microprocessors, in which case the case with the server; engineers linked two processor cores on the same chip.

The final step in reducing the enormous to the minute occurs in the field of biotechnology where scientists program squadrons of Nano robots or nanobots to attack viruses and tumors restoring health to the human body. Science hopes to miniaturize the huge machines used to irradiate cancer.

This work represents the culmination of my master of science in computer technology management. In the beginning, I compiled all my graduate papers. It became more when I realized the reports lacked a thorough explanation of Babbage, ENIAC, or Hollerith. As I progressed through the writing, I began to understand the difficulties encountered writing computers. When I began this project September 27, 2007, the ongoing debate among computer enthusiasts centered on which operating system users preferred. On one side, the proponents of the new operating system, Microsoft Windows Vista, I characterize these people as the corporate journalists with the million dollar syndication contracts. They would say anything to make a dollar and to get their opinions and names in print or on television.

On the other side of the champions of the older operating system, Microsoft Windows XP system, these people, I characterized as the home office types, business owners, working on shoestring budgets, wringing green tea from a greenback and expecting fifteen cents change. They are not paid for their opinions. They were just glad their company exists and turns a small profit.

Since September of 2007, Microsoft introduced an even newer version of its Windows Vista operating system, Windows 7. The advent of Windows 7 signaled the end of Windows XP (April 2014) and the end of the debate. Unlike Windows XP, Microsoft made Windows 7 to take advantage of the new Intel 64-bit microprocessors based on the multi-tile architecture.

What does it all mean? Besides the fact, Windows XP is going the way of the dinosaur. It articulates s a new direction for microprocessors. Look for a completely new generation of microprocessors that venture away from the serialized processing based on the Von Neumann four-cycle machines.

To make the original argument moot, Microsoft Corporation has issued two more versions of Windows, Windows 8, and Windows 8.1. Windows 8 ended Windows Vista likewise Windows 8.1 spelled the end for Windows 7. Many pundits say Windows 8 is an abomination. I found it very easy to use. It does not follow the interface established first with Windows 95. Instead, Windows 8 and 8.1 takes Windows-Intel computing in a new direction, the age of the tablet computer. One must remember the Windows key on the keyboard is a toggle switch that transfers you from the start page to a Windows 7 like environment.

If you installed Windows 8.1, this paradigm is more apparent. Keep in mind there is an arrow pointing towards the bottom of the screen in the lower left corner of the screen. By clicking or touching the arrow, you are taken to 8.1 environment that lists all the programs and apps on your computer. If one right clicks the mouse, one is given the opportunity to place the app or program on the start screen of the computer. I use Outlook, Word, and Excel often, so I placed on those applications on the start screen.

The detractors of Windows 8 have won, the new Windows 10 operating system is a cross platform system that does not forget the mouse and keyboard computer users. As mentioned before Windows 8.1 joins Windows 3.1, Windows 95, Windows 98, XP, Vista, and Windows 7 in the La Brea Tar Pits.

If you start an app and want to run a second app or program simultaneously, there is a plus logo on the lower right corner. If the plus logo is not visible, click the ellipsis logo. You will then be able to add tabs and run apps simultaneously.

This book is the conclusion to my first book The *Ordinary Man's Guide to Computer Science/Computer History*. It takes the reader beyond the confines of the desktop or laptop computer and examines network computing. In that section, I discuss everything from TCP/IP to the several incarnation of the Ethernet. I took the information directly from what I had learned studying the varying implementation strategies from a LAN.

During the first drafts, the book was concerned only with all I had learned about the history of computing. However, after writing and rewriting the text, before the discovery of the template, I realized this would not make a single volume. Several ingredients in the making of the computer were omitted from of similar books. For example, few writers of computer history discussed the contributions of Thomas Edison, Alexander Graham Bell, and Nikola Tesla. Still fewer discussed the contributions of African American inventors Granville Woods and Lewis Latimer let alone Mark Dean or John Henry Thompson and Phillip Emeagwali. I also added a section on pioneering women in computer technology.

There was just too much information to consider and I still had to start the discussion about the precursors of the modern network the telegraph and the telephone.

I hope you enjoy and comeback for more. I will be authoring a novel featuring time travel based on computer technology in the not too distant future. If you have a bone of contention over historical fact, please email me at mrhhardy@msn.com, subject line "ordinary man." If you wish to communicate about the book using any other subject line, you message will be sent to junk mail.

I hope my readers do not feel cheated; this is actually the third of three books. Books 1 and 2 are the two volumes separated, this the last combines the best of the previous two versions. Book Two, was simply too short.

I start my writing career in earnest, my first fiction will be semibiographical, and if you know me then you will recognize the events. If you do not know me, do not be surprised about my view of the world. Look for the Look Around in Anger in November 2014.

PART ONE

THE CALCULATING DEVICES
&
ELECTRICITY

1

Introduction

Traditional literature produced by computer scientists studying the history of computing devices, tends to divide or classify these ancient and antique calculating machines into eras or ages based upon the construction material of the machine. The division of the machines by construction material serves the purpose of suggesting a possible time frame in which the device was created. It also suggests that devices made of similar materials have similar purposes. By the same notion, the classification of computing devices by construction materials does little to determine the complexity or the necessity mandating the creation of the calculator. The five generally accepted ages or computing eras are Flesh Era, the Wood Era, the Metal Era, the Electromechanical, and the Electronic Era (Williams M. R., 2000, pg. 2).

The construction materials method of classification is similar to a method employed by archeologist and anthropologist to classify the technological development of ancient civilizations; Bronze Age and Iron Age are examples. It does little to examine symbiotic relationship between the cognitive enterprise and technological innovation. For this reason, I will use material's classification as a general framework for my study and not as a strict guideline. I will try to follow human ingenuity and innovation based on necessity and other social dynamics. To that purpose, this book includes a chapter on devices constructed to use electricity, an essential ingredient in modern digital computing.

In addition to the chapter on electricity, I have also included a chapter discussing alternative computing devices more specifically the cash register and the tabulating machine. Each variant when considered alone does little to aid in the comprehension of the modern digital computer's internal mechanisms or how the technology contributing to its implementation. In contrast, when one considers the overall complexity of the modern digital computer one must then realize, for example, how the telegraph contributed, as primitive as it is, two important ingredients to computing.

First, the telegraph demonstrates how electricity can be altered to send messages. Second, it demonstrates how to establish communications networks. This is a relevant point given the fact that a computer is a communications network unto itself, sending messages back and forth between the central processing unit and memory, from the keyboard to monitor to printer or from the keyboard to hard drive. The parallel is endless because of the innumerable methods the CPU uses to communicate with the other components of the computer. So, instead of confining the modern computer to the narrow definition of the Analytical Engine created by Charles Babbage—categorically accepted as the father of modern computing. We grace this study with a bit of diversity exploring the telegraph, Morse code, electricity, and the eccentricities of Nikola Tesla. Each variation breathes a little more life into what otherwise would have been a very dull book discussing metal computing tools.

Let us begin our journey through time by analyzing the sequencing of events according to materials: First, the Flesh Era of computing era of computing is a critical stage in the development of cognitive thinking in pre-historic humans. Unfortunately, there are no artifacts left to confirm my hypothesis about its conclusions. (One can observe children learning to count using their fingers.) The Flesh Era forced humans to develop language and writing to comprehend complex ideas and to present their ideas. The first extension of the hands and fingers were the written symbols. The scratches on the ground and on the walls of caves represent birth of the language and writing. The Flesh era did not occur overnight. It took thousands of years to accumulate the knowledge to coordinate spoken words with graphic symbols.

The Wood Era follows the Flesh Era in the study of human computing. The Wood Era created the foundation for the development of the rough mechanical calculating devices. These crude wooden devices were in all likelihood based on the hash marks found on the tally stick. Other wooden calculating instruments were the Salamis Tablet, Napier Bones, the yardstick, and the slide rule. The Wood Era did produced the two significant calculator breakthroughs in calculating machine technology—the abacus and the Calculating Clock.

The abacus invented about the fourth century AD was significant because it provided a means of representing numbers concretely. Another important calculator developed during the Wood Era was the first desktop calculator, the Calculating Clock of Wilhelm Schickard. I disagree with the materials classification method, which classified the Calculating Clock as a Wood Era device simply because of its construction materials. The Napier Bones, which the Calculating Clock superseded and manipulated, was of the Wood Era. The Calculating Clock on the other hand is far more though provoking. It exhibited all the attributes of the subsequent Metal Age calculator. It utilized buttons, levers, and keys to produce a digital solution. A concept that is totally unlike any other calculating device designed in the Wood Era that includes the abacus and the slide rule.

After the Wood Era came the Metal Era in the development of computing devices. It began in the 17th century, at approximately the same time Blaise Pascal built the Pascaline. The Pascaline was a crude chain-driven adding machine operated by means of dials and a stylus. Gottfried Wilhelm Leibniz admired the technology of Pascaline then created the Step Reckoner. Leibniz originally intended for the Step Reckoner to be an improvement over the Pascaline designing it to be capable of adding, multiplying, dividing, and subtracting; unfortunately, he failed.

After the Leibniz, failure came the most enduring of the Metal Age computing devices the Thomas Arithmometer. Charles Xavier Thomas of France invented it in 1822. The Thomas was long lasting because it was compact, portable, and capable of performing the four arithmetic functions. It had wide-ranging appeal because Thomas had the forethought to license the patent to numerous other companies to develop, improve, and manufacture the calculator. Consequently, the Thomas was also known as the TIM, the Archimedes, the Unitas, and the Peerless. Charles Xavier Thomas based his Arithmometer on the failed 17th century stepped drum technology imagined by Leibniz.

Sales of the Thomas-like calculators does not diminish until the arrival of the pinwheel calculators of Baldwin and Odhner in 1879, and then more rapidly with the arrival of the keyboard calculators. Even after the impact those innovations, the Thomas, and other stepped drum calculators, continued to capture a modest share of the calculator market until after World War I. The Thomas ceased to be a viable alternative to keyboard calculators after the introduction of the electric powered for calculators. Mechanical step drum calculators are still sold. The most popular step drum is the Curta.

By the late 19th century, society in both Europe and the Americas flourished as the Second Industrial Age spreads. The Second Industrial Age also produced the Robber Barons—a ruthless group of men and women with such extravagant wealth they seem beyond the reproach of law. The Robber Barons not only exploited oil, steel, and the railroad industries their influence reached the calculator industry. The atmosphere of business created by the Robber Barons manifested in the manner Burroughs, Brunsviga, NCR, and Remington-Rand dominated the final decades of the metal calculator era stifling competition by either eliminating competitors or purchasing a controlling interest of the competitors. Despite the pressure from the Robber Barons, of all the Gilded Age companies that began strictly as a manufacturer of calculators, only Burroughs and to a lesser extent Remington-Rand survived to compete in the Information Age.

The Electromechanical Era followed the Metal Era. Besides a technological succession, the Electromechanical Era gave rise to the Information Age in the form of the Hollerith punch cards. The punch cared created crude flat-file databases to replace the printed tape of the calculators. The Electromechanical Era began in 1887 during the height of the Metal Era calculators. The catalyst that spurred the Electromechanical Era was the logistics crisis encountered by the United States Census Bureau.

The first commercially successful electromechanical tabulating machine was the brainchild of Herman Hollerith who formed the Hollerith Tabulating Machine. HTM under the guidance of Hollerith controlled a very large portion of the tabulating machine industry during the early years of the Electromechanical Era. HTM laid the framework for the multinational conglomerate International Business Machines

4

Corporation (IBM). Thomas J. Watson succeeded Hollerith and managed IBM from 1924 to 1952. Under Watson's leadership, IBM became an economic world power. Other inventors and industrialists making significant contributions to the evolution of the computer during the electromechanical age were Konrad Zuse, George Stibitz, and Howard Aiken.

Following the Electromechanical Era was the Electronic Era. This age began with the invention of the Atanasoff-Berry Computer (ABC) in 1939 and ENIAC in 1946. At first, the change from electromechanical to electronic computing had little significance in the business world. Early electronic systems were predicated and dependent upon punch card technology developed in the previous era. IBM with Watson with Thomas J. Watson at the helm followed the business model status quo established by Hollerith, nee James Patterson of NCR. If IBM could not sell a company a computer, it rented the computer to the company along with punch cards and accessories. In the early years, this was both a blessing and a curse for IBM. It made clients entirely dependent on IBM for service and maintenance; it also created niche-computing markets for IBM competitors.

After launching it first series of electronic computers, the System 700 series, IBM dominated the world market manufacturing several computer models: 7000, 1401, 1600, and system 360. In the 1950s and 1960s, it was not uncommon in the computer industry to refer to IBM as the elephant in the dining room.

The classification of computing machines by the materials method is similar to a timeline. However, two exceptions contradict these (Hashagen and Rojas 2002) assumptions. The first exception is the Antikythera device. It is made of metal. It was invented more than thousand years before the Calculating Clock of Schickard. Although the Antikythera device is an analog solution to the nautical problems, it is never the less is regard as the first recorded evidence of a computing machine.

The second exception is the Schickard Calculating Clock. It is an exception because it is clearly a digital computing device and not an analog computing device like the slide rule of the Wood Era. It does not function as a ruler, slide rule, sextant, or other Wood Era devices. Instead, much like the Antikythera device, it utilizes a format common to the Metal Era.

The practice of dividing technologies is not obligatory in the history of computing literature but convenient. For example, three books used as references in the bibliography of this text:
1. The Universal History of Computing,
2. Computers the Story of a Technology, and
3. Computing Before Computers.

The author or authors, with the exception of Ifrah, performed a cursory acknowledgement of generational computing technologies, which included mathematics. Ifrah like me divided technologies according to innovation. The other two books divided computing devices according to materials.

In the first book, The Universal History of Computing the author alludes to the development of writing and counting as individually different in nomenclature. Mr. Ifrah implies that writing is a cognitive skill where phonetic sounds are associated with symbols. Numerology, on the other hand, is more structured and required deeper cognitive skills and comprehension. I differ, from Ifrah on this point. The concept that the acquisition of language and the acquisition of number are different is exotic. Perhaps his suppositions were based on the comprehension of algebra or calculus.

The comprehension of numbers is an extension of language acquisition and is learned by the child in the same manner as he or she learned the alphabet. I based that opinion on six years of graduate school and ten years of teaching. The social historians and the developmental cognitivists tell me the prehistoric people are re-experienced in the lives of children as they maturate. Each child in their own manner learn in a matter of months what it took the prehistoric people thousands of years to construct, a language, and number system. We humans, unlike the ancients, have an oral and written tradition that compensates for the instinctual trial and error learning of Cro-Magnon and Neanderthal. Classic and uncomplicated examples of number acquisition are found in conundrums and nursery rhymes *One Two, Buckle My Shoe,* and *This Old Man.*

Nursery rhymes are perfect examples of children creating numbers vocally and mentally in the same manner; they created the alphabet before grasping the full details of writing. The child acquires language by listening to parents, siblings then compares the sounds with observed actions and responses. Socialization of the child is accomplished in a similar manner by comparing the social morals of the home against the moral values of the group.

In the other two reference texts taken from the bibliography, neither author strives to adhere to the strict parameters of the material's method of classifying computing technology or on cognitive elements of human learning. First Swedin and Ferro, list a timeline of technological accomplishments. Then proceed to outline the major computing accomplishments of the previous generations. The two authors concentrate the exploration on the history of computing after the invention of ABC and ENIAC examining software, integrated circuits, and networking.

Finally, the third reference, which can be found online as well as in the library or in the stock of an online retailer, is Computers Before Computing edited by William Aspray. It is remarkable. This is not traditional exposition. It is a collaboration of the leading historians and computer scientist of the era of Mr. Aspray. This volume is a depth study of computing and the computing eras just prior to the transistor in 1945.

The remaining pages of this book transcribe a (not a concordance) history of computing milestones from the early analogs to present day. Unlike authors before me who have written the history of computers and calculating machines, I make no pretense of altruism for the development of the machines. Very little in the way of altruism, manifests itself in the history of computers with the exception of Pascal creating the adding machine for his father and Vannevar Bush's patriotism during the outbreak of World War II.

At first, this book was to contain all I had learned about the history of computing. However, after writing for a year, I realized I could not make a single volume. The first draft was more than two hundred pages and I was only to Edison. There was just too much information to consider in networking even though we touched upon it with discussions of the telegraph and the telephone. However, those discussions are not comprehensive. This book is the first of two volumes the first volume is called Two Chapters from The Ordinary Man's Guide to the History of Information Technology. The second volume is A Brief History of Computing. Volume 1 addresses the development of computing devices from the Salamis counting boards and the abacus through the modern personal computer. Volume 2 examines the technology and history of the Internet.

I hope you enjoy and comeback for more. I will be authoring a novel featuring time travel based on computer technology in the not too distant future. If you have a bone of contention over historical fact, please email me at mrhhardy@live.com, subject line "ordinary man." I imagine many of you will. The truth of the matter is, I am not the world's greatest typist, and the Microsoft Word spellchecker has its limitations. Added to the fact, I can no longer get to MSC to hire a typist. So! If you find an error, please notify me.

2

The Beginnings

The renowned reverend Herman Melville wrote, "…We cannot live for ourselves alone. Our lives are connected by a thousand invisible threads, and along these sympathetic fibers, our actions run as causes and return to us as results… (Voigt, 2010)"

The idea of writing words and numbers connect the thousand invisible threads of human activity described in the Melville quotation. Each connection coincides with our intrinsic need to communicate, congregate, and understand the world around us. The need to congregate is an instinctual trait found in animal as well as human proliferation. It also serves as the primary protection against predators and extinction. When humans developed language, it fulfilled an innate psychological need to describe the surrounding world and build emotional attachments. That corresponds directly to the modern pedagogical theories of human development. Infants like our primitive predecessors, instinctively learned language to explain their surroundings and establish emotional attachments.

The earliest evidence of a written form of communication dates back more than 25,000 years to the cave drawings of early humans and Neanderthals recounting their hunts for food. The ancient symbols of the boar, the bison, the star, and the earth found on the cave walls of Europe, Africa, and Asia represented the first strands of primitive writing. As primitive beings accepted the phonetic sounds for the boar, the bison, the star, and the earth, it marked the seminal beginnings of a formal writhing language and numeration (Robertson, 2004, p. 18–22). How many parents have washed the crayon cats, dogs, and trees off the walls before the child learned to write?

Anthropologist estimate—around 5300 BC—the beginnings of written languages coincide with humans transitioning from nomadic hunter-gatherer lifestyles to permanent settlements. For prehistoric societies, written languages were a not only for ciphering, it was necessity to avoid conflict. There was no medicine. A warrior getting injured during battle meant death from blood loss or infection. Written language let the tribal chieftains and heads of families set up treaties.

The pictographs once celebrating the hunt now represent the pathways to peace. The figures represent the boundaries of a homeland, the size of animal herds, and the size of the grain fields. The pictographs evolved into proto writing, then letters and words.

Once a written language was established, a number system soon followed. There is no doubt that the first computing device of prehistoric people was the flesh: fingers and hands. The limitations of the flesh were exhibited by modern primitive mechanical devices used to measure and record articulations of numbers—lines in the sand, tally sticks, knots on a rope, and pebbles in a bag. The primitive element of arithmetic was manipulation of real-world objects representing a one for one correspondence (Flegg, 1983).

After the proto-written languages came the pictographs or hieroglyphs. Hieroglyphs are found on the walls and clay tablets of ancient Egypt and Samaria. They provided the first glimpses formal writing by humans and the use of an organized number system. The crude symbols are reminiscent of the caves drawing. The Egyptian hieroglyphs represented units (ones) with a vertical hash marks scrawled onto parchment or etched into walls or clay tablets thusly |, | |, | | | as the equivalent of one, two, and three—the number 10 was created with a hump symbol ∩, the coiled rope represented 100, and the symbol for the water lily represented a thousand. (Table 1)

Table 1 Large Number Egyptian Hieroglyphs

Ancient Egyptian large number hieroglyphs	
100	1000
℮	⸮

The Babylonian glyphs are the exception. Babylonian writing described a number system entirely alien to the modern concept of numbers. Babylonian numbers were sexagesimal—that is, a number system based on 60 instead of five or ten—the fingers on the hands. The Babylonians, however, did not always utilize all 60 numbers. Perhaps an ancient monarch had six fingers on each hand. The backbone of the Babylonian number system was two symbols. For numbers from one through nine a narrow, they used a wedge-shaped mark or %. The Babylonians represented 10 with a symbol similar in shape to the modern mathematical symbol for less than symbol or ' .

The earliest record of mechanical devices (besides writing) humans used to compute were the balance scale and the tally stick. Both of these devices are analog tools. These objects came to no conclusions; they only simulated or mirrored the real life objects. Other records gleaned from the chronicles researchers state the text of ancient Romans record keepers reveal tax collectors for Israel and Judea documented their tax receipts with knotted cords.

The use of knots on a string was not isolated to the Ancient Hebrew communities. Researchers divulged that primitive societies in Germany, India, and China used knotted cords before the extensive use of a formal writing and number systems. Accordingly, Spanish conquistadors of the 16th and 17th centuries stated the Incas—a South American indigenous people that occupied the territories of modern Peru, Ecuador, Chile, and Argentina—also used knotted ropes to record taxes for population (Kidwell & Ceruzzi, Landmarks in Digital Computing, 2009).

The two ancient civilizations that had the greatest influence on modern society were ancient Greece and Rome. The Greeks gave us our first glimpses into the comprehension of democracy, human nature, science, geometry, and higher mathematics with the philosophies of Aristotle, Plato, Pythagoras, Euclid, and Zeno (Ifrah, 2001). For those who do not know, Zeno's Arrow gave us our fist glimpses of differential calculus.

The Romans copied much of the Greek culture, adopting Greek architecture, mythology, and art. In addition to being unflattering plagiarists of the Greeks, the Romans were remarkable engineers. The Romans built an infrastructure of highways to connect the vast arms of its empire and extraordinary viaducts to bring water to its urban centers. Yet for all its military prowess and feats of engineering, their lasting legacy to the modern world was the adaptation of Christianity and the Roman numerals. The Roman numerals—I, V, X, L, C—once the engines of commerce and science for more than a millennium, now quietly adorn the faces of clocks, the spines of books, and the suffixes of the National Football League championship games. The Roman numeral lost its influence in Europe and Western society with the arrival of the Islamic culture and the Hindu-Arabic number system.

Since the translation and adaptation of the al-Khwarizmi in the 12th century, the Hindu-Arabic number system has dominated every mathematical aspect of Western culture from scientific study to the conduct of commerce. The history of Hindu-Arabic number system began in the Indus Valley as a counting system called Brahmi more than 2000 years ago. The Arabs modified Brahmi during the Islamic expansion, when their armies conquered the Indus Valley during the seventh century. The new Hindu-Arabic number system did not become popular in Islamic society until the publication of the manuscripts of the al-Khwarizmi in 825.

The Hindu-Arabic number system migrated to Western Europe around 1120 AD when English cleric Robert of Chester translated the al-Khwarizmi text into Latin for the study of mathematics. It slowly replaced Roman numerals in Western European mathematics as papal resistance weakened (Flegg, 1983).

Table 1 Ancient Number Systems

Ancient Number Systems		
ones	tens	Civilization
I	∩	Egyptian Hieroglyphic approx. 3000 BC
◀Y	Y	Old Babylonian Cuneiform approx. 2350 BC (Ifrah 2001)
I	Δ	Acrophonic Greek Numerals approx. 700 BC
I	X	Roman Numerals approx. 500 BC (Flegg 1983)
א	׳	Hebrew Alphabet Numerals approx. 200 BC (Ifrah 2001)

A major catalyst for the invention of a calculating machine no doubt came with the creation of money. The first known records of precious metals used as medium for commerce traces back to the third millennium of ancient Egypt and Mesopotamia (Williams, 1997, p. 22).

Money added mobility to a society. People were free to shop and without the worry of spoilage or animal predation inherent with the older barter system. Money established the fabric of the social framework. For instance, transcriptions on ancient tablets of Hammurabi (king of Babylonia) and Eshnunna (the northern kingdom of Mesopotamia) described the laws that set forth the amount paid in silver or in grain for an agricultural worker as 12 se of silver (equal to a half a gram). In addition to wages, the law codes established the penalty for biting a person's nose as a mina of silver (half a kilogram) or a shekel (one-sixth a mina) for slapping someone's face (Williams, 1997, p. 18).

To account for their accumulation of monetary wealth, ancient monarchs and sovereigns commissioned the first mechanical counting machines to ease the burden of the one to one correspondence created by knots, notches, and bags of stones. The first known counting machine was the Salamis tablet. The Salamis tablet first appeared in ancient Babylonia between 300 BCE and 1100 BCE. Salamis tablets were made of clay, stone, or wood. The scribe accomplished an accounting of valuables by placing beads or pebbles in grooves on the board. It is not clear if the number system was base 10, binary, or octal.

The abacus was the first practical general-purpose calculating device. The Chinese invented the abacus between 500 and 1300 BCE. Later explorers and traders brought it to Europe and the Middle East. Ancient mathematicians, treasurers, and storekeepers used the abacus for addition, subtraction, multiplication, and division, as well as fractions and square root.

The abacus consisted of a four-sided wood frame surrounding a number of metal rods. A fifth wooden beam divided the abacus into two sections as shown in Figure 1. In the narrow portion of the abacus, each rod held two beads (possibly the hands) whilst in the lower section each rod held five beads (possibly representing fingers on the hand). Correspondingly, each bead in the upper portion of the abacus had a value of five, and each bead in the lower portion of the abacus had a value of one. (It takes no great leap of faith to see the relationship between the arrangement of the beads and the five fingers of the hand.) The right-most column of the abacus corresponded to the ones column in the decimal system and progressed accordingly leftward from the ones column to the tens column, hundreds column, etc. The Salamis tablet and the abacus had the same drawbacks, neither device was digital, nor could either print its results. Tallying of large numbers of silver or gold coins and ingots was trusted entirely on the agility, honesty, and skill of the accountant. After the tally, what a priest or steward wrote for the total on parchment became law.

Figure 1 Abaci Chinese and Roman

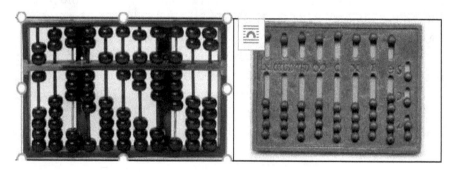

3

Early Devices

What is a computer? Some experts say a computer is an electronic device used for performing computations and making rational decisions. From the viewpoint of a technologist, the advent of the general-purpose digital computer was born from the necessity of humankind's efforts to automate and record mathematical computations with a mechanical device. The etymology of *computer* shows that it evolved from the modern French word *computeur* around the middle of the 17th century. It was roughly defined as "...someone who calculates numbers ..." (Microsoft, 2008).

The definition of a computer from the viewpoint of a historian says a computer is any device that helps humankind in the performance of various kinds of computations or calculations. Thus far, in my investigation, I have uncovered humankind's need for real numbers capable of describing abstractly the needs of commerce and science succinctly and coherently. I then coordinated that with an analysis of the family and economic forces, which compelled the invention of writing and numbers as prehistoric civilizations shifted from a nomadic lifestyle to agrarian lifestyles. Next, I learned there was a symbiotic relationship between money and numbers that spurred the necessity of inventing accounting machines. Finally, in my discussion of the ancient human computing experience, I have established that the inconsistencies of the ancient number systems based on hieroglyphics and the numerals of the ancient world obfuscated rather than clarified their real-world needs and equivalents.

THE ANTIKYTHERA DEVICE

When I began this project, the ideal of a computer was based on a machine seeking mathematical solutions, analog or digital. The Antikythera device is the one exception to logic of computer development sequential evolution of Flesh, Wood, and Metal. This exception occurs because the proponents of popular history—television—calls it the first computer.

The story of the Antikythera device begins on April 15, 1900 when a skin diver fishing for sponges off the coast of the island of Antikythera north of Crete finds the artifact and turns it over to a local archeologist. On first examination, many archeologist and historians thought the artifact originated in 14th century Europe rather than Ancient Greece because of the complexity of its mechanisms. However, after thorough examination with x-rays, studious research, and carbon dating historians surmised the ancient Greeks created the Antikythera device between 200 and 100 BCE. Another common mistake made by archeologists on first examination was the idea the Antikythera device was an astrolabe—a Greek navigation device based on the twelve constellations of the zodiac.

In 1956, Yale Professor Dr. Derek de S. Price stated in the article entitled "An Ancient Greek computer" published in the *Scientific American,* the Antikythera device was an elaborate calendar (Price, 1959). In a later study, Rob S. Rice (1995) at the USNA Eleventh Naval History Symposium wrote the Antikythera mechanism was an arrangement of calibrated differential gears inscribed and configured to produce solar and lunar positions in synchronization with the calendar year.

A second computing device proposed by popular historians, examined herein, is the mechanical theater of Hero of Alexander, built around 65 AD. The theater of Hero featured mechanical actors performing the play *Nauplius.* A series of pistons, pulleys, and ropes controlled the behavior of the actors. The theater tried to represent the actions of nature through mechanics. Ifrah classified the theaters of Hero as automata (Swedin & Ferro, 2007, p. 25–26) (Ifrah, 2001, p. 169). In answer to the question, was the Antikythera Device a computer? Yes, it was a computer, an analog computer.

Figure 2 Antikythera Device

JOHN NAPIER

John Napier was a Scottish theologian, mathematician, and inventor who etched his name into history when he, in 1614, invented logarithms, the decimal notation of fractions. Napier also created Napier Bones—an array of rods with printed digits used for calculating of products and quotients. The typical array or set of Napier Bones is comprised of ten rods or bones, nine of which display the multiples of a given number on the index between one and nine. The tenth bone or rod, is called the index, displays numerals 1 through 9. When aligned in ascending order the array resembles the multiplication table.

To multiply 6 by 58, the value of the index bone, 6, is aligned beside the 5 and 8 bones, respectively. The value of 6 times five in the 58 is read from the sixth location of the fifth bone, or 30. That total is placed in the hundreds column or third column left of the decimal, horizontally. Next, the value for 6 times 8 is found on the sixth location on the 8th bone, or 48. That total is placed in the tens column below the first product, horizontally. The columns are then added resulting in

17

a sum of 348. The modern multiplication table replaced Napier Bones. Napier Bones however proved instrumental in the creation of the first digital calculator.

THE SLIDE RULE

Another significant breakthrough in computing (technically calculating) occurred in 1620, when Edmund Gunter invented the forerunner to the modern slide rule. The device Gunther invented was actually a nautical aid to helped sailors. Edmund Gunther was born in Wales in the year 1581. He was a professor of astronomy at Gresham College in London, from 1619 until his death. Before his invention of the slide rule, he is most noted for his 1620 publication of the Table of Artificial Sines and Tangents (Canon Triangulorum) a seven-figure table of logarithms for sine and tangent functions. He is also credited with the invention of the words cosine and cotangent.

Three years after Gunther's breakthrough, William Oughtred made improvements to the Gunther invention and created the rudiments of the modern slide rule by adding an adjustable scale. The Oughtred slide rule was round. William Oughtred was born March 5, 1574, in Eton, Buckinghamshire, England.

Later, in 1654, Robert Bissaker made improvements to the Oughtred's slide rule adding an adjustable inner scale and changing the shape of the slide rule from round to a rectangle. In 1671, Seth Partridge repositioned the Oughtred scales on the slide, making it easier to perform calculations. John Robertson in 1775 made another improvement that allowed the settings to transfer to any of the parallel scales. Peter Roget (*Roget's Thesaurus*) added the logarithms scale in 1815 allowing calculations of the powers or square roots of a number (Ifrah, 2007, p. 156).

4

The First Calculators

The European Renaissance proved as fertile a ground for invention as it was for social change. Not only was it thought provoking for British inventors Robert Bissaker, William Oughtred, and Edmund Gunter with the development of the slide rule. It was also a fertile ground for Continental Europeans, particularly in Germany and France where the Metal Age of calculators took root in the form of Wilhelm Schickard, Blaise Pascal, and Gottfried Wilhelm von Leibniz. Between them, they blazed a trail in computing that shaped the future of the modern desktop calculator and was the harbinger of the modern computer.

Wilhelm Schickard

It was in the atmosphere of the European Renaissance that the Wood Era of computing ended and the Metal Era of computing began. This minor event occurred because of the inventiveness of the German scientist Wilhelm Schickard. What is often overlooked is the complexity of the Calculating Clock. In the heretofore Wood Era, inventions described were extensions of the hash mark on the tally stick. All that ended with the Schickard Calculating Clock. The Calculating Clock did not exhibit any of those qualities. It exhibited the qualities of calculating machines invented during the Metal Era of mechanical calculators.

19

No remnants of the Calculating Clock were found in the Tubingen, Germany where Schickard lived. The only evidence the machine ever existed was discovered when researchers found sketches and a description in letters written to renowned astronomer Johannes Kepler, in 1623. In the initial letter, Schickard describes his invention the Calculating Clock:

> "What you have done by calculation I have just tried to do by way of mechanics. I have conceived a machine consisting of eleven complete and six incomplete sprocket wheels; it calculates instantaneously and automatically from given numbers, as it adds, subtracts, multiplies, and divides. You would enjoy seeing how the machine accumulates and transports spontaneously a ten or a hundred to the left and, vice-versa, how it does the opposite if it is subtracting... "

Figure 3 The Calculating Clock

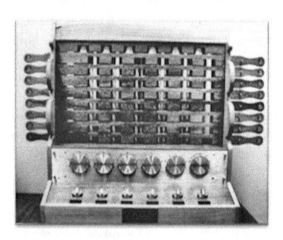

In subsequent letters to Kepler, Schickard sent more detailed descriptions along with sketches of the prototype, a six-digit calculator that not only added or subtracted (Figure 3) but performed multiplication and division by manipulating a set of Napier Bones housed in the top of the calculator.

Schickard is the first tragedy in the history of computing. He lived at the wrong time in the wrong place. He and his family met a premature death, falling victim to the Bubonic Plague during the Thirty Years War. For cyber historians, the story is even more tragic in that Schickard's only prototype was lost when his house was set ablaze to sterilize the neighborhood of the plague (Sandhills Publishing Company, 2008). IBM furnished the replica of the Schickard calculator (Figure 3).

BLAISE PASCAL

Figure 4 the Pascaline

The scientific quest to simplify the tedium of mathematical calculations did not end with Schickard's death. Instead, it began anew in the personage of French scientist and mathematician Blaise Pascal. Pascal was born near Lyon on July 29, 1623 in the Clermont region about 200 miles south of Paris.

Without any knowledge of the Calculating Clock, Pascal, in 1642, invented the Pascaline. The Pascaline (Figure 4) was different from the Schickard device. The Pascaline was made entirely of metal. It was a rectangular box about 36 centimeters (cm) long, 13 cm wide, and eight cm high. Pascal built several versions of the machine, one with five dials, a second with six dials, and a third with eight dials. The number of dials on the face of the machine determined the precision of the machine.

The Pascaline made its calculations using gears and sprockets in the same manner as the odometer display on the dashboard of an automobile, before the advent of the LED speedometers and odometers. To obtain the precision the gears needed to make the calculations with the Pascaline, Pascal trained himself in metal fabrication techniques. He did this because local machinists and clockmakers were not accustomed to the precision Pascal demanded.

Pascal built the Pascaline, shown in Figure 4, for altruistic reasons. He wanted to assist his father, Etienne Pascal, a tax collector, who often complained about being over burdened with the counting of taxes in Clermont (Karwatka, 2004). Historians infer that Pascal based the design of his calculator on the machines developed by Hero of Alexandria in ancient Egypt (Hoyle, 2004).

Numbers were entered into the Pascaline by rotating of the appropriate dials on the top or face of the Pascaline. The right most dial represented the one's column; the next column left represented the tens and so forth. Addition was accomplished by selecting the appropriate number on the dial and rotating the dial. To add a second number, repeat the process. The machine worked in a manner similar to the action of dialing a rotary telephone.

The viewing windows atop the Pascaline displayed the results of the operation. The viewing windows were divided into two sections by a brass slide, which covered the section not in use. The upper portion of the window was for normal addition. Since the machine could not move in reverse. It could not perform subtraction. The lower portion of the display showed the Nine's Complement of the number held in the register. The Nine's Complement is an ancient technique used for the purposes of subtraction. The Nine's Complement is explained in Dorr E. Felt section of Chapter 5.

The Pascaline was also the first calculator marketed to the public with any semblance of commercial success. All records indicate Pascal was able to sell 50 of his mechanical calculators, hardly a roaring commercial success, but a step in the right direction (M. Williams, 1990, p. 39) (Ifrah, 2001, p. 122).

Gottfried Leibniz

Gottfried Wilhelm von Leibniz was born in Leipzig, Germany, in 1646. He is noted in this calculator history for expanding upon the concepts of Blaise Pascal when he created the Step Reckoner in 1671. The machine Leibniz envisioned far exceeded the capabilities of the Pascaline. It was supposed to be the first mechanical calculator capable of performing all four arithmetic operations: addition, subtraction, multiplication, and division. However, Leibniz's vision was not to be, the Step Reckoner was a failure. Leibniz did make a number of pioneering breakthroughs in calculator technology with the Step Reckoner. Among them was the first inscriptor window, which allowed the operator to see the number entered into the machine before processing.

Figure 5 The Step Reckoner

The Step Reckoner, also, introduced the concept of the stepped drum, a gear that used progressively larger teeth or sprockets as a method of selecting the correct number. The stepped drum mechanism of Leibniz influenced the design of future calculators far more than the Pascaline. The stepped drum technology with a continuing number of improvements was the technical foundation for mechanical calculator design well into the early twentieth century.

Leibniz introduced the world to the Step Reckoner with a demonstration of a wooden prototype at a meeting of the British Royal Society in London, in 1672. Unfortunately, the wooden prototype failed to work correctly. Sympathetic members of the Royal Society allowed Leibniz to withdraw his calculator until the necessary corrections were made (M. Williams, 1990, p. 42) (Swedin & Ferro, 2007, p. 12).

The reason for the failure of the Step Reckoner originated with two flaws in the design. First, the Step Reckoner suffered from a lack of precision. As it was with Pascaline for Pascal, Leibniz and the Stepped

23

Reckoner suffered from substandard metal fabrication techniques. The calculator required a very complex and intricate gear works requiring a person with specialized mechanical expertise to construct it. The second flaw researchers found was in the carry mechanism. The lack of precision in the carry mechanism caused the machine to produce erroneous totals.

Essentially, The Step Reckoner failed to carry tens correctly when the multiplier was a two or three digit number. The flaws became evident when archeologist and engineers were dissected one of the two prototypes Leibniz had constructed. The prototypes had sat in the attic of the University of Gottingen until a school custodian discovered it in 1879 (M. Williams, 1990, p. 42).

After his failure at the London Royal Society, Leibniz, over the next 45 years, constructed several prototypes trying to correct the flaw in his design. There is no evidence he ever resolved the mechanical flaws in his calculator. Centuries later, historian attempted to build a Step Reckoner by deconstructing the prototypes. Additionally the researchers attempted to construct a Leibniz Reckoner from the numerous drawings he left behind. In both incidents, the historians failed to overcome the errors found in the prototypes. Because Leibniz never built a fully functional stepped drum calculator, many historians credit Philipp Matthäus Hahn as the creator of the stepped drum calculator.

In the book *Computing Before Computers* (1996), computer historian and author Michael Williams, wrote,

> Leibniz died on November 14, 1716, enfeebled by disease, harassed by controversy (not the least of which with Newton's claims for the invention of calculus), and embittered by neglect...
>
> His death went unnoticed by the school he founded in Berlin and in London where his benefactor, the House of Hanover ruled (Soylent Communications, 2009).

A record left by a funeral attendee tells us "...he [Leibniz] was buried more like a robber that what he really was, the ornament of his country (M. Williams, 1996)."

Historians recognized Leibniz more for his contributions to mathematics than his calculating machines. He and Isaac Newton share credit for the creation of calculus. Although his invention, for the most part, went unrecognized, the stepped drum approach to calculator mechanics was the only practical solution to the construction of mechanical calculators until the Baldwin pinwheel calculator and the Felt keyboard comptometers in the late 19th century.

Almost simultaneous to Leibniz's efforts to build the Step Reckoner was Samuel Moreland attempt to build a calculating device to count British currency. The calculator was so difficult to use that the operator required an assistant. Historians refer to the Moreland reckoner as only slightly better than the Pascaline.

The machines invented by Pascal and Leibniz provided the foundations for a number of future scientist in our investigation of the sources and history of the computer. Such esteemed inventors as Poleni, Leupold, and Gersten built calculating machines during the 18th century that improved upon the either the Pascal or Leibniz designs (Soylent Communications, 2009).

A brief summation of their contributions follows: The first of these inventors was Giovanni Poleni who in 1709 built a calculator based on the works of Pascal and Leibniz. When he heard reports that a rival had built a competing machine, Poleni destroyed his device. All that remained of his efforts were his notes. Jacob Leupold followed Poleni in an attempt to improve the Step Reckoner for personal gain. Historians at IBM were able to re-create his stepped drum device from the notes left behind (Figure 7). C. L. Gersten, who in 1735 followed in Leupold footsteps, invented a calculator that, like the Pascaline, could only perform addition (Redin, 2007) (M. Williams, 1990) (Chase, 1980).

Philipp Matthäus Hahn

Philipp Matthäus Hahn was born on November 25, 1739, in Scharnhausen, Germany. Hahn was a clergyman and a skilled clockmaker when he successfully built the first fully functional calculator based on the Leibniz Step Reckoner in 1773. Insofar as can be determined from research, one cannot—at this time—ascertain whether Hahn reinvented the stepped drum apparatus or borrowed the idea from Leibniz.

Figure 6 Hahn Calculator

Hahn's calculator included a set of 12 drums arranged in a circular configuration actuated by a crank located in the axis of the arrangement. The machine was capable of making calculations as large as 12 digits. Some scholars believed that Thomas de Colmar used the Hahn's machine and not the Step Reckoner as the prototype for his calculator the Thomas Arithmometer (Thomas for short). After Hahn's death in 1790, his two sons and his brother-in-law, Johann Christopher Schuster, continued to manufactured the calculator for a profit until the mid-1820s (IBM, 2008) (Redin, 2007) (Chase, 1980).

Jacob Leupold

Jacob Leupold was born in Germany in 1674. In Germany, he

Figure 7 Leupold Calculator

was a very distinguished machinist and mining engineer (Gale Virtual References 2005). He is best known in the annals of technology for his book *The General Theory of Machines*, which by coincidence was published in 1727 the year he died.

In the history of computing machines, he is noted for successfully building a calculator based on the Leibniz stepped drum technology. He borrowed the circular style from the Hahn calculator.

Leupold proposed using a counter to vary the sprockets engaging on each turn of the handle and disengaging the geared wheel where necessary. Leupold never marketed his calculator because the similarity in construction to the Hahn designed. IBM archivist reconstructed the Hahn calculator shown in Figure 6 from notes recorded by the designer (IBM 1990).

Figure 8 Thomas Arithmometer

Charles Xavier Thomas de Colmar was born in France in 1785. He is famous because he built the Thomas Arithmometer in 1820. The *Thomas* became the first commercially successful mass-produced calculating machine. The *Thomas* weighed approximately forty pounds and filled the surface of a medium-size desk. Charles Xavier Thomas like Hahn before him based his new calculator on the Leibniz technology of the stepped drum built 150 years earlier. The Thomas Arithmometer (shown in Figure 8) like the Step Reckoner performed the four basic arithmetic operations. The technology used to create the Thomas Arithmometer was so successful variations of it were used well into the twentieth century until the advent of the electric adding machine (M. Williams, 1990).

The innovations introduced by the *Thomas* vastly improved the operations of the Leibniz-Hahn stepped drum calculator. The first innovation was revising the alignment of the gears. In the Step Reckoner the gears on a horizontal axis were sliding. In the *Thomas*, the gears were fixed on the axis. Second, the *Thomas* used a pinion to engage the gears rotating around the axis (Ifrah, 2001, p. 127).

Unlike Leibniz, Thomas created an efficient carry mechanism (M. Williams, 1990) that reduced the registers to zero. Next, Thomas added a blocking lever, a series of springs that stopped the machine's operation when it reached the correct place position (Ifrah, 2001, p. 127).

The most beneficial innovation introduce by the *Thomas* (World-Information Organization, 2007) was its ability to reverse the operating function in the result registers (up to sixteen digits), which permitted reliable and stable calculations over extended periods without the need for gear realignment. The *Thomas* was marketed for ninety years by several companies under several different names—Unitas, MADAS, TIM, Archimedes, Peerless, and Saxonia—well into the twentieth century (Ifrah, 2001, p. 127) (IBM Archives, 2009).

David Parmalee

David Parmalee, in 1849, was the first American inventor to make a significant contribution in the development of the digital calculator when he constructed the first adding machine with a keyboard. The machine was awkward and could add only one column of digits. Parmalee filed a patent for his adding machine in 1850, U.S patent number 7074. Despite his breakthrough with keyboard technology for calculators, the adding machine proved impractical for business or science and never achieved commercialized success.

Victor Schilt

The story of the Victor Schilt Adding Machine is an intriguing mystery in the history and development of digital computing. The mystery begins with Schilt's appearance at the Great London Exhibition of 1851 with a new keyboard-style adding machine.

Schilt, a Swiss clockmaker, misrepresented himself as the patent holder of the adding machine. In blunter terms, Schilt was disingenuous fraud. This deception, he perpetrated for two years on officials and visitors of the Great London Exhibition held in the Crystal Palace Exposition Hall. His deception even allowed him to claim the coveted Crystal Palace Exposition Bronze Medal for technical ingenuity.

The new-fangled device described as a rectangular box that featured nine keys, 1 through 9, on one face or top of the box. Also on the face of the box was an aperture that displayed two or three digits. Adjacent and to either end of the group of apertures were two knobs.

Twenty-first century scholars have unraveled Schilt's deception. In the essay *An Early (1844) Key-Driven Adding Machine* (2008), French scholar, Denis Roegel states Schilt stole the design for the prize-winning calculator from the French architect and clockmaker Jean-Baptiste Schwilgue of Strasbourg. To substantiate the above assertion, Roegel uncovered three sources that refute the Schilt's claim on the key driven calculator.

Figure 9 Schilt Calculator

First, Roegel's search of nineteenth century French patent records reveal a copy of Schwilgue's original 1844 patent application for the adding machine in question. The document does not mention Schilt as contributor. Second, were the first hand accounts of witnesses to Schilt's behavior at the London exhibition. Many describe Schilt, after receiving more than 100 orders for the adding machines, as anything but joyful. Accounts state, Schilt appeared apprehensive or angst-ridden. The final proof of Schilt's deception, Roegel presents in the form of statements transcribed by J.A.V. Turck—noted calculator historian, author of *Origin of Modern Calculating Machines*, and manager of Felt & Tarrant Comptometer from 1930 to 1953—show that Schwilgue employed Schilt as a mechanic, from 1847 through the end of 1848, to build the machine..."

Roegel explains the scholarly oversight was due in part to errors by several historians beginning in the 1920s who erroneously proclaimed the calculator as Schilt's machine. Making the calculator earliest known European key driven adding machine. Roegel attempts to clarify the errors in this fashion. Renowned historian Maurice d'Ocagne stated, "He (d'Ocagne) was aware of Schwilgue's claim on the invention but never found the time to inspect Schwilgue's machine or review the patent." Consequently when he wrote his history, the Schwilgue episode was not corrected. As a result d'Ocagne's neglect, other historians, following the in the footsteps of the highly regarded opinion of d'Ocagne, reiterated the error in their histories of calculating machines.

Finally, Roegel states even the trusted and reliable Turck added to the confusion when he (Turck) erroneously stated in his book *Origins of Calculating Machines,* that D.D. Parmalee keyboard adding machine predated Schilt's chicanery in US patent records by one year. A negative proof, none the less, it was evidence of the existence of a machine by Schilt (Turck, 1921) (Roegel, 2008).

Thomas Hill

As the Industrial Revolution progressed on the North American continent, during the period known as the Antebellum, several inventors emerged to challenge the European dominance of the mechanical calculator industry by the *Thomas Arithmometer.* Among them was Thomas Hill of Waltham, Massachusetts who in November of 1857 built a keyboard style

Figure 10 Hill Arithmometer

calculator he called an arithmometer. The *Thomas Hill Arithmometer* was the second North American adding machine to utilize the keyboard technology for a calculating machine (IBM Archives, 2009). The *Hill Arithmometer*, as it was called, utilized a totalizing wheel. Additionally, for the first time in calculator technology all the keys were controlled by a lever, which produced different rotations of the totalizing wheel (Roegel, 2008).

Hill, like many of his contemporaries and predecessors, never advanced his invention beyond the experimental stage. Consequently, general knowledge of his contributions to the history digital calculators and computing machines were esoteric relegated to patent office records and the readers of 19th century scientific journals. This machine was the antecedent of the keyboard technology introduced by Dorr E. Felt, William Hopkins, and William Seward Burroughs some thirty years later.

THE LEONARDO AFFAIR

People often think of events in history as isolated moments of destiny. They think of history as Archimedes did with his emotional outburst, "Eureka, I have found it." Life however is not static, it waxes and wanes with the tide of human emotions and events which circumscribe our being. For example, beginning in 1642, a series of calculator innovations built upon the Step Reckoner and the Pascaline led the *Thomas* by Charles Xavier Thomas in 1822.

Then there are aberrations in the history of technology. One of the aberration we discussed the Antikythera device. A 20th century archivist in Madrid Spain found another aberration to the logic of calculator development. This exception to the logic of scientific development is described by the discovery of the Codex Madrid (a set engineering notes and sketches by Leonardo da Vinci dating back to 1493. At the time of its discovery, historians believed the Codex Madrid was a momentous discovery that demonstrated the genius of da Vinci was ahead of its time.

How this discovery affects calculator history? The story begins in the 1960s da Vinci when was a very popular subject for historians, researchers and teachers. On February 13, 1967, a group of American researchers, working in the National Library of Spain in Madrid, discovered two heretofore-unknown collections of Leonardo's manuscripts, the Codex Madrid I and Codex Madrid II. Spanish museum officials later explain the discovery by stating the manuscripts, not seen for almost two hundred years, were mislabeled.

After careful study, the researchers believed they had discovered the origins of the world's first digital calculator. Coincidentally, IBM archivists hired Dr. Robert Guatelli, a renowned expert of Leonardo da Vinci artifacts, to verify the da Vinci manuscripts. Guatelli specialized in recreating replicas of machines found in the da Vinci manuscripts and sketches. After reviewing the documents at the Massachusetts Institute of Technology, Guatelli remembered the Codex Atlanticus, which depicted a similar machine. Dr. Guatelli combined the two descriptions and drawings, and built a replica of the Codex Madrid in 1968. Shortly thereafter, IBM displayed the da Vinci Codex Madrid calculator its traveling exhibition of antique calculating machines.

After a year of touring the United States, the da Vinci exhibit on the IBM traveling museum became the object of controversy, as two opposing factions argued about the purpose the machine.

The two factions represented the most talented scientific minds in the nation. On the one side were those that believed the findings of Dr. **Guatelli** were not accurate. They believed Dr. **Guatelli** had grievously erred. On the other side, were those proponents who sided with IBM and Dr. Guatelli. To resolve the feud, an academic trial was held at the Massachusetts Institute of Technology, to ascertain the correct intent of the **da Vinci Codex Madrid**.

To summarize the academic trial, the dissenters prevailed with their position was proved. The machine proved too impractical to be an adding machine. The supposition was based on fact that when one considers the last digit (the last wheel) would have to turn an astronomical 10 to the 13th power (10^{13}) if the Codex Madrid calculator was truly an adding machine.

Figure 11 Leonardo's Calculator

5

Calculating Engines

Originally, the term computer referred to human beings. In the 19th century, a computer was a clerk who performed mathematical calculations in accordance with known methods. These human computers performed calculation nowadays carried out by one form of electronic calculator or electronic spreadsheets in a computer. The term calculating engine in the 19th century referred to an entirely different class of computing machine hitherto not discussed. These machines did not fit in the framework of desktop calculators, arithmometers, or comptometers built by the aforementioned Schickard, Leupold, Hahn, Schwilgue, or Thomas. Nor did they fit into the class of pinwheel or keyboard calculators invented by Felt, Burroughs, or Baldwin in the latter half of the 19th century. Leading the way among the inventors of the calculating engines was Charles Babbage of Great Britain. However, he would not be the last.

Babbage, known as the father of modern computing, called his first attempt at transforming calculator technology the *Difference Engine*. The Difference Engine had more than 8,000 parts, weighed five tons, measured eleven feet long, and stood seven feet tall. It was supposed to be a general-purpose digital computing device built for automating the production of mathematical tables—logarithmic, trigonometric, nautical, astronomical, actuarial, and differentials. The Babbage Difference Engine was comprised entirely of metal mechanical parts—

brass gear wheels, rods, ratchets, pinions, etc. Electricity in 1822 was still a magician parlor trick. The computation of numbers was performed decimally by positioning a ten-toothed metal wheels mounted vertically.

Historians have classified these machines as the harbingers—at least in the case of Babbage—of the modern computer. Although there were many subsequent difference engines, Babbage alone receives the accolades of scholars for his unique approach to digital computing. Babbage disciples include Ada Lovelace, Georg Scheutz of Sweden, Martin Wiberg of Sweden, and George Grant of the United States.

Charles Babbage

Probably the most admired person in annals of computing science history is Charles Babbage. His work is considered visionary because it exceeded the scope of early 19th century British calculator technology. Historians applaud Babbage for his theoretical logic and mechanical solutions for complex calculation with calculating engines, the Difference Engine of 1822 and the Analytical Engine of 1842. Babbage envisioned a calculating machine—a difference engine—capable of automatically producing error free calculations for mathematical tables publication avoiding the errors normally produced by manual production of actuarial and scientific tables (Wilkes, 2003).

His plan for a difference engine began while he was still a student at Trinity College in Cambridge. John Herschel, a colleague and mentor at Cambridge, encouraged Babbage to fulfill his dreams after listening to a presentation. The proposed results were would be accomplished, for example, by representing a trigonometric function, such as sine or tan, as a polynomial. The degree of complexity of the function was determined by the required accuracy of the tables—four or five digit decimals. By using a finite method, the calculation of said polynomial substitutes were reduced by repeated addition of only the differences in each resulting equation (Bromley, 2003).

In 1823, Babbage proposed to Parliament that building such a machine would aid the British government with its actuary tables as well as the scientific, nautical, and business communities. To prove the project was viable, Babbage built a smaller prototype of the Difference Engine that handled only six digit numbers and capable of processing the formula: $T = x^2 + x + 41$ (Bromley, 2003). After a successful demonstration of the prototype, he initially received £1500 funding from the British government (Swedin & Ferro, 2007). The support from the government eventually grew to more than £17,000 for the project (Bromley, 2003).

Figure 12 Babbage Engine

The Difference Engine, had it been built, would have had more than 25,000 parts and weighed more than three tons (White, 2004, p. 5). Despite the utility of the Difference Engine as a practical aid to printing tables, it is, in the mathematical sense, according to Broomley, an extremely limited instrument. Consequently, Babbage sought new avenues to solve his automated table production problems. Referring to the Broomley (2003) "Analytical Engine" text once more, Babbage realized the second difference in the in the equation $T = x^2 + x + 41$ was constant because it was a quadratic.

To automate the second difference into the calculator operations, Babbage modified the gears of the Difference Engine so that the tabulated values of the second difference were feedback into the machine. The results of which would cause the values of the function to be calculated without an intermediate polynomial. Babbage attempt to rationalize the second difference in the equation as a constant manifested with a modification to the original configuration of the Difference Engine. The new configuration however could not perform the required multiplications of the new equation $\triangle 2 \sin(x) = -k \sin(x)$.

The modifications Babbage imagined for the Difference Engine resulted in the ideal for the Analytical Engine, which would have been in principle the first fully programmable, general-purpose, automatic digital computer (Wilkes, 1992).

The Analytical Engine contained the four basic components found in the von Neumann architecture required for modern computers: memory, CPU, input and output. The Analytical Engine design consisted of these four components: the mill, the store, the reader, and the printer.

The mill was the calculating unit, consistent with the CPU of a modern computer. The store was where the Analytical Engine held data prior to processing, which is consistent with memory and storage in modern computers. The reader and printer are self-explanatory and the equivalent to the input and output devices. Input for the Analytical Engine was performed using a series of punch cards reminiscent of Jacquard's punch cards and the cards Hollerith (IBM) would use 60 years later during the electromechanical and electronic eras. (Bromley, "Analytical Engine," 2003).

Popular legend would have the casual historian believe Babbage and the Difference Engine succumbed to the same engineering problems that befell Leibniz and the Step Reckoner. After further investigation of Babbage, the author discovered the reasons behind the failure to complete either the Analytical Engine or Difference Engine had little to do with the engineering skill or technological savvy of Britain during the Industrial Age. The opposite was true; the skills the Babbage staff gained as a result of working on the difference engine fortified British engineering and proliferated throughout the nation. Elements of the techniques employed by Babbage trained engineers supplanted known methods in the textile industry and influenced the development of new machinery across England and later the United States (Williams M. R., The Difference Engines, 1979).

What caused Babbage's failure to complete either project had more to do with his hubris, his personality, his eccentricities, his inability to cope with people or the ever-changing fabric of British society during the Industrial Revolution more than any technological shortcomings (Bromley, 2003). Compounding the aforementioned factors contributing to his downfall was the loss of his father and his own chronic poor health.

Financial problems were a secondary contributor to his downfall. Although the project was government sponsored, it was plague by irregular funding intervals, which created disgruntled employees causing several work stoppages. With each work stoppage, Babbage was forced to furlough old and trusted employees then for some unknown reason hire untrained replacements, which complicated the setbacks the project experienced. The final cause for Babbage's failure to produce either Difference Engine or the Analytical Engine was due in part to the fact he began to think of the projects as an academic exercise rather than a commercial enterprise (Swedin & Ferro, 2007).

Ada Lovelace

Of all the people I researched for this project, Augusta Ada Lovelace was the most mysterious a disciple of Babbage. This much is for sure; she was the daughter of Anna Isabella Milbanke and Lord Byron—the famed British romantic poet and satirist. She was born in London in 1815, the only child of a loveless marriage and Byron's only legitimate child. Lord Byron removed himself from his daughter's life by relinquishing parental rights to his wife in 1816. The mother, not wanting her daughter to inherit or pursue the enigmatic and scurrilous lifestyle of her poet father, had the child educated in mathematics and science. At the age of 13, Augusta surprised her mother with a design for a flying machine. In spite of her creativity for design, mathematics proved to be her true calling. By age 20, Ada had married William King, the Earl of Lovelace in 1835. We also know she befriended Charles Babbage in 1833, then a professor of mathematics at Cambridge University (Smart Computing, 2010).

From there, fact and fiction merge as to the exact role of Ada Lovelace's contribution to computer science and as the world's first programmer is unclear. I have researched eight sources of information. Thus far, six of which are listed in the bibliography of this book. Five on the list—Bromley, "Difference Engine," 2003; Bromley, "Difference and Analytical Engines," 1990; Stein, 1985; Wilkes M. V., 2003—paint Lovelace as something other than the popular legend. Wilkes is the most generous stating that escapades of her mathematical agility were grossly exaggerated. While Bromley's 1990 article in the book edited by William Aspray (Aspray, 1990, pp. 88–89) *Computers Before Computing* is the most disparaging stating, "…there is no evidence that Lady Lovelace ever prepared a program for the Analytical Engine nor had the knowledge to do so…"

Of the remaining sources, which compel evidence corroborating that she was the world's first computer programmer, there are three. The most confusing are the statements made by M. V. Wilkes and recorded by George Ifrah in his book, The Universal History of Computing (Ifrah, 2001, p. 190–194).

Let me explain: the controversies and complications surrounding the story of Lady Lovelace began in 1842 when Babbage traveled to Turin, Italy, to deliver a series of seminars on the intricacies of the Analytical Engine (Bromley, "Difference and Analytical Engines," 1990).

All sources cited herein credit Lady Lovelace for her skillful translation of the Italian mathematician Luigi Menebrea's memoirs about the Analytical Engine from French to English. Each source states that in the Menebrea memoirs, Lady Lovelace added extensive notes. All agree that the notes she added were prepared under the close supervision of Babbage (Bromley, "Difference and Analytical Engines," 1990).

As the Lovelace legend grew, it gave rise to overstatements about her mathematical ability and importance in the saga of Charles Babbage (Wilkes M. V., 2003). The overstatements have led many to believe that Lady Lovelace wrote intricate programs for the Analytical Engine. Babbage's memoirs suggest it was Lady Lovelace's idea to write a program that allowed the machine to calculate Bernoulli numbers (Smart Computing, 2010). Others postulated that Lovelace found "bugs" in programs that Babbage prepared (Bromley, "Difference and Analytical Engines," 1990).

The reasoning behind the growing legend of Lady Lovelace is the tendency to apply the 20th century notion of sexual equality to 19th century English society. Furthermore, upon closer examination of the correspondence between the Babbage and Lovelace there was no evidence that she prepared a program for the Analytical Engine nor had the knowledge of the Jacquard punch cards (Bromley, "Difference and Analytical Engines," 1990).

Besides Bromley and Wilkes, other cyber historians have affirmed the myth of Ada Lovelace as the first computer programmer as without foundation. In her book Ada, a Life and a Legacy (Stein, 1985, pp. 92–110), Dorothy Stein argued Babbage wrote the programs as evidence to this affect; she cites the book Passages from the Life of a Philosopher, on page 136, Babbage (1864) wrote:

"Sometime after the appearance of his memoir on the subject in the "Bibliotheque Universelle de Geneve," the late Countess of Lovelace informed me that she had translated the memoir of Menebrea. I asked why she had not herself written an original paper on a subject, which she was so intimately acquainted. To this, Lady Lovelace replied that the thought had not occurred to her. I then suggested that she should add some notes to Menebrea's memoirs an idea, which was immediately adopted.

We discussed together the various illustrations that might be introduced: I suggested several, but the selection was entirely her own. So, was the algebraic working out of the different problems, except, indeed, that relating to the numbers of Bernoulli, which I had offered to do it to save Lady Lovelace the trouble? This she sent back to me for an amendment, having detected a grave mistake, which I had made in the process... (Babbage, 1864)"

From the viewpoint of Stein, Wilkes, and Bromley, it seems that Lovelace was merely a vessel of information distribution. A practice often employed by Babbage to distribute information about his Analytical Engine to the public. To substantiate this point of view historians refer to a similar incident that occurring ten years earlier when Babbage used a similar tactic featuring the journalistic skills of one Dionysius Lardner—a British professor and technical writer—to disseminate information about the Difference Engine to the general populace. Lardner, like Lovelace, had become a popular read in the circle of mechanical scientists near the mid-19th century. Undoubtedly, it was through the writings of Lardner that Scheutz enhanced his understanding of the Babbage Difference Engine (Bromley, "Difference and Analytical Engines," 1990).

Differing from that line of thought and the Lardner incident, Georges Ifrah in his book The Universal History of Computing (Ifrah, 2001, pp. 190–194) wrote, "Lovelace was a competent writer of computer programming." The exact quote from the Ifrah document reads as follows, "...this lady mathematician transformed the driest mathematical formulae and the most off-putting technical descriptions into the most exquisite algorithmic poems..."

That is not all; in the next paragraph on the same page Ifrah states, "Ada Augusta Byron, the Countess of Lovelace...the first weaver of coded instructions on a punch card..." Finally, on the last paragraph of that page, Ifrah states, "She was a woman of some ability and had a clear grasp of her subject..."

The issue would not be as disconcerting if the two sides had separate sources. However, as stated above, the only source used by renowned computer historian George Ifrah was authored by M. V. Wilkes (Wilkes, 1956), Automatic Digital Computers. Ifrah continues the popular historic point of view of Lovelace by citing Babbage as the source of the compliments to Lovelace in a set of papers translated by Maurice d'Ocagne (Ifrah, 2001, pp. 190–194). Ifrah did qualify his position on Lovelace and Babbage controversy by returning us to reality—neither the Analytical Engine nor the Difference Engine was ever built.

Georg Scheutz

Figure 13 Scheutz Difference Engine

Georg Scheutz was born in born in Jonkoping, Sweden, on September 23, 1785. He was the son of Frederik Christian Scheutz and Andreas Lenaeus Scheutz. The parents were ordinary people without academic degrees, the father was an innkeeper, and the mother wrote hymns. The Scheutz Inn had the reputation of being one of the better rest stops when visiting the hamlet.

Starting in 1803, Scheutz attended the University of Lund where he studied law. In 1805, he took a judicial examination that led to his appointment as vice-actuary with the Gotha Supreme Court, and part time judge. In 1812, Scheutz moved to Stockholm and worked in one of the government ministries before taking a job as an auditor with the Swedish military—the job only gave him a title, it paid no salary (Merzbach, Georg Scheutz and the First Printing Calculator, 1977).

From 1815, Scheutz found work as a publisher of a Swedish magazine *Anmdrkaren*. In 1819, Scheutz created a new journal; *Anmdrkarne* that eventually became *Argus Magazine; Anmdrkaren* went to another publisher. His most notable accomplishment in publishing was the translation of the works of William Shakespeare into Swedish. However, it was his interest in science and technology in the publishing industry that led to his first encounter with the works of Charles Babbage (Merzbach, *Georg Scheutz and the First Printing Calculator*, 1977).

In 1843, Georg and son Edvard built the first fully operational difference engine, in Sweden, (Bromley, Difference and Analytical Engines, 1990). The story of the Scheutz Difference Engine began when the elder Scheutz first encountered the works of Charles Babbage in 1832, He read the Swedish magazine the *Journal for Manufakturer:* The publication was about Charles Babbage's book *Economy of Machinery and Manufactures* (Merzbach, Georg Scheutz and the First Printing Calculator, 1977).

In that journal, Scheutz studied the academic career and accomplishments of Charles Babbage, a banker's son, who studied mathematics at Trinity College, in Cambridge, England (Merzbach, Smithsonian Digital Depository, 2007). While at Trinity, as an undergraduate student, Babbage cofounded the Analytical Society. The Analytical Society was student organization created to promote the mathematical methods, notations, and techniques found in the works of Lagrange, Laplace, Lacroix, and other continental mathematicians, who adhered to the calculus traditions created by Leibniz—inventor of the Step Reckoner—in opposition to the British borne Newtonian calculus method (Merzbach, Smithsonian Digital Depository, 2007).

A few years later, Scheutz discovered more details about the Babbage machine, in the *Edinburgh Review* written by Dionysius Lardner. The same Dionysius Lardner mentioned in the previous section. Lardner used the publication as an opportunity to describe in detail the three major difficulties with the publishing of mathematical tables: First, Lardner briefly described the problems with several major mathematical tables produced over the last 50 years. Second, he used these tables to dramatize the importance and obstacles to producing large quantities of error free data cheaply and quickly. Third, Lardner described, for his readers, in layman's terms, the Babbage concept for a new mechanical calculator (Computer Museum of America, 2008).

After reviewing Lardner's article on the Difference Engine, Scheutz sought a detailed history and status on the construction of the Babbage Difference Engine (Merzbach, *Georg Scheutz and the First Printing Calculator*, 1977). Once he had familiarized himself with the computational and the construction techniques used in the Babbage engine—without sketches or blueprints—he and Edvard built a small prototype of a difference engine from wood, wire, and cardboard.

They called the prototype the Scheutz Calculator. The Scheutz Calculator (Scheutz Difference Engine) was the first machine to create, calculate, and print nautical, actuarial, and mathematical tables. Unlike the Babbage's Difference Engine, which operated on the principle of seven difference engines, the Scheutz Difference Engine operated on just three difference engines.

Scheutz and his son constructed two metal versions of the wooden prototype, one in Stockholm in 1853, the other in London in 1859. The Dudley Observatory of Albany, New York, purchased the Stockholm machine, demonstrated at the Paris Universal Exhibition in 1856 for 1000 pounds sterling. The Observatory used the Scheutz Difference Engine for a short time until 1858. The observatory used the Scheutz Difference Engine to print the Nautical Almanac Office for the United States Department of Navy.

The General Register Office in London used the second engine as it was intended to print and produce the 1864 English Life Table— statistics on life expectancy by age and sex(actuary tables). However, as stated earlier, the Scheutz Difference Engine use of only three difference engines instead of the prescribed seven difference engines postulated by Babbage. Consequently, the accuracy of actuary tables produced by the Scheutz Difference Engine came into question because it produced inconsistent results.

Some historian speculated the problems that arose with the Scheutz Difference Engine stem from the shortcuts the inventors used to avoid the production problems encountered by Babbage during the construction of both the Analytical and Difference Engines. Consequently, the Scheutz Difference Engine made only a marginal contribution to the printing of the English actuarial tables. For this reason, the hoped-for commercial success of the calculator, Scheutz desired, never materialized (Bromley, *Difference and Analytical Engines*, 1990).

MARTIN WIBERG

Figure 14 Wiberg Difference

In Sweden, Martin Wiberg followed in the path of fellow Swedish inventor Georg Scheutz when he created a difference engine in 1860. Wiberg was born in 1826 in Visby, Scandia, Sweden. He matriculated at Lund University in 1845 and received a Doctor of Philosophy of Science in 1850. Initially, he became interested in the printing industry when he saw there was a demand for accurate mathematical tables for trigonometric and logarithmic functions. Wiberg wanted to use the Scheutz Difference Engine to compose, compile, and print the tables. However, these plans changed when he discovered that the Scheutz Difference Engine had been sold to the Dudley Observatory in the United States and the General Register Office in London.

Undaunted by the setback, Wiberg set out to design and build his own difference engine. By 1860, he had successfully built a difference engine based on the Babbage and Scheutz machines. The Wiberg Difference Engine was about the size of a sewing machine. Wiberg's calculator was more compact than the Scheutz or Babbage difference engines because of an innovation he substituted into the design. Instead of the metal disks used by both the Babbage and Scheutz difference engines for the counting wheels, Wiberg arranged them in a linear fashion along a common axis. The Wiberg difference engine had all the capabilities of the Scheutz Calculator, and more reliability. His machine was successfully used to print logarithmic, actuarial, and trigonometric tables.

Wiberg was a remarkable engineer and a prolific inventor, whose contributions ranged from difference engines to heating devices for railroad carriage components, to the speed controls of match-manufacturing machines, and self-propelled torpedoes. Wiberg also invented an automatic breech-loading weapon. For all his genius, he was unable to bring any of his inventions to commercial success. He is remember in this text for his ability to shrink the size of the difference engine from a device that weighed tons to a device small enough to fit on a desktop (Merzbach, Georg Scheutz and the First Printing Calculator, 1977).

GEORGE GRANT

George Grant is another disciple of Charles Babbage. He is mentioned in this text because he also invented a difference engine in 1876 to print a variety of mathematics' related tables. George Barnard Grant was born in Maine in 1849 to a shipbuilder and his wife. For his early education, he attended the Bridgton Academy in Maine. He began his college education at the Chandler School of Science at Dartmouth College in New Hampshire before enrolling in the Lawrence School of Science at Harvard in Cambridge, Massachusetts. At Harvard, Grant earned a bachelor's degree in 1873.

Figure 15 Grant Difference

Grant's interest in building complex number calculating machines began when he was deducing computing tables while building excavations and embankments. His first attempt to construct complex number calculators were made while he was still attending the Lawrence School Science at Harvard. According to his notes, he failed because constructing the machine was more difficult than he anticipated. In 1870, however, he learned of the Babbage difference engine and proceeded to design a difference engine. His second attempt to build a difference engine was met with skepticism by colleagues causing him (Grant) to lose confidence in himself and to set aside his plans.

A year later, after encouragement by members of the Harvard faculty—professor Wolcott Gibb and Henry Lawrence Eustis president of the Lawrence School of Science—and other prominent scientists in the New England area, Grant made a third attempt to build a difference engine. Grant described the machine he designed, in the August 1871 issue of the *American Journal of Science*, as being influenced by the antecedent difference engines of Babbage and Scheutz. Grant also acknowledged Dionysius Lardner whose article appeared in the 1834 edition of the *Edinburgh Review* magazine as having influenced the design of his difference engine. Grant also stated the 1854 British patent specifications of the Scheutz Difference Engine and Babbage's own writings describing his vision of advanced calculating engines influenced his difference engine.

After graduation, Grant's benefactors supported his continued development of the difference engine. In 1874, the Boston Thursday Club raised funds for the continued construction of a machine, which was supported by Philadelphia sponsor, Fairman Rogers. He encouraged Grant to exhibit the difference engine at the 1876 Centennial International Exhibition at Philadelphia. The difference engine Grant built was approximately 2.5 meters long and 1.5 meters high. It was operated either manually or with a power source. Operated manually it made calculated 10 to 12 terms per minute. When operated with a power source the calculating capacity doubled.

Despite the exposure afforded it at the Centennial International Exhibition the Grant Difference Engine faded into obscurity. Grant's future lay not in the development of difference engines and calculating machines but in tools. As it was with Babbage, fifty years earlier, the need for precision gears proved a necessity for success. So it was for Grant, the skills required to develop gears for his difference engine were pioneering and far more advanced than skills found in comparable tool and machine shops in New England. The fortuitous opportunity allowed Grant to found a groundbreaking gear making company, Grant Gear Works. From this extremely lucrative business, two subsidiaries, Philadelphia Gear Works and the Cleveland Gear Works were born.

Torres Y Quevedo

Leonardo Torres y Quevedo was born on December 28, 1852, in Santa Cruz de Iguña in Molledo, Cantabria, Spain. He is mentioned here for the building of several relay-activated, electromechanical calculating machines, which of all things "played" chess. The electromechanical machine, or "automaton," that Quevedo built in 1890, which he named "El Ajedristica," were modified chess playing computer. It processed algorithmic calculations in a manner similar to an adding machine.

The machine Torres y Quevedo constructed played a king and a rook endgame against an opposing king (played by a human opponent) and was able to achieve checkmate from any starting position in a few moves. The machine consisted of a metal base that made contact with the squares of the board to enable the computer to identify the king's square via electric currents. This device was recognized as theoretically related to the Analytical Engine Charles Babbage imagined almost 80 years earlier (Vernet, 2008).

Torres y Quevedo is listed in this section of the book, because according to historians, he is the logical electromechanical successor to Charles Babbage. Second because he credited Babbage as the major influence for his interest in electromechanical calculating devices. According to George Ifrah *Universal History of Computing* (Ifrah, 2001, pg. 201) Gonzalvo, the son of Torres stated in 1953 "My father did not construct an analytical engine, but he established its principles—which is similar to modern machines... He did construct a demonstration model which calculated the formula a= (p x q) – b..."

6

The Gilded Age

The Gilded Age describes an era during the American Industrial Age that began in the years following the Civil War and ended just after the close of World War I, in 1919. The origin of the term is usually associated with the novel of the same name co-authored by Mark Twain. The term is a metaphor that defines an obsession with golden objects, which has both positive and negative connotations. On one hand, the term gilded refers to things of beauty and value. On the other hand, the term refers to items that are cheap, plated, commercialized, painted, and fake.

Twain's novel describes social climbers and get-rich-quick scam artists, who have no substance, like a gold-painted trinket. Additionally, Twain (Samuel Clemens) suggests the term is a fascination with the wealth and power that gold symbolizes. Finally, the Gilded Age refers to the Golden Age of mechanical calculators, which were trendsetters when introduced.

Figure 16 Baldwin Pinwheel

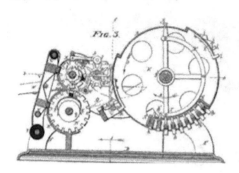

To get a clear picture of the Gilded Age, one must take into account the toll taken on the ordinary citizen of the United States. Historians and writers often juxtaposed the hardships endured by the ordinary citizen struggling to survive deprivation against opulent wealth of J. P. Morgan, James Fisk, Jay Gould, Cornelius Vanderbilt, and Andrew Carnegie. The *robber barons*, who made enormous fortunes—yet displayed charity towards none—forced thousands of their fellow citizens to endure intolerable socioeconomic degradation. The Gilded Age was also an era dominated by four social dynamics: the unbound wave of immigration, the economic upheaval due to the industrial revolution, the end of slavery, and the relentless westward expansion.

Against this backdrop of willful greed and poverty emerged new technologies: the telegraph, the automobile, the airplane, the telephone, and the electric light. Together the inventions transformed the quality of life for the ordinary person. Calculator technology also transformed society, especially in the world of business. During the Gilded Age, for the first time, the epicenter of calculator technology shifted from Europe (Paris & Berlin) to the Americas, Chicago, and Saint Louis.

For the first time, the genius that created the new calculators, with the exception of Hollerith and Hopkins were journeymen who learned their trade through apprenticeships and had little or no formal training in physics, mathematics, or engineering. These innovators learned their trade through, practice, observation, and imagination. Together they were able to skillfully bring about a renaissance to the calculating machine industry.

Also for the first time the calculating machine used new technologies instead of the 17th century stepped drum of Gottfried Leibniz. When Baldwin replaced the cumbersome stepped drum (Figure 17) with the smaller streamline pinwheel (Figure 16), it paved the way for calculating machines that were based on 19th century technology and science.

The golden age for the calculating machines began with the Baldwin Pinwheel Calculator of 1872 and ended with the absorption of the Moon-Hopkins Billing Machine Company by the Burroughs Adding Machine Company in 1921. The golden age of mechanical calculators also includes the likes of Thomas Edison, John Patterson, Charles Raleigh Flint, Thomas J. Watson, and Herman Hollerith all of whom were key players in the grand scheme of the electric tabulators the forerunners of the electromechanical calculator.

During the Gilded Age, three significant scientific breakthroughs occurred in the technology of mechanical calculators. The first, the invention of the pinwheel calculator, which ended the monopoly of the Leibniz, stepped drum style calculator. The second calculator technology breakthrough was the invention of the keyboard. The keyboard eliminated the dial and stylus that predominated the calculator since the Pascaline (1642). The final breakthrough was the introduction of electricity as a source of power to propel the gears of the calculators (Kidwell, 2000).

Figure 17 Step Drum Mechanism

Dorr E. Felt

Dorr E. Felt invented the first commercially successful keyboard style calculator, in 1884. The calculator Mr. Felt invented was called the Comptometer. It was capable of processing two of the four basic arithmetic calculations, addition, and multiplication (Kidwell, 2001). Subtraction on the Felt Comptometer required the use of the Nine's

Figure 18 Felt Comptometer (1890)

complement. Division with the Comptometer was not possible. Figure 20 shows the 1887 version of the Comptometer.

I stumbled across the Nine's Complement of subtraction by addition, while studying unusual math techniques and tricks for middle school teachers while attending Lesley University Graduate school of Education in 1994.

The Nine's Complement is a mathematical technique used to find the remainder of a subtraction problem using addition instead of normal subtraction procedures. To find the difference to subtraction problems using the Nine's Complement, one has to find the nines complement of the subtrahend. For example in the following problem: subtract, the subtrahend, 231 from, the minuend, 789. First, find the nine's complements of the subtrahend 231 which is 768 then add that to 789. The answer is 1557. Disregard the one as a marker for thousands and add it to the one's column of the remaining three digits transforming 557 to 558, which by the way is the answer of the original subtraction problem, what is 789-231?

The Felt Comptometer keyboard had a full complement of 81 keys, 1 through 9. In the original configuration of the keyboard there was no zero, the absence of a keystroke in a column or blank space in the column represented zero (Redin, 2007). However, by December of 1889, Felt and Tarrant had overcome the zero issue with the keyboard. In 1886, Felt applied for a patent and received it in 1887 (Kidwell, 2001).

Dorr Eugene Felt was born in Rock County, Wisconsin on March 18, 1862. Lacking any formal education past the ninth grade, he honed his mechanical skills by working in a machine shop near Beloit, Wisconsin. In 1882, he moved from Wisconsin to Chicago where he worked with the maintenance crews of a Pullman Company. Shortly after a promotion to crew chief, he left the railroads and took a job as a sewing machine sales representative. Dissatisfied with the life of a travelling sales representative, Felt returned to his infatuation with calculators.

After returning to Chicago, he took a position with Ostrander and Huke machine shop. He got the inspiration for the Comptometer while at work; he observed the intricate controls of a planing machine. It was making cuts of varying lengths and depths for the fabrication of sheet metal. During the Thanksgiving holiday, of 1884, he fashioned a prototype of the Comptometer in a wooden macaroni box (Figure 21). He improvised the components for his calculator from meat skewers, staples, string, wire, and rubber bands which, when combined emulated the action of keys (Kidwell, 2001).

Figure 19 Macaroni Box

FELT
"MACARONI BOX"
(1885)
64-K-61

In 1886, he acquired funding for the project from a cousin, Chauncey Foster and then acquired tools to construct the calculator from the A. B. Lawther machine shop. Felt produced several prototypes of his adding machine, which he believed were suitable for marketing. He filed for a patent early in 1887 and received it in July of 1887. He began marketing the Comptometer to Chicago area merchants. The machines eventually caught the attention of Robert Tarrant, who decided to support Felt with funding and marketing campaigns (Kidwell, 2001).

The two men formed a partnership in 1887 and founded the Felt and Tarrant Manufacturing Company. In 1889, Felt added printing capabilities to the Comptometer calling the new device the Comptograph. By 1902, Felt and Tarrant had decided to end their partnership. The terms of their separation stated that Felt should retain the company name and rights to the Comptometer. Tarrant, in turn, agreed to form a new company, the Comptograph Company. This new company, as the name implied, would retain the rights to the Comptograph. By 1914, the Comptograph Company had discontinued business for lack of sales, in Great Britain (Kidwell, 2001).

In 1915, Felt introduced the Felt & Tarrant Model-F. It had an error detection key and a correction key on the keyboard. Both the keys proved highly profitable, and by 1920, Felt & Tarrant had sold 42,000 units, twice as many units as any previous Felt & Tarrant comptometer model. The last model that Felt personally supervised production was the Model J in 1929. He died a year later in 1930.

The Felt and Tarrant Manufacturing Company went public on the stock market in 1946. In 1957, the company changed its name to the Comptometer Corporation. In 1961, after a merger with the Victor Adding Machine Company, it changed its name to the Victor Comptometer Corporation. In 1986, the Victor Comptometer Corporation changed its name to Victor Technologies (Kidwell, 2001) (Ifrah, 2001, p. 131) (M. Williams 1990) (Thomson Gale, 2005) (Aspray & Campbell-Kelly, 1996, pp. 30-31) (Kidwell, 2001) (Thomson Corporation, 2005).

Willgodt Theophil Odhner

Figure 20 Brunsviga Mini

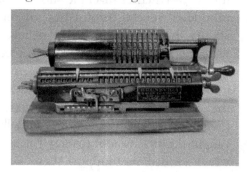

Three years after Baldwin introduced his new calculator technology, a Swedish inventor by the name of Willgodt Theophil Odhner, while living in Russia, filed a patent for a pinwheel or cogwheel mechanism similar to Baldwin's device. As time passed, the names of the two mechanisms became synonymous (Redin, 2007). However, it was Franz Trinks, head of the German firm Grimme, Natalis & Company of Braunschweig of Germany, who realized the full potential of the Odhner pinwheel calculator and acquired the rights to the patent in 1892.

Grimme, Natalis & Company manufactured and marketed the calculator as the Brunsviga. Grimme, Natalis & Company continued to develop and refine the Brunsviga calculator over a 30-year period producing several different variations and models of the calculator.

Between 1905 and his retirement in 1925, Trinks received over 40 US patents for innovation made to the Brunsviga. The Brunsviga became one of the most successful calculators in Europe. According to company records, Grimme, Natalis & Company sold more than 500,000 calculators. Figure 19 shows the Brunsviga mini (Wolff, 2007).

In 1927, the company changed its name to Brunsviga Maschinenwerke Grimme, Natalis & Company AG, then later to Brunsviga Maschinenwerke AG or Brunsviga Machine Works. After World War II, the company resumed production of the Brunsviga with a model 13 machine. In 1957, it first collaborated with Olympia, then in 1959 merged.

Even though the new Brunsviga pinwheel calculating machine was an improvement over the old stepped drum machines. The pinwheel calculators were better suited for scientific applications than for the tedium of business. Whereas scientists used the machines to verify result, commerce required the addition of long lists of numbers. For example, to set up a placement digit on the machine required the setting a lever for that digit. This made operation of the machine slow and frustrating. What commerce most desired was speed, a machine with a keypad and a printer (Williams M. , 1990).

Frank Stephen Baldwin

Frank Steven Baldwin was born in New Harford, Connecticut in the year 1838; he grew up in Nunda, New York. He attended Union College in Schenectady, but withdrew from college to take over the family architectural business. The outbreak of the Civil War interrupted his plans. Believing President Lincoln's explanation that the war would last no longer than few months, Baldwin volunteered for service with the Union Army. At the end of his enlistment, it was apparent to Baldwin, after the fierce early combat, the Rebels were a formidable determined lot that planned to endure at all cost. He then decided against any further service in the military (Kidwell, 2000).

After the Civil War, Baldwin moved to Saint Louis and worked at Peck's Planing Mill. While working at the planing mill, he invented a device that measured the board feet lumber. The device measured the lumber's length by turning a knob. A tape measure gave the width of the board. The length totals were accumulated on one or more sets of dials (University of Saint Andrews Scotland School of Mathematics and Statistics, 2009) (Kidwell, 2000).

Charles H. Peck, co-owner of the planing mill and the President of St. Louis Life Insurance Company allowed Baldwin an opportunity to examine the design and construction of the company owned Thomas

Arithmometer. Shortly thereafter, Baldwin filed a caveat with the U. S. Patent office for the invention of his own calculator in 1872.

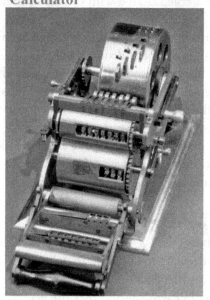

Figure 21 Baldwin Pinwheel Calculator

The innovation, known as the Baldwin Principle, featured a single pinwheel mechanism rather than several intertwined gears and sprockets. It was a revolutionary concept that eventually replaced the bulky 17th century stepped drum calculator technology (M. Williams, 1990). Pinwheel calculators remained a viable sales commodity until the 1950s and the advent of the transistor (Kidwell, 2000).

Some historians have contested the originality of Baldwin's innovation. Some have gone so far as to say that Baldwin was not the first to employ the pinwheel technology for a calculator. They have claimed that Giovanni Poleni (1683-1761), Anton Braun (1686-1728), Izrael Abraham Staffel (1814-1885), Didier Roth (1810-1885), and Leibniz all built calculators that used the pinwheel technology long before Baldwin filed a patent to claim the technology.

All the assertions about the originality of the Baldwin pinwheel calculator are true, but they are all irrelevant. It matters not that Philippe Vayringe (1684-1746) sold a handful of machines based on the Braun design for a pinwheel style calculator. What the Baldwin detractors failed to elaborate or recognize is that all of the aforementioned pinwheel designs remained in the experimental stage of development because each lacked commercial success. Remember the vacuum tube was actually invented by Thomas Edison but he is seldom credited with the invention because he did not understand the technology or know how to exploit the discovery (Kidwell & Williams, 1992, p. 12).

The mechanics of the stepped drum calculator consisted of nine geared wheels surrounding a central gearwheel shaft that had teeth or cogs increasing in size depending on the number entered by the operator. A results wheel (Figure 17), at the end of the square shaft, was rotated to any of ten different positions to register the digits 0 to 9 (M. Williams, 1990).

The Step Reckoner when the operator entered a number into the machine by setting the small pointers—that controlled the position of the gears on the square shafts—then turning of the crank caused all the stepped drums to rotate and add the appropriate digits to the accumulator. To add eight, for example, it was only necessary to cause the square shaft to rotate eight steps. This was accomplished when the small gear on the shaft meshes with eight teeth on the large drum. To multiply a number by 5, the operator turned the crank five times (M. Williams 1990).

In contrast to the complicated and redundant operation of the stepped drum calculator, the pinwheel configuration contained a single set of movable pins on a single shaft, one pin per digit, which protruded or retracted according to the requirements of the user. The cam mechanism rotated by means of a lever eliminating the need for the stylus or the reversing mechanism common on the stepped drum (the *Thomas Arithmometer*) devices (M. Williams 1990).

Arithmetic operations for the pinwheel calculator, again in contrast to arithmetic on the stepped drum, began when the cam contacted various spring-loaded rods of the pinwheel; the spring-loaded rods extended from the surface of the disk according to the operator's need. For instance, if the operator sets the lever to the fifth position, this resulted in the cam having five protruding gear teeth, when rotated; the number five is added to whatever amount that is stored on the accumulator (M. Williams 1990).

Figure 18 shows a photograph of the Baldwin Pinwheel Calculator, circa 1873. Baldwin received the patent for his invention in 1875. Baldwin and associates (Kidwell, 2000) attempted to market the new calculator machine but were unable to generate much interest. Baldwin believed there was a market for his calculator in the financial centers of the East Coast. After a two-year effort, he sold only five machines. After failing to market his machine, Baldwin returned to Saint Louis and resumed his career as an architect. All the same, he remained interested mechanical calculating machines and took out several more patents on calculators in the twentieth century (IBM, 1994) (Kidwell, 2000).

In 1900, Baldwin patented the Baldwin Computing Engine. Another patent on the Baldwin Calculator followed the Baldwin Computing Engine in 1902. Neither machine achieved the desired commercial success Baldwin desired. In fact, Baldwin did not achieve any real commercial success until he collaborated with Jay Randolph Monroe in 1912.

Monroe suggested the Baldwin Calculator adapt the 81-key keyboard format used by rivals. The two men formed the Monroe Calculating Machine Company. A decade later, the Monroe Calculating Machine Company pioneered electro-mechanical calculators. The company changed its name to the Monroe, The Calculator Company.

According to folklore, William Seward Burroughs, the founder of the Burroughs Corporation, built the Baldwin pinwheel calculator in the Saint Louis machine shop of his father, Edmund Burroughs. After further investigation, city records indicate that Edmund Burroughs did not live in the Saint Louis area until the late 1870s. Furthermore, his son William did not move to Saint Louis until 1881. Popular legend makes the assertion that the younger Burroughs was given the opportunity to examine the 1875 Baldwin Pinwheel Calculator in or around 1881, however, there is no substantive evidence to support the notion either (Kidwell, 2000).

William Seward Burroughs

The discussion of the company created by William Seward Burroughs is a vital component in the history of the mechanical adding machine. Created during the Gilded Age, it alone was the only 19th century adding machine company capable of making the transition from the Gilded Age (post-Civil War) to the Information Age and the arrival of the transistor. Some might argue that Victor Technologies, Hollerith Tabulating Machines, and National Cash Register made the transition. However, let me point out that neither Hollerith Tabulating Machines nor National Cash Register began operations exclusively as a digital calculator company. The former was essentially a 19th century version of a computer company. The latter was a cash register company. Victor Technologies never expanded beyond business calculators. Victor did not make computers.

An Ordinary Man

William Seward Burroughs was born near Rochester, New York in 1855. Burroughs grew up and lived in and around the cities of Rochester and Auburn New York until 1881. According to historians (Kidwell, 2000), the Auburn city records indicate that Burroughs worked as a clerk and accountant in several area banks. While working as a bank clerk at the Cayuga County National Bank, he became interested in creating an adding machine to assist banking clerks and accounting (Massachusetts Institute of Technology, 2002).

Albany city records, also, show he worked in a lumberyard as a boxer and a planar (Kidwell, 2000). His father, Edmund Burroughs, moved to Saint Louis, Missouri in the late 1870s and William followed him to Saint Louis in 1881. While working in Saint Louis, the younger Burroughs had several jobs, which provided him with the manufacturing and mechanical skills he needed to succeed later in life.

William Seward Burroughs achieved fame and fortune because of the mechanical calculating machine he invented in 1884 and the company that displays his name. The adding machine featured the 81-key keyboard format. It also contained an accumulator at its rear that displayed a running total and a printed record of the input and results. Burroughs named his new calculator the *Arithmometer*, receiving a patent on the design in 1888. In 1886, he and three other men—Thomas Metcalfe, Richard M. Scruggs, and William Pye—founded, in anticipation of the patent approval, the American Arithmometer Company of St. Louis.

In 1889, Burroughs renamed the adding machine the Bankers' and Merchants' Registering Accountant. During the initial testing of the calculator several flaws were revealed in the machine's design causing it to fail the trial. The setback caused Burroughs and company to simplify the operation and design of its calculator, primarily changing the printing mechanism, and simplifying the operating handle (Kidwell, 2000).

In 1892, he presented a revised version of the Bankers' and Merchants' Registering Accountant to the local banking community for a second trail-run. The second set of tests proved the revisions successful; and, the American Arithmometer Company ordered 100 machines from its manufacturer the Boyer Machine Company for marketing to the local business community. Despite the machine's high price, $475, it soon found a niche market amongst the banks and insurance companies of Saint Louis.

Figure 22 Burroughs' Accountant

American Arithmometer shortened the name of the calculator to the Burroughs Registering Accountant. In 1895, the American Arithmometer Company assumed responsibility for the manufacture of the Burroughs Registering Accountant, and for the first time, it paid dividends to its investors.

In 1896, American Arithmometer hired William H. Pike as a supervisor to oversee cost reduction and increase efficiency. He improved the machine and filed three patents in the process on the Burroughs Registering Accountant. For his efforts, Pike was rewarded with a $40 a week salary and $3000 in bonuses. Pike was promoted to factory supervisor of the newly establish Burroughs Adding and Registering Machine Limited, a subsidiary licensed to manufacture and sell the Burroughs's Arithmometer in Great Britain (Kidwell, 2000).

In 1904, the American Arithmometer Company moved from Saint Louis to Detroit, Michigan and changed its name to the Burroughs Adding Machine Company—honoring its founder, William Seward Burroughs. In 1953, the Burroughs Adding Machine Company changed its name to the Burroughs Corporation when it began making computers and computer accessories. In 1986, the Burroughs Corporation merged with the Sperry Corporation to form Unisys (Hancock, 1988) (Kidwell, 2000) (Nebeker, 2004) (Aspray & Campbell-Kelly, 1996, p. 31).

William Hopkins

The story of William H. Hopkins was one of the more curious and twisted episodes of the Gilded Age. The Hopkins brothers', William and Hubert, story gave birth to the 10-key keyboard format for adding machines and three calculator companies but in the end, neither brother acquired lasting fame or fortune. William Hopkins' story not only marked the apotheosis of the Gilded Age (Kidwell, 2000), it also marked the end of the individual challenging the corporate giants—Burroughs and NCR.

William Hopkins was born in 1850. He lived with his parents on a farm in central Indiana until he left for Indianapolis in 1868 to attend Butler College to study engineering. He did not graduate because of chronic illnesses. After recovering from ill health, he became a missionary with the Christian Church, first in Minnesota and later in Wisconsin. The church recognized had no formal ecclesiastical infrastructure and the ministers were not regularly paid (Kidwell, 2000).

During this period in his life, William supported himself for-the-most-part by teaching. However, ailing parents, beset with financial difficulties, caused him to return to his parent's farm. Upon his return, Hopkins supported himself with inventions he created through his knowledge of engineering. He received his first patent for a simple adding machine that did not have the ability to borrow during the subtraction process. This machine did not create much interest among possible investors and did not go into production.

He did better with his second and third inventions (a knockdown chair and a patent for the scale). The knockdown chair (predecessor to the folding chair) took care of all family expenses. His efforts to manufacture the scale were less successful and eventually caused the family to relocate in western Kansas. In 1885, the Hopkins family moved to Saint Louis.

While in Saint Louis, he became an evangelist, and then served as a chaplain, eventually graduating to pastor of the Second Christian Church of Saint Louis. It was during this period, 1888 that he came up with the idea for a second adding machine based on a ten-key keyboard.

In 1892, Hopkins completed the design for the machine. It proved to be a revolutionary innovation and changed the face of contemporary adding machines that until then featured keyboards with 81 or more keys (Kidwell, 2000).

The Hopkins calculator was easier to use, more reliable, and less expensive than calculators produced by rivals. Not only was the Hopkins calculator capable of addition, it could perform subtraction as well. The device, also, printed the numbers entered by the operator and the arithmetic results on a paper tape.

In 1892, Hopkins filed an application for a patent, which he did not receive until 1894. Before he filed the patent, Hopkins in collaboration with Joseph O. Heimbach and Hubert Hopkins—William's younger brother and a mechanic in his own right—produced a working prototype for demonstration at the offices of St. Louis patent attorney A.C. Fowler. Fowler was greatly impressed with the invention and recommended it to officials of the St. Louis Mechanic's Bank.

The clerks at the Mechanic's Bank were less than enthusiastic about the new adding machine because of flaws in its operation. The bankers did not like the way the device required the operator to set the place value for each digit. Invigorated by the criticism, William Hopkins proceeded to redesign the adding machine according to the specification of the clerks at the Mechanic's Bank. The newly designed machine came with two modifications, a tabulating key, and a place order key. With these modifications in place, the operator need only push a key to shift the carriage to the appropriate position before entering data (Kidwell, 2000).

In the spring of 1891, Hopkins hired James Whitelaw, a St. Louis machinist, to build a model based on his redesign. Whitelaw completed it in January 1893 at a cost of $1,000, which the stockholders of the Standard Adding Machine Company paid. The redesigned adding machine—now called the *Standard*—was once again placed at the St. Louis Mechanic's Bank for a trial period of one year.

After a successful trial period, the officers of the Standard Adding Machine Company showed little or no interest in marketing or manufacturing the Standard. Consequently, William formed the Hopkins Adding Machine Company with the exclusive license to manufacture and market the *Standard*.

Figure 23 The Standard

At the National Banker's Convention held in St. Louis in 1896, Hopkins circulated a flyer announcing a new and improved Hopkins 10-key adding machine was available. Shortly thereafter, the Standard Adding Machine Company reacquired the rights to production of the machine. The *Standard* proved a very successful contender in the St. Louis and national adding machine markets.

The Standard Adding Machine Company displayed the Hopkins 10-key adding machine at the Louisiana Purchase Exposition held in St. Louis in 1904, which awarded it the Grand Prize for Instruments of Precision and Philosophy by a panel of international judges. By 1906, Standard Adding Machine Company had sold more than 3,400 of the machines. By 1907, the company marketed several models of the *Standard* some of which had the capabilities to add fractions as well as whole numbers. Besides being able to add and subtract the new models were capable of multiplying and dividing. The *Standard* had a price that ranged between $185 and $225.

The fortunes of the Hopkins brothers and the Standard Adding Machine Company were to undergo major changes when Hubert Hopkins decided to take his skills to the competing Dalton Adding Machine Company. This change in loyalty occurred because William began to devote more of his time to other projects, the development of brakes for railroad cars, and the ministry.

In 1902, Hubert demonstrated his ideas for a new adding machine to James L. Dalton and St. Louis patent attorney John D. Rippey. So enchanted by the technology of the new adding machine the two executives agreed to form the Addograph Manufacturing Company making Hubert the company treasurer and Simon Lederer the vice president (Kidwell, 2000).

Hubert's escapades demonstrated the increasing difficulty facing start-up companies in the increasingly competitive adding machine industry. When Addograph applied for patents on Hubert's design, Joseph Boyer, president of American Arithmometer (Burroughs), challenged Rippey and his associates on the grounds of patent infringement. The resulting trial forced Addograph to make extensive modifications to the design of the machine before the United States Patent Office granted their application. Because of the continual conflict with Boyer and American Arithmometer, Addograph did not receive its patents until 1912.

According to court records, conflict between the rival companies peaked during May of 1903 when Joseph Boyer engaged in a clandestine plot, along with Addograph executive Simon Lederer, for a hostile takeover of Addograph by American Arithmometer. Court records further indicate that by July, Hubert Hopkins had joined the Boyer-Lederer conspiracy against his own interest with Addograph (Kidwell, 2000).

Upon learning about the conspirators, James Dalton acted quickly to thwart any takeover of his investment. He hastily convened a meeting of the Addograph board of directors to gain their proxy and dash Boyer's efforts. With this majority, Dalton convinced loyal board members to grant him exclusive licenses to manufacture the Dalton Adding Machine under the Hopkins's patents. In late July 1903, Dalton restructured Addograph forming the Adding Typewriter Company of St. Louis (later renamed the Dalton Adding Machine Company) to execute the license agreement. Dalton moved the company to Popular Bluff, Missouri. Then in 1914, Dalton moved to the company to Cincinnati, Ohio leaving Missouri forever.

The Dalton Adding Machine was one of the most popular 10-key adding machines of the early twentieth century. Early models of the Dalton Adding Machine used glass inserts as enticements, which allowed a customer to gaze at the machine's intricacies as it calculated the totals. Rand-Kardex acquired a majority interest of the Dalton Adding Machine Company through a merger in 1927. Rand-Kardex later merged with the Remington Typewriter Company and the Powers Accounting Machine Company to form Remington Rand (Kidwell, 2000).

Figure 24 The Dalton

The modern configuration of the 10-key adding machine with the familiar arrangement of three rows of three keys owes its existence to David Sundstrand who applied the innovation to adding machines he produced at the Sundstrand Adding Machine Company in 1923 (Redin, 2007). Sundstrand Adding Machine Company was sold to Underwood, which merged with Olivetti before entering the electronic age.

In 1904, Hubert and William Hopkins made a last stand against the corporate giants Burroughs, Monroe, and National Cash Register. They, working in conjunction with the Moon Brothers Carriage Company, founded the Moon-Hopkins Manufacturing Company. In 1906 or 1907, the company renamed itself the Moon-Hopkins Billing Machine Company.

The Moon-Hopkins Billing Machine Company was the last attempt of the individual to build a company, from the ground up, in the adding machine industry. From its inceptions, Moon-Hopkins produce a brand of office machine that was superior or equal to any machine produced in the Saint Louis area.

Historians describe the efforts of the Moon-Hopkins Billing Machine Company to build a competitive adding machine as the last stand of the small businessman. After the sale of the Moon-Hopkins to Burroughs in 1921, the adding machine became the domain of the corporate entity and tycoon. The Moon-Hopkins Billing Machine shown in Figure 25 was a final testament to the Hopkins brothers' skill and ingenuity. The walls of the machine were glass, designed to entertain the operator and casual observer as well as discharge billing. For this purpose, it not only carried out the functions of an adding machines but incorporated functions of a typewriter as well (Kidwell, 2000).

It performed as well as the Burroughs' Registering Accountant when printing the results of addition and multiplication. In the same manner, it rivaled the *Standard* and the *Dalton* adding machines, utilizing the 10-key adding machine keyboard configuration. Like the *Universal,* the Moon-Hopkins Billing Machine printed parallel columns of numbers. By 1911, the company had replaced the hand crank driver with an electric motor (Kidwell, 2000).

Despite the machine's superior quality, the Moon-Hopkins Billing Machine Company was not able to manufacture enough machines to compete in the markets outside the Saint Louis area. To complicate matters even more, Moon-Hopkins was beset with a series of lawsuits from rival manufacturers, which included the Dalton Adding Machine Company of Cincinnati and the Burroughs Adding Machine Company of Detroit. Even though Moon-Hopkins eventually prevailed in the courts by 1918, the continual legal struggles placed an undue financial burden that drained profits (Kidwell, 2000).

The company's troubles mounted when William Hopkins died in 1918 and Hubert was in failing health and unable to assume leadership of the company eventually withdrawing from the company operations. Sensing bankruptcy, the Moon-Hopkins Company board capitulated to the Burroughs Adding Machine Company and petitioned the U.S. District Court in Detroit to permit a takeover by the Burroughs Adding

Machine Company without violating the 1914 Anti-Trust Act (Kidwell, 2000).

During the Gilded Age of calculators, inventors created hundreds calculating devices many of whom the author did not mention. This is not an oversight. In this author's opinion, many of the calculators of this era did not change technology already described. Some were merely new takes on the dials first presented by the Baldwin and Odhner pinwheels. Some machines such as the *Dalton* and the *Standard* were victims of mergers to form larger companies like Burroughs, National Cash Register, and Monroe.

Figure 25 Moon-Hopkins Billing Machine

Still other firms such as Comptograph Company, the Morse Manufacturing Company, and the American Adding Machine Company, found the competition too fierce, failed to produce enough revenue to compete with the likes of Burroughs or Monroe, and went out of business. Other examples of companies agreeing to merger partnership as did the New Hiett Machines Manufacturing, the Sundstrand Adding Machine Company, the Underwood Typewriter Company, Ellis Adding-Typewriter, and the Brennan Adding Machine Co (Kidwell, 2001) (Kidwell, 2000).

7

Cash Registers, Typewriters, and Tabulators

Thus far, in my quest to trace the origins of the computer from antiquity through the Industrial Age and into the present day has followed the narrow focus of the evolution of the digital calculators. This discussion revealed three prevailing calculator technologies: the step-drum, the pinwheel, and the keyboard driven.

Because this chapter diverges from the tried and true, I will summarize what has been discussed thus far. In Chapter 2, I elaborated the analog devices of the *Flesh* and *Wood Era*. The context of the chapter discussed yardsticks, Salamis boards, and slide rules. Then in Chapter 3, The First Calculators, the discussion analyzed calculators of the *Metal Era*. The discussion led us to discover Wilhelm Schickard created the first desktop calculator, the Calculating Clock.

Pascal unknowingly followed Schickard and found moderate commercial success with the invention of the Pascaline, selling approximately 50 machines. He in turn was the inspiration for Leibniz to attempt to improve upon the Pascaline. Leibniz masterminds the creation of the stepped-drum technology, a technological breakthrough. However, his calculator the Step Reckoner is a failure. The stepped-drum technology festers with minor commercial success for one hundred and fifty years before it rises again in the form of the *Thomas Arithmometer*. Once Thomas perfects the stepped-drum technology, it dominates sales in the metal calculator era for the next hundred years. The *Metal Era* of mechanical calculators ends shortly after World War II with the introduction of solid-state technology and the transistor.

In Chapter 5, The Gilded Age there begins a shift in calculator economic power from Europe to North America, from London, Paris, and Berlin to Saint Louis, Detroit, and Ohio in the United States. Out of necessity, the pinwheel and the step drum calculating technologies integrate with the keyboard as buttons supplant the dial and the stylus.

The purpose of the divergent in chapters seven and eight is to examine parallel solutions in other industries. The parallel technologies are a necessary because the ABC or ENIAC computers were not isolated spontaneous events. The alternative solutions speak for themselves as the forces of industry and commerce shaped their existence in the business world.

The study of these variations to the mechanical calculator is also necessary to change the lexicon that the rudiments of the computer—the digital calculator—had its beginning with the cold steel of the Charles Babbage Difference and Analytical Engines. Albeit true, that Babbage envisioned a mechanical device with a memory, an input/output, arithmetic-logic unit, and a control unit, in the early 19th century. By the latter half of the 19th century, His ideas were no longer unique but eclipsed. Christian Hamann, Martin Wiberg, and Bernard Grant all had built a difference engine. All three of the Babbage disciples produced portable difference engines that surpassed the machines Babbage envisioned in technological acumen, reliability, and functionality. By the end of the 19th century designers of digital calculators during the Gilded Age—not immune to the purposes of the difference engines—had incorporated the two of the four basic computer elements—memory and input/output into their adding machines.

It is necessary to study alternatives to the digital calculator because of the advancements made by NCR and HTC. Both companies learn how to resolve the shortcomings that were endemic to metal digital calculating devices. By looking at the problem from the perspective of National Cash Register and the Hollerith Tabulating Company, the feasibility of an electronic computer draws nearer.

That being said, this chapter, Cash Registers, Typewriters, and Tabulators, focus on three emerging 19th century technologies that when looked at separately are insignificant to the development of the modern computer. However when combined along with the technology already discussed the computer is inevitable. The first of these innovations is the cash register. The second technology diversion is an investigation of the electric tabulating machine. Finally, we examine the origins of the typewriter. When combined, the modern personal computer contains ingredients from each diversion.

In Chapter 8, A Brief Course in Electricity, I stray even further from the original definition of the computer, this time examining events that occur completely outside the realm of a calculating and computing technology. In examining these aspects of the Industrial Revolution, I circumvented clumsy explanations as to why mechanical ingenuity failed to achieve the desired outcome and side step the problems that eventually were the undoing of Charles Babbage. Also in Chapter 8, I examined the implications of the incandescent lamp, the biographies of Tesla, and Edison, the role of Westinghouse and Morgan, and the influence of electricity, electronics, and radio had on the building of ABC and ENIAC. Then if good fortune prevails, by the end of the Chapter 8, I will find myself in a position to continue along the original path, with these accessories in tow, towards the implementation of the digital computer.

THE CASH REGISTER

The history of the first commercially successful cash register culminates with the story of James and John Ritty, of Dayton, Ohio, in the year of 1879. The history of the cash register begins with the antecedent of the cash register, the cash drawer. The cash drawer was the prevalent business tool in the majority of retail establishments worldwide by the mid-nineteenth century.

The basic advantages of the cash drawer were its dividers for holding coins and paper currency. The basic disadvantages of the cash drawer were two major defects. First, it lacked an audit trail. Specifically, the cash drawer did not record transactions or detail items purchased. Second, the cash drawer did not have a totalizer or printer. As a result, transactions made at the cash drawer were often the focal point of intense acrimony. It is at the cash drawer that customers often accused storeowners and their employees of theft.

James Ritty opened his first saloon in Dayton, Ohio in 1871 billing himself as a connoisseur of "Dealer in Pure Whiskies, Fine Wines, and Cigars." Despite the popularity of his saloons, Ritty was not immune to allegations of theft customers made about his employees. The claims levied against his saloons caused to Ritty to suspect employees were pilfering a portion, if not all, of the customer's payments. However, without proof, Ritty was powerless to intervene.

In an effort to save his sanity, Ritty took a vacation to get away from the day-to-day operations of his saloon. While on vacation, he contemplated a resolution to his cash drawer problems. Popular legend states he found the solution while on a cruise ship touring Europe. Supposedly, he stumbled upon the idea while visiting the pilothouse of the cruise ship and observing a machine counting the turns of the ship's propellers.

What is fact, when Ritty returned to Dayton; he had a clear idea of how to solve his restaurant problem. He explained his idea to his brother John, a mechanic by trade, and together they designed and built the first cash register. It had buttons arranged along the lower third of the device the upper half resembled a clock face. The buttons recorded the sale; the arms on the face of the cash register worked like the arms of a clock, displaying the cost of each item.

Within a few months of his initial showpiece, Ritty introduced improvements. Among the improvements to the cash register were the familiar pop-up flags and a bell replacing arms of the clock to indicate the price of each item. The original cash register did not have a cash drawer that came with a later version (Massachusetts Institute of Technology, 2002) (HighBeam Research, Inc, 2001).

Ritty applied for and received a patent for the cash register in 1879. He named the device the "Ritty's Incorruptible Cashier." A short time later, Ritty opened a small factory to manufacture the Incorruptible Cashier. Ritty advertised the Incorruptible Cashier as a storekeeper's dream come true. The first Incorruptible Cashier was no more than an adding machine with a bell. The updated version of the original featured pop-up flags indicating the purchase price of an item and an accumulator displaying a running total and final cost. The presence of the cash register in his saloon effectively ended most of the animus between customer and clerk.

Ritty was an exceptional saloonkeeper as he opened several others in the Dayton area. It was second nature to him. He could not, however, find the time to manage his saloons and to manage the manufacturing and marketing of the Incorruptible Cashier. Overwhelmed by the success of the Pony House Saloon and other establishments in and around Dayton, Ritty sold his patent rights to the Incorruptible Cashier cash register to Jacob H. Eckert in 1881. Eckert hoped to capitalize on the pragmatism of the cash register formed the National Manufacturing Company. Sales of the new cash register were slow and Eckert did not profit as he anticipated.

In 1884, John H. Patterson and his brother Frank were the owners of a successful business selling coal and mining supplies. Their only fault was their recordkeeping. It was as unorganized as the brothers were shrewd. One of their many problems was the growing number of unrecorded bills of sales and accounts payable on the ledger in their office. While in search of a solution to their dilemma cash flow problems, John read an article about the National Manufacturing Company's cash register and purchased two machines. Within the year, the Patterson brothers were able to reduce their accounts payable from $16,000 to $3,000. John's success with debt reduction prompted him and Frank to purchase the National Manufacturing Company from Eckert for $6,500, renaming the company, in the process, as the National Cash Register Company (NCR).

After purchasing the National Manufacturing Company, John and his brother discovered it was a money losing enterprise. At first, they asked Eckert to nullify the deal and offered him a $2000 bonus to reacquire the company. After Eckert refused, the Patterson brothers set about making sure their National Cash Register Company began to make a profit.

Figure 26 Ritty's Incorruptible

John assumed responsibility for the training of the employees who were to sell the cash registers to retailers and restaurateurs. He implemented new policies that would have a huge impact on the way corporate America developed executives and sales crews. It is said that by 1930 one in six of the top executives in the United States were trained at NCR (Knipple, 1998) (IEEE, 2008).

CHARLES KETTERING

Besides the Patterson brothers, another influential person at NCR was Charles F. Kettering. Most people associate the Kettering named as founder of automobile battery manufacturer DELCO, for his work with General Motors, or for his charity at the Sloane-Kettering Cancer Institute. He is considered one of America's great inventors; Charles Kettering holds more than 180 patents and has had an unrivalled impact on the conduct of commerce in American life. Few Americans know of his contributions to commerce and computing devices because of his contributions to automobile starting systems.

Kettering was born August 29, 1876 on a farm near Loudonville, Ohio. After graduating from the Ohio State University with a degree in electrical engineering, Kettering began work for NCR as an experimental engineer. During his five-year stay with NCR, the company saw an unprecedented growth in technological acumen. Among his many innovations came a credit verification system better known as the "OK Charge Phone." Kettering integrated the use of a telephone to verify individual credit at department stores. It was the forerunner to the credit card. Kettering added a low cost electric motor for the printing cash register to NCR's war chest. The motor eliminated the need for a hand crank to operate the cash register. These two advancements move the cash register from high business tool to ordinary business tool. In other words, the improvements made to the cash register widen the market of consumers for the cash register. The lower price made the cash register available to small business owner. For his encore with NCR, Kettering invented the Class 1000 Register Accounting Machine for banks, hotels, and insurance companies. The Class 1000 Register Accounting Machine had the ability to track transactions from multiple clerks. The Class 1000 was the forerunner to future computerized models of cash accounting machines produced by NCR (Charles F. Kettering, 2003). After his tenure with NCR, Kettering formed the Dayton Engineering Laboratories Company (DELCO) with the financial support of NCR.

ACCOUNTING MACHINES

In 1921, NCR's efforts to outdistance of the competition led to the development of the Class 2000 Register Accounting Machine. The Class 2000 Accounting Machine evolved from the Kettering Class 1000. It was a cash register that had a line printer and printed data an inserted form card. It was the perfect accounting tool for banking, insurance, and the hospitality industry. The Class 2000 Accounting Machine had the ability of track and produce separate totals for 30 separate clerks. The Class 2000 was the precursor of NCR's entry into electronic data processing and the point of sale computer.

After the introduction of UNIVAC by Remington Rand in 1952, NCR acquired control of the Computer Research Corporation (CRC) to propel itself into the electronic data processing industry. Four years later, in 1956, CRC under the aegis of NCR introduced the Class 29 Post-Tronic electronic computer form of the earlier Register Accounting Machines. The Class 29 Post-Tronic Computer utilized magnetic strips for data storage.

In 1962, NCR revolutionized the industry's electronic memory market with the introduction of an innovative mass storage technology for its Model 315 mainframe computer with a technology known as card random access memory (CRAM) instead using the conventional magnetic tape or punch card. Each CRAM card measured 14 inches long and 3 ½ inches wide. A single card consisted of a Mylar surface with seven data recording tracks, which the computer used for reading and writing of data for future use (NCR, 2008). Each track had a storage capacity of 3,100 characters making the total storage capacity of each card was 21,700 characters. A stack of CRAM cards created a CRAM file. The CRAM file handled a stack of 256 magnetic cards with a total storage capacity of 5.5 million characters per stack (NCR, 2008). CRAM mass storage technology was a viable and successful   alternative to magnetic tape in the 1960s until the development of disk drive technology.

THE FALL AND RISE OF NCR

In 1991, American Telephone and Telegraph (AT&T) purchased a controlling interest of NCR. In 1994, AT&T changed the NCR name to Global Information Solutions (GIS). Five years later in 1996, NCR re-emerged in the corporate world, when AT&T decided to divide itself into three independent publicly traded companies Lucent, AT&T, and GIS. AT&T divided itself partially because the courts decided it was a monopoly and partially because it wanted to compete better in the ever-changing telecommunications industry. After the announcement of AT&T's breakup, GIS renamed itself NCR.

The resultant AT&T breakup caused the three spin off companies to narrow the focus of their business mission. For example, Lucent specializes and markets telephones, networking equipment, microprocessors, and other computing accessories. AT&T focuses on providing the public with long-distance telecommunications services for landline and cellular telephones. AT&T recently purchased a controlling interest in the cellular telephone provider Cingular. While NCR manufactures automated teller machines (ATMs), various electronic office equipment, supermarket scanners, semiconductors, and networking systems (NCR History Timeline, 2009).

Since reemerging from the shadow of AT&T, NCR has evolved into an entirely different company. Prior to the breakup of AT&T, NCR was a hardware-only company. After reestablishing itself, NCR became a full solutions provider when it purchased Compris Technologies, Inc. Compris Technologies was a leading provider of management software and store automation for the food-service industry. To complement its acquisition of Compris Technologies, NCR purchased Dataworks, a developer of check-processing software.

In 1998, NCR concluded its transformation from a hardware only manufacturer to a differentiated software and services company with the sale of their hardware-manufacturing branch to Solectron. To assure its position in the software services market, NCR, in 2003, received a patent on its signature capturing software. It continued to solidify its position in the software and services market by acquiring Kinetics and Galvanon leaders in the self–service travel and self–service health care industries, respectively. In 2009, NCR moved its national headquarters from Dayton to Duluth, GA (NCR History Timeline, 2009) (Massachusetts Institute of Technology, 2000) (IEEE, 2009).

Electric Tabulators

Herman Hollerith and the electric tabulator came to the forefront of American technology because of a logistical nightmare at the United States Census Bureau in 1885. As the 1880 census progressed, the Census Bureau found itself on the horns of a dilemma. It still had millions of uncounted census forms in 1885. Bureau officials realized the difficulties manifesting itself with the 1880 census would double if not triple for the 1890 census. The population growth and unbound immigration, raised alarms in the minds of Bureau officials causing them to estimate that a hand-count of the 1890 census would take approximately 13 years. That would violate the mandate authorized by the Congress—a census of the entire country every ten years. Bureau officials did not want to contemplate starting the census of 1900 while it was still tabulating the data for 1890 (Meyer, 2002, p. 80).

This logistical crisis came about for a number of reasons. The primary cause of the problems was the technology employed by the United States Census Bureau. The USCB required a hand count of every enumeration form. The policy developed by the Census Bureau to hand count the population originated in the 18th century. By the middle of the 19th century, that policy became obsolete (Heide, 1997). The second factor contributing to the crisis—according to 19th century Census

Bureau officials—was the Constitutional mandate that required a count of the United States population every ten years. Historians, on the other hand, state prior to 1902, a major contributor to the logistical crisis of the Census Bureau were it was a temporary agency that had to be reconstituted every ten years. To comply with Constitutional mandates, Congress merely appropriated funds to hire a completely new staff every ten years to organize census operations. The haphazard method Congress used to manage the census revealed obvious flaws to the continuity in the day-to-day management of the census. Temporary employment yielded temporary ideas and commitments. Second, technological research and ingenuity to cope with the logistics of the census policies and procedures was non-existent.

THE CENSUS

For the first six censuses, from 1790 to 1840, the basic enumeration unit employed by the Census Bureau was the household. The census of 1840 recorded just over five million families (households). Beginning with the 1850 census, the Census Bureau initiated several changes to the enumeration protocols. The protocol change did not speed the job of the census. The change in protocol extended the job of the census enumerators.

The first protocol change was a shift in the emphasis of the enumeration unit from the family to the individual. A second protocol change was made in the requirements of the individual enumerators. From 1850 forward, enumerators were mandated, by federal statue, to make personal inquiries at every dwelling and account for each family member. This one change in protocols made the job enumerator more labor intensive. The increased detail requirements of the 1850 census caused the workload to increase by a factor of almost five, recording twenty-three million inhabitants instead of 5 million families.

Another protocol change that was initiated with the 1850 census required the enumerator to make two additional copies of enumeration records. Prior to 1850 only one set of records was required for each district. The new changes required the enumerator to make copies of his or her records for the Census Bureau, as normal, plus one copy each for the clerk of the county court and the secretary of state of the state or territory for each enumeration district (Szucs, 1998) (AncestoryInc.com, 2009). Even with the required changes, the census took only five months to enumerate. The 1850 census was called the first modern census not because it included a more complicated form but because it also recorded the number of slaves in a household. Free persons were listed individually on one form. A second form recorded the slave members of the household – separate but not equal.

THE ISSUE

From 1850 to 1890, the amount of work required of census marshals or clerks to count the population—despite the carnage of the Civil War—grew almost threefold as the population grew from 23 million citizens in 1850 to 63 million citizens in 1890. The growth in statistical records was observed in the number of tables Congress required the Census Bureau to enumerate. In 1850, the entire census had only 60 table; by 1890, the number of tables in the enumerations had grown to almost 1700 tables (Heide 1997).

Logistical problems began to manifest with each new census. Take for example the problems occurring between 1860 and 1870. Whereas the 1860 was conducted during a civil war, the census showed the population of the United States as roughly 31 million citizens, the form required only 13 questions. With relative calm, the census of 1870 showed the United States with a population of roughly 40 million and required the answer to 17 questions. The 1880 census required the enumerator to solicit the answers for 25 questions, keep in mind there is no permanent staff or director.

The new census forms and the 23 percent increase in population were secondary to the underlying issues at the Census Bureau. Since 1850, when the tally system was initiated, technology for counting the census forms remained stagnant. Then in 1872, the chief clerk of the census Charles Seaton improvised a machine that enabled several tally sheets to be counted mechanically. A gracious but still nearsighted Congress considered Seaton's invention a significant breakthrough and paid him the equivalent of a clerk's salary for 29 years (U. S. Census Bureau, 2008) (Campbell - Kelly 1990, p. 37) (Heide 1997).

Some final notes about the census of 1880 can be summarized thusly: the contentious predicates of selfishness, corruption, and malevolence permeating the Gilded Age private industry also infected the Census Bureau. The season was ripe for corruption, backroom politics, and scandals: The Compromise of 1876, the Crédit Mobilier, the bribery of Secretary of War William Belknap, the Fiske and Gould gold market scheme, and Whiskey Ring Scandal. The atmosphere of corruption manifested itself at Census Bureau in the form of political chicanery and outright corruption. Politicians demanded detailed statistical data from the census to vindicate funding request and pork barreling, which resulted in more changes to the census forms and more calculations. At one point, due to their substantial workload, members of the Census Bureau suggested a Constitutional change to reduce the frequency of the census.

THE COMPETITION

In an effort to avert the impending disaster of 1890 and avoid the wrath of Congress, the Census Bureau solicited bids from the private sector for a logistical solution. The solicitation offered as a reward to any company capable of meeting the logistical challenge an exclusive government contract worth millions of dollars. The scope of the solicitation was simple, shorten the time required to compile and count the data from the census of 1890. Three men stepped forward to accept the challenge described in the solicitation: Charles F. Pidgin, William C. Hunt, and Herman Hollerith (Aul, 1972).

Each of the competitors made oral presentations to Census Bureau administrators describing the virtues of their data processing system. Two of the three competitors, Pidgin and Hunt, described systems that required human intervention of the tabulation with hand transcription and manipulation of data forms prior to the actual tabulation of data. The first competitor was Charles F. Pidgin. Pidgin called his data processing system the *Chips System*. It was very similar to the Hollerith tabulating system. What distinguished the *Chips System* from the Hollerith Tabulating Machine was the method of tabulation. With the *Chips System* data gathered by an enumerator was transcribed by hand onto cards, color-coded cards, and then hand-counted. Each color of the cards represented a certain class of data such as age, sex, or occupation (Heide 1997) (Williams M. R., 1996, p. 124).

The second competitor was William C. Hunt. Hunt utilized a system of data processing called the *Slip System*. The *Slip System* as the *Chips System* required the sorting according to color-codes and counting of information by hand together with transcribing the data using different color-coded slips (Wolf, 2000, pg. 37). The Hollerith data processing system, which did not require color-coding or any human intervention with machine operations after loading the cards onto the automatic card counter, won the contract easily (Heide, 1997).

A summary of the events surrounding Hollerith's victory began in 1887 with a series of tests to assess each competitor's data processing capabilities. The first assessment for the tabulating machines called for the compiling of the mortality statistics for the city of Baltimore. A second assessment called for the machines to compile the medical statistics also from the city of Baltimore for the Office of the Surgeon General of the Army (Campbell - Kelly 1990) (Heide, 1997).

The final assessment came in 1889 at the behest of the director of the census, Robert P. Porter who stated the tabulating system winning this trial wins the contract to count the 1890 census. The assessment of the tabulating machines involved the tabulation of the questionnaires for the St. Louis district from the 1880 census, a task that required the counting of more than ten thousand individuals (Campbell - Kelly, 1990).

What made Hollerith's system a clear-cut winner was the fact his machine performed the sorting and counting automatically. Once the machine counted the population or performed a rough count, Hollerith—as Jacquard did with the automated silk looms of Paris before—selected different variables or classes to elaborate during the count. In addition to the rough count or total sample population, his machines tabulated the occupation, age, gender, race, and ethnicity for sample population of the Saint Louis trials.

For the census of 1890, Hollerith's machines counted the entire United States population in six weeks. The Census Bureau was delighted; the rough count set the population of the United States at 62,947,714 people. After the rough count, the machines tabulated each class of the citizen by sex, age, gender, occupation, race, ethnicity, income, housing, geographic area, and education. Economic factors it tabulated were number of workers in specific industries. Two and a half years after it began, Hollerith and his machines had tabulated, printed, collated, and sent to Congress the entire 1890 census report, which included more than 1700 tables. A stupendous feat when compared to the tabulating time of seven years required for the census of 1880. The entire 1890 census report was 2640 pages. All told, Hollerith earned $11 million dollars (U. S. Census Bureau, 2008).

The key to Hollerith's success was his punch card. It measured 6 5/8 inches in length with a width of 3 1/4 inches (Figure 27). Each card contained space for 288 punches. The card's lower right-hand corner was clipped to provide the card proper orientation in the machine as it passed through the system. The leftmost 48 punching positions on the cards contained the four-digit codes representing the enumeration district. The data for an individual was recorded on the right side of the card with 240 punching positions. Data categories were recorded in several of irregularly shaped regions, or fields, on the card, beginning at the top, left of the enumeration districts, then moving roughly clockwise around the card.

For example, the third field recorded the race of the individual. The fourth field recorded the gender. Field 5 recorded the age. Field 6 represented the age of the individual within a range of five-year periods (0-4, 5-9, 10-14... etc.). The seventh field recorded marital status of the individual (married, unmarried, widowed, divorced). All total the card contained twenty-one fields. Enough space to record the information the enumerator gathered from the citizenry (Campbell-Kelly, 1990).

The data was recorded using the pantograph punch. The punch had a pre-drilled guide plate bearing an image of the card to the front and a carriage for a blank card to the rear; by depressing an index pin into a hole in the guide plate, a hole was punched with accurate registration in the corresponding position in the card.

The Hollerith Tabulating Machine revolutionized business by reducing the time required to process large volumes of data. The success Hollerith achieved during the census of 1890 led to additional contracts from private industry and foreign governments. By 1891, Hollerith machines were used to count the census of Canada, Norway, and Austria (Campbell-Kelly, 1996). The machines were easily adaptable to business operations and soon were placed in the offices of railroad shipping companies and utility companies. In 1896, Hollerith formed the Tabulating Machine Company (TMC).

Figure 27 Hollerith Card

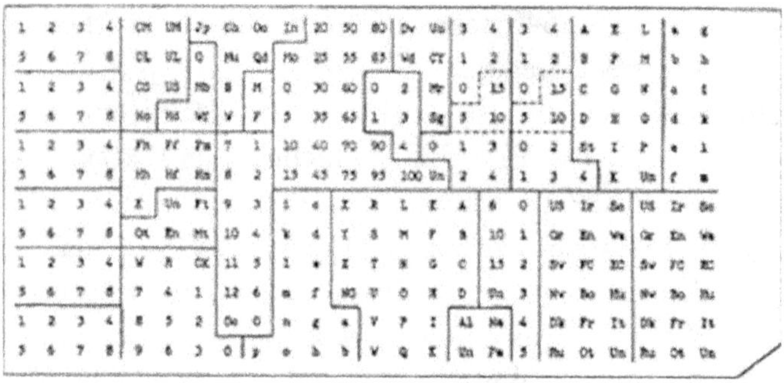

After completion of the census of 1900, Hollerith and the new Census Bureau director S.N.D. North began negotiations for the census of 1910. The two men were unable to agree to terms—mainly because of the rental price of the tabulating machines. TMC wanted to raise the prices it charged the Census Bureau to rent its machines. The Bureau believed the new prices were too high. Because of the failed negotiation, TMC lost the Census Bureau contract for the 1910 census. By 1907, Hollerith had put the Census Bureau contract in the past and began to expand TMC to foreign markets and the private sector (Campbell - Kelly, 1990).

The Census Bureau decided to build its own tabulating machine. Using the Hollerith Tabulating Machine as a template, Census Bureau employees, under the auspices of James Legrand Powers, developed its own tabulating machine, by 1907. In addition to the automatic feeder, common on the TMC machine, Powers incorporated a card sorter and a printer to the machine for use by the Census Bureau. The innovations were a marked improvement over the machine offered by TMC (U. S. Census Bureau 2008). In 1911, Powers, who held the patent on the improved tabulator, left the Census Bureau and founded Powers Accounting Machine Company. Powers' enterprise was soon the most successful automatic tabulation company on the market. In 1927, Powers Accounting Machine Company merged with the Remington

Typewriter Company and Rand Kardex to form Remington Rand (U. S. Census Bureau, 2008).

Despite the setback, losing the contract for Census of 1910, TMC continued to expand and secured contracts with prominent business entities such as the Atchison, Topeka, & Santa Fe Railroad and at Denver Gas & Electric Co. and Taft-Pierce. Hollerith pioneered business practices still used today (by IBM) such as renting data processing equipment instead of selling and requiring renters and owners to purchase data processing supplies exclusively from TMC. The sale of cards was so profitable that Hollerith made no improvement to the machines at all.

HERMAN HOLLERITH

Herman Hollerith was born Feb. 29, 1860 in the city of Buffalo, New York. He received his education at the City College of New York and Columbia University, graduating in 1879. After college, he worked as a statistician for the Department of Vital Statistics, compiling data on the nation's manufacturers. His work revealed there was a problem dealing with large amounts of data by hand. While on the job, he Hollerith met Dr. John Shaw Billings the head of the Department of Vital Statistics. Billings took a liking of Hollerith for two reasons, first because he liked to mentor talented new employees of the Department of Vital Statistics. Second, because Hollerith was dating his daughter. For this reason, Billings provided Hollerith with the inspiration for the development of an electric tabulating machine.

After explaining to Billings the problem he was having with compiling large amounts of data by hand, it was recommended he study the works of Joseph Marie Jacquard (1752-1834). Jacquard was a French industrialist who invented the automated programmable silk weaving loom. Jacquard accomplished the task with punch cards made of stiff pasteboard or cardboard. The cards contained various patterns of punched holes which in turned control the thrust of knitting needles creating various patterns in silk fabric. Each throw of the loom's shuttle (drawing horizontal threads) was monitored by a punch card controlling an array of the knitting needles. The pattern of holes on each punch card determined whether a needle would pass through the fabric. The cards controlled the loom the in the same manner a computer's operating system controls the input and output of data on a computer. The Jacquard system gave weavers increased productivity, better efficiency and greater flexibility in elaborate weavings of silk and other fabrics (Gale Virtual Library, 2008). Hollerith adapted the Jacquard principle of on and off (binary math) to computing, the rest is history.

In 1911, Hollerith merged the Tabulating Machine Company with the companies of Charles Ranlegh Flint, International Time Recording Company (TRC) and the Computing Scale Company (CSC), to form the Computing Tabulating Recording Corporation for 1.2 million dollars. Hollerith stayed on with the merged companies as a secondary consultant until 1921. In 1924, under the leadership of Thomas J. Watson Sr., the company changed its name to International Business Machines or IBM (Campbell-Kelly, 1996).

Figure 28 Hollerith Tabulator

The significance of the Hollerith triumph was not lost on the inventors of the first digital computers. The punch card theory Hollerith used easily transferred to electromechanical and to electronic calculators. The use of on or off, ones or zeroes scheme for tabulating machines is the basis for the binary code used in the programming language of digital computers. The punch cards made it easy to enter data into the computer. Engineers favored it to the reconfigurations of switches and wiring in a computer, which was the case for the original ENIAC when it first went into service.

The first coding scheme for the punch cards to represent characters that human comprehended was EBCDIC (Extended Binary Coded Decimal Interchange Code)—the equivalent to text in computers and devices that utilized text.

American Standard Code for Information Interchange (ASCII) replaced EBCDIC as the primary exchange code when the personal computers became predominate. ASCII was developed using the same principles that created the Morse and Baudot codes. Unicode replaced ASCII as the medium of communication. Unicode is a computing industry standard for the consistent representation and manipulation of text expressed in most of the world's writing systems.

THE TYPEWRITER

Figure 29 Typewriter circa 1878

The first patent on a typewriter was filed by Henry Mill of Great Britain, in 1714 (World - Information.Org, 2007). William Burt invented the typewriter in the United States in 1830 (Wikipedia.Org, 2010). This invention, he called the Typographer, printed words one letter at a time. Following Burt's Typographer, there was an abundance of proto typewriter designs, which had patents from Italy to Brazil. Most of the erstwhile inventors of the typewriter found little commercial success, and the enthusiasm for their typewriters waned soon after its introduction. In 1867, the American inventor Christopher Latham Sholes read an article in the journal *Scientific American* describing a new British-invented typewriter. It was enough to inspire Latham along with Carlos Glidden, and Samuel Soule to build the first commercially practical typewriter.

Sholes and associates tinkered with the invention and produced a second model in 1868, which he received a patent. The 1868 machine wrote at a rate that far exceeded the speed of the pen. Still it was crude, and Sholes made numerous improvements to the typewriter over the next few years. Despite the writing speed, despite the numerous innovations, commercial success eluded the small group of partners.

It would take Sholes and associates another 8 years along with numerous revisions including a QWERTY-style keyboard and a second patent before finding financial backing. Then in conjunction with a business promoter, James Densmore they were able to convince Philo Remington—of E. Remington and Sons, the small arms manufacturer, to produce the machine. Once Remington agreed to manufacture the typewriter, Sholes and associates were paid $12,000 for the rights to the patent.

It took Remington another five years to sell the first 1000 typewriters. The first Sholes, Glidden, Soule typewriter Remington marketed used upper case letters only. Remington overhauled that shortcoming by adding a lower typeface to the keys. By 1880, E. Remington and Sons were making more than a 1000 machines a year (Aspray & Campbell-Kelly, Computer: A History of the Information Machine, 1996, pp. 24-29).

The modern computer keyboard is based on the innovations initiated by Remington on the Sholes, Glidden, and Soule typewriter. The most important innovation was the staggered QWERTY key arrangement, which made typing easier and ended key jamming.

The modern computer keyboard owes its touch-tones to the digital telephone. Each tone of a touch-tone telephone emits its own sound. The sound has a numeric value that the computer describes with ones and zeroes. Likewise, the symbols on the keys of the computer keyboard are assigned numeric values. For your information, Thomas Edison created one of the first electric typewriters when he electrified the typewriter using an electromagnet.

8

A Brief History of Electricity

This chapter in the history of the modern digital computer highlights some of the major events in the domestication of electricity. The age of electric wonderment—as far as the computer is concerned—began in the 19th century with the invention of the Cooke-Whetstone telegraph. The telegraph was followed by the invention of the telephone, the electric light, the electric tabulator, and finally the radiotelegraph.

The first of the electric miracles was the telegraph. It linked the nation from Atlantic to Pacific supplanting the optical telegraph, the newspaper, the locomotive, and the Pony Express for speed and convenience in telecommunications. Prior to the invention of the telegraph the time required to send a message by locomotive, from Baltimore to the District of Columbia was roughly an hour. The time required to send a letter from Washington D. C. to San Francisco by locomotive (the fastest form of transportation in the 19th century) was eight days. The telegraph narrowed the communications gap to a matter of minutes for communications between Baltimore and Washington and to a matter of a few hours for communications between San Francisco and the District of Columbia. The telegraph proved electricity was not merely a source of entertainment regulated to the parlor tricks of charlatans and would-be magicians but a valuable utility.

The telegraph with its crude relays and switches that sent messages through copper wire serves as a forerunner to the Electromechanical Era of human computing. To talk about computing without including a discussion of electricity is like eating oatmeal (not granola) without the milk. True Burroughs, Felt, and Hopkins were able to develop machines with a limited artificial memory for the immediate job of printing on paper tape. However, the neither the metal calculators nor the computing engines could not send the records across town or thousands of miles across country without the use of horse and rider or locomotive.

The miracle of the telephone invented in 1867 by Antonio Meucci followed the telegraph. The telegraph had linked local and national events from coast to coast giving notice of the assassination of President Lincoln, and the end of the Civil War are examples of its capabilities. The telephone did for communications on a micro level what the telegraph did on a macro level. Father living in Baltimore could talk with a child living in San Francisco as if standing in the same room.

The incandescent lamp, the light bulb, invented in 1879, follows the telegraph and telephone, proving that electricity has versatility. It culminated several millennia of human efforts to bring the light of day inside the homes after dark. With the invention of the electric lamp, Edison proved electricity was more than a conveyor of messages but a source of power. Applications using the lessons learned from the incandescent lamp proved more valuable than either the telegraph or the telephone.

Edison later discovered a mysterious thermionic discharge (originally known as the Edison Effect) from the light bulb while he was trying to solve the problem with the blackening of the inside of the incandescent lamp by the filament. To resolve the problem, Edison inserted a second electrode or anode and experimented with the polarity of the filament. He noticed that when the second electrode was made positive with respect to the first (the filament), a current traveled through a vacuum. When the polarity reversed, the blackening of the interior of the light bulb did not occur. Edison fascinated by the phenomena, but could not find a use for it (Poole, 2010).

The next electric miracle was the Hollerith Tabulating Machine. The Hollerith Tabulating Machine changed landscape of computing forever when it conquered the overwhelming Census Bureau crisis of 1890 in a matter of six weeks. The prodigious accomplishment marked the simultaneous beginnings of the Information Age and the Electromechanical Computing Era.

After the demonstrations of the Hollerith Tabulating Machine computing power, businesses and nations around the world jumped at the opportunity for it services. For the majority of the small businesses, companies that had only a few hundred customers chose to stay the course electing to use an array of desktop calculators produced by Monroe, Burroughs, Dalton, or Felt-Tarrant.

The last of the great 19th century invention based on electricity and electromagnetism was the radiotelegraph. The radiotelegraph paved the way for the modern radio, television, wireless computing, and the cellular telephone. Guglielmo Marconi invention of the radiotelegraph (1896) linked the world without wires in the same manner as Morse linked the world with wire. The radiotelegraph did for the ships at sea what the Synchronous Multiplex Railway Telegraph (1887) invention of Granville Woods did for communications between moving locomotives and railroad stations. Prior to Marconi's invention of the radiotelegraph, communications between Europe and North America was through the Transatlantic Cable, which sometimes could take hours or days because of the effect of the salt water had on the copper cables and the natural impedance of electrons. An in depth discussions of the telegraph, telephone, and radiotelegraph are found in Chapter 16: Networks.

By the end of the Gilded Age, nothing was immune to the influence of electricity, not even the trustworthy mechanical calculator. After World War I, electric adding machines and typewriters were commonplace in the office. Electric power had displaced the venerable horse as the main source of power for public transportation in cities with the trolley car, subway, and elevator.

Although these modern miracles by themselves seem trivial and insignificant, they are when combined with the other principles of physics define the precursors of computing. One must remember scientific discovery is not a cut and dried static event. Just as the discovery that salt is bitter and sugar is sweet has led to numerous cooking innovations. Likewise has it been with scientific discoveries. No one disputes the validity of Pythagorean Theorem led to trigonometry. Likewise, no one doubts Archimedes when, he used a beaker of water to determine which had the greater volume a squared ingot or an irregularly shaped ingot of silver. Scientific discovery is based on the accumulation of knowledge and observations made over years, decades, or even centuries by dedicated investigators who recorded their experiments with unexplained phenomena.

ORIGINS

Since the dawn of civilization, the bolts of lightning in the heavens above have aroused human curiosity. The ancient civilizations like the Greeks through mythology imagined the bolts of lightning as the wrath of the god Jupiter. Oddly enough, the etymology of electricity evolved from the Greek word *elektron*—meaning amber. In her book, *Empire of Lights* (2003, p. 17) Jill Jonnes recounts how the Greek philosopher Thales of Miletus, in 600 B.C., discovered that amber when briskly rubbed with a cloth became electrified (magnetic) attracting leaves, straw, and feathers.

Human understanding of electricity or electromagnetism would remain stagnant for almost two thousand years until William Gilbert (1544–1603) of London replicated Thales's experiments with amber (Jonnes, 2003, p. 18). Gilbert's testing did not stop with amber. He expanded Thales's discovery with tests of several different materials: glass, rock crystal, sulfur, and sealing wax. Gilbert called the phenomena of static electricity "electrical effluvia" (Jonnes, 2003, p. 23).

Otto von Guericke (1602–1686) followed Gilbert in the progression of human comprehension of electricity or electromagnetism. Better known for his work in creating a vacuum, von Guericke invented the first electrostatic generator in 1661 in the town of Magdeburg, Germany. The generator consisted of a sulfur ball mounted on a pole inside a glass globe. A hand crank rotated the sulfur ball. The rotating sulfur ball rubbed against a leather pad generating sparks of static electricity. Otto von Guericke had no idea what the sparks were, nor did he advance the study of the phenomena except to notify other scientists of his findings (Jonnes, 2003, p. 20).

An Ordinary Man

It would be another 48 years, before Francis Hawksbee (1666–1713) (sometimes-spelled Hauksbee) of England, in 1709, expanded upon the human understanding of electricity and electromagnetism. Hawksbee reproduced von Guericke's experiment creating an electrostatic generator using a hollow glass sphere (in place of sulfur) excited by a rubber tube (a short adjustable column stuffed with leather) provided the friction which produced the static electricity. Hawksbee set the standard for building electrostatic generators. The Hawksbee generator became the primary source of electricity for scientific experiments and the parlor tricks of charlatans and magicians during the 18th century (Jonnes, 2003, p. 20).

Only recently in human history—from the Renaissance forward—has man learned how to harness the mysterious powers of electricity. The first of these discoveries came with the invention of the Leyden jar.

The first invention to actually harness electricity was the Leyden jar. Its invention was credited to three individuals. The first was German professor of philosophy, Georg Matthias Bose (1710–1761). Bose published a paper on how he had drawn "fire" from electrified water. He had built an electrostatic generator following Hawksbee's guidelines and used it to electrify water and produce sparks that ignited the vapors of the liquid, alcoholic spirits. He promoted the importance of electricity throughout Germany through his discovery (Keithley, 1999, p 21 - 22).

The second person credited with the invention of the Leyden jar was Ewald Georg von Kleist (1700–1748). Kleist a Prussian educated physicist at the University of Leiden. He became excited about electricity when he learned about the Bose's experiments. His aim was to repeat the Bose experiment with the electric charge in alcohol. He built the first Leyden jar by accident. During one of his experiments in 1745, he placed a nail in the mouth of a medicine bottle containing alcohol and touched it to an electrostatic generator. To his surprise, he received an unpleasant jolt when he touched the nail (Keithley, 1999, pp. 21 - 23)

Scientific historians credit Dutch scientist Pieter van Musschenbroek (1692 –1761) with the actual invention of the Leyden jar, in 1745. It was his friend, attorney Andreas Cuneus, who while seeking diversion from his practice of law, seized struck upon the idea of an electrified water storage container. Cuneus touched a wire protruding from a jar of water with an electric charge. After receiving quite an unpleasant jolt from the wire, he described the events to Musschenbroek (Jonnes, 2003, pp.).

Musschenbroek re-created Cuneus unfortunate event, this time charging the wire in the jar with an electrostatic generator. After he received a very uncomfortable jolt himself, he advised others not to repeat his mistake. Musschenbroek discovery of the Leyden jar was by accident. Without any knowledge of von Kleist, he stumbled upon the device according to French essayist Voltaire when he—like von Kleist—accidentally shocked himself (Fara, 2002, p. 52). The Leyden jar was the first known capacitors. The capacitor—originally called a condenser—is a passive electronic device that is capable of holding a charge in an electrostatic field. A capacitor is not to be confused with a battery, which is capable of generating its own electricity internally. A capacitor, only receives the electricity from an external source.

These early capacitors provided many opportunities for the inquisitive experimenters to demonstrate the power of electricity without the presence of an electrostatic generator. A typical 17th and 18th century Leyden jar consisted of a glass jar partially filled with water sealed with a cork at the top. A thick conducting wire (brass or copper) capable of storing a significant amount of electric charge protruded through the cork. The Leyden jar received its initial charge by bringing it into contact with an external source, a friction-generating machine (Fara, 2002, pg. 54) (Virtual Museum of Old Electric, Electronic, and Electrochemical Instruments, 2009).

The next milestone in the harnessing of electromagnetism occurred when Benjamin Franklin (1706–1790), one of the Founding Fathers of the United States. Franklin was able to prove that electricity and lightning were one in the same (Abbott, 1981). Franklin had long thought lightning was the natural occurrence of static electricity. He had observed the similarities between lightning and manmade electricity. To prove that lightning and static electricity were one in the same, he designed an experiment to determine verify lightning would pass through metal. The story of how Franklin accomplished the proof by flying a kite in a thunderstorm to electrify a key is taught to every elementary school child in the United States. It is part of the American cultural mythology. Franklin, without a doubt, was one of the greatest American scientist of his time.

Franklin's discoveries led to the invention of the lightning rod to protect homes and ships from the damage caused by lightning (Library of Congress, 2009). However, Franklin's hypothesis describing electricity as a fluid proved incorrect. He based his theory on the fact that an object's electrical changed charges when rubbed. The object either gained or lost electrons becoming either positively or negatively charge. Objects with opposite charges attract each other; those with the same charge repel one another. Franklin's error occurred because the existence of the atom—protons, electrons, and neutrons—was unknown. Today some modern historians believe Franklin's theory was referring to the atom and the flow of electrons from negative ions to positive ions not liquid (ABC - CLIO, 2003).

Another step towards the understanding of electricity occurred with the invention of the battery by Italian physicist Alessandro Volta (1745–1827) in 1800. Unlike the Leyden jar, which required charging from an external source, Volta's battery created electrical energy internally. The voltaic pile—as it came to be known—relied on the conversion of chemical energy into electricity. The voltaic pile consisted of alternating disks of zinc and copper or silver with each disk separated by brine soaked cardboard. The voltaic battery provided the first practical method of generating continuous streams of electricity. The voltaic battery also created the sustainable first electric circuit (Jonnes, 2003, pp. 31-32) (Smithsonian Institution Libraries, 2001).

Figure 30 Volta

The battery invented by Volta was a wet cell battery. In 1887, German scientist Carl Gassner invented the Galvanic Battery—creating the first dry cell battery of zinc and carbon (Ikenson, 2004, p 73). A dry cell battery is a battery with an electrochemical cell with a low-moisture content electrolyte or a pasty electrolyte, not actually dry. An electrolyte is any substance containing free ions, which behaves as an electrically conductive medium. The most common electrolytes are salts, acids, and bases (bases are the opposites of acid). For his battery, Gassner (Ikenson, 2004, p 73) used a zinc container with a porous substance to absorb the electrolyte then sealed the dry cell across the top with bitumen.

Another prominent scientist following in the footsteps of Volta and Franklin was Michael Faraday (1791–1867)—remembered is in history for his understanding of electromagnetism. Faraday built the first electric motor in 1831 when he discovered that moving a magnet inside wire coil created electricity. He later built the first generator and transformer.

In 1820, Michael Faraday, in London, discovered that a wire passing through a magnetic field developed a current. He also demonstrated how the relationship between electric current and magnetism could produce motion, by creating a primitive motor. Roughly, ten years later, in 1831, Faraday discovered the principle of the generator when an electric current in a wire moved near a magnet (Smithsonian Institution, 2002).

The following year, Frenchman Hippolyte Pixii (1808–1835) created the first dynamo for generating electrical current (Karam, 2005). Based on the experiments of Oersted and Faraday we are able to conclude the following:

a) An electric current produces a magnetic field
b) A magnetic field produces a current in a wire (Wallace, 1991, p. 52).

In 1826 William Sturgeon(1783–1850), another British inventor, demonstrated the Faraday magnetic effect increased when electric current is passed through a wire wrapped around an iron bar. Later, Sturgeon went on to create the commutator and the first practical electric motor.

American inventor, Joseph Henry, using the Sturgeon and Faraday discoveries was able to create powerful electromagnets capable of lifting more than a thousand pounds. The first practical business application of electricity and magnetism came in the form of the telegraph. More information on the history of the telegraph and the telephone is found in Chapter 16 "Networks."

History of the Light Bulb

Unlike the telegraph and the telephone, the inventor of the lightbulb has a murky past. For example if one were to ask an American who invented the light bulb: The American automatically responds Thomas Edison. However, if one were in Great Britain, the term light bulb might evoke the name Henry Swan. In Germany, the same question produces a response of Heinrich Göbel. Some fanatical African Americans will insist that Lewis Latimer invented the first commercially successful incandescent lamp and passed the information on to Edison. The point to remember is that Edison's lightbulb was not serendipity, a happy accident. Numerous inventors prior to him invented a lightbulb, but because lack of interest, lack of financial backing, or some other frustrations did not follow through with the idea.

The chronological history of the incandescent lamp or smokeless torch has a more circuitous route than either the telephone or telegraph. The quest to illuminate the dark inside home has primitive roots, with the earliest known records dating back to the domestication of fire, by the Neanderthal and the Cro-Magnon.

No doubt the first attempts at illuminating the home were burning sticks or lumps of burning coal captured in a brazier. The exact origin of the first oil burning lamp, is unknown, but anthropologist have uncovered evidence devices for artificial light (a bowl shaped rock, a large shell or the like filled with a moss or a similar organic matter soaked with animal fat) was used in the middle east and east Asia as early as 70,000 BC (Bellis, 2009).

More recent evidence of artificial lighting was found in hieroglyphs of the ancient Egyptians, as early as 2000 B.C. Ancient Egyptians used a saucer shaped lamp for indoor illumination. The first of these lamps were open vessels made of stone, clay, bone, pottery, or shell. The fuel burned was olive oil, beeswax, fish oil, whale oil, sesame oil, nut oil, or animal fat.

Artifacts of lamps did not appear in ancient Greece (the cradel of democracy) until 700 B.C. The lamps resembled the lamps described in *A One Thousand and One Nights* assembled from Middle Eastern and Arabic Literature. The Greeks, like their Egyptian predecessors, made their lamps of pottery, stone, or clay then later of bronze. The Romans developed a terra-cotta lamp similar in shape to the Greek lamps. Later the Roman lamps took the shape of animals and vegetables.

In the 18th century, a major improvement occurred in the design of the oil buring lamp when the central burner (wick) was invented. The fuel source instead of floating in an open resevoir was enclosed tightly in a metal can or glass vase. The oil flow was contolled by an adjustable metal tube surrounding the wick.

The introduction of petroleum based products made kerosene lamps more economical in the 19th century. By the middle of the 19th century, natural gas and petroleum based products were used to light the streets and homes of many Old World cities and cities of the western hemisphere (Microsoft, 2009) (Bellis, 2009).

All told there were at least seven attempts to create an incandescenat lamp prior to the successes of Swan in 1878 and Edison in 1879. Sir Henry Davy of Great Britian invented the first electric incandescent lamp in 1812. Davy theorized he could maintain an incandescent light between two carbon filaments. His experiment was simultaneously a success and a failure. The lamp Davy invented was not suitable for indoor use. It was however suitable for the outdoor lighting of streets and waterfronts. What Davy invented was the framework for the arc light or lamp.

In 1820, Warren De la Rue enclosed a platinum coil in a vacuum tube and passed an electromagnetic current through the wire. It was the first incandescent lamp. His lamp design was a scientific success but the price of the few grams of platinum—worth more $300—made De la Rue's invention commercially impractical.

The first patent issued for an incandescent lamp was issued to Frederick de Moleyn in 1841 of Great Britain. His lamp like that of De la Rue used platinum coils for filaments. Another feature in the de Moleyn bulb not present in the De la Rue bulb was a partial vacuum which added an inert gas to retard the rapid disintegration of the filiament. Never the less, the de Moleyn version of the incandescant lamp suffered from the same economic restrictions that doomed the failed De la Rue' lamp. In 1878, Joseph Wilson Swan successfully created a near perfect vacuum in a glass bulb and invented the first incandescent lamp with a carbon filament.

Thomas Edison is credited with the creation of the first commercially practical incandescent lamp. Edison was awarded a patent for his lamp because he arrived at the same conclusions as Swan without any prior knowledge of Swan's efforts. From 1879 forward, Edison was forced to fight law suit after law suit to defend his claim on the incandescent lamp against Swan until the two merged efforts (Smithsonian Institution, 2002) (Bellis, 2009) (Microsoft, 2009).

Thomas Alva Edison

Figure 31 Edison
Light Bulb

We study the life of Thomas Edison here because he was an example of the American success story and a shrewd entrepreneur who over reached his success, crumbled, and started over. In his lifetime, Edison received more than 1000 patents. He won everlasting fame for his innovations in telecommunications with such inventions as the printing telegraph. The improvements he made to the Bell telephone are still the basis of the modern telephone. Then he topped his success with telegraph and telephone with the light bulb (Figure 31). After his fall from the summit of the electric industry, the crafty Edison introduced the phonograph and the motion picture each are etched into the mantra of modern society and the history of electrical engineering.

Moreover, as important as the perfection of the light bulb became to modern civilization, more impressive was many of his inventions that were the precursors of future electronic innovations such as the vacuum tube, magnetic tape, and optical disk. When he placed a metal plate at the base of his incandescent lamp (light bulb), he created a diode or the thermionic valve, a one-way valve to regulate the flow of electric current.

What he observed and recorded, he called the "Edison Effect" which became the basis for vacuum tube electronics, which played a significant role in the future of radio, radiotelegraphy, telephone technology, and computers. The printing telegraph was the basis for future inventions such as Telex.

During his lifetime, Edison was the most prolific inventor in American history. He was born on February 11, 1847 in the town of Milan, Ohio, the seventh of seven children. During the Civil War, Edison learned about the attributes of electricity while working on the Grand Trunk railroad between Port Huron and Detroit selling newspapers and sundries. When idle he read books he borrowed from the local library (Jonnes, 2003).

By 1868, at age 21, he received his first patent for the telegraphic vote-recording machine. The following year, he invented an improved version of the stock ticker tape creating the printing telegraph. The Edison version of the stock ticker printed stock quotations and gold prices in plain text rather than Morse code. The image of the Edison printing telegraph under glass became the iconic symbol of Wall Street. For printing the telegraph, Edison received $40,000, which is the equivalent to $700,000 in 2008 (Massachusetts Institute of Technology, 2009). In 1874, Edison reaped more rewards by selling his quadruplex telegraph to Jay Gould for $30,000 (Woodside, 2007, p 24).

In 1876, Edison established his famed research laboratory at Menlo Park, New Jersey. It was the first of its kind, a laboratory dedicated to industrial research in the field of electromagnetism. After the establishment of the Menlo Park laboratory, Edison did not disappoint. Starting in 1877, Edison demonstrated his genius when he received a patent for improvements to the Bell telephone speaker. A year later, Edison invented of the phonograph. On December 31, in 1879, Edison demonstrated his version of the light bulb. For his creative ingenuity, a gracious public gave him the nickname "Wizard of Menlo Park (Ikenson, 2004, pp. 32 - 36)."

Before Edison created his version of the electric lamp, a number of cities had already granted franchises to local utility companies to light their streets. Many North American and European cities alike chose the electric arc lights for public lighting, New York, London, and Paris the most prominent.

The arc light, based on the Davy invention, had several drawbacks, the most obvious, was its unsuitability for indoor use. Another major drawback with arc lights was the power source, alternating current (AC), in 1879, was considered too dangerous for public use. Wires were suspended overhead or placed under thoroughfares without the proper insulation were dangerous. The most annoying drawback of arc lights was its incessant, irritating flicker (like a discordant strobe light). Finally, arc lights were expensive to maintain. The filaments of an arc light required constant replacement. The steady glare of Edison's incandescent lamp easily superseded the arc light for outdoor use (Morgan Reynolds Inc, 2005, p. 12).

Prior to the Edison breakthrough, the alternative to outdoor arc lighting was gaslight. In 1880, gaslights proved to be a thriving industry and a worthy adversary to Edison's business acumen. Many cities and towns across the United States relied on gas for both residential lighting and heating in addition to lights for public safety. These cities— Baltimore the most prominent—had set up utility commissions, which granted franchises to local companies to provide gas to the public. The

19th century gaslight and heating utility companies provided similar conveniences provided by present day utility companies (Smithsonian Institution, 2008).

Edison realized that his display of lights on New Year's Eve would be just a sideshow if he and his colleagues could not develop an infrastructure to challenge the gas utilities. To meet the challenge and to sway customers away from the gas utilities, Edison created and patented all the necessary components to make electricity available and affordable: bulbs, sockets, switches, wires, junction boxes, power meters, coils, voltage regulators, and insulation to connect customers' homes to the power source. To his chagrin, Edison discovered that many of his financial backers refused to invest in an unproven system. Undaunted by the lack of support, Edison was able to raise enough funds privately from friends and associates to complete his vision.

To highlight the efficiency and practicality of the electric light, Edison founded the Edison Illuminating Company and built the Pearl Street (power) Station at 255-257 Pearl Street in the heart of the financial district of New York City. On September 4, 1882, Edison introduced America to the first electric generating power plant. It served an area one square-mile. Clients included the wealthy and the influential: J.P. Morgan, the New York Stock Exchange, and a number of the nation's largest newspapers including the New York Times (WGBH/PBS, 2000).

Edison began a marketing campaign to seduce customers from the gas utilities, which inferred the incandescent light provided a brighter, safer, and better way to light the home. To hasten the replacement of the gas utilities, Edison purposely patterned his electric light utility after the infrastructure of the gas utility. Wherever gas companies offered lighting, Edison would challenge by offering his incandescent at a light cheaper rate. Where gas companies laid pipes under the streets to distribute gas for indoor use, Edison paralleled their efforts building power stations and laying underground conduits to carry electricity. Every convenience the gas utility offered, Edison planned to have his electric company equal or surpass (Smithsonian Institution, 2008).

In 1890, by combining his various enterprises, Edison formed the Edison General Electric Company to sell a wide range of consumer products from electric light bulbs and lamps to electric heating. A few years earlier, the Thomson–Houston Company—this is significant because of the eventual merger with Edison General Electric—was formed in 1883 when a group of investors from Lynn, Massachusetts led by Charles A. Coffin purchased the American Electric Company.

Polite history states that as both Thomson-Houston and Edison General Electric expanded into new economic frontiers. It became apparent to both companies that neither company individually could gather the necessary resources to complete with the likes of the powerful Westinghouse Electric Company. Therefore, out of a necessity to survive, the two companies combined in 1892 to form the General Electric Company (GE) (General Electric, 2009). Edison would later sell his stock in the company to pursue other ventures such as motion picture studios and the phonograph companies (New York Times, 1892).

The true history of the era tells a different story. As it became apparent that George Westinghouse and Nikola Tesla would prevail in the "War of the Current," J.P. Morgan and the board of directors at Edison General Electric decided to embrace alternating current instead of continuing with Edison's obstinate fight against it. Morgan led a revolt to force a merger with rival Thomson-Houston. The revolt ended with the removal of Edison as company president and his name removed from the company: changing Edison General Electric to General Electric.

Electromagnetism

There are four fundamental forces found in nature: electromagnetism, gravity, the weak force, and the strong force. The four fundamental forces govern how all objects or particles interact. The fundamental forces are based on the following four criteria: the types of particles that experience the force, the strength of the force, the range of force, and the nature of the particles that negotiate the force. Sir Isaac Newton in 17th century Great Britain described gravity. Newton stated gravity acts upon all objects having mass; it causes apples to fall from trees and determines the orbits of the planets around the Sun. On Earth, objects fall at a rate of 32 feet per second per second. It does not matter whether the falling objects are positively charged or negatively charged; all objects fall at the same rate whether the object is one ounce or one ton.

The weak force is found in radioactive decay and neutrino emissions. The weak force has a very short range. The strong force describes the binding of quarks together in atomic clusters to make more-familiar subatomic particles, such as the atomic nucleus and interactions between all particles containing quarks. Like the weak force, the strong force has a very short range and does not appear in the macro world of physics.

The fourth force is electromagnetism (EM). EM has an unlimited range and unlimited strength. As a weak force, it affects very little. As a strong force, it creates magnetic fields that can deflect harmful radiation from the sun. Physicists and scientist describe electricity or electric current as electromagnetism. The EM spectrum is a label describing the various kinds of EM radiation. The electromagnetic spectrum consists of the following: visible light, radio waves, microwaves, infrared light, ultraviolet light, X-rays, and gamma rays.

Electromagnetism occurs both naturally and artificially. Each version of EM is described by the attributes of naturally occurring electromagnetism. Examples of the occurrences of electromagnetism spectrum are the polar Aurora Borealis created by radiation from the Sun and the lightning from weather anomaly such as a thunderstorm, volcanic ash cloud, or sandstorm. It is the flashes of lightning that woke human curiosity. Flashes of lightning are described as bolts of electricity. A bolt of lightning travels at a speed of 186,000 miles per second (the speed of light) and reaches a temperature of 50,000 degrees Fahrenheit (Ultimate Reference Suite, 2008).

Artificial electric current or manmade electricity comes in two forms: stationary electricity also known as static electricity and moving electricity also known as current electricity. An example of an everyday static electricity occurs when a person walks across a dry carpet and creates a spark just before touching a metal handle of a door or cabinet. An example of current or moving electricity occurs when an electrical appliance is activated in a home or office. Current electricity is called moving electricity because it is continuously moving along a defined pathway as oppose to the random and isolated discharges of static electricity.

Scientists and engineers group electric current into two subcategories: direct current (DC) and alternating current (AC). The names of the two forms of electricity are demonstrative of their differences. The electrons produced in direct current flow in one direction. The current produced by batteries is an example of direct current. The electrons produced in alternating electricity flow in one direction then reverse and flow in the opposite direction. An example of alternating current is the electricity that flows through the wires of your home, supplied by the local power company.

Direct Current

The heyday of direct current occurred during the first half of the Gilded Age when Thomas Edison, in 1879, created the first commercially successful incandescent lamp or light bulb. During the 1880s, in the United States direct current was almost synonymous with electric power. Today, direct current is the exclusive domain of automobiles, radios, semiconductors (memory chips), subway trains, and microprocessors (Meyers & Jernigan, 2003, pp. 257 - 259).

The main attribute of direct current is that it flows in one direction and one direction only making it safer than alternating current, which flows in two directions. Direct current is not dangerous unless used at very high levels. Direct current generators—or dynamos as Edison called them—were easily linked in parallel. The main purpose of linking dynamos in parallel is it permits the increment or decrement of power. If you go into the study of electrical engineering, you will learn more about parallel linkage and series linkage of electric appliances. Another advantage of direct current is that it is easier to understand. Two easy to use, easily understood, algebraic formulas explain the basic concepts of direct current, direct current power distribution, and power dissipation.

The main drawback to widespread usage of direct current during the 1880s was it had a transmission limitation of one mile—half that if transmitting more than 200 volts. Another drawback to using direct current in the 19th century was the transformer. A transformer allows electricity to be generated at very high voltages and sent or transmitted to other locations and distributed at lower voltages. At its destination, the transformer allocates the proper amount of voltage for the destination albeit 110 volts or 220 volts. However, in the 1880s, transformers for direct current were non-existent. Therefore, clients of direct current power companies all had to use the same voltage levels. That scenario grew more unwieldy because even in the 19th century, there was job specialization in the neighborhoods and the work place. Job specialization required different kinds of equipment (incandescent lamps, motors, elevators, trolleys, and subway systems) which required different levels of voltages.

The inability to transform direct current electricity severely restricted its trade. For example, if the electricity required to power light bulbs in a factory required 60 watts of power, then the power transmitted by the power station was 60 watts. If machinery at the same factory required 100 watts of power to operate, the factory owner had to buy electricity from a source other than provider powering the light bulbs or purchase bulbs that used 100 watts of power.

In the 1960s, transforming of direct current from high voltage to low voltage and vice versa stopped being a problem. Science bridged the technological differences that separated Nikola Tesla and Edison in the late 19th century. Today, the only differences between the two power sources are the needs of the customer. With power converters that regulate the flow of current between electrical appliances, the worry of over which form of electricity is most beneficial is moot.

Nikola Tesla

Thomas Edison may have pioneered the use of electricity and the electric lamp (light bulb) but it was the genius of Nikola Tesla that created the modern infrastructure we use today to consume electricity. His accomplishments when compiled completely overshadow the 1879 accomplishments of Thomas Edison in electric distribution. Never the less, it was Edison's company General Electric that profited the most from Tesla's genius. When all the legal and political wrangling had finished, General Electric dumped Edison and went on to become one of the largest and most profitable corporations in the world. For all his genius and creativity, Tesla never won the Nobel Prize. His work with alternating current rivals the genius of Einstein, Bohr, and Marconi. Tesla throughout his long career filed hundreds of patients on both direct current and alternating current engineering application. He received patents for dynamos, generators, alternators, transformers, motors, wireless transmissions (radio), x-rays, and florescent lights. Yet, he is the forgotten man in the annals of history of the United States. A Google search of the Internet shows that only two schools were named in his honor, while every major city in the United States has at least one school named in honor of Thomas Edison.

Nikola Tesla was born in the Austro-Hungarian Empire on July 9, 1856 in a mountainous area of the Balkan Peninsula known as Lika

(Cheney, 198, p. 25). Tesla began his education at home and later attended school in Carlstadt, Croatia where he excelled in studies. At an early age, Tesla demonstrated his genius by solving mentally problems in integral calculus (Cheney, Uth, & Glenn, Tesla, master of lightning, 1999, p. 9).

How alternating current became the staple of energy in the United States begins with the arrival of Nikola Tesla in New York City in 1884. Armed only with a letter from a colleague of Edison, Charles Batchelor, as means of introduction, Tesla was able to gain an interview with the great Edison in Menlo Park. At first, Edison scoffed at the recommendations Batchelor made in the letter. However, after Tesla was able to elaborate his experiences with electricity and electrical engineering, he won Edison's favor and received a conditional job offer to work at the Menlo Park laboratory. The stipulation for employment required Tesla to repair the dynamos Edison had installed on the USS Oregon moored at the New York shipyards.

"Yes indeed," replied a confident Tesla who hastened to the shipyards and went to work immediately making all the necessary repairs. Tesla worked feverishly through the night repairing the countless short circuits and broken circuits on the ship. By dawn, with the assistance of the ship's crew, he had finished job (PBS, 2004).

Stunned by Tesla's speed and efficiency, Edison gave Tesla a job at his Menlo Park laboratory. Tesla's first assignment from Edison was to redesign the Menlo Park shop. Tesla completed the task in about a year. Although an avid proponent of alternating current, Tesla dampened his enthusiasm with innovations. Tesla convinced Edison to let him redesigned the DC dynamos to make them more efficient. Edison—a shrewd, irascible businessman—and always interested in making money, agreed to Tesla's proposition. In exchange, Edison agreed to pay Tesla $50,000 if he improved the efficiency of the dynamos.

Several months later, Tesla completed the work on the dynamos and then to his dismay Edison reneged on his promise. When Tesla asked him to explain, Edison stated he thought Tesla understood the offer was made in jest. Tesla did not see the humor in the explanation and immediately resigned his Menlo Park position (PBS, 2004) (Morgan Reynolds Inc, 2005, p. 47) (Cheney, Uth, & Glenn, Tesla, master of Lightning, 1999, p. 20).

After leaving Menlo Park, his reputation preceding him, Tesla was able to form several business partnerships. The first of these partnerships was with a group of crafty investors who established the Tesla Light and Manufacturing Company. The investors wanted Tesla to focus on improving the system of arc lights already in place in many American and European cities (Jonnes, 2003, p. 11).

On March 30, 1885, Tesla filed for his first patent, a design improvement for the arc lamp that addressed the major problems with its use, the annoying flickering, maintenance costs, and reliability. The newly formed Tesla Light & Manufacturing Company was a success and making money. However, when Tesla attempted to persuade the investors fund the building of an electric motor, they balked. They were not interested in such a project. To compound his difficulties with his new company, the investors refused to pay him for his improvements to the arc light. Penniless and desperate, Tesla took a job as a ditch digger to provide himself with food and shelter during the winter of 1886-1887 (Seifer, 1998, p. 41) (Morgan Reynolds Inc., 2005, p. 48).

In the spring of 1887, Tesla's luck changed for the better when he met the personage of A.K. Brown of the Western Union. Brown read about Tesla's genius in a publication, the Electrical Review. Brown recognized the advantages alternating current had over direct current and thought Tesla would be the perfect cornerstone to establish an electric empire. He quickly formed a partnership with Tesla then added attorney Charles Peck to the partnership and established the Tesla Electric Company. Later Peck was able to convince financier J. Pierpont Morgan to subsidize the Tesla Electric Company. Overjoyed by his newfound benefactors, Tesla threw himself wholeheartedly into the job. He worked so furiously, that many of his colleagues worried about his health (Cheney, Tesla: man out of time, 1981, p. 58) (Seifer, 1998, p. 42).

Soon, with the aid of a friend, newly immigrated friend Anthony Szigeti, Tesla produced the foundations for a new alternating current industry. Tesla and Szigeti built dynamos to generate the current, the transformers to contain the power, and the foundation for an alternating current infrastructure, just as Edison had done ten years earlier for direct current. Tesla also produced the Tesla Coil, an induction coil widely used in modern radio technology.

Tesla was reluctant to go public with his new inventions because of past ordeals first with Edison and the investors of the Tesla Light and

Manufacturing Company. He did not trust American businessmen. He wanted financial rewards for his sacrifice. After getting advice from his company's patent attorneys, Tesla, on May 15, 1888, presented his philosophy in a monograph to the membership AIEE (American Institute of Electrical Engineers), "A New System of Alternating Current Motors, and Transformers (Morgan Reynolds Inc, 2005, pp. 52 - 54) (Seifer, 1998, p. 45)."

Tesla carefully explained the possibilities of alternating current were endless: The basis of his theories for alternating current was its flexibility and unbound transmission limitations. Direct current was inflexible and required a powerhouse every other mile because of power degradation. Because of the proximity of the power stations, cables carrying direct current had to be buried under the streets. Alternating current, on the other hand, can travel hundreds of miles without power dissipation. As Tesla explained, with his technology powerhouses that generated electricity are located in isolated places not in the middle of the city. Electricity generated at Niagara Falls could carry thousand volts of electricity hundreds of miles to New York City safely high over the heads of the people.

The key to the Tesla infrastructure was his newly invented polyphase transformer. The polyphase transformer was capable of manipulating two or more current levels simultaneously with their phases overlapping. It increased the voltage of current as it left the power station and decreased the voltage to an appropriate level for the safe delivery to homes, business, or factories. With the introduction of the Tesla inventions, the War of the Currents began. Tesla and associates faced stiff competition from the Edison Empire (Morgan Reynolds Inc, 2005, p. 55) (Jonnes, 2003, p. 154).

War of the Currents

The "War of the Currents" was not a war between two great armies colliding on the field of valor; it was not a war where victory was measured by feats of bravery. In fact, it was not a shooting war at all. The "War of the Currents" was an ideological war that pitted two opposing technologies and business philosophies.

On the one side were the proponents of scientific advancement, technological achievement, and sound business practices—the proponents of alternating current. On the other side, stood the proponents of superstition, stubbornness, and the last sanctuary of direct current, Edison General Electric. At the heart of the conflict was the intractable, irascible Thomas Edison, the champion of direct current electricity. His opponent, the champion of change, progress, and alternating current the eccentric Nikola Tesla and his supporter the shrewd industrialist George Westinghouse. There were many skirmishes between the opposing sides, but the war focused on two major battlefields the Chicago World's Fair (the Columbian Exposition) and the Niagara Falls power generation project.

At the start of 1880s, Edison General Electric held every major patent for the distribution and creation of direct current. Additionally, Edison General Electric held patents for the production of the incandescent lamp. Any investor or industrialist that wished to build an electric power company using direct current had to pay royalties to the Edison General Electric Empire or attempt to break ground using the still unreliable and somewhat dangerous alternating current (Jonnes, 2003, p. 47).

Alternating current was not an entirely unused source of power during the 1880s. It was used as the source of power for the arc light, a product that provided public lighting in many European and North American cities. The most prominent users of alternating current in the United States were the Westinghouse Electric of Pittsburgh and the Thomson-Houston company of Lynn, Massachusetts (Jonnes, 2003, p. 36).

The first breakthrough for proponents of alternating current came with the invention of the Gaulard–Gibbs transformer in 1881 (improved by William Stanley in 1885). The new transformer allowed Westinghouse Electric and the Thomson-Houston Company to mount cursory challenges to the Edison General Electric monopoly. The companies could build power plants well outside of commercial or residential services areas. Then transmit the electricity to the customer without the blighting the service area with the unsightly smoke stacks inherent with direct current power plants. The new transformer allowed the transmission of electricity at very high voltage and then transforms it or step it down for delivery to individual customers.

The Gaulard-Gibbs was the first transformer created, although Tesla is sometimes credited with the invention of transformer. Until Tesla's innovations, existing AC systems use the Gaulard–Gibbs a single-phase transformers. AC suppliers were in some ways strapped with the same limitations Edison had with direct current power. However, multiple installations of the transformer proved more flexible overall and began to erode the Edison General Electric grip.

The limitations of the Gaulard-Gibbs were one thing. In the public eye, alternating current was still dangerous. This misconception favored the Edison General Electric because of the AC power lines were overhead not in the ground were another (Jonnes, 2003, p.123) (Smithsonian Institution, 2002).

The great changed in the way America consumed electricity began in 1888 with the Tesla inventions. Tesla invented the polyphase transformer, a brushless AC induction motor, and an AC power generator. The advantages Edison and Edison General Electric had enjoyed for nearly a decade began to evaporate. The Tesla inventions were revolutionary and changed the landscape of the electric power industry breaking the grip of the Edison General Electric monopoly.

The Tesla polyphase transformer added flexibility never known with the Gaulard-Gibbs transformer. For the first time, the source voltage levels did not matter. The new Tesla transformer changed the high voltage from the source to the lower voltage level required at the destination. Edison instead of acknowledging the advantages of the Tesla electrical system and jumping at the opportunity to invest in the new technology for Edison General Electric launched a public tirade against the use of alternating current.

George Westinghouse—owner of Westinghouse Corporation of Pittsburgh—unlike Edison did not hesitate and jumped at the investment opportunity. He made an offer of $60,000 to Tesla for all of his patents. The offer consisted of $5,000 in cash and 150 shares of stock in the Westinghouse Corporation. He also agreed to pay Tesla royalties of $2.50 per horsepower the Tesla Induction Motor produced (Cheney, Tesla: man out of time, 1981, p. 63).

Edison's campaign of debauchery against Tesla, alternating current, and Westinghouse was designed to sway the public in favor of direct current. The content of the campaign appealed to superstition and ignorance. Edison resorted to the use of fear mongering to frighten the public into believing the Tesla system was dangerous. One example of Edison's tactics occurred when he hired schoolboys to steal the pets of the neighbors in West Orange, New Jersey to demonstrate the dangers of accidental electrocution with alternating current.

This mindset led Edison to recommend to the state of New York use alternating current as a humane method of executing prisoners. Edison also recommended that the state name the new electric chair "Westinghouse." He then dubbed the electrocution process as being "Westinghoused" (Morgan Reynolds Inc, 2005, p. 60).

The campaign did not inconvenience Westinghouse or his method of doing business. By using Tesla's polyphase alternating current technology, he won for the Westinghouse Company the exclusive rights to provide lighting for the Columbian Exposition in Chicago over the favored Edison General Electric Company. Next, Westinghouse armed with the Tesla patents decisively outclassed Edison General Electric efforts to harness the power of Niagara Falls and provide electricity to both Buffalo and New York City.

After losing the Columbian Exposition and the Niagara Falls project, Edison and colleagues switched tactics replacing the street level fear mongering and thuggery with courtroom litigation claiming patent infringement. They relied on the skills of their legal department to challenge the legitimacy of the Westinghouse incandescent lamp; claiming Edison General Electric did not grant license to Westinghouse to manufacture and was due compensation (Smithsonian Institution, 2002).

The new tactics were too little, too late; they were not enough to allay the fears of billionaire financier J. P. Morgan and the Edison General Electric board of directors. The legal battle with the Westinghouse Company had drained the Edison General Electric's coffers. The war of currents had cost the company its dominance of the electric industry. Enough was enough; led by Morgan the board of directors began merger talks with the Thomson-Houston Electric Company. From the board of directors' point of view it was essential to stay competitive with Westinghouse and gain a piece of the lucrative alternating current market.

While Edison continued to bicker with Westinghouse in the courts, Charles A. Coffin president of Thomson-Houston negotiated the merger with the J. P. Morgan and Edison General Electric board of directors. The first action of the newly formed company was to abandon direct current in favor of alternating current. This action effectively terminated Edison's leadership role at EGE. For his long and devoted service to Edison General Electric, the board of directors gave Edison a pension that consisted of twelve and a half percent of the company stock and a pension of $600 a week.

After the ouster of Edison, billionaire and financier J. P. Morgan became the majority stockholder of Edison General Electric. With Morgan as chief executive officer (CEO), the board of directors named Charles A. Coffin as first president of General Electric (PBS, 2004) (General Electric, 2009) (Massachusetts Institute of Technology, 2009) (Smithsonian Institution, 2008).

With controlling interests of General Electric in his pocket, J. P Morgan, attempted but failed to seize control of Westinghouse Electric and form a monopoly. This feat was averted because of Tesla's devotion to the partnership with Westinghouse. Westinghouse, in deep financial trouble, appealed to Tesla to tear up his royalty contract, worth millions of dollars, in order to save Westinghouse Electric. Tesla, fearing a Morgan takeover would ruin his financial future obliged Westinghouse. However, Westinghouse did not feel obligated to return the favor to Tesla with a new royalty contract after stemming Morgan's efforts. After saving Westinghouse Electric from the hands of Morgan, George Westinghouse abandoned Tesla.

Nikola Tesla is the tragic character in the history of the United States and electric power industry. He began life as a child prodigy who should have enjoyed the fruits of his genius. Instead, his life was filled with corrupt people that took advantage of his inexperience with others. His inventions should have made him a millionaire a thousand times over. Instead of enjoying the fame and wealth he earned, he spent the last years of his life in obscurity feeding pigeons. He had no legacy and died in obscurity and abject poverty—in comparison to contemporaries Westinghouse and Edison—in 1943, in a two-room suite at the New Yorker Hotel.

Ironically, in 1943, a few months after his death, the United States Congress awarded the patent for the radiotelegraph to Nikola Tesla, reversing the decision of the patent office, which had awarded a patent to Guglielmo Marconi. Nikola Tesla had filed a patent on the basic components of the radio in 1896. In addition, Tesla published schematics describing all the basic elements of the radio transmitter that Marconi later used. Since Tesla had no heirs, the decision was moot.

Alternating current is an electric current that reverses the flow of its energy or polarity at regular intervals. The current surges or flows in one direction until it builds to a maximum then drops to zero. The current then surges or flows in the opposite direction, building to a maximum and again dropping to zero. At which time it resumes its original course.

The two consecutive surges, one in each direction, is one cycle. The number of cycles repeated in the span of one second is the frequency at which the electricity flows. Alternating current displaced direct current as the standard for residential and industrial use in the decade leading up to the twentieth century. At the dawn of the 20th century, AC was distributed more economically because of the invention of the transformer that raised and lowered the voltage to a desired level for use in either the residential, commercial, or industrial settings (Stross, 2007, p. 175) (PBS, 2004).

Electric Circuit

Figure 32 series circuit

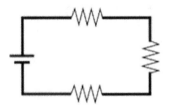

An electric circuit is a system or network designed to control the pathway of electric current for particular purposes. An electric circuit consists of at least three elements. The first is the wires (conductor). The second is the power source. Technically speaking, the first two elements can form an electric circuit, however; the wire or conductor would soon burn out or short circuit without the third component (the load) to dissipate the energy from the power source. The primary purpose of the load is to consume or burn the electricity in the circuit. The load could be an electric motor, an incandescent lamp, or a radio. Besides the aforementioned definition, an electric circuit may consist of several different electrical components: potentiometers, transistors, resistors, capacitors, diodes, relays, and switches.

An electric circuit has two basic forms series, parallel. A circuit may also be a combination of both series and parallel circuits. The image in Figure 32 is a basic series circuit. The definition of which states that there is only one path for the electricity to flow.

In contrast, a parallel circuit has multiple paths for the flow of electricity. In Figure 33 electricity flows down several paths, each with a load to dissipate the energy of the current. Figure 33 illustrates a fundamental parallel circuit.

Figure 33 Parallel Circuit

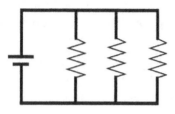

People just beginning the study of electricity; learn the intricacies of direct current before tackling alternating current. The reasoning behind this is twofold. Studying direct current makes it easier to grasp the theories of alternating current. Second, there is no danger of accidental electrocution as there is in alternating current.

Learning direct current is very straightforward. Connecting wires to power sources using direct current is based upon two fundamental theories developed by scientists in the 19th century. The first is Ohm's Law. The ohm is a measure of resistance. It is named in honor of the German scientist Georg Simon Ohm who discovered that all conductors resist the flow of current to some extent. Ohm's Law states that the amount of current (I) in a conductor is equal to the voltage (E) divided by the resistance (R), when these values are measured in amperes, volts, and ohms. It can be express in three simple algebraic equations:

1. $E = IR$,
2. $I = E/R$,
3. $R = E/I$.

The second fundamental theory to comprehend in the study of direct current is Kirchhoff's Law. Kirchhoff's Law is almost as easy to comprehend as Ohm's Law is. In fact, it is based upon the principles of Ohm's Law. Gustav Robert Kirchhoff a German born scientist postulated about the laws of conservation regarding the radiation of heat and applied it to parallel circuits. His findings are summarized in the following two statements:

a. The algebraic sum of current into any junction is zero
b. The sum of current into a junction equals the sum of current out of the junction.

The underlying reasoning for beginners learning direct current first is the more people use direct current for the pursuit of hobbies such as kit building, computer enthusiasts, and amateur radio. Each starts out by building circuit boards.

Second, the study of alternating current requires a good understanding of algebra and beyond more so than the basics expressed in Ohm's Law. To comprehend AC, one has to comprehend the principles of impedance, polarity, the sine wave, wave angle, and waveform.

To summarize, the study of electricity study begins with the three basic methods units: resistance, amperes, and volts.

A review of the terms used in the discussion about the pioneers of electricity follows:

1. Ohms—an ohm measures the resistance between two points on an electric circuit. The ohm was named in honor of the German physicist Georg Simon Ohm who discovered the relationship between the flows of current through a conductor is directly proportional to the voltage. Resistance or Ohms in a circuit is calculated with the following formula $R = E/I$.

2. Ampere—an ampere is a unit of electric current, or amount of electric charge. The ampere honors French scientist Andre Marie-Ampere who is credited with the discovery of electromagnetism. An ampere is calculated with the following formula $I = E/R$.

3. Volt—a volt is defined, as the electric potential difference required moving one ampere of current through a conductor with one ohm of resistance. The volt is named in honor of the Italian scientist Alessandro Volta who invented the first battery, the Voltaic pile. A volt in an electric circuit is calculated with the algebraic expression $E = IR$.

4. Conductor–A conductor is any material that can carry an electric current. Most metals are considered conductors. Copper and aluminum are used to wire homes while gold and silver are used to build circuits in computers and other portable devices.

5. The opposite of a conductor is an insulator. Insulators such as rubber, wood, and paper are very poor conductors of electricity.

6. Electric current—electric current is the rate of the flow of electrons at any given point through the wires of a circuit.
7. Parallel circuit—a parallel circuit is a closed electrical circuit in which the current is divided into two or more paths
8. Series circuit—a series circuit is an electrical circuit that has just one path from the source to the ground.
9. Transformer—a transformer is a mechanical device that is capable of increasing or decreasing the voltage of an electrical circuit.
10. Polyphase—is an electrical system that uses or generates two or more alternating voltage levels at the same frequency but differing in phase angle multiphase electricity.
11. Direct current—is an electrical current that flows in one direction only. Automobiles and many battery-powered portable devices use direct current.
12. Alternating current—is electrical current that reverses direction periodically. The number of times it reverses back to the original direction during a second is the frequency. Electric utilities distribute alternating current to their customers.

The discussion thus far has focused on the discoveries of the pioneers of electricity, Franklin, Oersted, Tesla, Edison, etc. Those pioneers laid the groundwork for modern electronic computing. Of all the inventions involving electricity in the 20th century the most valuable, the most important is the creation of the transistor and the integrated circuit. From vantage point of the modern computer, the creation of the integrated circuit is the greatest invention of the 20th century. Without the invention of the integrated circuit, the modern personal comforts we take for granted would not be possible. Without the technology gained from building transistors the integrated circuit would not be possible.

TRANSISTORS

Figure 34 illustrates how the integrated circuit has changed the face of electronics since the invention of ENIAC. The photograph contains the relative size of the three stages of electronics, on the left is a vacuum tube used in the first generation or big iron computers such as ENIAC and some second-generation computers. In the middle of the photograph is a transistor used in second-generation solid-state computers such as the IBM 1401. On the right of the photograph— what appears to be a dot or an imperfection of the photograph is the integrated circuit. The electronic component is found in computers from the size of the laptop to the IBM super computer Watson. The microprocessor compared to a transistor is but a speck of dust (IBM Archives, 1964).

Figure 34 Vacuum Tubes, Transistors Microchips

Prior to the invention of the transistor portable electric appliances were virtually nonexistent. There were a few portable devices prior to the invention of the transistor—the exception the walkie-talkie and the police radio. For the most part, electronic appliances were stationary, attached to an electric wall outlet. As the transistor grew in importance, it began to replace conventional electronic circuit featuring vacuum tubes.

The basic building blocks of the integrated circuit is the electronic device it displaced, the transistor, which was, invented by William Shockley, John Bardeen, and Walter Brattain of Bell Laboratories in 1947. The transistor is a solid-state device consisting of a tiny piece of a semiconductor material such as of carbon, silicon, or germanium. The typical early transistor had at least two electrodes but no more than three electrodes. The transistor replaced the vacuum tube in the operations of all electronic appliances by 1964.

Jack Kilby invented the first integrated circuits in 1958 working for Texas Instruments. In 1959 by Robert Noyce Fairchild

Semiconductor in California invented a second form of the integrated circuit. The United Stated Patent Office decided to award the patent to both individuals because of minor variations of manufacture. The Kilby idea was to make all the components and the chip out of the same block (monolithic) of semiconductor material. The Noyce integrated circuit like the Kilby device was monolithic; however, the manufacturing process used by Fairchild Semiconductor was the planar process, which creates tiny lines of metal to act as connectors between semiconductor substrate (Mueller, 2004, pg. 17).

INTEGRATED CIRCUITS

An integrated circuit (IC) is a miniature electric circuit. It is no more than a very advanced electric circuit. An electric circuit is made from several electrical components transistors, resistors, capacitors, and diodes, that when connected in various ways behave differently.

The transistor is the switch. It turns electricity on, off, or amplifies current. The resistor limits the flow of electricity controls the amount of current passing through a circuit. The capacitor collects electricity and releases it quick burst like the Leyden jar. The diode stops the flow of electricity. It also allows electric current to flow under certain conditions. These components are the building blocks of electrical applications such as radio, television, and computers. The integrated circuits place all the components of an electronic circuit in miniature onto a single silicon wafer drastically reducing the size and cost of the circuits.

The integrated circuit grew out of necessity. When the transistor went into production, each circuit was handmade soldered to electronic circuit boards with other components (resistors, capacitors, inductors, diodes, etc.). This method of production was acceptable as long electronic applications were not overly complicated. However, as scientific knowledge grew, so did the number of transistor and other electronic components needed to satisfy scientific curiosity. Eventually, this method of construction reached its limit. New application requiring circuits based on individual transistors became too large and too difficult to hand assemble. Noyce and Kilby decided instead of making transistors one-by-one, several transistors could be made at the same time, on a single semiconductor. An integrated circuit differs from a microprocessor in that microprocessor contains the entire computer on a chip. The IC is for individual electronic components.

An integrated circuit is etched onto semiconductor material, a crystal of germanium or silicon. Computer manufacturers enclosed the IC in either a hermetically sealed case or a non-hermetic plastic capsule. The case or capsule has leads or connectors extending from it to permit information input, output, and a power-supply.

When first introduced to the computer industry, the integrated circuit was not readily accepted by the electronics industry when introduced in 1959. That attitude changed, however, when the National Aeronautics and Space Agency (NASA) showed an interest in the IC for the Gemini and Apollo spacecraft. The IC was small, lightweight, a prized alternative to bulky transistors and even clumsier relay switches common to computers of the 1960s. A second government initiative by the Department of Defense authorized the use of the integrated circuit as the guidance mechanisms for the Air Force's land based Minuteman intercontinental ballistic missiles and the Navy's submarine based Trident and Poseidon intercontinental ballistic missiles (ICBM) (Ceruzzi, 1999, p. 188).

Integrated circuits have two group types depending on the transistors contain within, bipolar integrated circuits, and Metal-oxide-semiconductor (MOS). Bipolar integrated circuits contain two junction transistors as their principle elements. Metal-oxide-semiconductor (MOS) is a special type of field-effect transistor that works by varying the width of the channel, which carries electron flow. The wider the channel, the better the device conducts current. Some integrated circuits contain hybrids transistors (Whitaker, 1996, p 654).

A second method of classifying an integrated circuit is by the number of transistor-based circuits placed on a single chip. Under this method of classification, the first generation of microprocessors were described as being small-scale integration (SSI) chips that had less than 100 transistor-based circuits and components. The next size chip was classified as medium scale integration (MSI) chip. It contained more than a 100 transistor-based circuits but less than a 1000 transistor-based circuits. Correspondingly, a microchip with more than a 1000 transistor-based circuits but less than 10,000 transistor-based circuits was a large-scale integration (LSI) chip. An integrated circuit with from 10,000 to 100,000 transistor-based circuits was a very large scale integration

(VLSI). Microchips having more than 100,000 transistor-based circuits were ultra-large-scale integration (ULSI) (Swedin & Ferro, 2007, p. 68).

ELECTRONICS TERMINOLOGY

Now that you are familiar with some of the attributes of an integrated circuit, the following list provides definitions for some terms common to the electronics industry.

1. Semiconductor—a semiconductor is a material that is neither a conductor of electricity such as copper or a good insulator of electricity like wood or rubber. Atomic elements that make good semiconductors are carbon, silicon, and germanium. Most semiconductors are made of silicon and germanium crystals. If impurities—called dope or dopant—are added to the crystals, the semiconductor ability to conduct electricity increases.

    a. Semiconductors have two types of impurities acceptor impurities and donor impurities.

    b. Semiconductor crystals that contain donor impurities are negative or n-type semiconductors. Donor impurities because of their atomic structure donate an electron or have a negative charge.

    c. Semiconductor crystals with acceptor impurities are positive, or p-type. Acceptor impurities because of their atomic structure accept the extra electron. Transistors, resistors, capacitors, and diodes found in modern integrated circuits are all products of semiconductor technology.

2. Transistors—Bell Laboratories invented transistors to replace vacuum tubes as regulatory switch in an electronic circuit. Transistors are comprised of three levels of semiconductor materials. Transistors amplify, reduce, or stop the flow of current and voltage through an electronic circuit. The room on/off switch for the lights in your home is a real world example of a transistor.

3. Resistors—a resistor, as its name suggests resists electric current through a circuit. It is a two-terminal electrical or electronic component. Resistors are color-coded to specify its capacity for resistance. A resistor's capacity to produce a voltage drop is measured in ohms. In the real world of electronics, variable

116

resistors known as rheostats and potentiometers regulate the volume on radios, stereo receivers, and amplifiers.

4. Capacitor—a capacitor or condenser (as it was originally called) is a passive electronic device that collects and stores electricity in an electrostatic field that measured in by units of capacitance. The buildup of electricity in camera is an example of capacitor collecting electricity from a battery to power a flash bulb. The Leyden jar represented the first use of a capacitor.

5. Diode—The diode or rectifier is any passive semiconductor device through which electricity can flow in only one direction, essential for the operation of a radio. A diode prevents the flow of electricity in some conditions and permits the flow of electricity when the conditions change. For example, the photocells on a garage door opener, the door will close as long as the light beam is unbroken. If by chance a child or pet breaks the beam of light between the photocells, the diode stops electricity flow causing the door to stop and open. The diode is the simplest possible semiconductor device (Whitaker, 1996, p. 278).

6. Rectification—Rectification is the process of changing alternating current to direct current by blocking the reverse flow of current.

7. Electric circuit—an electric circuit is a closed pathway through which electric current travels.

8. Microchip—a microchip is a small piece of semiconductor material carrying many thousands or millions transistor based circuits.

9. Integrated circuit —an integrated circuit has two definition the first defines an integrated circuit as a tiny electronic circuit. The second definition read thusly a tiny complex of electronic components contained on a thin chip or wafer of semiconducting material (Microsoft, 2010).

10. Microprocessor — a microprocessor is the central processing unit that performs the basic operations of a computer; it consists of an integrated circuit contained on a single chip.

FINAL NOTES ON ELECTRICITY

Final observations on why I included of a chapter on electricity. Many of the conveniences we enjoy today rely on electrical power.

Edison's attempt to resolve the blackening of the incandescent lamp indirectly led to the creation of the vacuum tube and later the basis of the radio. The vacuum tube was the basis of all early electronics and eventually led to the invention of the transistor. The transistor led to the invention of the integrated circuit, which led to the invention of the microprocessor. Electricity added versatility never achieved with strictly mechanical (metal) computing.

Figure 35 Early Microprocessor

9

Twentieth Century Pioneers

History marks 1937 as the dawn of the Electronic Era of computing, the same year John Atanasoff and Clifford Berry built the Atanasoff-Berry Computer (ABC) at Iowa State University in Ames, Iowa. An actual working model was not completed until 1939. For more than 32 years, the scientific world ignored the Atanasoff-Berry invention. The reason for the oversight was due in part to ENIAC built by John V. Mauchly. Prior to building ENIAC Mauchly took a four-day vacation to Iowa State University to visit Atanasoff and Berry. During his stay at Iowa State, Mauchly examined the ABC, reviewed its design specification, and discussed with Atanasoff every aspects of the computer's operations. Once he had returned to the University of Pennsylvania and the Moore School of Engineering, proceeded to design and build his own computer. Mauchly collaborated with John Presper Eckert and built the world's first general-purpose electronic computer, ENIAC in 1946 (Aspray, Broomley, Ceruzzi, & Williams, 1990).

The trip proved Ames, Iowa to be very opportune for Mauchly and associates because gave him and Eckert a blueprint for success. At the time of Mauchly and Eckert's breakthrough, a number of other physicists and engineers were on the verge of a making similar technological breakthrough. Among them working towards a digital

119

solution were John von Neumann, Konrad Zuse, and Howard Aiken all were very close to the same conclusions made by Atanasoff and Berry. The next few pages will briefly examine the contributions of the twentieth century computing pioneers.

Konrad Zuse

The first pioneer of the 20th century discussed herein is Konrad Zuse of Berlin, Germany. Born in 1910, Zuse became famous because of his efforts in the developing the Z1 relay circuit computer (electromechanical). (Historians refer to the Z1 as both a calculator and a computer.) The Z1 was a binary computer, capable of solving linear algebraic equations (Ifrah, 2001, pg 206). The computer also produced output in the floating-point format (whole numbers with decimal fractions.). Zuse fashioned the computer's memory out of metal plates cut with a jigsaw. He made the calculating unit made from secondhand telephone relays switches, and the program instructions were recorded on discarded motion picture film instead of cards similar to the cards used by Hollerith or Jacquard (Ceruzzi, Relay Calculators, 1990).

In 1938, Zuse filed a patent in the United States for the Z1 a year before Atanasoff and Berry had completed their preliminary work on the ABC. The patent office denied the Zuse application because the details of his work were too vague (Swedin & Ferro, 2007, pg. 36).

Zuse, also, claimed he built the Z3, which, if properly presented, would have been the world's first general-purpose program-controlled electro-mechanical computer. The Z3, he claimed had the following arithmetic and algebraic properties: addition, subtraction, multiplication, division, square root, and floating-point decimals. His claims were never verified because the United States and the United Kingdom were at war with Germany. Most likely, the Z3 and its documentation was a casualty of Anglo-American bombing of Berlin.

Zuse attempted to build a fourth computer the Z4, but work on the Z4 was suspended when Germany surrendered. A few years after World War II, Zuse resumed his efforts to build the Z4. He completed the Z4 in Switzerland, not Germany, in 1950. That was four years after Eckert and Mauchly announced ENIAC. Zuse moved the Z4 from Switzerland to France later in 1950. The French used the Z4 used until 1960. The Z4 was Europe's first commercial digital computer. Most records of Zuse's work were lost during the World War II or not recognized as original because of the disdain of the Nazis (Swedin & Ferro, 2007, pg. 36).

George Robert Stibitz

George Robert Stibitz is known as the father of the modern digital computing. He was born on April 20, 1904, in York, Pennsylvania. His college education began at Denison University in Granville, Ohio where he earned a bachelor's degree in 1926. He enrolled in Union College and earned a master's degree in 1927. Following a year working as a technician with General Electric in Schenectady, Stibitz enrolled at Cornell University and received a PhD in mathematical physics in 1930. After graduating from Cornell, the next job Stibitz landed was with the Bell Laboratories (IEEE Computer Society 2009).

While working at Bell, Stibitz earned everlasting fame when he invented a relay-based calculator with circuits capable of performing binary addition and subtraction in 1937. He named the new relay computer, the Model K. The K stands for kitchen, where he built the computer.

A relay switch is an electromechanical device activated by electricity passing through an electromagnet. Samuel F. B. Morse utilized the switch for his telegraph of 1844 to regulate the length of electric pulses—then classified as either dots or dashes—to send messages. A relay is binary device that functions in either one of two states: on or off. As the use of electric pulses for communications grew more sophisticated, the on and off signals of the switch became ones and zeroes—the binary language of the computer (Ceruzzi, Relay Calculators, 1990, pg 208).

Georges Ifrah (2001, pg. 207) states that Stibitz received his inspiration for the Model K relay computer while watching the pari-mutuel totalizer boards tabulate the odds on wagers made at the horse track. In 1939, Stibitz and colleague Sam B. Williams built a larger more complicated machine based upon the principle of the Model K dubbed the Complex Number Calculator (CNC). Cyber historians recognized the CNC as the first electromechanical binary computer, ahead of Zuse and the Z1.

On September 11, 1940, Stibitz accomplished another computing first when he connected to the Complex Number Calculator at the Bell Laboratories in New York to a remote teletypewriter at Dartmouth College in Hanover, New Hampshire. It marked the first time in history a computer was accessed remotely via the telephone.

The members of the American Mathematical Society at Dartmouth sent very complex mathematical problems to the CNC location and received their answer a minute or two later.

The CNC was born when Stibitz realized that groups of relay circuits linked together were capable of performing more than routine processing phone numbers. A summary of his observation are listed below:

1) Some circuits converted numbers dialed (no touch-tone in the 1930s) by the customers into a numerical format suitable for routing and automatic switching,

2) Some circuits stored information—the dialed numbers— while the system searched for an open telephone line from the central office,

3) Some relay circuits displayed information about the internal workings of the telephone network.

In other words, the telephone company's relay circuits performed all the functions of an automatic calculator, even though the circuits were not designed to "calculate" in the commonsense of the word.

When first built, the Complex Number Calculator performed only multiplication and division. However, after Stibitz and Williams made a few modifications, the Complex Number Calculator could also add and subtract. The machine output was in the decimal format, four relays coded each digit (Ceruzzi, Relay Calculators, 1990, pg 207-213).

By 1940, Stibitz had adjusted the machine so that it was capable of outputting floating-point decimals, which permitted the multiplication and division of very large numbers by 10, 100, or 1000 (Ifrah, 2001, pg. 209).

In 1964, Stibitz became a research associate at Dartmouth Medical School. There he achieved his greatest distinction as an engineer pioneering the development of computer applications (programs) for biomedical research. His applications monitored the movement of oxygen through the lungs, mapped the brain cell structure, and analyzed the diffusion of nutrients and drugs in the bloodstream (Ifrah, 2001, pg. 209) (Encyclopedia Britannica, 2008).

An Ordinary Man

Howard Aiken was born in Hoboken, New Jersey in the year 1900. His family later moved to Indianapolis where he grew up. Aiken completed undergraduate studies at the University of Wisconsin in Madison receiving a degree in electrical engineering in 1923. While studying at the University of Wisconsin, he worked for a Madison Gas Company. After graduation, the company promoted him to chief engineer. After working almost ten years as an engineer, Aiken decided he wanted to build computers and enrolled at the University of Chicago. There he studied mathematics and physics. He later enrolled at Harvard University earning a PhD in 1939.

Aiken gained notoriety when he designed the Harvard Mark I, an electromechanical computer. Aiken, while on the faculty of Harvard and in concert with the engineers of IBM laboratories, built the Harvard Mark I computer—originally named the Automatic Sequence Controlled Calculator (ASCC). The ASCC was capable of performing the five basic arithmetic operations addition, subtraction, multiplication, division, and comparison. It also had the ability to reference previous results.

The ASCC as the machines produced by Zuse and Stibitz machines used relay switches to perform operations. It was an enormous machine; it stood more than 8 feet high, was almost 51 feet long, and weighed more than five tons. The ASCC contained 765,000 parts, which included 1400 switches, 3,300 relays, more than 175,000 connections, and over 500 miles of wire. The ASCC was programmed by one of three methods, punch cards, perforated tape, or by physically reconfiguring its 1400 switches.

The computers built by Aiken, Zuse, and Stibitz shared three common characteristics: first, they were adding machines or calculators. Second, they were binary devices based on the electric relay. Finally, each used some form of perforated tape or punch card to input information into the machine. An electric typewriter provided the displayed output (Ceruzzi, 1990, pg 213 - 219).

Grace Hopper is the first person to coin the phrase "computer bug," when she literally removed insects from the circuitry of the computer. She made the statement while working inside the superstructure the Harvard Mark I. She achieved lasting fame among her peers for her work on software and computer programming. Her work with Flow-Matic provided the foundations for the programming language COBOL (Common Business-Oriented Language). Her software engineering skills were game changing not because Hopper was a woman but because they changed the way the computer received instructions.

She was born Grace Brewster Murray on December 9, 1906 in New York City. She was the eldest child of Admiral Walter Fletcher Murray and Mary Van Horne Murray. She attended the Hartridge School in Plainfield, New Jersey a prestigious preparatory high school. After graduating from high school she attended Vassar College, graduating in 1928, Phi Beta Kappa with a BA in mathematics and physics. She accepted a teaching post while pursuing graduate degrees at Yale University, completing her MA in 1930 and a PhD in mathematics in 1934. In 1930, she married Vincent Foster Hopper, an English instructor with the New York School of Commerce.

After the start of World War II, Grace followed family tradition and enlisted in the Navy as a member of the WAVES (Women Accepted for Voluntary Emergency Service) in December of 1943. She received a commission as a Navy Lieutenant in July of 1944. Service in the navy gave Grace the extraordinary opportunity to work with the development of cutting edge computing machines, when she joined Howard Aiken on the Mark I project.

While working on the Mark I project, she wrote a 500-page manual on the operations for the Automatic Sequence-Controlled Calculator (ASCC). In it, she outlined the fundamental operating principles of computing machines. Her work did not go unnoticed and she was retained to assist Aiken to work on the Mark II and Mark III computers.

In 1946, she became a naval reserve officer and joined the Harvard faculty as a research fellow, where she continued her computing research until 1949. In 1950, Grace joined the Eckert and Mauchly Computer Corporation. While at EMCC, where she helped developed the UNIVAC. After Remington Rand purchased EMCC, she devised the revolutionary computer-programming concept of the compiler. She developed the compiler because she believed that computers should be programmed in a language that resembled human communication. A compiler, when defined succinctly, transforms human readable source code into machine-readable code. She was influential in the developed of several programming languages for UNIVAC. Among them Mathmatic and Flow-matic, two programming languages she laid the groundwork for her design of COBOL (Common Business Oriented Language) in 1959 (Riddle, 1995). COBOL was used on IBM mainframes until the microprocessor revolution. Java, C, C++ are compiler based programming languages.

Colossus

Colossus is listed out of place here with the machines of the electromechanical era. Technically Colossus was a programmable, all-electronic, special-purpose computing device created during World War II. Colossus contained more than 2400 vacuum tubes and was controlled in the same manner as ENIAC with switches and patch cords. It was not the first electronic digital computer; the ABC predates it by six years. (It does not qualify as a computer because it had a single purpose, counter espionage.) Colossus was born in London out of the creative genius of Alan M. Turing, and colleagues. Turing a remarkable English mathematician and logician formed the current theories of the universal computer—known popularly as the Turing machine—influenced the development of digital computers throughout the 1940s and 1950s.

After the fall of France in 1940, Great Britain fought the war alone against the powerful German military until December 7, 1941, when the United States entered the war. Colossus decoded the Enigma radio signals of German spies inside Britain and alerted British Intelligence about German tactics.

Unlike the three previously described electromechanical devices—the Complex Number Calculator by Stibitz, the Z3 by Zuse, and the Harvard Mark I developed by Aiken—the logic circuits of Colossus performed Boolean math instead of the binary functions. That is instead of adding, subtracting, multiplying or dividing integers (real numbers); Colossus sole purpose was to read, compare, and decipher one value to another, one string of electronic pulses with another string of pulses. An overly simplified example of a Boolean math problem asks Colossus to determine whether following equation conforms to the algebraic laws of associativity: $x \wedge (y \wedge z) = (x \wedge y) \wedge z$, true or false. Once the computer determined the value of the equations were true or false, it allowed British Intelligence to decipher and translate the encoded message to English (Williams M. R., 2000).

The Colossus had a high-speed internal operation. As was the case with machines produced by Zuse, Stibitz, and Aiken the outcomes of Colossus changed by the altering of the sequence of switches. It had no built-in memory. Various cables plugged into the machine, changed outcomes generated by Colossus. The plug cable characteristics gave Colossus sophistication not found in the previously mentioned electromechanical relay calculators (Williams M. R., 2000).

ATANASOFF-BERRY COMPUTER

The Atanasoff – Berry Computer (ABC) was the first electronic digital computer ever built. Professor John Atanasoff and his graduate assistant Clifford Berry built it, in 1939 on the campus of Iowa State University in Ames, Iowa. What they envisioned was a hard-wired calculating machine capable of processing the arithmetic sequences necessary to solve simultaneous linear systems.

The ABC was about the size of a large office desk (Winston, 1998, pg. 67). It weighed only 700 pounds. It contained a little more than 300 vacuum tubes, and a mile of cabling (Anderson, 1994, pg. 393). It was miniscule when compared with the ENIAC and other first generation computers. The ABC had an eye-popping processing speed of one operation every 15 seconds (fast for 1939). A snail's pace when compared to the modern desktop computer capable of processing more than 150 billion operations in 15 seconds. The ABC utilized modern computing methods such as binary arithmetic and electronic switching elements. The computer had up to eight digits of precision.

By 1939, the prototype was capable of processing 29 variables in two simultaneous linear equations. This process is similar – in the general sense – to the algebraic method for solving three simultaneous linear equations with three unknowns with the squared array.

The Atanasoff and Berry prototype functioned properly in every manner except for its input-output device. The machine relied on punch-card technology to enter and retrieve data but it made just enough errors to prevent reliable, accurate solutions for every equations (Mackintosh, 1987). Atanasoff and Berry were never able to complete the numerous cures required to perfect the computer because of the start of World War II. Their service commitments sent them to opposite ends of the nation, Atanasoff to the District of Columbia, Berry to the Bay Area of California (Ceruzzi, 1999, pg. 230).

The efforts of Atanasoff and Berry were vindicated in 1973 when Judge Earl Larson of the U.S. District Court of Minnesota voided the Eckert-Mauchly patent. He based his decision on three facts. The first was the weeklong visit Mauchly made to the laboratory of Professor John Atanasoff at Iowa State University in Ames, in 1941, which Mauchly allowed to examine the ABC prototype and review its blueprints. The second fact was the regular correspondence between Mauchly and Atanasoff about the capabilities of the digital computer (Mackintosh, 1987). The third fact that influenced Judge Larson was the behavior of John Mauchly. Shortly after his trip to Ames, he enrolled in special classes in electronic engineering at the University of Pennsylvania's Moore School of Engineering. He did this to familiarize himself with the most recent developments in the field of electronic engineering (Ceruzzi, 1999, pg. 238).

After the Larson decision, ENIAC was recognized as the world's first general-purpose digital computer while the Atanasoff-Berry Computer was recognized as the world's first special-purpose digital computer (Williams M. R., 2000).

ENIAC

The name ENIAC is an acronym for the Electronic Numerical Integrator and Computer. John Presper Eckert and John William Mauchly built ENIAC in 1946. The dimensions of the first digital computer are gigantic. ENIAC was roughly eight-feet tall, three feet wide, and almost one-hundred feet long. It weighed approximately 30 tons (60,000 pounds). ENIAC contained more than 17,000 vacuum tubes, 70,000 resistors, 10,000 capacitors, 1,500 relays, 6,000 manual switches, and miles of cable.

Eckert and Mauchly began work on ENIAC in 1943 after receiving a commission for funding from the United States Department of the Army to build a machine to calculate its artillery ballistics. Eckert and Mauchly completed their task shortly after the close of World War II in 1945. The Department of the Army formally accepted ENIAC in July of 1946. Shortly thereafter, Mauchly and Eckert commercialized their efforts with ENIAC forming the Electric Control Company (ECC). The ECC was renamed the Eckert-Mauchly Computer Corporation (EMCC). The primary mission of EMCC was to build ENIAC style computers for the Defense Department contractors, quasi-government agencies, large universities, and large corporations.

Coincidentally, the world's first digital computer programmer of ENIAC was Mrs. Adele Goldstine. Mrs. Goldstine was the wife of Henry Goldstine one of the scientist that helped build ENIAC. Mrs. Goldstine's contribution to ENIAC also included writing the documentation manual for its operations. In fact, the first people to program the behemoth ENIAC were all women: Kay McNulty, Betty Snyder, Marlyn Wescoff, Ruth Lichterman, Betty Jennings, and Fran Bilas. The team of women came to be known as the Women of ENIAC. Remember to control the behavior of ENIAC required the reconfiguration of its 6,000 switches. I have included a very brief biography of their academic accomplishments before they came to ENIAC:

1. Marlyn Wescoff graduated from Temple University in June 1942 with a major in social studies and English and a minor in business.
2. Fran Bilas graduated from Chestnut Hills College for Women with a major in mathematics and a minor in physics in 1942.
3. Betty Snyder graduated from the University of Pennsylvania's school of Journalism in 1939.
4. Kay McNulty graduated from the Chestnut Hills College for Women with degree in mathematics.
5. Ruth Lichterman graduated from Hunter College with a degree in mathematics
6. Betty Jennings came to ENIAC after graduating with a degree in Mathematics from Northwest Missouri State Teachers College.

The first EMCC commercial contract was to build the Binary Automatic Computer (BINAC) for the Northrop Corporation (now Northrop-Grumman). BINAC was the first computer to use magnetic tape as storage medium (Aspray & Campbell-Kelly, 1996, pg. 95 - 99). The next project EMCC undertook was to deliver UNIVAC—an upgraded version of ENIAC—to the United States Census Bureau, in 1951 for roughly the same reasons Herman Hollerith won the contract to count the Census of 1890.

Even though the Census Bureau had awarded EMCC a $300,000 contract to deliver UNIVAC, poor fiscal policies and management decisions allowed the hostile takeover of the company by the

Remington-Rand Corporation. To bolster the sagging spirits of the former EMCC employees and stakeholders, Remington-Rand changed the company's corporate name from EMCC to UNIVAC a Division of Remington-Rand.

In November of 1952, as a publicity stunt, Remington-Rand boasted to political pundits and journalists that UNIVAC could predict the winner of the presidential election between World War II hero five-star General Dwight David Eisenhower and Illinois Governor Adlai Stevenson. (At the time of the election, only two five-star generals, George Washington and Ulysses S Grant, had become president of the United States.) UNIVAC, using only a small sampling of the popular votes cast, one percent, correctly predicted General Eisenhower as the winner and next President of the United States.

Both broadcast and print media as well as the wire services (United Press International, Associated Press, and Reuters) decided not release UNIVAC's prediction to the public fearing it would lead to voter apathy. Instead, the press led with a story stating UNIVAC was unable to decipher the results. The handwriting was on the wall, none of the executives and business leaders associated with the project ignored the elephant at the dining room table. The UNIVAC predictions made it clear that computers were the future of business. In 1955, the Sperry Corporation purchased Remington-Rand to form the Sperry Rand Corporation. Later the company shortened its name to Sperry. In 1986, Sperry and the Burroughs Corporation merged to form Unisys (Ceruzzi, 1999)

IBM

Although history credits Eckert and Mauchly with the building of UNIVAC as the seminal step towards modern computing and computer technology, any discussion about the embryonic days of electronic computers or computing is incomplete without a discussion about the role of International Business Machines (IBM). Since its formation by Herman Hollerith as the Tabulating Machine Company, IBM has made great contributions to the economic prosperity and safety of the United States starting with the logistical nightmare facing the United States Census Bureau in 1890.

Without the support of the IBM Corporation, the United States would not have landed a man on the moon. Without the support of the IBM Corporation, the United States would not have been able to secure itself from nuclear attack. The United States also owes IBM a great deal for the Naval Ordnance Research Calculator (NORC). Until the onset of the personal computer, IBM and computing were synonymous.

At the close of the Gilded Age roughly 1920, only four major companies Remington-Rand, Burroughs Adding Machine Company, NCR, and IBM competed for the lucrative office machine market. Of the four competitors, IBM (then known as the Computing Tabulating Recording Corporation) was the smallest. By 1921, IBM was undergoing major internal changes to management that would make IBM the world's largest data processing company (Swedin & Ferro, 2007, pg 24).

The rise of IBM's corporate dominance of office machines and computing technology begins in 1911 when Herman Hollerith sold the Tabulating Machine Company to Charles Ranlegh Flint. Flint supervises the merger of TMC with the International Time Recording Company (TRC) and the Computing Scale Company (CSC) to form the Computing Tabulating Recording Corporation (CTRC).

In 1921, Flint hires Thomas J. Watson Sr., then the second in command at NCR, as the new general manager of the floundering CTRC. The company Watson took over specialized in scales and measuring devices. Borrowing from his former mentor John Patterson at NCR, Watson initiates several policy changes in the form of executive directives.

The first directive was to change the focus of CTRC to its most lucrative and technologically advanced department, the tabulating machine department. From that moment on, the company would focus on providing mechanical accounting solutions to the business world. The second directive, he explains, "Each individual customer has an individual solution." Finally, to augment his challenge to sales staff, Watson initiates the practice of paying bonuses to sales agents exceeding their quota (Waldman, 1998, pp. 131 - 152).

IBM's initial entry in computer age began with the ASSC, the Harvard Mark I, the electromechanical computing machine built under the auspices of Howard Aiken. In 1946, IBM's entry into the *Electronic Era* occurred when the Selective Sequence Electronic Calculator (SSEC) made its debut. The SSEC was a hybrid of the traditional IBM punched-card technology and Howard Aiken's ideas about relay circuits (Ceruzzi, 1990, pg 244).

Instead of using Harvard Aiken expertise to build the SSEC, IBM built the SSEC under the guidance of Professor Wallace Eckert of

Columbia University and the Watson Scientific Computing Laboratory. The SSEC was not an electronic computer, because it used both vacuum tubes and electromechanical relays. The approach was used because the SSEC was considerably faster than its predecessor the ASSC.

The SSEC combined the speed of electronic circuits with a storage capacity of 400,000 digit enabling it to do thousands of calculations per second. Its operations relied on 12,500 vacuum tubes and 21,400 electrical relays. The SSEC was 40 feet by 60 feet by 80 feet along the periphery of a room at the IBM New York City headquarters. IBM displayed the SSEC until 1952 when the 701 computer replaced it.

The incentive to build the 701 computer was the partially due of Thomas J. Watson patriotism. At the outbreak of the Korean War in June 1950, Thomas J. Watson, Sr., asked the U.S. Government what the IBM Corporation could do to assist. The government's response to Watson, build a large-scale scientific computer. A computer that will be useful in the design of aircraft, the development nuclear weapons, and the manufacture munitions. The 701 was a landmark computer because it was:

1. The 701 was only one-fourth the size of the SSEC and 25 times faster.
2. The 701 was IBM's first mass produced large-scale electronic computer.
3. The 701 was IBM's first scientific computer available commercially.
4. The 701 series computers were the first computer memory stored internally in an addressable electronic memory.

In 1952, Thomas J. Watson Junior succeeded his father as head of the company. Between 1952 and 1960, IBM began to assert its domination of the data processing industry. Following the lead of such Gilded Age pioneers as George Westinghouse and John Patterson the younger Watson hired all the available physicists and electronics engineers to spearhead his campaigns in research and development efforts to dominate computer technology and to curtail competition.

The 1952 emphasis on research and development began to pay dividends for IBM by creating new markets worldwide in both the government and commerce. By the mid-1950s IBM had introduced the first computer to use solid-state technology entirely. Solid-state devices, based on the transistor, were smaller, more reliable, more economical than computers based on vaccuum tubes. The transistor use less power and and did not required refrigeration (air conditioning) to cool its circuits. In addition, during the late 1950s, IBM introduced two of its most financially successful computers systems, the 1401 business computer and the 1620 scientific computer (IBM Archives, 2009).

SAGE

The creation of the 701 computer also marked the beginning of a long and fruitful partnership with the United States. The two would team up again to implement the SAGE project. SAGE is an acronym for Semi-Automatic Ground Environment; it was the brainchild of the United States Defense Department and the United States Air Force. The SAGE project integrated radar technology and computer technology to provide a systematic automated tracking and interception of unidentified aircraft flying over North America.

The idea for SAGE began in 1949 at the start of the "Cold War" following the Soviet Union's explosion of its first nuclear bomb in Siberia. The United States Department of Defense (DoD) grew fearful that aircrafts from the Soviet Union could carry nuclear weapons over the North Pole to attack the United States or Canada. Adding to this fear was the widespread commercialization, the polar airspace between Europe, South Korea, Japan, and North America. Under these circumstances, it was clear to many in the military and the State Department that North America geographic isolation policy was no longer a plausible defense strategy for national security. To placate the widespread fear of a preemptive Soviet nuclear strike, the Department of Defense was compelled to develop an information system capable of distinguishing friendly aircraft from aggressor aircraft.

SAGE was the remedy to the panic in the Department of Defense. SAGE when fully deployed was a network of more than 20 computers spread across the continent. Its primary purpose was to detect Soviet (Communist) aircraft carrying conventional and nuclear weapons aimed at targets inside the United States and Canada. The total cost of the SAGE project was 8 billion dollars when completed in 1963.

Although the project turn into a huge white elephant for the government once the Soviets developed intercontinental ballistic missiles (ICBM)—undercutting the project's original purpose. SAGE did spawn several innovations worth commercial exploitation, which included a modern programming language (FORTRAN), cathode ray tube (CRT) displays, printed circuit boards, core memory, mass storage devices, and the mouse. Other innovations credited to the SAGE project included the first full duplex computer network to connect radar arrays. SAGE, also, created the first wide area network.

The SAGE computer network utilized The AN/FSQ-7 computer—it was the largest computer ever built. It contained more than 55,000 vacuum tubes, occupied approximately a half-acre of floor space, and weighed 275 tons. It consumed almost three megawatts of power.

IBM and the Department of Defense were able to salvage the SAGE initiative with the development of the North American Aerospace Defense Command (NORAD). Computer alignments in NORAD were able to monitor and detect aircraft and missile launches inside the Soviet Union, Communist China, and Warsaw Pact communist governments.

In conclusion, the SAGE project made IBM the dominant world power in the computer industry. At the peak of the SAGE project, IBM employed between 7000 and 8000 computer engineers. The SAGE project enabled IBM to grab the industry technology lead in mass storage devices, processor technology, and real-time processing technology it never relinquished. After the SAGE project, the journalist and economic observers of the computer industry referred to IBM as Snow White and the seven dwarves—IBM and the seven dwarves. SAGE was replaced by the Worldwide Military Command and Control System (or WWMCCS) to detect missile launch shortly after the Cuban Missile Crisis. Later the United States and Canada integrated satellite surveillance into their defense computer network. The original 20 computer locations across the continent of SAGE grew to 27 computer locations with the merger of satellite, radar, and computer technology.

SABRE

While IBM was at the forefront of the SAGE project, opportunity came knocking at the corporate venue. Several major corporations were seeking unique solutions for their own logistical problems. One the companies needing one of the specialized solutions, IBM promised—Thomas J. Watson's second directive individual customers have individual solutions—was American Airlines. Towards the end of the decade of the 1950s, American Airlines faced a logistical crisis worth of the Census Bureau in 1890. Its reservation system was overloaded and the constant source of customer dissatisfaction.

To resolve American Airlines reservation system crisis, IBM initiated the SABRE an acronym for Semi-Automatic Business Environment Research. SABRE paved the way for the IBM to create a virtual monopoly in the niche of tracking in real-time reservations for passengers.

SABRE was second major contribution made to modern computing by IBM. When fully implemented in 1963, SABRE, linked two IBM 7090 mainframe computers—one live, the other on standby—over 10,000 miles of leased telephone lines to more 1100 ticket agents in 50 cities across the United States to coordinate seat inventory and passenger records. The system was capable of processing 10-million reservation request per year (Aspray & Campbell-Kelly, 1996).

IBM began work on project SABRE in 1957 and completed it in 1960. SABRE reduced the time a ticket agent was required to wait to confirm a passenger's reservation on a flight with American Airlines from 90 minutes to three seconds. The SABRE project was so successful that IBM built similar reservation systems for Pan American Airlines, Delta Airlines, and Eastern Airlines. Before it was completed in 1960, SABRE turned out to be the largest civilian computing project in the nation's history. It employed more than 200 computer programmers who produced more than a million lines of programming code. The technology that made the SABRE project possible was the real-time computing developed by IBM during the SAGE project. The internet travel agency Travelocity is a subsidiary of the American Airlines' reservation system (Aspray & Campbell-Kelly, 1996).

IBM CONTRIBUTION TO HUMANITY

All to often historians become overwhelm by the economic and technological power IBM amassed over the last 125 years of existence. Despite some unpredictable misstep at the outbreak of World War II— who could have predicted the Holocaust—IBM has continually contributed to the arts and culture of not only the United States but the world.

On their website is a link IBM100. It takes the vistior to the 100 projects around the world IBM actively participated. The projects include mapping the Genome of the coca plants of West Africa. The projects help West African farmers select the fittest seed for the growing of coca trees and increased production of coca. Providing a DNA transistor to map individual gene sequences. Other projects IBM helped bring to fruition were the National Malaria Control Program, preservation of culture through technology, and exploring the ecosystems of the oceans.

Final Notes

Figure 36 Von Neumann architecture

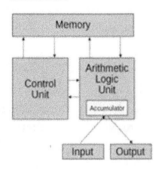

Modern computer architecture is based on the theories of John von Neumann. He stated that a computer should have these four basic components: memory, a control unit, arithmetic-logic unit, and an input/output unit.

John von Neumann was a gifted Hungarian born physicist who moved to the United States—shortly after the rise to power in Germany of the National Socialist Party—in 1933. Prior to World War II, von Neumann worked as a professor at Princeton University. After the start of World War II, he worked on several project for the Department of War (Department of Defense) including the Manhattan Project with such scientific giants as Enrico Fermi, Albert Einstein, and Robert Oppenheimer who were instrumental in the development of the atomic bomb that led to the defeat of Japan in the Pacific theater of the War.

In 1944, he was transferred to the U.S. Army's ENIAC computer project designed and managed by J. Presper Eckert and John W. Mauchly. His most important contribution to the project was making the suggestion to modify ENIAC to run as a stored-program machine. A von Neumann machine has one large singular RAM structure, which contains both program memory and data memory.

10

Kinds of Computers

When I began this discussion, it was assumed the first computing devices contrived by humans were indeed the hands and fingers but there were no artifacts to confirm my assumptions. One could only surmise the first mechanical computing devices were based on hands and fingers because the early number systems and counting devices were conveniently group into units of five or ten. Examples of this supposition are the first computing tools, the abacus, and Roman numerals. Both were grouped into multiples of fives, of course every number system begins with one. Artifacts developed by civilizations other than the Romans do not support the above theory.

The ancient civilizations of Egypt, Israel, and Babylonian showed a remarkable inconsistency with both five and ten. For example, the cubit—a measure of length from Jewish as well as Egyptian civilizations—was the distance between the tips of the middle finger to the corner of the elbow. After looking at both basic numbers, there is no elaboration of their numbers. The Babylonians used a sexagesimal number system based on wedges and inverted triangles. It did not resemble the space between the forefinger and thumb, as did the Roman symbol for five, V. Two hands V, V or X look like the V stacked.

The Egyptians were even less uniform with their number system; they represented computations with pictures of plants and animals (pictographs). Another measure taken from a Biblical reference was the span. A span was the distance from the tip of the thumb to the tip of the little finger. The ancients soon realized that not all people were the same size and a standard was need. The length of the monarch's arm and hand became the accepted standards for the cubit and the span. These measures changed of course with the succession of the new monarch. The continued references to physical measures instead of set standards guaranteed the first rudiments of counting and computing analog.

Even after the Hindu-Arabic system was introduced, it took several generations before Schickard introduced the digital calculator to take advantage of its flexibility. The following sections examine computing devices from the late 19th century forward after the introduction of electricity.

ANALOG COMPUTER

The analog computer's place in the history of human computing fulfills the primitive human curiosity to question why certain events occur. Analog computers represent the physical events that pure mathematics could not describe, predict, or explain. Analog calculating machines have been with us since antiquity. They range in complexity range from a simple sundial to complex differential integrators (a device used to compute the area contained within closed curves). Classic examples of analog computers from antiquity include *Stonehenge* in Great Britain and *Piedra del Sol* in Mexico City. Smaller analog computers from antiquity are the Antikythera device of 300 BC and the slide rule of late Medieval Europe.

The most enduring analog devices include the slide rule, the abacus, and the Antikythera device. These ancient of analog devices illustrate the basics use of analog computing. It is a device that performs computations by continuous measuring physical variables, which are analogs of the actual items being computed. The analog built between the two world wars solved mathematical problems beyond the mathematical capabilities the average student. The AC Network Analyzer solved problems by modeling the events directly proportional to its size. The Profile Tracer and the Differential Analyzer solved difficult problems by continuously measuring the events the lay of the terrain or arcs of parabolas, etc.

The apex of the analog computer occurred in the 1920s, when complex analog calculating machines called differential analyzers were built to solve problems in ballistics, electric power generation, and simulate industrial controls (Kidwell & Ceruzzi, Landmarks in Digital Computing, 2009). Twentieth century analog computers perform in the much the same manner as its antique counterparts only instead of being restricted to monitoring the behavior of natural occurrences it monitors man-made occurrences such as the electric power grid of Mississippi and Alabama or the wave action against the Zuider Zee seawall in the Netherlands. The most famous analog computers of the twentieth century include the Product Intergraph, the AC Network Analyzer, and the Differential Analyzer of Vannavar Bush (Bromley, The Analog Computers, 1990).

Between the two world wars—that is between 1918 and 1941—complex analog computers were the primary computing devices of commerce, science, and the military. Analog computers solved problems using one of two methods. The first method used to solve problems with an analog computer was by recording the physical event. The Tide Analyzer of Lord Kelvin used this solution in the 19th century. The Tide Analyzer marked on paper the daily occurrences of tide levels.

A second type of analog computer was the scale model analyzer. This form of analog computer a simulator is built to scale to solve electric power generation problems, controls for hydroelectric dams, and coastal seawalls. These analog computers were some of the most complex and powerful computing devices ever built. Yet, despite their computing power, the arrival of the digital computer, in the late 1940s, overshadowed them and rendered them obsolete within a decade (Kidwell & Ceruzzi, 2009).

Some of the reasons the analog computers vanished was due to the fact they were specialized computing devices. The analog computer was inflexible and therefore inappropriate for general business or scientific computing which required the flexibility of a calculator. A second reason for the demise of the analog computer is the transistor.

As the electronic component began to play a prominent role in the digital computer, it was obvious the computing power of the digital computer was significantly faster than its analog counterpart. With the advent of the transistor, the cost of computer manufacture was reduced significantly. Thus making the manufacture of intricate integrator wheels, output gears, and precise torque amplifiers necessary for the analog computer proved prohibitive. Lastly, analog computers were never in widespread use. the 2nd generation computers digital computers, IBM 1401, and to a lesser extent the first generation (big iron) computers easily outpaced the analogs built to solve military ballistics, combat avionics, and huge commercial or construction projects of industry, business, and education (Bromley, The Analog Computers, 1990).

Analog computers, either mechanical or electromechanical, provided solutions to complex non-linear equations and simulation of multi-dimensional, parallel, and continuous processes heretofore requiring hundreds if not thousands of man hours. One such analog device although much simpler was the Powles Calliparea of 1870; it was the alternative to the mathematics of Ohm's law. It measured, without calculation, the cross-sectional area of a wire to determine its resistance to conducting electric current (Bromley, The Analog Computers, 1990).

The analog era ended because it was inflexible. Even the magnificent Differential Analyzer of Vannevar Bush could not be given new instructions to concentrate their attention to counting the census or tracking Soviet aircraft nearing Canadian airspace. Analogs ended because scientific advancements needed crisper and faster solutions (Aspray & Campbell-Kelly, 1996, pp. 60-62).

VANNEVAR BUSH

Most people associate the name Vannevar Bush with the development of the atomic bomb. However, prior to the war, Vannevar Bush was one of the nation's leading engineers and computer scientist pioneering the development of several analog computing projects. He was the first vice president and dean of engineering at the Massachusetts Institute of Technology (MIT) and president of the Carnegie Institution. Vannevar Bush was born March 11, 1890, in Everett, Massachusetts. He received both his bachelor's and master's degrees in mathematics from

Tufts College. He received his doctorate in engineering from the Massachusetts Institute of Technology in 1916.

His rise to prominence began with the invention of a simplistic analog computer surveying tool named the Profile Tracer. The profile tracer plotted the traverse of the land and reproduced it on paper. Over a nine-year period between 1922 and 1931, Bush became recognized by his peers the preeminent computer scientist of the United States for the invention of several electromechanical analog computers, which included the Product Intergraph an analog computer that solved simple equations and the Differential Analyzer. The Differential Analyzer or the Rockefeller Differential Analyzer (as it eventually became) was Bush's attempt to reproduce or re-invent the Babbage Difference Engine (Redshaw, 1996).

The Rockefeller Differential Analyzer was one of the most powerful analog computers ever built. It could solve differential equations with as many as 18 independent variables. The Rockefeller Differential Analyzer weighed 100-tons, contained 2000 vacuum tubes, and 150 electric motors.

Almost simultaneous to the invention and building of the differential analyzers came Bush's development of a "network analyzer." The network analyzer was an analog computer that solved electricity distribution problems. It was a miniature version of the large electrical networks in the southern and western portions of the United States.

Bush's scientific success with analog computing, allowed him to become the chief scientific advisor to President Franklin Delano Roosevelt. With Roosevelt's backing, Bush was instrumental in mobilizing the United States' scientific community prior to the outbreak of hostilities with Germany and Japan in World War II.

At the behest of Vannevar Bush, President Roosevelt created the National Defense Research Committee (NDRC), to organized, and coordinated federal government scientific research relating to national defense. A year later, Bush asked the President Roosevelt to create the Office of Scientific Research and Development (OSRD), which superseded the NDRC. As the primary administrator of the OSRD, Bush was instrumental in spearheading the Allies' development of radar and the atomic bomb before the Axis powers.

One final note, Vannevar Bush was credited with the invention of hypertext, a forerunner of HTML, with a theoretical machine called Memex. With Memex, it was the intention of Bush to create a machine that mirrored human memory (Griffin, 2006). Some psychiatrist, associate Google, and Bing search engines with human memory stating that access to the voluminous amounts of data contained in the search engines has affected the way people recall events.

RISE OF THE DIGITALS

The moment in history when general-purpose computers began supplanting analog computers occurred in 1945 shortly after the conclusion of World War II. The events that precipitated the change transpired when the Department of the Navy's commissioned the Massachusetts Institute of Technology's Servomechanism Laboratory to build a universal flight simulator to train its future and current pilots.

During World War II, before potential pilots—for either the army or the navy—could fly military aircraft, they had to undergo a rigorous training program that included both textbooks and servo-mechanical aircraft simulators. The existing simulators the armed forces used to replicate the cockpit environments of its combat aircrafts had several shortcomings. The most perplexing fault of the aircraft trainer was the arduous task of reconfiguring the servomechanisms, relays, and hydraulic lifters for each of its different aircraft. The second fault of the trainer was the inflexibility of its control unit, which also required a complete set of instructions for each aircraft.

The task of finding a universal flight trainer was the responsibility of the Aircraft Stability and Control Analyzer (ASCA) project. The Office of Naval Research in partnership with the Massachusetts Institute of Technology Servomechanisms Laboratory initiated the project in 1944. The new control unit for the simulator had to be capable of reproducing the navigational and cockpit environments for each military aircraft without the arduous and labor-intensive reconfiguration process of the old simulator.

The ASCA flight simulator project was originally conceived as an analog computer but after the program's executives learned of ENIAC. The focus of ASCA shifted from building an analog simulator to building a large-scale high-speed multitasking digital computer-based flight simulator. The code name for the project was Whirlwind. As a result of the shift in focus, Project ASCA was removed from the auspices of the Servomechanisms Lab to the MIT Digital Computer Laboratory.

The Navy brought in J. W. Forrester to serve as director of the Digital Computer Laboratory's Whirlwind in 1947. While presiding over the new computer, Forrester, in 1955, invented the basis for random-access memory (RAM), Coincident-current Magnetic Storage, or magnetic core memory. Magnetic core memory became the logic-standard for RAM memory in digital computers for the next two decades. Core memory replaced vacuum tube memory and was utilized until the invention of semiconductor memory. In 1956, Forrester received a patent for magnetic core memory. The change to magnetic core memory provided Project Whirlwind with the needed high levels of speed and reliability necessary to replicate an aircraft's cockpit environment.

Project Whirlwind eventually became the Semi-Automatic Ground Environment or SAGE used by the United States Air Force North American Aerospace Defense Command (NORAD) at Cheyenne Mountain in Colorado Springs. The flight simulators for both civilian and military aircraft are descendants of SAGE and Project Whirlwind. SAGE demonstrated the overall versatility of the general-purpose digital computer and its overall superiority to analogs. Consequently, as the notoriety of SAGE grew increasingly popular, so did modern general-purpose digital computers. The overall effect on the entirety of the computer market was the decline in use of analog computers for business, scientific, and educational projects. One derivative of SAGE/Project Whirlwind was MITRE. MITRE Corporation, a not-for-profit corporation, formed to develop new technologies for United States government (M.I.T. Libraries, 2009).

The development of the modern digital computer evolved from the history of mechanical computing, beginning with Wilhelm Schickard's Calculating Clock in the 16th and concluding with the invention of the Atanasoff Berry Computer and ENIAC. Digital computers fit awkwardly into three categories: personal computer, mainframe, super computer. There are several gray areas in the three areas of digital computing where the boundaries overlap. The personal computer has three deviations. The most common deviation of the personal computer is the laptop or notebook and the desktop. The third and often-overlooked variation of the personal computer is the file server or minicomputer. Another gray area in the classification of computers comes in the classification of the mainframe and the supercomputer. Although the term mainframe is passé, the term supercomputer has, in every way, replaced the term mainframe for complicated and arduous processing. Likewise, the laptop or notebook computer has deviations of the portable personal computer. Then there is a third deviation, the Personal Digital Assistant. For some people this has become a blackberry or IPhone. However, Palm HP, Sony, and Dell to name a few manufacturers still make the digital assistant. The PDA come loaded software products ranging from Microsoft Office to a low-end generic office software suite. All of the PDA come equipped with notepad, datebook, and Bluetooth.

The second variant is the netbook. A netbook as the name implies is a personal computer designed for use on the internet. Recently, Google and several other manufacturers came out with the Chrome Book. This is a computer designed to stream online business software instead of purchasing it from the online retailer or brick and mortar supplier. Google provide its software free on the Chrome book and for anyone else who is tired of purchasing the updates to popular software suites. The problem with this arrangement, 76% of the world's computers use Microsoft Windows software. Sun Microsystems (Java) also provides its online office suite software free. Although it is installed on the hard drive, Microsoft charges an annual fee to download and use the latest incarnation of its Office Suite. Adobe charges a monthly fee to download and use their most up to date software suites.

A third variation of the notebook or laptop computer is the tablet computer. The tablet computer is a touch screen device that is sensitive to movement on it main output device the screen. All tablet computer come without keyboards or mouse. Like the PDA, it provides a virtual keyboard to input data. A variation of the table computer is the e-reader. For the remainder of this chapter, I will discuss the various types or styles of computers.

MAINFRAMES

Figure 37 inside ENIAC

The term mainframe or big-iron computer applies to the first-generation computers. The name is indicative of the majority of electronic computers built between 1939 and 1950. The term is, also, emblematic of large-scale, second-generation computers manufactured after the advent of the transistor. Without reference to exceptions, the characteristics of first-generation mainframe computers were enormous frames covering hundreds of cubic feet and weighing thousands of pounds. These computers contained thousands of vacuum tubes, relays, switches, and miles of electric cable. ENIAC, Colossus, UNIVAC, and EDVAC were classic examples of the first-generation mainframe computer. The lone exception to the above description was the ABC built by Atanasoff and Berry at Iowa State University in Ames, Iowa.

The end of the Big Iron computer era came about because of three revolutionary advancements in electronic technology: the printed circuit board, the transistor, and the integrated circuit. The first breakthrough was the printed circuit board (PCB), invented by Paul Eisler of Great Britain in the 1943. The printed circuit is an electrical device where the wiring for a circuit and components consist of a thin coat of electrically conductive material instead of conventional copper wire. Printed circuit boards were partly responsible for the reduction in the overall size and weight of equipment while improving reliability and uniform size and volume compared to the hand-soldered circuit boards (Carano & Fjelstad, 2004, pg 4-7).

The second advancement in electronics was the invention of the transistor in 1947 by William Shockley, John Bardeen, and Walter Brattain. The transistor replaced the vacuum tube and attributed greatly to the reduction in the size of the computer and other electronic devices. The third advancement in electronic engineering was the invention of the integrated circuit by Robert Noyce and Jack Kilby in 1958. The integrated circuit replaced the transistor and further reduced the size of electronic devices.

The technologies of the transistor, the printed circuit, and the integrated circuit changed forever the size and shape of the computer. For example, the typical first-generation computer was completely hand built. It was the size of a living room and weighed tons, the typical second-generation computer was, for the most part, massed-produced then assembled. It was the size of a dinner table with several china cabinets. The third generation computer was completely massed produced. It was the size of a portable record player turntable. When the first-generation computer, in Figure 37, is compared to the second-generation computer, the IBM model 1401, in Figure 38, the differing architectures are profound.

ENIAC was 100 feet long, three feet wide and 8.5 feet tall. It

Figure 38 IBM 1401 Computer

contained more than 17,000 vacuum tubes, 70,000 resistors, 10,000 capacitors, 1,500 relays, and more than 6,000 manual switches. It weighed 60,000 pounds. UNIVAC, a second-generation of ENIAC, was 14 feet long, eight feet wide and 8.5 feet tall. It contained more than 5,600 tubes, 18,000 crystal diodes, and 300 relays. Univac occupied 952 cubic feet and more than 112 square feet of floor space. UNIVAC weighed 29,000 pounds and consumed 125 kilowatts of electricity.

The IBM 1401, in contrast, was typical of second-generation computers. It contained only 4,350 transistors and 6,213 diodes. It occupied a mere 33.8 square feet of floor space and weighed between

3,000 and 11,000 pounds, depending on the number of accessories printers, magnetic tape readers, punch card readers, and disk drive storage devices, etc. added. The computer consumed a maximum of 12.5 kilowatts of electricity one-tenth the consumption of UNIVAC. Notice also, that while there are people at the controls of the 1401 in Figure 38 and ENIAC in Figure 37. The people in Figure 37 are inside the super structure of the computer; technicians are programming or verifying the circuits within the structure of ENIAC.

Despite its compactness, the IBM system 1401 still conformed to the sequential nature of the von Neumann architecture. The foreground, in Figure 38 shows a keyboard for input, moving left is an early disk drive storage device, to the left and rear of the disk drive is a card reader. Behind the card reader is another storage device a magnetic tape drive, finally to the right of the person seated is a printer (Aspray & Campbell-Kelly, 1996, pg. 131) (International Business Machines Corporation, 1961). All the technicians working with the 1401 system are outside the superstructure of the computer.

Some of you might wonder why fourth generation computers (microprocessor) computers were not discussed. The cabinetry and the size of a third generation computer and a fourth generation computer do not differ greatly. What differs is the superior computing power of the fourth compared to the third. Third generation computers were miniature reproductions of 2nd generation computers. The technology the microprocessor had not been perfected with the advent of the 3rd generation computers. Third generation computers still had individualized ALU, control units and accumulators instead of a monolithic CPU. Fourth generation computers combine all the components of the computer on a microprocessors. For this reason, owners of fourth generation computers are not compelled to purchase accessory extension cards to add a mouse card, sound card for audio, and modem card for telecommunications as they were with third generation computers.

The Fall of IBM

The decline of the mainframe computer and the decline of IBM as a dominant computer maker correspond directly with the advent of the fourth generation personal computer. A number of issues contributed to the decline of IBM from an economic world power to just another computer company. The primary reason contributing to IBM's downfall is the hesitancy to embrace the microprocessor as a solution to its own internal difficulties and contemplate how it affected industry trends. The remainder of this section examines briefly the IBM decline.

I have already discussed IBM's birth as Tabulating Machine Company with the logistical crisis of the Census Bureau in 1880. I also addressed Herman Hollerith relinquishing power in favor of Charles Ranlegh Flint, the rise of T. J. Watson Senior and the emergence of IBM as an economic powerhouse in the late 1950s. Trouble began for IBM after it introduced the System 1401 in 1959. It sold more than 12,000 machines the first year. That total surpassed the combined sales of IBM's next seven largest competitors (Aspray & Campbell-Kelly, 1996, pg. 135).

The greatest difficulty confronting IBM after the introduction of the 1401 came from within not its competitors. It had seven models of computers. Each computer IBM developed had a specialized task for its customer's particular niche in the economy. An inadvertent consequence of such dedicated software was specialization was compatibility. IBM had produced seven computer, each model incompatible with the six other models. To complicate matters even more was the fact that a good portion of IBM customers still relied on punch card technology. These complications combined to increase the company's overhead.

For example, a customer that owned or rented the 7000 model computer—used to start SABRE for American Airlines—could not expand its computing power by adding the model 1401 or 1600. Special software engineering was required to link model 1401 with model 7000. It was easier for a customer to purchase the newer product along with its accessories than to have engineers write software to adapt each new generation of equipment to the accessories of the older units than to pay for the continued upkeep of hybrid computing.

Competitors recognized the compatibility problems of IBM and sought methods to leech customers away from the computing giant. The most effective method of leeching customers was reverse engineering or cloning of an IBM computer.

By cloning the IBM computers, competitors gained several advantages over IBM. For example, Honeywell—creator of one of the more successful cloned computers—undermined the IBM hardware development cycle. First, the clone computers were a spur of the moment development. The cloned computers did not have the enormous financial commitments IBM made to the development of hardware. Second, the clone makers did not have any fiscal commitments or responsibility to development of new software or legacy software. They merely reverse engineered the IBM products. The Honeywell cloned computers ran the IBM 1401 proprietary software without the complicated software engineering prominent at the offices of IBM clients. Finally, the cloned computers were not constrained to the IBM business model or marketing strategies. Clone makers leeched clients from IBM wherever possible. To add insult to injury, the cloned computers were not only cheaper but used the newest semiconductors innovations, circuit boards, and integrated circuits.

Hypothetically, a company renting an IBM 1401 for $3500 a month could return it to IBM and purchase a new Honeywell cloned computer for less than the annual rental price of the 1401. During the first week the Honeywell made the cloned 1401 available to the public, it siphoned away 400 of IBM's once loyal customers (Aspray & Campbell-Kelly, 1996, pg. 136).

In response to the threat of the cloned computers and growing manufacturing and maintenance costs of incompatible computer models, IBM built the System 360. IBM designed the System 360 for two purposes. First, the 360 was to deliver a coup de grace to the clones of Honeywell and similar computer manufacturers. Second, the 360 was the bridge to the compatibility problems IBM had with its own product line. The main feature of the System 360 was its versatility; it was compatible with any previous computer IBM model computer and required no specialized software engineering. The first week the System 360 was on the market, IBM sold 9000 units.

The System 360 was a mainframe computer smaller and more powerful than any of the previous seven IBM computers. It was an awesome display of one-upmanship and engineering acumen. The System 360 was the prefect computer, except for one fatal flaw, its builder lacked of a clear vision of the future. Almost as soon as IBM delivered System 360, RCA and General Electric offered cloned versions of the model for a fraction of the cost. Burroughs, Control Data, Honeywell, NCR, and Sperry-Rand recognized the absence of time-sharing software (MULTICS) in the 360 and identified niche markets in science, education, and commerce to sell their own cloned versions of the IBM 360 with time-sharing ability.

Accelerating the downfall of IBM in the mid-1970s was its resistance to the use the integrated circuit. The integrated circuit came about because of IBM's influence over NASA and the Apollo Man on the Moon project. IBM's convinced its partner NASA the integrated circuit was the solution to the space and weight limitations of the Apollo lunar module and the solution to the navigation and guidance controls of the Apollo command module.

For some reason, IBM—after witnessing the computing prowess of the integrated circuit on the Apollo missions—instead of investing in integrated circuit technology, stubbornly continued to rely on solid-state mainframe computer technology to dominate the computer industries. In the world of computer science IBM became a victim of commodification—any competent manufacture (fool) can build a mainframe.

Consequently, smaller manufacturers seeing an opportunity rushed in to fill the technology gap IBM abandoned after the lunar missions. The integrated circuit was an inexpensive alternative to solid-state transistor circuit board technology. The integrated circuit made computer technology cheaper and available to a larger portion of the economy and population. In spite of itself, the popularity of the integrated circuit, IBM continued to maintain high margins of profits, even though its market share of computer manufacturing fell from 75% to 50% of all the computers produced in the Free World.

New competitors Data General, DEC, Xerox, Osborne, and Apple joined the fray with the older rivals Unisys, GE, RCA, and Honeywell contending for customers and a share of the computer manufacturing market. Although it fought vigorously against these new threats by producing the IBM AT and XT personal computers—machines capable of interfacing with its mainframe computers—IBM failed to maintain the dominance it enjoyed in the 1960s and 70s. Its market share, as the 1980s ended, declined to just over 20% of all the computers made throughout the world.

Another reason for IBM's downfall emanated from the shift in the data processing business models—away from hardware centric and centralized computing to the distributed or networked computing models—that emphasized software rather than hardware. The new business model emphasized the integrated circuit and microprocessor ergo the personal computer rather than the solid-state technology of the mainframe. Instrumental in changing the emphasis of data processing from centralized computing to distributed computing was a small firm named Novell.

Novell a Utah based software firm was founded in 1983. It introduced the distributed business model with its Netware network operating system. Novell was the first company to sell local area network (LAN) operating system software, capturing roughly seventy percent of the market for large and small companies. NetWare's success was based on its ability to link personal computers using a DOS operating system to a network server. In turn, Netware allowed the personal computers to share files and services.

The final contributing factor to the decline in the dominance of IBM in the computer industry stems from its heritage. The working model IBM inherited from Herman Hollerith and later Thomas J. Watson was developed when data processing was based on punch card technology during the late 19th century and first half of the 20th century. Hollerith made as much from the rental of equipment and the sale of punch cards as he made from the sale of his tabulating machines. The empire he passed to Watson and IBM was a hardware-based technology.

IBM translated that hardware-based heritage first from the tabulating machine to the electromechanical computer and later to the mainframe electronic computer. At the dawn of the distributed computing age, the sales tactics—each individual customer has an individual solution—passed to Thomas J. Watson from John Patterson and initiated at IBM was no longer relevant because of the sway of the personal computer. Many inside the computer industry and data processing industry believed the personal computer was a solution looking for a problem.

The IBM strategies for hardware and centralized computing became obsolete as software based companies transformed the data processing landscape reducing the cost of doing business with less equipment and expensive software engineers. Software based companies like Novell and Microsoft, further diluted the importance of IBM hardware. Microsoft in particular developed a single software suite that was simultaneously suitable for work, school, laboratory, college, and the home. Owning a computer was no longer the symbol of the powerful and the prestige of the wealthy. The computer in the workplace became as commonplace as the pencil, the typewriter, and accounting ledger (Aspray & Campbell-Kelly, 1996, pp. 131-156).

One last comment about IBM, it became an industrial giant because it accepted computing challenges from commerce, education, and government no other company was able to undertake. It created an empire building equipment for Project Whirlwind, SAGE, SABRE, NASA's Gemini and Apollo spacecraft, and the Cheyenne Mountain NORAD ballistic missile defense system. Ironically, in February of 2005, IBM sold its personal computer division to Lenovo a multinational corporation sponsored by "Cold War" mortal enemy the People's Republic of China.

PERSONAL COMPUTERS

Figure 39 IBM PC2

The personal computer (PC) is characterized as a low-cost computer designed for use in the office, school, or home. The price of a PC ranges from the $100 model, designed for use by children in remote third-world villages, to several thousands of dollars for the powerful high-end computers used by scientists to decipher the human genome, create artificial life, or by cinematographers to animate motion pictures. Personal computers are divided into two subclasses: stationary (desktop) and portable (laptop or notebook).

Stationary computers or desktops personal computers are designed for numerous scenarios ranging from the corporate office to the individual home. All modern personal computers built in 2011 are fourth-generation computers. The fourth-generation PC differs from third-generation PC in that fourth-generation computers utilize microprocessor technology while third generation computers utilized integrated circuit technology. Some may feel that the explanation is an exercise in semantics but it is not. Third generation computers contained multiple integrated circuit chips. In fact third generation computers are miniature versions of 2nd generation computers. The fourth generation computer differs because it has the entire computer built on a single silicon wafer.

151

The difference between the two technologies is extensive. Third generation computers were larger, slower, consumed more electricity, and cost more. The differences can be compared to that of bookkeeper and an accountant. The 3rd generation computer represents the bookkeeper and the 4th generation computer represents the accountant.

Bookkeepers perform the mundane tasks of recording day-to-day transactions of the employers. Bookkeepers follow the direction of their supervisor, which is usually an accountant. The accountants performs the same tasks as the bookkeeper however, accountants are licensed by the state in a manner similar to attorney licensing. The licensing of an accountant requires college studies beyond the bachelor degree and the passage of a state administered accounting exam. Once the accountant passes the state test, he or she is designated as a certified public accountant. The CPA audits and inspects the financial records of individuals or businesses. Then prepares financial statements, creates a budget, audits the assets and investments, and files tax reports for his client. The CPA is responsible for all of the client's records.

The personal computer is capable of producing a multitude of documents far beyond the basic tasks of the early digital calculators, tabulating machines, and electromechanical devices discussed earlier in this text. People use personal computers for a plethora of tasks from the design of superstructures for bridges, skyscrapers, and aircraft. Personal computers are the sharp point of the spear in the fight against disease. Desktop computers were made IBM compatible because before the shift from hardware centric computing the personal computer had to be able to communicate with the mainframe computer, which was 90% of the time an IBM mainframe. Apple and UNIX computers are the lone exception to that rule. The major manufactures of the modern desktop are Lenovo, Gateway, Toshiba, Samsung, Dell, Hewlett Packard, Acer, and Apple. The majority of personal computers have a starting price of $399 then ranges on upward toward $2599 for high-end home computers to $10,000 for cinematographers.

HISTORY OF THE PERSONAL COMPUTER

The personal computer began as a cottage industry for computer enthusiast and hobbyist in 1974. The first personal computers were compact versions of mainframe computers. Unlike its mainframe counterpart, which used solid-state transistor technology, the personal computer used the integrated circuit and later the microprocessor.

The first personal computers were sold as kits—the buyer assembled—by Micro Instrumentation and Telemetry Systems (MITS) Altair 8800. MITS advertised the computer kit in the magazines Popular Electronics and Popular Science for the price of $397. The Altair 8800 (Figure 40) was primitive looking compared to the modern personal computer. It looked more like a movie prop in a bad science fiction movie rather than a computer.

The Altair 8800 had neither mouse, keyboard, nor monitor common elements of the modern personal computer. The on-board random access memory (RAM) was a monstrous minute 256 byte; the microprocessor was the Intel 8080. To input data, the operator toggled the individual switches on the face of the machine. The data output generated by the Altair 8800 consisted of a series of flashing bulbs also found on the face of the computer.

Figure 40 The Altair 8800

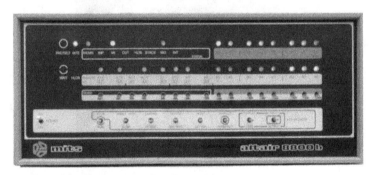

Despite its awkward appearance and obvious shortcomings, the Altair 8800 was a commercial success and soon fostered competitors who produced their own kits. Among the competitors were the Heath kit Model EC-1 Educational Analog Computer, the IMS Associates kit 8000 (IMSAI 8000), the South West Technical Products (SWTPC) 6800 Computer kit and the Apple I by Apple Computers.

As the popularity of the personal computer grew beyond the enthusiast, manufacturers began producing preassembled personal computers. The preassembled computers came with keyboards and a video adapter to connect the television. Some of the more popular brand names of preassembled computers included the Commodore-64, the Apple II, the Osborne, and the Tandy Radio Shack (TRS-80).

As the popularity of the preassembled computers grew, it came with monitors instead of video adapters to view the keyboards input and output. To save projects, the user connected to an audiocassette tape recorder in the same manner as the mainframe computer did the miniaturization of hard disk technology in Figure 38. In pricier preassembled models, manufacturers included or offered a pair of floppy disk drives. The price for a computer already assembled ranged from $260 for the Commodore-64 to $1300 for the Apple II, Figure 41. To add a 5¼-inch disk drive to the Apple II cost another $400, for the Texas instruments TI-99 the cost of a floppy drive was almost $750.

Figure 41 Apple IIe with disk drives

The breakthrough that made fourth-generation personal computers possible occurred in 1969 when Busicom a Japanese firm contracted Intel to build a handheld calculator. Intel assigned Ted Hoff to design the processor for the calculator. Hoff advised Busicom that the calculator they wanted designed would cost about the same as the Digital Equipment Corporation (DEC) PDP-8A microcomputer ($5800), which relied on a series of small integrated circuits produced by Intel.

To circumvent the exorbitant costs, the Intel Corporation under the aegis of Hoff built the first microprocessor. The microprocessor was a radical departure from regular practices. Instead of creating a series cost prohibitive complex integrated circuits to form the processing element, Hoff revolutionized the manufacture of computers. He proposed etching the entire computer circuitry onto a single silicon wafer creating the first microprocessor, known as the 4004. The name 4004 referred to the number of transistor-based electronic circuits 4,004 on the chip. Two years later in 1971, Intel produced the 8008 microprocessor. The 8008 as its name indicates has twice the processing power as the 4004 microprocessor. Intel has since the creation of the 8008, has introduced a new microprocessor every eighteen months (Ceruzzi, A History of Modern Computing, 1999, pg. 218).

A second problem arose during the design of the 4004 microprocessor, how to give it instructions. To resolve this issue Intel contracted Gary Kildall to write a programming language for the 40004. Kildall created Programming Language for Microcomputers (PL/M). PL/M evolved into Control Program for Microcomputers (CP/M) as the sophistication and complexity of the microprocessors increased.

Prior to the IBM entry into the personal computer market, CP/M was the de facto industry standard for a personal computer operating system. It sold for $75. It was not however the only operating system available. Those dissatisfied with CP/M could choose PC-DOS (MS-DOS) that sold for $25 (Slater, 1992).

Then 1983, IBM decided to enter the personal computer market and approached Microsoft's Bill Gates and Paul Allen in the belief that they owned CP/M. They advised the IBM repreesentatives Microsoft owned PC-DOS that Gary Kildall owned the CP/M software. The subsequent negotiations between IBM and Kildall did not go well. IBM returned to Microsoft headquarters and asked Gates and Allen to build an operating system for its new personal computer. In the first months after the introduction of the IBM personal computer, Microsoft sold two million copies of MS-DOS six times what CP/M and Kildall sold.

Microsoft developed MS-DOS using Beginner's All-purpose Symbolic Instruction Code (BASIC) programming language— considered inferior by programming purist—made Gates and Allen billionaires a hundred times over. BASIC had a distinct advantages over CP/M. First, besisdes controlling the input and output of a computer, it was a programming language. Second, as a programming languge, it could be used to create end-user applications that seamlessy interfaced with the operating system (Slater, 1992). CP/M had to specialize to adapt software.

LAPTOP

Figure 42 Laptop

A laptop or notebook computer is the mobile counterpart of the desktop. A laptop performs the same functions as the desktop. What separates the two is the construction. The desktop computer is compartmentalized, while the laptop or notebook computer has one conjoined framework. All the four components of the von Neumann architecture the screen, memory, keyboard, storage, and microprocessor all fit neatly together inside a case no larger than 20 inches by 2 inches by 17 inches. Portable computer are more expensive than desktops even though they have less computing power than desktop computers. The price range for portable computers was from $599 (with exception of the third world computer) to $3599.

What makes the portable computer valuable to its owner is its ability to connect to networks with or without wire. It connects to a LAN by accepting RJ-45 or USB cable connections. Laptops also have built-in wireless Ethernet better known as Wireless Fidelity (Wi-Fi). The Wi-Fi format is an industry standard that allows authorized users to seamlessly connect to the private or public intranets of public library systems or corporate networks. Wi-Fi is so popular that it has penetrated the home market allowing millions of home users to sidestep buying multiple subscriptions for internet service.

Wi-Fi was originally implemented to supplement wired local area networks (LAN) of large and small business firms. Wi-Fi is not 3G or 4G. 3G or 4G are broadband technologies provided by wireless telephone providers as an augment to cell phone or cable subscription.

Although Wi-Fi and 3G appear redundant applications, they connect to networks differently. Wi-Fi connects through an access point attached to a wired network via standards stipulated by the IEEE 802.11 *b, g,* or *e.* The broadband technologies, 3G or 4G, must access the wired network or home network via a gateway provided by the cell phone company. A computer network gateway is a screening device that converts data packet protocols of 3G and 4G to data packet formats understood by the wired network or vice-versa.

Figure 43 Osborne

The Learning Research Group at Xerox PARC led by Alan Kay first conceived the ideal of a portable computer system in the late 1960s and early 1970s. This original thinker gave birth to the Dynabook. The Dynabook was essentially a tablet computer that later adapted a keyboard. The original intent of Kay and associates was to provide children a digital experience. However, because technology in the 1970s was not as advanced as technology in the 21st century the Dynabook became a passing thought, never operational (Lees, 1980).

The first commercially successful portable personal computer was the Osborne I by the Osborne Corporation (Figure 43). It was portable in the sense that it was easily transported from one location to another. The processor was the Zilog Z80 operating at the eye-popping speed of 4-MHz. The computer featured a 5-inch visual display with two built-in 5¼-inch floppy drives. The Osborne I weighed approximately 24 pounds and ran on either batteries or 110 AC volts. (My Dell XPS 8700 with Intel I-7 microprocessor desktop with terabyte hard drive weighs only 14 pounds.) The Osborne I sensation created a niche market of similar portable computers. There were several competitors with designs similar to the Osborne I differentiated with slight upgrades. For instance, the Kaypro II was identical in every way to the Osborne except it featured a nine-inch screen.

The downfall of these portable Osborne-like computers was the operating system. All save the Compaq were built for the CP/M operating system, which was not compatible with the new IBM personal computer operating system using MS-DOS.

The first computer considered a laptop, was produced in 1982. It was called the GRID Compass. The computer featured a modified version of the clamshell design. The design differs from current laptops in that the visual display covers the keyboard and overlaps over the battery pack, Figure 44. The computer was extremely expensive costing more than eight thousand dollars. The microprocessor for the Grid was the Intel 8086 and it operated at 8-MHz. The Grid featured 256K of RAM and had internal 384K bubble RAM. The machine weighed roughly 10 pounds. External storage was with floppy disk, which was available through a separate unit. The machine was originally designed for corporate executives but found its way to missions aboard the NASA space shuttle Discovery in 1985.

Several computer manufacturers followed the GRID Compass design of the modified clamshell. Among the copycats were IBM Convertible, the Zenith MinisPort, and the Apple Macintosh portable. The first computer manufacturer to use the familiar clamshell design used by laptops and notebooks of the 21st century was Apple when it produced the Macintosh PowerBook in 1992.

NETBOOK

Figure 44 Grid Compass

New to the personal computer scenario is the netbook. The netbook is a smaller less powerful version of the laptop computer that is specifically designed for use on the Internet. The netbook supersedes the connotation notebook. Originally, the notebook computer was a smaller less powerful version of the laptop computer. However, the term laptop and notebook became synonymous during the 1990s as quantitative differences between the two models became so minute it made the distinction passé.

The netbook computer when originally conceived as an augment device between the laptop and the PDA. Most featured the Intel Atom microprocessor with pre-loaded software because it did not have a disk drive. The original netbooks were small equipped with 8-inch screen, one gigabyte (GB) of RAM and small hard drives from 5 to 8 GB. However, in 2008 as their popularity grew net books became less powerful laptops. However as the popularity of the Apple IPad grew, the sales of the netbook plummeted.

To counter the popularity of the tablet computer manufactures started producing inexpensive netbooks such as the Ultra books. The Ultra books feature an 11-inch screen with an Intel microprocessor much faster than the Atom. Ultra books still feature preloaded software and 4 gigabytes of ram. To increase the speed of the Ultra Book, manufacturers added solid-state disk drives to augment load time from the hard disk.

One of the most popular netbooks is the Google Chrome book. The Chrome book unlike the Ultra Books operated only when connected to the internet. It is an example of a ThinNet client. Google provides a series of software suites that mimicked the popular Microsoft Office Suite of business software. All data produced by the Chrome Book is stored on Google Cloud computing. It has Google's Android operating system that was originally developed for smartphones and tablet computers.

Some manufacturers advertise the netbook computer as small notebook computer that takes advantage of the Internet's server-side processing or perform task too difficult for the PDA or smart phone.

TABLET COMPUTER

Apple Computers began selling the IPad tablet computer in 2009. It was a radical departure from the previous incantations of the tablet computer, which were based on hardware reconfiguration. The early tablet computer was a laptop computer with a keyboard that was hidden by a monitor capable of rotating 180 degrees to enable or activate the tablet mode. Once the user was finished with tablet tasks, the computer was returned to the traditional laptop clamshell for word processing, spreadsheets, etc. The earlier tablets came with handwriting-recognition software and conveniences associated with paper and pencil day planners and general ledgers.

The Apple IPad, created by Steve Jobs, dissolved the notion of the hardware reconfiguration in favor of a small, inflexible device that fitted inside the conventional leather portfolio case. The departure from the old incantation of tablet computer along with touch screen technology made the IPad an instant commercial success. Additionally, the customer could purchase specialized computer applications that gave the computer more flexibility not found in traditional tablet, laptop, or desktop computers. These applications had the versatility to provide the IPad user with numerous functions such as comparison-shopping and a portable library.

The success of the IPad has spawn a new generation of tablet computers using the Android operating system. The new Android tablets mimicked the IPad. All have virtual keyboards, touch screen technology, and for an additional fee, one can purchase a conventional keyboard to increase productivity of the tablet for such applications as spreadsheets and word processing.

Figure 45 Microsoft Surface Tablet Computer

The Microsoft Corporation entered the tablet computer fray in June of 2012 with the Surface Tablet hybrid laptop computer. The Surface debuted two models the Surface RT (Figure 45) and the Surface Pro. The 10.5-inch RT model was a low cost Windows answer to the IPad. The Surface Tablet featured the Windows 8 operating system, front and rear cameras, 2 GB of ram, and 32 GB of storage. The tablet has a slot for micro SD chips to expand RAM. It also has a USB slot to connect or charge the computer. the Surface easily converts into a laptop (Ultra Book like) computer with an inexpensive attachable keyboard. The software on the Surface like the Ultra Book is preloaded. It features a cut down version of Microsoft Office. The Surface Pro is an upgraded version of the RT model with more bells and whistles. It has Wacom drawing tablet technology. In addition to the Office suite, Surface has 4 GB of RAM, a hard disk size of 64 GB. The storage disk is a solid state disk drive. Like the RT model the Surface Pro converts to a laptop with the addition of a keyboard. Best of all it has a National Football League contract that puts it in front of millions of viewer every week.

The new tablet is inexpensive. Unlike first-generation tablet computers, which cost $1700, and up, the new tablets highlight portability and affordability starting at $250. Most come with wireless networking capabilities either Wi-Fi or 3G. All tablets can be added to a wired network with the aid of a USB port.

E-READER

A variation to the tablet computer is the e-reader. The e-reader is less a sophisticated version of the tablet computers described in the previous sections. Their primary purpose of the e-reader is to do for books what the MP3 player did for music. The convenience of the e-reader allows the user to purchase a book without visiting the traditional brick and mortar bookstore. The most popular of the first generation e-readers are the Amazon Kindle and the Barnes and Noble Nook. There are several competitors Sony Reader Digital Book, Kobo e-reader, Velocity Micro Cruz e-reader, and the Pandigital Multimedia Novel e-reader.

Most e-readers have limited internet access although some feature full service internet browsing to challenge the Nook and Kindle domination of the market. With the exception of Sony, Kobo, and Apple's IPad, most e-readers depend on the Amazon or Barnes & Noble library of eBooks. Both Sony and Apple have the own libraries of books, although Apple has license to access both the Barnes and Noble library and the Amazon library. In November of 2011, both Barnes & Noble and Amazon released new versions of their e-readers. The new e-readers featured better multimedia functions and Internet browsing capabilities along with color visual displays.

FILE SERVER

Externally, the physical appearance of the file server is identical to the desktop personal computer found in the majority homes, schools, and offices. File servers evolved from the multiuser minicomputer while the microprocessor supplanted older transistor and integrated circuit based computers. Prior to the introduction of the core processors, one could distinguish a file server from a personal computer by the number of microprocessors it contained. A personal computer had only one microprocessor. A file server had at least two microprocessors and as many as eight microprocessor attached to its chassis depending upon its workload. With the advent of the dual microprocessor, the distinction between a server and a personal computer begins to blur.

Another means of distinguishing a file server from a personal computer was its LAN (local area network) connections, and software. The file servers could handle 200 simultaneous connections, while a personal computer has just one connection. Finally, the file server's network operating system is more complicated than the desktop computer software. The operating system software of the file server is more concerned with network security than word processing and spreadsheets typical of the personal computer.

PDA

A PDA or Personal Digital Assistant is a handheld electronic communications device that has a limited computing capacity. It is an example of a thin-client on a distributed network. PDA devices have a number of computing applications which allows the user send to text messages, read email, maintain a personal contact list or directory, a notepad, a calculator, a datebook, storage for music replay, and handwriting-recognition software. A PDA pushes data to the server, which performs the processing. PDA devices are not standalone processers capable of editing or creating databases, complicated word processing, or spreadsheets. The popularity of the PDA hinged on its ability to use 3G or Wi-Fi to contact WLAN, WAN and LAN networks (Walters, 2001, pg. 125).

The term PDA was supplanted by the term smartphone with the advent of the iPhone created by Apple Computers and the BlackBerry by Research in Motion. The smartphones and BlackBerrys possess all the features of the PDA and it has a telephone capable of voice mail, texting, and taking photographs.

SUPERCOMPUTER

A supercomputer is a computer that can have a dozen or more microprocessors to work in the parallel processing of data. Parallel processing allows the computer to function at a high rate of speed. A supercomputer is loosely defined as the fastest processing computer of a given time period. It is said that the first generation supercomputer of the 1970s, the CRAY I, had less the computing power than the Intel Core 2 computers processors. (First generation Core 2 processors have more about 291,000,000 transistor-based circuits. Microchips made during the decade of the 1970s had, at most, only 29,000 circuits.) A supercomputer is a specialized computer. It works on large processing projects such as global warming prediction or mapping the human genome (Walters, 2001, pg. 121).

APPLE

Steve Jobs and Steve Wozniak founded the Apple Computer Company in 1976. From its inception, the Apple computer was the exception to the Intel-IBM compatibility rule. While other companies were compelled to switch operating systems from CP/M to MS-DOS, Jobs and Wozniak built a computer based on the MOS Technology 6502 microprocessor for the Apple II and a modified version of DOS, Apple-DOS. The Apple II was much easier to use than its IBM counterparts. Consequently, it became an immediate success with the public. Apple established its foothold of about 20% of the computer market with the help of innovative programs like VisiCalc.

In 1984, the Apple Computer Company, now Apple Computer Incorporated, introduced the Macintosh. The Macintosh featured a graphical user interface (GUI). It was a complete break from the traditional DOS text-driven command line interface produced by IBM and its clone competitors. The Macintosh GUI required the use of a mouse as the initiator of action clicking icons on the desktop to open programs instead of opening the command prompt and typing in the name of the program.

While Apple introduced the Macintosh as the new computer standard for business and higher education, Apple promoted its DOS based Apple II-style computers as the machine for home and school. When it was introduced in 1977, the Apple II cost $1350. What made the Apple II so popular were its multiple expansion slots. These allowed the customization of the machine for the niche it was servicing. Sales of the Apple II reached a remarkable 985 million dollars in 1983. After the introduction of the Macintosh, Apple failed to introduce an enterprise version of its operating system and began to fall behind Microsoft and IBM clones in usage in the business world. Microsoft reversed engineered Apples operating system and attached it to its NT technology allowing it to participate in Windows's business local area networks (LAN). Apple had not response. As a result, of this indecision Apple share of the computer market fell to approximately five percent.

Apple and IBM attempted to build a cross platform computer based on the PowerPC microprocessor in the 1990s. The PowerPC microprocessor was a hybrid of the Intel and Motorola microprocessors. It was a processor capable of reading and writing to applications produced by both the Motorola 6500 series processor and the Intel x86 processors. IBM abandoned the partnership and Apple took possession of the PowerPC for future use with its own hardware. The processor (produced by Motorola) was the basis for several innovative computers produced by Apple the iMac, the G4 and the Mac Book.

Apple rejuvenated itself with the introduction of the IPod in October of 2001. The iPod became the de facto industry standard for MP3 players capturing 92% of the MP3 player market. An MP3 player is a compact digital music player. Unlike compact disk players that required CD-ROM to play music, the MP3 player has internal storage capacity eliminating the need for external sources.

The Apple iTunes store became the de facto industry standard for digital music stores. The iPod was a phenomenal success because Jobs did for iPod and iTunes because what Edison and Tesla did for the electric power industry in the 19th century, Apple did for the MP3. He created an MP3 player infrastructure for the player and the store. Apple also insisted major recording studios adopt the iTunes file format instead of the Windows Media File (WMF) format to sell music.

Apple followed the iPod with the iPhone, which quickly became the best-selling cellular telephone on the market. Each new iteration of the iPhone is expected to sell at least 10 million units. In 2008, Apple changes its name from Apple Computers to Apple Inc. to reflect the fact the focus of the company was no longer exclusively computers.

11

Computer Architecture

Computer architecture in this text refers to the entire structure and detail needed to make a computer functional for human use and consumption not just the dynamics of the microprocessor. If you will recall in Chapter 9, "Pioneers of the 20th Century," it was established that computers shall adopt the von Neumann architecture also known as the Princeton Architecture, which stated all digital computers should have four distinct components: memory, a central processing unit (control unit, arithmetic-logic unit), and an input/output unit.

Adaptation of the von Neumann model led designers of early computers to discover a bottleneck in the processing pathways (bus) between the CPU and the peripheral devices. Two factors contributed to the bottleneck. The first problem with the von Neumann architecture was bandwidth. It was inappropriately small between the CPU and memory compare to the overall memory available. As a consequence, for large projects the end-user had a considerable downtime. Downtime is the waiting period between the end of one project and the start of another.

The von Neumann bottleneck was resolved with several mechanisms:

1) a cache between the CPU and the main memory,

2) Separate buses or separate access paths for data and instructions using the Modified Harvard architecture.
3) Add branching predictor algorithms (Wikipedia.org, 2009).

CENTRAL PROCESSING UNIT

At the core of every computer is the central processing unit (CPU) without it a computer is no more than a fifteen-pound paperweight. All the other components—the speakers, the CD-ROM, the keyboard, and the mouse—serve as auxiliary devices to the interface of the central processing unit. The CPU has two sub-components, the arithmetic-logic unit (ALU) and the control unit (CU) (Weems, 2007).

The concept of the central processing unit dates back the infancy of the electronic computer, to ENIAC in1946—and to a lesser extent the ABC of 1937. In the early days of the electronic computer era, the CPU was indistinguishable from the rest of the computer. That was due in part to the way ENIAC was constructed. The task of programming ENIAC was a very complex and labor-intensive task. For instance, to change the programming in ENIAC from solving ballistics problems to counting the census, engineers were required to change the physical configuration of hundreds if not thousands of relays and switches.

The process required several teams of technicians, mathematicians, physicists, and engineers to work arduously for several days and sometimes weeks. First, the mathematicians designed the math problem for ENIAC solve. After the mathematicians were sure, the equations would yield the proper results, the engineers transferred the equations to a storyboard prototype. The storyboards were preparation to configuring the many switches and relays contained in ENIAC. Once the engineers were assured the storyboard rendering of the circuits would yield the correct results, they and assistants proceeded to configure the circuits according to plan.

After the configuration of the circuits was complete, the scientist and engineers began testing. The tests they performed confirmed the machine was free of short-circuits. The short-circuit test was followed by a verification cycle test (VCT), which in turn was followed by implementation of operations. The VCT tested the circuits and established the machine computed correctly. The VCT also certified that ENIAC produced the correct information, the engineers and technicians tested the machine with known solutions for integrals or differentials.

For example, what is the solution the following differential: $y = \int(x) = \sqrt{2x-1}$, if $x = 5$ or 4 or 3, etc. In this equation, $y = \int(x)$ represents a distance and x represents time. Therefore, Δy (the change in y) represents the distance traveled in the time Δx (the change in x); hence, $\Delta y / \Delta x$ (the change in y divided by the change in x) equals the average velocity, etc., etc.

The first modification to CPU technology occurred when John von Neumann theorized ENIAC use stored memory. John von Neumann detailed EDVAC, Electronic Discrete Variable Automatic Computer, in a publication in 1945. It was the first computer designed to use stored memory. The reason EDVAC had a significant impact on computer technology was von Neumann's theories stated that all computers should have four basic components:

1. a central arithmetic unit or arithmetic-logic unit (ALU), which performs mathematical and logic computations;
2. memory (RAM) and storage in the form of punch cards, punch tape, and later magnetic tape;
3. a control unit, which directs and controls CPU access to peripherals and how fast the CPU should retrieve and process data or instructions from memory;
4. Input and output are the components that have the ability to interface with humans.

The addition of memory and storage eliminated the need to reconfigure of ENIAC for each solution. The addition of memory provided the computer flexibility, redundancy, and portability. It gave the computer engineer the ability to verify data integrity and reliability without labor-intensive reconfigurations activities. Flexibility, redundancy, and portability are three characteristics found in modern personal computers, computer programs, and local area networking.

Input and output, the fourth characteristic of the von Neumann architecture, gave the computer operator the flexibility to change input and have a hardcopy of the data outcomes, instead of copying dials and displays. Today the redundancy of storage on semiconductor chips replaced the constant need for paper and punch card technology.

Figure 46 Handmade Transistor board

Another milestone in CPU technology that made a significant impact on computer architecture was the transistor. The transistor revolutionized the construction of computers and its CPU. It changed one's perspective of the computer because it changed the outwards appearance of the computer. With the transistor, computers were no longer the hulking, power-hungry, behemoths epitomized by ENIAC. The transistor reduced the size of the computer, eliminated its thirst for electric power, and removed the untrustworthy vacuum tube.

In addition to changing the computer's physical appearances, the transistor opened the door for more innovative business and scientific uses of the computer. The benchmark for the transistorized computer was the IBM 1401 computer system—about the size of a standard home washer and dryer combination.

Another radical change occurred in computer technology in 1959, with the invention of a new semiconductor technology, the integrated circuit (Figure 35, page 119). The integrated circuit eliminated the need to build discrete electronic components—as shown in Figure 46. The birth of the integrated circuit created the third-generation computer. The integrated circuit evolved into the microprocessor, and the fourth-generation and current generation of computer technology. The microprocessor merged the discrete components of the CPU—the control unit, the arithmetic logic, and cache memory onto a single silicon wafer. Ted Hoff constructed the first microprocessor in 1969. From that moment forward, the destiny of computers was set; all had their control unit, memory, and ALU placed on a silicon wafer.

ARITHMETIC-LOGIC UNIT

The action performed by the arithmetic-logic unit (ALU) determines what the computer actually does with a given set of program instructions. As stated previously, the ALU performs five basic arithmetic operations. It manipulates numbers by comparing, multiplying, dividing, adding, or subtracting the numbers to produce a desired outcome.

To send a letter from the computer keyboard to the computer monitor the ALU compares the series of ones and zeroes to a database of zeroes and ones designated as letter. If it finds a match, it loads the output to the monitor. If it does not find a match, it compares it to commands already in memory and performs the instructions. The instructions may ask the computer to print on the screen, save to a disk, or print on paper.

To get a better understanding of how the ALU accomplishes this task. Think of the old Morse code. Each letter in Morse code was represented by a series of dots and dashes or long and short bursts of electricity. The modern computer system uses the same ideal only skips the long and the short in favor of a series of on and off signals or zeroes and ones to create the ASCII (American Standard Code for Information Interchange) system then later into Unicode. ASCII and Unicode are more complicated than Morse code.

ASCII has 256 different combinations of zeroes and ones to represent the twenty-six letters of the alphabet, numbers and special characters such as the ampersand compared to the 36 characters of Morse code. Every time the end user presses a key, he or she camouflages themselves as an old time telegrapher then sends a message to a portion of the computer system. Every time the ALU reads a code it acts as the receiving telegrapher and records the message for the customer, in this case the correct piece of peripheral equipment albeit monitor, printer, disk drive, or Internet. Each letter has either a binary, octal, decimal, and hexadecimal equivalent used in the same manner as the dots and dashes of Morse code. For instance, Morse code wrote "c-a-t" with dash, dot, dash, dot or c; dot, dash or a; and dash for t, ASCII told the computer to write 67-65-84 to represent the word cat.

Computers, however, do not think in decimal numbers. The decimal output is strictly for human consumption. Computers operate in binary code or machine language. The binary code is formed into chunks of information for easy transport. Hexadecimal code provides 256 combinations of binary groupings thirty-two 8-bit words or 16 16-bit words. (The larger the word the faster the computer operates.) The hexadecimal format gives the computer greater range in delivering information for human consumption. For most of us, when we write the computer is reading special instructions given it by a word processing program to perform a special method of addition known as concatenation to deliver the value of words to the screen (Abd-El-Barr & El-Rewini, 2005, pg. 273). Unicode began replacing ASCII code in 1987.

CONTROL UNIT

The primary function of a computer's control unit (CU) is to control and coordinate the operations of the CPU. Essentially, the CU regulates the flow of information through the processor. The CU reads the instruction from memory then coordinates the four-step cycle fetch, decode, execute, and store. No matter the size or the purpose of a computer, the control unit operation does not vary. It does not matter whether the computer is performing a basic end-user task such as word processing or a server task such as securing end-user logon. The CU operates according to the program requisites regulating the receiving, decoding, storing managing the flow of information through the CPU (Abd-El-Barr & El-Rewini, 2005, pg. 273).

MICROPROCESSORS

At first glance, this section might appear to be duplication in light of the three previous sections discussing of the central processing unit. Inasmuch as the subject matter is the same and despite the fact the terms CPU and microprocessor have become synonymous in the minds of many people; there is still a lot to differentiate the two. For starters, the microprocessor is the physical container of the CPU etched onto a silicon wafer.

The term central processing unit originated before integrated circuits, before microprocessors. The central processing unit or CPU was developed by von Neumann to identify the portion of the computer that performed the actual processing. As computer technology, transformed form vacuum tubes to transistors to integrated circuits the CPU started to shrink in size. The first-generation computer consisted of thousands of vacuum tubes, switches, relays, and miles of wire that required huge amounts of energy, space, and maintenance. The invention of transistors began the miniaturization of the CPU.

With the advent of the integrated circuit, the computer was made even smaller. The first computers to utilize the integrated circuit were the minicomputers. The once large and bulky CPU was reduced to sheets of circuits on a motherboard. The invention of microprocessor reduced the size of the computer and the minicomputer became the file server replacing the mainframe.

At one time, there were four general-purpose microprocessors manufacturers servicing the United States Intel, Motorola, Advance Micro Devices (AMD), and Cyrix. However, since 1990 changes in the United States economy and the overall computer market has forced Cyrix dropout of competition in the United States out, leaving only Motorola, Advanced Micro Devices to compete with frontrunner Intel (Wikipedia, 2009).

The Intel Corporation microprocessors set the industrial benchmark for CPU circuitry and performance for the last few decades. The Pentium microprocessor marked the end of the old x86-style of computers—originally built for Intel by Ted Hoff—introduced in 1993.

What made the Pentium microprocessor superior to previous iterations of the x86-style microprocessor was the combining of memory and ALU on the same chip as the CU. This change would later produce clock speeds over 3,000 megahertz. In 2006, Intel discontinued the Pentium class microprocessor in favor of the more versatile Core 2 class microprocessor.

According to Intel, the Core 2 is the eighth-generation of the original x86 the architecture. All that means is that Intel has built its chips to be backwards compatible with the original x-86 architecture. The boast of backwards compatibility is a jab at Apple Inc., which, if you remember, came out with two lines of computers the Apple II series and the Macintosh. They were not compatible. The newer computer, the Macintosh, could not read the files of an Apple II (Walters, 2001, pg. 119).

Actually, the Intel Core microprocessor ends the almost 60 year strict adherence to the von Neumann computer architecture theory with the emergence of a CPU capable of parallel processing instead of sequential processing. In addition, Intel Core 2 style microprocessors signaled an end to the tradition of limiting home computers to one CPU.

The second-generation Core microprocessor contains two, four, or six microprocessors and brings the power of the office workstation to the home (Walters, 2001, pg 119).

Intel's chief rival in the United States is Advance Micro Devices (AMD). AMD produces the Athlon and Phenom microprocessors, to name a few, for general-purpose computing in the office and the home. The architecture of the original Athlon class microprocessors were, at first, direct copies of the Intel x86 classes of microprocessors. Later AMD negotiated with Intel to produce a clone of the x86-processor architecture. Legal wrangling caused AMD to reverse engineer the Intel microprocessor to match the Intel microprocessor benchmarks.

Since the issuance of the original manuscript, Intel has produced three new microprocessors that is not counting the microprocessors developed specifically for use as file servers. The first three chips were named I-3, which has two microprocessor cores, the I-5, which had two to four microprocessor cores, and the I-7, which has 4 to six microprocessor cores.

Another Intel competitor, the Motorola Corporation developed general-purpose microprocessors for Apple computer companies. It is famous for developing the microchips to run operating system of the early Apple Macintosh computers. Apple's Macintosh was the primary alternative to Intel Windows based personal computer. Eventually Apple chose another path to challenge the Intel-Windows dominance with a new operating system based on a variation of the UNIX operating system (Wikipedia, 2009). Apple is now more famous and profitable because of its cell phones, MP3 players, and tablet computers than it is for desktop and laptop computer manufacturing.

Motorola, also, for a short time, beginning in 2002, was in a partnership with IBM, to develop the Power Macintosh microprocessor, later renamed by IBM as the PowerPC microprocessor. The microprocessor was for a brief moment thought to be a hybrid of the Macintosh-Intel microprocessors. However, Apple Computers abandoned the project and Motorola processors, 3 in favor of Intel microprocessors in 2005 (Wikipedia, 2009).

The one time fourth competitor was Cyrix. Unlike AMD, Cyrix microchip designs were never the results of license negotiation between it and Intel. Cyrix microchips were always the result of research and reverse engineering of the Intel hardware. Cyrix eventually went out of business in the United States because it merged with companies that did not want to compete with Intel or AMD (Walters, 2001, pg 113).

Microcode

Contrary to the notion all Intel computer are alike. The opposite is true. Consider this; compare a Dell Inspiron XPS with a Dell Inspiron 17. Although both computers are made by Dell and each shares the same Dell ISA or EISA proprietary architecture, one is a 17-inch laptop, the other a desktop. Their parts are not interchangeable. Notwithstanding the obvious structural differences, the microprocessors are not compatible. One is manufactured by AMD the other manufactured by Intel. Each computer is different because the computer manufacturer uses a different set of codes or more precisely microcodes to control microprocessor behavior. For example, the XPS uses an Intel I-5 microprocessor, while the Inspiron uses an Intel I-7 microprocessor. That is not to say the I-7 or I-5 processors are not interchangeable with similar products, they are because the computers are mass-produced. The difference is the date of manufacture.

To summarize, Intel introduced its new line of microprocessors, it indicated the I-3 would be the first and the I-7 the more advanced of the three. However, the rolls can reverse when the date of manufacture is considered. For example, Intel stated its I-5 microprocessors, in general, has either two four microprocessor cores and up to eight logical cores. The Intel I-7, on the other hand, has between four and eight microprocessor cores and two logical cores for each microprocessor present on the motherboard of the computer.

The main function of the logical core is to decrease the number of instructions on the pipeline. It takes advantage of superscalar architecture (multiple instructions operating on separate data in parallel). Ordinarily the I-7 computer would be considered the more powerful of the two microprocessors. Yet, when date of manufacture is considered, the logic may reverse.

In 2010, the Inspiron personal computer with the I-7 microprocessor used the 32-nanometer a 2-D (planar) device manufacturing process. Normally the Dell XPS I-5 microprocessor is considered the smaller and slower of the two. However, in 2011 Intel began manufacturing microprocessors with 3-D Tri-Gate transistor 22 nanometer (Intel, 2011). How does this affect the workings of the computer? Clearly, transistors circuits manufactured in 2014 are denser than microprocessors manufactured prior to 2011.

The code guiding the CPU is called the microcode. It differs from code written in C++ because it is not software like *Call to Duty* or *Excel*. It is not user accessible except when updates are sent by the manufacturer, nor can it be removed from the computer without doing irreparable harm to the computer. It is an essential ingredient to the computer. If the CPU is, the brain of the computer then microcode is the nerve cells of the brain.

Microcode is the lowest level of instructions in the computer. It resides in a separate high-speed memory cache and works as a translation layer between the machine instructions and the circuitry of the computer. Microcode allows designers to create machine instructions without having to design electronic circuits.

Engineers write the microcode instruction during the design phase of the computer construction. One unit of microcode is called a microinstruction. A microinstruction is the most elemental instruction for a CPU. It may cause the CPU to move the contents of a register to the arithmetic logic unit (ALU) (PC Mag.com, 2011). It requires several microinstructions to fulfill complex machine instruction (CISC). Microinstruction is also called a "micro-op" or "μop."

Microinstructions differ from computer to computer by vendors and even within same computer family. For example, microcode written for a Gateway 420 desktop computer using a Pentium 4 microprocessor will incapacitate a Toshiba laptop computer using the same Pentium 4 microprocessor or a Gateway 420 using an Advanced Micro Devices Pentium 4 equivalent microprocessor. More specifically microcode written for an Lenovo T420 using a Pentium 4 microprocessor with a NetVista 02r4079 motherboard will not run on the Sony Vaio using the same microprocessor on a NetVista 02r4076 motherboard (Walters, 2001, pg. 162) (Wikipedia, 2009). Many manufacturers update flaws in the microcode with patches provided online or sent to the customer via CD ROM.

Assembly language was the first attempt by computer programmers to interface and direct computer operations. Assembly language is an ancient ancestor of C++, COBOL. It is not microcode. Microcode guides the CPU telling it how to analyze, reconstruct, and recover interface data.

A final definition for microcode suggests it is a set of instructions not accessible by ingenuity or program. The software programmer never sees microinstructions, and it is not documented for the public. Many microprocessors use microcode to handle machine instructions and assist with chip's operations. The update for microcode comes in the form of firmware, which replaces the existing microcode with updates. Since this code is not accessible while the hardware is running. There is typically a specific way that the new microcode needs to load on the device (WiseGeek, 2003).

Firmware

The term firmware is very confusing. For some hardware vendors, IBM for example, the term microcode is synonymous with firmware—even though as explained in the previous section, microcode directs the CPU actions, and can vary from computer to computer. Other manufacturers simply describe ROM as firmware. Another point of confusion arises when manufactures describe the code used to regulate the CPU access to the hard drive as microcode. Firmware is software stored on a non-volatile memory chip that holds program instructions in a computer or computer device instead of being part of a program such as the operating system.

Using the above definition firmware and ROM are identical. ROM is often associated with the bootstrapping of a computer and is often referred to as ROM Basic Input Output System (ROM-BIOS). ROM-BIOS differ from microcode in that one can change the ROM configuration in microprocessor before the CPU retrieves the operating system. This is accomplished by typing a rare combination of keys on the keyboard during startup. Instructions to access ROM-BIOS are often printed on the screen during start up. For Example, the bootstrap tells the user to hold down or press F2 before the Windows Logo appears on the screen. I apologize to Apple. I am not active in the classroom any longer and do not have access to a Macintosh. Once inside the ROM-BIOS the user can for instance change the system boot procedure.

Four-step cycle

In addition to the interface, microcode directs the CPU method of retrieving and processing instructions and data. Until the advent of the multicore computes, most CPUs utilize a four-step cycle to execute data. Computer scientist developed the four-step CPU cycle to exploit the von Neumann architecture. The four steps are as follows: fetch, decode (analyze), execute, and write-back (store). Steps 1 and 2, in newer computers, are called the *fetch cycle* and are the same for each instruction. Steps 3 and 4 are called the *execute cycle* and will change with each instruction.

During the fetch stage, the CPU retrieves information, instruction, or data, from memory or input. When the CPU retrieves instruction from a memory location, it retrieves data internally. When the CPU retrieves online input, it retrieves data externally. Once the data is retrieved, the second stage in the CPU cycle begins.

The second stage in the CPU cycle is the decode step. Once the CPU retrieves instructions and data, it decides what to do with the information. For example if an instruction requires the addition of the number 3 at memory address (hexadecimal location) 16FA, with the number 4 at memory address 22DB, a fetch instruction retrieves the two numbers. The decode step necessitates the preparation of the instructions for the execute step in the CPU cycle. The preparation phase includes choosing the correct computer components, memory location, and output devices for the execution of the instructions.

During the execute stage the CPU performs the processing. The ALU component of the CPU also works during the execute step; it performs one of five operations with the decoded information: addition, multiplication, division, subtraction, or comparison. Once the execute stage has completed, the CPU brings online the appropriate devices to complete the task.

The final stage is the write-back; write-back stores the results of the previous three steps. The write-back stage of the four-step cycle saves the instructions either in main memory (address F1AD) for future execution, sends the results to output (monitor or printer), or writes the results to the hard disk for storage (Walters, 2001, pg. 14).

CISC AND RISC

The discussion about Complex Instruction Set Computing (CISC) and the Reduced Instruction Set Computing (RISC) microprocessors add to the current knowledge of computer architecture. CISC and RISC are the two sub categories of general-purpose computer microprocessor architecture. All general-purpose computer processors work in the same way by completing a set of operations--usually mathematical or logical. Each processor operation has a set of commands associated with its routines. With the RISC design, each command generally requires the processor to perform a single operation. Whereas the CISC based microprocessor command results in several consecutive operations are performed.

The first microprocessor was the Intel 4004; Ted Hoff introduced it in 1971. The 4004 microprocessor was a 4-bit processor. Over the past 40 years, as microprocessors became more complex, the technology evolved into faster microprocessors 8-bit, 16-bit, 32-bit, and 64-bit processors. The most commercially successful line of microprocessors are produced by Intel was the 16-bitl 8086, which set the standard for future Intel x86 architecture. The x86 processors belongs to the CISC subcategory of microprocessors primarily because its instructions are very complex and of variable length.

A CISC microprocessor uses program instructions at the Assembly Language level. Assembly language is a low-level computer programming language in which each statement corresponds to a machine instruction. CISC instructions expedite the manipulation of low-level computer elements and events such as memory, binary math, and address location. Implementation of CISC microprocessor architecture requires small binary files. The advantages of CISC computer are as follows:

1. Micro programs are easily implemented, less expensive than hardwire control units.

2. The microcode is easily updated with firmware instructions, which allows designers to make CISC machines backwards compatible to earlier versions of microprocessors. New microprocessors are capable of using the software of earlier computers because the new computer contains a superset of the instructions used by the earlier computers. For example, a Core duo microprocessor can read the code and run the software written for an Intel 286 microprocessor. s

3. Fewer instructions could be used to implement a given task as each instruction became more capable. This occurs because the instructions make efficient use of slower main memory.

4. The compiler less complicated because microcode instruction sets can be written to match the paradigms of high-level languages.

The IBM Research Laboratories introduced the idea of RISC computer architecture in the 1970s. Engineers at IBM discovered not all the instructions written for a CISC microprocessor was executed. By reducing the sets of instructions on an existing CISC machines to the instructions used most frequently, the programming code ran two or three times faster (Walters, 2001, pg. 26-28).

A RISC uses a limited number of instructions. The instructions for a RISC are of fixed length, and of the same format. RISC operations are performed on registers only, which are available in larger numbers than on CISC processors. The only memory operations are load and store. The hardware in RISC processors is simpler in principle, because the RISC architecture relies more on the compiler and software for sequencing complex operations. Another important difference in the two chips is that CISC depends on microcode while the RISC depends on hardwired control units and machine instructions. All RISC processors despite manufacture had the following characteristics:

1. one cycle execution time
2. Pipelining is a technique that allows a CPU to perform multiple tasks during the four-step cycle: fetching, executing, storing, analyzing.
3. large number of memory registers

The most popular RISC microprocessor was the PowerPC produced by the partnership of Apple, Motorola, and IBM. The Sun Systems Scalable Processor Architecture (SPARC) was second. Sun like Apple used the Motorola 68K processor. Sun Systems later designed its own processor (Intel, 2011) (Walters, 2001) (Hannibal, 2004).

SIMD

A technology related to RISC is Single Instruction Multiple Data (SIMD). SIMD has two versions MMX or multimedia extension and SSE streaming single–instruction. With the MMX version, a 64-bit floating pipeline can work on the same calculation on four 16-bit or eight 8-bit numbers simultaneously.

Intel offers its more recent version of SIMD SSE, which uses two floating-point pipelines to do the same as MMX but on twice the data. SIMD only works on parallel data schemes (Walters, 2001).

SUPERSCALAR

A computer that has more than one pipeline is classified as superscalar. Superscalar computers allow for branching predictors and speculative execution. Branching circuitry is designed to deal with the typical computer programs. Branching pipelines consume a lot of memory space and to compensate, the branch predictor jumps ahead of the ALU and predicts when the CPU should take a branch in its routine.

The speculative execution performs the branch after an appointed time for a branch just in case the branch is needed or needs to be removed from memory. Speculative execution and branch prediction are paired to increase the CPU's ability to perform several computations simultaneously (Walters, 2001).

VLIW

Another method used to increase microprocessor capacity is parallelism. Parallelism as the term indicates features the simultaneous processing of data by a microprocessor instead of serial processing, common in the original von Neumann style computer. One technique of parallelism is Very Long Instruction Word (VLIW). The idea behind VLIW implies that if the processor accepts longer words, 64-bits instead of 16 or 32-bits, it will work faster. The CPU accommodates the long instructions with wide pipelines that execute the multiple opcodes in multiple operands. With VLIW processors, multiple instructions are executed simultaneously; the VLIW codes are fetched and decoded in parallel. The task of ensuring there are no unwanted (unmatched) dependencies between instructions executed is the responsibility of the software (compiler) rather than the processor. VLIW and superscalar processing are similar but differ in that the processing in VLIW is performed in parallel instead of serially (Walters, 2001) (Intel, 2011).

EPIC

As manufactures try to squeeze as much out of the circuits printed on silicon, the physical limits for the microprocessor technology manufacture will inevitably reach capacity. As a consequence, the performances of processors will stagnate. In order to sustain future advances in microprocessor technology it is necessary for a manufacturer to develop processors that are more efficient. One solution for microprocessor technology limitations is the Intel Explicitly Parallel Instruction Computing (EPIC). EPIC is the culmination of a partnership between Intel and Hewlett-Packard. EPIC combines the best features of RISC technology and VLIW technology. The basis of EPIC technology is software should be able to indicate the inherent parallelism in programs explicitly, rather than obligating the processor to reconstruct it from a particular sequence or series of operations (Intel, 2011).

INPUT

The keyboard and mouse are the primary means of human-computer interface. Secondary input methods include portable storage devices (CD-ROM, floppy disk, DVD, and magnetic tape), computer-to-computer telecommunication, and voice recognition. To better comprehend how data input works, it best to look back at the history of the computer. As stated in the chapter Pioneers of the Twentieth Century, early data input consisted of platoons of scientist arranging and rearranging the tons of switches vacuum tube, relays, and circuit breakers to achieve a desired outcome. The task was so arduous and tedious it often took weeks to complete.

Then John von Neumann postulated computers would be more practical with self-contained memory. That idea eliminated the squadrons of engineers and technicians. Despite the advancement of computer input technology, 19th century punch card was the basic input device. Engineers adapted the keyboard as an input device after Stibitz proved computers were capable of remote connections. The mouse as input device was the direct result of SAGE research.

OUTPUT

Output is the results of the manipulation of data as requested by the computer operator. Output can be as simple as the printing of letters or listening to music played by the CD-ROM drive. Output is the desired information that a computer provides the user. Output devices are printers, modems, monitors, speakers, DVD, CD-ROM, telecommunication connections (Internet) to other computers, and email. Output by definition is the opposite of input.

BUS

The 'Bus' on a computer is not a ride on public transportation or a former running back for the Pittsburgh Steelers named Jerome. The bus on a computer is an integral part of its overall operation. The bus is the highways or pathways, on which information is carried to and from the CPU. More specifically, the bus is a series of wires that stream data into a computers microprocessor, memory, and out to other components. There are two kinds of bus. There is the internal bus that the CU fetches from memory and passes it to the ALU for processing then sends it to RAM, the printer, the monitor or the hard drive. Then there is the external bus, which accesses, input from a USB port, a digital camera or external hard drive (Walters, 2001, pg 60).

REGISTER

A register on a computer is a temporary storage space where CPU can retrieve information quickly. Registers are part of the ALU, but not the ALU itself. The register is the top portion of Random Access Memory (RAM). Imagine RAM as a triangle, at the very pinnacle is the CPU follow by the registers. Registers have different task within memory. Some of the common terms applied to the task the registers in main memory perform are general purpose, addressing, accumulator, and storage. The following list defines the purpose of these specialized registers:

1. An address register is a special register in the computer's memory. It is not to be confused with its IP address on a network. An address register in memory is the location where the CPU finds data. Therefore, in the four-stage cycle, the ALU will retrieve information from a memory location defined by a number. In the modern computer, that number is 2^6 or 64 bits long. To state simply an address on a computer is any location in memory that computer may retrieve data.

2. While executing a program, the CPU tracks the address of the next instruction it fetches from the instruction memory. This address is kept in a special register called the program counter or the accumulator.

3. A general-purpose register stores (saves) outputs and results as required. The manufacture of memory components in the pyramid increases from bottom to top.

Although the price of hard drives has gone down, a secondary hard drive will still cost approximately $59 per terabyte. That may seem inexpensive but it is not, compared to memory optical disk that do not require an independent power source (Walters, 2001, pg. 45) (Hennessy, Patterson, & Goldberg, 2003, 92).

12

Operating Systems

The operating system, although it was not defined in either of the Von Neumann and Harvard computer architectures, is another very important component of the modern digital computer. Since the advent of stored memory, the software-based operating system has played a vital role in the operations of the computer as it became more automated. The purpose of the operating system is to serve as an interface between the hardware of the computer and its human user. The operating system automates the management and control of computer resources such as memory, input, output, device control, storage, microprocessor operations, BIOS management, and application management.

Modern operating system software contains four characteristics: redundancy, integrity, scalability, and reliability. Redundancy is needed because systems need to track and record what it operations. An operating system has integrity because it must continually calculate solutions. An operating system needs to be reliable, the average computer will start anywhere from eight to eleven thousand times during its lifetime. Each start must be like the previous so the operating system must know where it saved data, what equipment is available to it, and the capacity of memory and storage. Finally, the software must be scalable for future needs. The next few pages tell the story of how the modern operating system was created.

The first computers, the ABC, and ENIAC, did not have an operating system as we understand the term today. Operations of the first general-purpose computer, ENIAC, required a team of technicians and engineers to walk through the chassis of the computer flipping switches, changing relays, and manipulating plug boards. Before memory was added, if reconfiguration was not required, these early behemoths received instructions for a task from a stack of punch cards or spools of punch tape then later magnetic tape.

When John von Neumann introduced the EDVAC (Electronic Discrete Variable Automatic Computer) concept of stored memory, the way computers operated began to change. Instead of massive reconfigurations of switches, computers received instructions electronically. Moreover, the programs were coded with binary codes of zeroes and ones, which were kept in the same place that held the data the computer processed. By letting a program treat its own instructions as data offered the engineer tremendous advantages. First, it accelerated the work of the computer. Second, it simplified the circuitry, and making possible the ideal of programming and programming languages.

To make the early computers successful, two major innovations were necessary. The first was the development of a high-level programming language—FORTRAN (Formula Translation) invented in 1957 and two years later COBOL (Common Business Oriented Language)—and a control program or function. Today the control functions of a computer are called the operating system, or OS. The concept of a computer operating system began as a result of the programming.

Batch

The introduction of the transistor in the mid-1950s changed the computer fundamentally. No longer were squads of engineers and technicians parading through the chassis of the computer. Overnight computers transitioned from big iron computer with cavernous chasses to mainframe computers. The computer was no longer seen as the successor of the Babbage Difference Engine. The transistor made the computer a dependable tool. It was now reliable enough to manufacture and sell to paying customers. Customer had the expectation that the computer would function long enough to get some meaningful work completed. For the first time, there was a job specialty in computer science. Computer scientist was no longer an all-encompassing term. There were now specialist designers, builders, operators, programmers, and maintenance personnel (Tannenbaum, 2002).

The transistor marked the beginning of the 2nd Generation of computers. To perform tasks a programmer would write a program in FORTRAN. He would then hand the cards over to a technician who would transcribe the program onto the punch cards. After the programmed was placed on punch cards, it was taken to the computer room where the operator would place them in position for the computer to process. If the computer was busy, the program was placed in file cabinet until the current program finished processing. The problem with method of programming was time lost waiting. This waiting period was called down time.

The high cost of the equipment, spurred companies to utilize the wasted down time. One solution-adopted industry wide was the batch system or batch programming. The idea behind batch programming was to collect the problem in a tray. The tray was filled with punch cards for the various jobs in line for processing. Instead of waiting for the main company computer to read the cards and process the data, the punch cards read onto a magnetic tape by a smaller, less expensive computer, such as the IBM 1401. The IBM 1401 is very good at reading cards, copying data on to magnetic tapes, and printing output. However, the 1401 is not the perfect computer for numerical calculations. Other, much more expensive machines, such as the IBM 7094, were used for the real company computing.

The first attempt at reducing the down time came in the form of the Fortran Monitor System" or FMS for the IBM 709 (Larner, 2014). The Fortran Monitor System controlled mainframe computers with batch programming. The Fortran Monitor System (FMS) included the compiler and card loader, and the controls for processing and execution of jobs for the primary company computer. IBSYS was, the equivalent of FMS, it was developed for the IBM 7094 (Tannenbaum, 2002).

General Motors promoted the development of the modern operating system, when scientist it employees created the General Motors Batch System. Batch programs ideally eliminated the need for human intervention in the loading of punch card programs or tape into the computer. The batch program would read the program and execute it to completion. When one program completed, the batch program or Job Control Language (JCL) would tell the computer to start another stack of cards. Header cards would tell the computer which compiler to use (Fortran or Cobol) to complete the project (Milo, 2009). Header cards in the deck acted as the "job control." Header cards indicated when a project was over and when to start a new project.

For those of you not old enough to remember Windows 3.1, it contained two batch programs that always needed attending, Config.sys and Autoexec.bat. Config.sys and Autoexec.bat resided in the boot directory of DOS. (Windows 3.1 rested on top of DOS. At that time, it was not an independent operating system.) Config.sys listed the hardware the operating system was to load before going live. An example of a line adjusted in Config.sys: DEVICE=C:\WINDOWS\HIMEM.SYS. HIMEM.SYS is a DOS device driver, which allowed DOS programs to store data in extended memory. The device driver is important because Microsoft Windows ran on top of the DOS required HIMEM.SYS before it could operate.

IBM attempted to create a universal computing operating system with the introduction of the System 360 Operating System in 1962. The 360 OS was compatible with all previous IBM operating systems and many non-IBM computer systems or clones. The System 360 OS contained four distinct operating systems BOS, DOS, and OS/360. BOS was the acronym for Batch Operating system for small computers. TOS was the operating system for medium size magnetic-tape computers. DOS was the operating system for medium and large computers. System OS/360 totaled more than a million lines of code and was supposed to lift computing to levels beyond clone capabilities.

The 360 OS despite all its fanfare was a little more than a batch processing system. The 360 OS, often scorned because of the unusual number of errors, did not fulfill the mission T. J. Watson transferred to IBM from NCR, "Each individual customer has an individual solution." The IBM 360 operating system was a boondoggle that damaged IBM's prestige in the computer industry and wallet, eventually costing IBM five hundred billion dollars (Aspray & Campbell-Kelly, 1996).

The Burroughs Corporation made its contribution to batch programming by creating the Burroughs 5000 Master Control Program (Hayes, 2003). The Burroughs 5000 Master Control Program added a critical feature to batch processing, the ability to run several processes at once. UNIVAC made its contribution with the EXEC I. The EXEC I

186

program allocated memory, scheduled I/O request, and scheduled CPU request.

Time Sharing

Although batch programming was useful, it did not provide an efficient solution to the use of the CPU. During batch processing, the computer processed programs sequentially, only one program at a time. The next step in the development of an operating system occurred with the invention of time-sharing. Time-sharing allowed the computer to process two or more programs simultaneously. Time-sharing took advantage of the idle time that occurred with batch programming. During batch processing once the processor has outputted the data, it sits idle until the output has finished printing.

Time-sharing allowed multiple users to share the idle time of the CPU from remote terminals. The first time-sharing programs were developed by the Massachusetts Institute of Technology (MIT) and Dartmouth College. MIT developed the Compatible Time Sharing System (CTSS. Dartmouth sponsored the Dartmouth Time Sharing System (DTSS).

The MIT concept was the first time-sharing system implemented, 1961. It set the stage for other colleges and universities to do follow-up research and innovations on time-sharing. The original MIT implementation allowed three research assistants to access the computer and work independently. While the MIT project was designed for the computer professional, the Dartmouth project had a broader aim. Dartmouth designed its time-sharing program for a wider variety of computer user. CTSS eventually became Project MAC part of ARPA (Aspray & Campbell-Kelly, 1996).

Another prominent computer operating system was the Multiplexed Information and Computing Service (MULTICS), invented by MIT in 1963. MULTICS was an ambitious project MIT developed originally for IBM. However, MULTICS was not ready until after IBM had introduced the System 360 computer. IBM balked at revising its 360 OS to accommodate MIT. In addition, IBM believed MULTICS software would aid cloning of its products. General Electric (GE) replaced IBM as sponsor of the project because it wanted MIT to use MULTICS for the GE model 645 computer. The new partnership between GE and MIT added a third collaborator Bell Laboratories, now Lucent, to develop the software. As it turned out, the partnership was beneficial for GE, because it made their mainframe computing division profitable. MULTICS was capable of supporting 1000 remote terminals, 300 simultaneously (Aspray & Campbell-Kelly, 1996).

Multitasking

Although there are other mainframe operating systems worthy of mentioning, MULTICS provides a convenient segue to discuss the personal computer operating systems. Records indicate the origins for operating systems on personal computers stem from the minicomputers using MULTICS. MULTICS was designed as time-sharing program for second-generation mainframe computers with limitless resources. As the market for the minicomputer developed, software engineers faced a new set of problems adapting MULTICS.

Minicomputers were not as versatile as their mainframe counterparts were. The primary concern, they had very limited resources. The minicomputer, costing a tenth as much as a mainframe, performed only a limited number of tasks, such as accounting, research, classroom, and enrollment. After the introduction of the integrated circuit, minicomputers evolved into servers. The integrated circuit harkened the 3rd generation computer. The third generation computers were indeed mini mainframe computers.

One of the first operating systems adapted for the minicomputer (then later for the microcomputer or personal computer) was UNIX. Another operating system adapted for the minicomputer was Virtual Memory System (VMS). Both of these operating systems were multitask capable, multi-user operating systems. Project Whirlwind, which became SAGE, influenced the Digital Equipment Corporation's development of VMS. UNIX, developed by Bell Laboratories was influenced by MULTICS. Multitasking, loosely defined, states that a computer operating system has the ability to perform simultaneous operations.

The first operating system specifically designed for the personal or microcomputer was CP/M. It was scheduled as the operating system for the IBM personal computers. How Microsoft was chosen to write the code for the IBM personal computer operating system known as PC-DOS is another story. PC-DOS became an instant success because IBM was still a trendsetter in the computer industry. The partnership of IBM and Microsoft dissolved in 1987 over the OS/2 – Windows 3.1 licensure.

Bell laboratories perceiving an opportunity adapted UNIX to the personal computer in an effort to challenge the IBM – Microsoft partnership. They were too late. The popularity of Microsoft Windows 3.1 exploded. Microsoft hedged its bets on its own future producing a competing version of UNIX, Microsoft Xenix (Tannenbaum, 2002).

DOS

DOS is a 16-bit operating system for the personal computer. It is a command line operating system. In other words, unlike present day computers where the user points and click on an icon or hyperlinks to implement a command or operation, DOS users would open the command line and type a command such as "DIR/W" on the keyboard. The computer would respond by displaying the contents of the hard drive in a directory consisting of filenames. The filenames would display horizontally because of the "/W" limiter. To run a program, the user would search the directory for a filename with a suffix ending with com, bat, or exe. The suffix in a DOS file system was the three letters immediately after the dot in the file name. (That same format is used in photograph files GIF, bmp, PNG, or jpg etc.) For example, a popular spreadsheet program during the DOS era was Quattro. To run Quattro, the user was supposed to type Quattro.exe. After newer versions of DOS (DOS 4.0) were published, computer operations were simplified and users need not bother typing the suffix.

MS-DOS was the predominant software for IBM computers and the clones in the 1980s. It gained popularity because it was easily adaptable as a client for use in computer networks. There were two approaches for DOS networking, which can be called the "PC centric" and the "UNIX centric" approach. PC centric networking adapted the system to a Novell Netware like network. The UNIX approach adapted the operating system to the protocols of TCP/IP with PC-IP.

Graphical User Interfaces

The origins of the graphical user interface trace back to Vannevar Bush. Bush envisioned the first GUI or graphical user interface in 1945. In the article "As We May Think" published in the Atlantic Monthly, Bush explains that Memex would be an index of what a person has read, written, and communicated. According to varying interpretations, the Memex rolodex worked in the same manner as hyperlinks on a webpage or in search engine.

After Bush left DARPA, Douglas C. Engelbart picked up on the Memex ideal and is credited with the development of hypertext, graphical user interfaces, and the computer mouse (Hermida, 2001) (SRI International, 2011).

By 1971, Engelbart had moved to PARC a division of Xerox. At PARC, he and colleagues built the first personal computer using a GUI (graphical user interface) operating system, the Xerox Alto, in 1973. The machine was designed for use by an individual. It had a single purpose to replace the large and expensive mainframe computer. The asking price for the computer was $40,000.

Xerox did not find a market for the Alto. Eight years later, Xerox made a second attempt to market the computer with the GUI operating system. During the second marketing attempt, Xerox redesigned and renamed the computer, the Xerox Star. Despite the over haul of chassis, the computer was still very expensive costing approximately $16,000. Again, Xerox failed to find a market for its GUI operating machine. Xerox had missed its opportunity to corner the personal computer market.

The PARC effort to develop the GUI operating system did not go unnoticed. Steve Jobs after visiting PARC and observing the Xerox Star GUI system, embarked upon building an Apple computer with GUI operating system. The fruit of Jobs first efforts produced the Apple Lisa. It like the PARC Xerox Star proved too expensive for the small office – home office user, sporting a price of $5000. Jobs' second effort at producing a computer with a GUI operating system was more successful. The public knows the second machine as the Apple Macintosh. The Macintosh was immensely popular because people who knew nothing about computers could use it without studying technical manuals necessary to use an IBM-clone computer for hours.

The Apple Macintosh creation greatly influenced the way computers operated in the future. Microsoft co-founder Bill Gates after viewing a demonstration of the Macintosh, had his company produce a GUI operating system for the IBM-style computer. In 1985, Microsoft developed the Windows operating system.

In 1995, However, Microsoft produced a freestanding version of Windows, Windows 95. Windows 95 replaced the underlying DOS system. As newer Windows rolled off the production line, Windows became more sophisticated. Sophistication of Windows led to increased popularity and the demise of computers using DOS.

In 1999, Microsoft produced Windows NT it became the basis for all future versions Windows for home and business. Windows NT combined the best attributes of all previous versions of Windows and DOS. When Microsoft adapted TCP/IP to Windows NT, it supplanted Novell's Netware as the favorite Network Operating System. TCP/IP connected UNIX, Apple OS, DOS, and Linux under the Windows GUI environment (Tannenbaum, 2002).

ANDROID

A new competitor on the operating system scene is the Android operating system. The Android operating system built on the Linux kernel. It was originally built for touchscreen mobile devices such as smartphones and tablet computers such as Amazon's Kindle Fire. It is not an enterprise operating system in the sense of IOS, Windows, and Linux. Although it is possible for an engineer to network a pair of Android computers in P2P LAN, it has not happened on a wide scale basis to threaten Windows or UNIX's X-Windows.

CONCLUSION

The standalone computer is an obsolete business model of the 1950s. It is inconceivable to purchase a computer that does not have networking capabilities. Operating systems proliferate because of their operating system's networking ability. Windows outpaced X-Windows, Novell Netware, and Apple Talk because Microsoft made an effort to produce an enterprise operating system fit for the school, home, and business environments. The $100 copy of the Windows's software on the majority of home computers seamlessly interfaces with the $5000 network operating system Microsoft installs at businesses and government agencies even though the two systems are different.

Another reason Windows is the preferred operating system over UNIX, Netware, and Apple Talk is that Microsoft incorporated TCP/IP (the worldwide de facto internetworking standard) into the software making it network ready out of the box without any specialized programming.

TCP/IP is on UNIX but original versions requires a few hours of study to adapt. Apple does not have enterprise software. Netware used IPX/SPX as it networking protocol. Only in the last five years has Novell incorporated TCP/IP into its OS.

13

Programming Languages

Programming languages are the backbone of software applications and the bases for all operating systems one might use on a computer. Programming languages are the only method of communication or interface humans can use to control the behavior of a computer.

There are hundreds of different programming languages. Machine and Assembly language were the first attempts by humans to give instructions or program a computer. Machine Language was a binary numeric codes. It consisted of long strings of 0s and 1s. Machine language programs were used to represent computer routines, such as addition or perhaps to locate the next string of instructions. Machine language was difficult to read and write, because its nature. It does not resemble human language or mathematical notation. Another drawback to Machine Language, there is no standards as with the more modern programming languages.

Assembly Language represents a second attempt to program a computer. Assembly Language is a low-level programming language a step above Machine Language. It embodies the first attempt to make computer programming palpable for the programmer. Its design based on machine language rather than human interaction. It allowed the use of short mnemonic codes, which referred to actions and blocks of data rather than machine addresses. So instead of writing "0110101100101000" for a computer operation, the programmer wrote A--25--S (ignore the hyphens). The A was synonymous with add. Twenty-five was the decimal address of the "short." Short defines the number as an integer not a floating point number with a ceiling less than approximately 32,000.

Assembly Language did not provide a method of organizing or manipulating complex information. As with Machine Language, it required the programmer to have detailed knowledge of the internal architecture of the computer (Aspray & Campbell-Kelly, 1996).

Any number of methods can classify computer languages: interpreted, compiled, scripted, object-oriented, or batched to name a few. For the remainder of this chapter, I will attempt to present the computer languages to you in their historical context regardless of format.

The barrier to understanding the history of computing occurs when cyber historian occlude, rewrite the history of programming. A few days ago, I read an article that stated clearly that Beginner's All-purpose Symbolic Instruction Code (BASIC) was the basis for batch programming of the Dartmouth Time Sharing System (DTSS). It was designed for business and liberal arts majors who did not have mathematical background of computer science majors. BASIC was strictly a tool of educators when Microsoft used it to build the DOS operating system for the IBM and the early Apple personal computers. FORTRAN was also instrumental in the development of BASIC.

FIRST PROGRAMMING LANGUGUAGES

Jacquard was the first machine programmer. He programmed the silk loom, bearing his name Jacquard, with a series of punch cards similar to the Hollerith Cards of the 19th century. The punch cards Jacquard used guided the needles to the looms that weaved intricate embroidered patterns in fabric.

Charles Babbage and Ada Lovelace King followed Jacquard introducing punch card technology to metal adding machines. Legend has it that Lovelace was skilled enough to instruct the Babbage Difference Engine to compute Bernoulli numbers.

The next person to employ anything similar to the Jacquard punch cards was Herman Hollerith used punch card technology as a tabulating media. The Hollerith punch card machines opened the door to databases and information technology.

BATCH PROGRAMMING

One of the first attempts to automate computer programming was batch programming. Early batch programs were no more than a list of commands for a computer to execute. Some of the early batch programs were the General Motors Batch System, the Fortran Monitor System, and the Burroughs 5000 Master Control Program. These programs eliminated the need for a human to load punch cards more than once to insure the computer was active. When one program completed its output, the batch program insured the next program would start automatically.

The normal routine from loading batch programs followed a pattern where a series of batch programs were recorded on a magnetic tape by a low-end computer (the 1401) then placed on the input spool of the high-end computer (the 7000). The batch programs on the spool caused the high-end computer to execute the program and write the results to an output magnetic tape. After all the batch programs were executed, the output spool was removed to the low-end computer for printing.

MODERN PROGRAMMING LANGUAGES

Programming languages for this text are divided into six overlapping categories: procedural or object oriented, compiled, or interpreted, scripted or markup. The early languages, assembly language and machine language, were low-level languages because they mimic the language of computers. To make programming easier to implement, computer scientist needed a programming language in a form easily understood by humans. One of the first programs to meet the criteria of making programming of computers easier was FORmula TRANslation (FORTRAN). FORTRAN a general-purpose, procedural, imperative programming language was well suited for numeric and scientific computation. A team of programmers at IBM under the auspices of John Backus developed FORTRAN. In 1957, FORTRAN was standardized and published. A sample of FORTRAN is listed below:

```
$ vim helloworld.f
program hello
print *,"Hello World!"
end program hello
```

Another early high-level programming language that met the criteria of making programming easier was the Common Business Oriented Language (COBOL). COBOL like FORTRAN was a procedural programming language. Unlike FORTRAN, COBOL was developed for the business community instead of science and mathematics communities. A group of computer professionals called the Conference on Data Systems Languages (CODASYL) developed it in 1959. The development of COBOL was greatly influenced by Flow-matic, the programming language developed by Grace Hopper. A sample of COBOL follows:

```
IDENTIFICATION DIVISION.
PROGRAM-ID. HELLO.
ENVIRONMENT DIVISION.
DATA DIVISION.
PROCEDURE DIVISION.
PROGRAM-BEGIN.
DISPLAY "I said, Hello world".
PROGRAM-DONE.
STOP RUN.
```

PROCEDURAL LANGUGES

Procedural programming languages are a top to bottom programming language. Procedural programming languages are described as a list of instructions, that tell the computer, what to do (procedure-by-procedure) step-by-step. The programmer then systematically breaks the overall problem down into sub problems (sub procedures). This is called functional decomposition, which continues until a sub problem is straightforward enough to be solved by the corresponding sub procedure. Procedural programming is built like a pyramid. As the problem is worked out, the pyramid expands proportionally until the sub-procedure of the sub-procedures resolve the issue.

The difficulties with this type of programming, is that software maintenance can be difficult and time consuming. When changes are made to the main procedure, the changes cascade to the sub-procedures and the sub-procedures of the sub-procedures and so on. The change may affect all procedures in the pyramid. The most popular procedural languages were C and BASIC. A definition of procedural programming reads as follows:

> Procedural programming is a programming paradigm based upon the concept of the modularity and scope of program code (i.e., the data viewing range of an executable code statement). A main procedural program is composed of one or more modules (also called packages or units), either coded by the same programmer or pre-coded by someone else and provided in a code library.

> Each module is composed of one or more subprograms (which may consist of procedures, functions, subroutines, or methods, depending on programming language). It is possible for a procedural program to have multiple levels or scopes, with subprograms defined inside other subprograms. Each scope can contain names, which cannot be seen in outer scopes (WordiQ.com, 2010).

BASIC

Beginner's All-purpose Symbolic Instruction Code or BASIC was and is another procedural programming language. The rage of computer science at the advent of personal computers became another footnote in computer history with the advent of scripting and object oriented programming. John Kemeny and Thomas Kurz of Dartmouth University invented BASIC in 1964. BASIC was developed as a teaching tool to teach non-mathematic majors the fundamentals of computer programming. There are many versions of BASIC, however, the one that was the most popular was the BASIC produced by Microsoft.

The original BASIC was also an interpreted language. Bill Gates and Paul Allen made billions of dollars when IBM chose Microsoft to create a disk operating system (DOS) for their new personal computers. Gates and Allen used BASIC to create PC-DOS, which had to be compatible with the IBM mainframe computers. In the late 1990s, it introduced QBASIC. In the mid-1990s, Microsoft changed the direction of the language to accommodate the growing popularity of computers using a graphical user interface (GUI). In this format, the user is shielded from programming and only has to drop and drag objects onto a template to produce a desired procedure. The latest iteration of BASIC is Visual Basic 2010. A sample of the original version of BASIC is listed below:

```
10 PRINT "Hello World!"
20 A=A+1
30 If A ≥10 then 10 else 400
40 End
```

C

C is another procedural programming language. C, the preferred programming language by many professional programmers and educators because BASIC lacked the qualities of a structured programming language. Dennis Ritchie and Ken Thompson developed C in 1974. C grew popular because it was CPU neutral and associated with UNIX the operating system at many colleges. C derived from Assembly language. C became so popular that many organizations began to publish their own version of C. In response to the widespread pervasion of C, the American National Standards Institute (ANSI) published a standardized version of the language in 1983. Thousands of universities, companies, and research facilities used C as a teaching tool.

C is a compiled programming language. That means after you compile the code you will not have access to correct flaws in the program. To correct flaws the programmer rewrites the raw source code. A sample of a C program is listed below:

```
#include<stdio.h>

int main()
{
  printf("Hello World\n");
  return 0;
}
```

C unlike BASIC requires the programmer to specify which library of expressions to include with the program to insure it runs properly.

OBJECT ORIENTED LANGUAGE

OOP is an acronym for Object Oriented Programming. OOP is a programming design philosophy. It differs from procedural programming in that everything in OOP is grouped as self- sustainable objects. My personal experience with OOP tells me it is a programming philosophy where the programmer describes an object, functions, and variables that are visible in some modules and invisible in others. One thing the programmer must understand about an OOP program, it exists in skeletal form as a list calling different modules to execute data.

One of the advantages of object-oriented programming techniques have over procedural programming is that it encourages programmers to create modules that it need not changed when a new data type (Ford for example) is added. A programmer can simply create a new module that inherits many of the features from existing automobile objects. This makes object-oriented programs easier to modify.

Sun Microsystems the publisher of JAVA states object-oriented programming is a method of programming based on a hierarchy of classes, and well-defined and cooperating objects. The predominant OOP programming languages are Visual Basic, Visual C++, C#, and JAVA. Coding for both C++ and JAVA resemble the sample coding for C shown above. C# pronounced C sharp does not require the include statement for the libraries to output data as with JAVA and the incarnations of C++.

SCRIPTING LANGUAGES

A scripting language is a programming language that allows the programmer to gain control of one or more applications. "Scripts" are distinct from the source code of the application, as they are usually written in a different language and often created or at least modified by the end-user.

scripting languages are often called little languages because it solves relatively small programming problem that do not require the overhead of data declarations and other features found in JAVA, Python, or C++ programming languages. Scripting languages are used for writing operating system utilities, printing files on a web page, and control aspects of file manipulation for special-purposes. Some of the popular scripting languages are PHP, JavaScript, ASP, and Visual Basic script. A sample of JavaScript follows to demonstrate how it is merged with the HTML markup language

```
<HTML>
<HEAD>
<TITLE> Hello World </TITLE>
</HEAD>
<BODY>
```

The following is a sample of JavaScript added to the HTML code ordinarily it is in a separate file.

```
<SCRIPT LANGUAGE="Javascripthelloworld"
SRC="Javascriptsource.js">
<PRE>
<SCRIPT LANGUAGE="Javascripthelloworld">
Document.writeln("Hello World");
</SCRIPT>
</PRE>
</BODY>
</HTML>
```

MARKUP LANGUAGES

A markup language refers to a language that specifies the format of the text displayed in a web browser. The de facto standard in markup languages is Extensible Hypertext Markup Language (XHTML).

XHTML was based on HTML or Hypertext Markup Language. Prior to XHTML, HTML was the predominant markup language for Internet and private intranets. HTML was a subset of Standard Generalized Markup Language (SGML). SGML was complicated, difficult to implement. HTML on the other hand was simple to implement and easy to learn. The major drawback to HTML was it was inflexible. HTML lacked definition. Coders could not store data on a webpage except in scripting languages. All programs written in HTML were the same.

However, with the advent of XML or Extensible Markup Language, the inflexible components of HTML were mitigated. Coders could now store information on a webpage and display the data. The World Wide Web Consortium (WC3) decided to merge the two markup languages producing XHTML in 2000.

COMPILED LANGUAGES

Computers do not really process the code written in JavaScript or C#. The language of the computer is machine code. The language of C# resembles human communications. To process the code natively and convert it into an executable file or correct errors in the code, requires access to an interpreter or a compiler for the programming language.

A program that uses a compiler is called a compiled language. Compiled languages were the first languages created by computer programmers. FORTRAN, COBOL, and Assembly language were all compiled programming languages. A compiler processes the code for a program into an executable program. The definition of a compiler in most major American dictionaries states the compiler is a program that translates high-level programming language into machine code.

Most computer scientist will tell you a the compiler first parses or analyzes all of the language statements syntactically in a sequential manner and then, in one or more successive passes, builds the output code, ensuring that statements that refer to other statements are referenced correctly in the final code. The code is linked to various libraries, which are common code sections found in many programs. The use of libraries helps keep redundant coding to a minimum. The compilation output is sometimes referred to as object code or an object module. (Note that the term "object" as used in this instance does refer to object-oriented programming. The object code as used here refers to machine code that the processor executes one instruction at a time.)

The best way to understand the previous paragraph is to download a public domain compiler of C from Tucows, CNet or a copy of the Java compiler from Sun Microsystems. Once you have a copy of the compiler you will see that if you do not end the statements with a semi-colon, the compiler will tell you it is an error. If you should refer to the same variable first with an uppercase x and then with a lower case x, the compiler will tell you it is an error. These are the easier errors. Should you be expert enough to build programs—because all of these languages can utilize object oriented programming—the compiler will tell you where error exists. Interpreting error messages is one of the finer qualities of a programmer.

High-level programming languages that are compiled and are not limited to computer architecture but are limited to a computer platform, Linux, Windows, Mac OS. They contain words and phrases that are easily comprehended. Compiled languages are faster than interpreted languages. The only drawback to compiled languages is the correction of errors. The compiler allows one to run test-trials the software application inside its shell on the desktop.

INTERPRETED LANGUAGES

Programming languages that are processed line by line are interpreted programming languages. The definition of a program interpreter states that it is a program that translates programming code one line at time, executing each line as it is translated, in much the same manner as a high school student learns a foreign language.

Interpreters generate code in the same manner as compilers but the output of the interpreter differs because it never compiles the source code. Instead, the program code is interpreted each time the program executes.

That gives the interpreted program several advantages. First, an Interpreted programming language is it easier to learn, BASIC and Python are easy to learn. Second, interpreter lets the programmer know immediately when and where problems with the source code exist. Finally, interpreted languages are available for several platforms, Windows, Macintosh IOS, and Linux.

.NET FRAMWORK

The dot net framework or Net Framework programming environment is an innovation developed by the Microsoft Corporations. It is a programming environment that is a comprehensive programming platform to build applications that run computers using the Windows Operating System. Net Framework includes a large library of language interoperability coding. Net Framework allows code written in one language (Visual Basic) to be used across several other programming languages.

The remarkable achievement of Net Framework is accomplished using a unique software environment. Microsoft accomplished this remarkable feat with the use of a technology known as the Common Language Runtime or CLR for short. Net Framework is housed in a very expensive software package entitled Visual Studio.

This current use or development of software is contrary to software use or development for ENIAC and early computers. In the early years of computers, programming languages such COBOL and FORTRAN were developed to run on a particular mainframe computer.

The Microsoft innovation is not unique to computer programming. The Sun Microsystems developed the JAVA programming language as a cross platform tool in 1995. Sun Microsystems touted write the code once run anywhere programming language is loaded. The basic difference between and Net Framework is that Net Framework has a copyright and patent. It use is licensed jealously guarded by the Microsoft Corporation. JAVA is an open source programming language that was essentially released to the public for any modifications. When Oracle Corporation purchased Sun Microsystems, it began to reign in control of the product and judiciously gain rights to the several versions. As of this moment, Oracle can use the word JAVA as a programming platform. Oracle still allows beginners and crafty programmer free access to software development environment.

The ideal of using software as a means of better computing is not unique to software development. Remember in earlier discussions IBM fell from the throne of world leader of computer manufacturer because of the inability to adapt their multitude of computers to a single programing language. The groundbreaking IBM 701 ran computer

202

networks for Social Security, the FBI, and the Census Bureau. The 701 could not communicate with the newer, faster IBM 1601 or the IBM 1401 found in college research centers and defense department research centers.

IBM's inflexibility left the door open for companies like Novell, to developed Netware and build computer-networking systems that deemphasized the use of large million dollar mainframe computers in favor of cheaper minicomputers and IBM clones from competitors such as Burroughs, Control Data, Honeywell, NCR, and General Electric using new semiconductors and transistor based circuits.

Software powers the transistor and microprocessor revolution, which paved the way for the laptop and desktop computers of today.

14

Memory

Of all the secondary components in your computer, the hard drive, the operating system, the keyboard, and memory. Memory is the most important, without it, your computer would work in the same manner as the old big-iron computer ENIAC. Alternatively, computer memory would consist as a series of trade-off technologies similar to the first cylindrical Edison phonographs, or the Hollerith punch cards. We are lucky in that the science of computing learned early on that sound, is another form of data that could be stored on Mylar plastic tape magnetically. We are truly fortunate there existed technology such as NCR's CRAM (card random access memory) and the hard drive.

We can reasonably say modern storage evolved from the punch card and the Edison phonographs. Modern memory migrated from the vacuum tube to core memory in the 1960 with the implementation of SAGE. Magnetic core memory is one of the earliest forms of random access memory (RAM) on a digital computer. It was comprised of small magnetic rings, cores, through which wires were threaded to store information in an electromagnetic field. Eventually, computer engineers replaced the core memories with semiconductor memory based on the transistor circuit.

Memory becomes active on your computer from the moment, you power up your computer until the moment the computer is turned off. Your CPU is continuously interacting with all the various forms of memory on the computer EPROM, ROM, EEPROM, RAM, virtual memory (hard drive), and storage (hard drive). In all likelihood, the start-up scenario invokes the following sequences:

1. The computer is started.

2. The computer loads data from read-only memory (ROM) chip stored on your motherboard and performs a power-on self-test (POST). The POST ensures that all the major components (keyboard, monitor, mouse, and memory are functional). Part of the POST test, the memory, and controllers verify all memory registers are quick, read/write, and certified.

3. The CPU then loads the basic input/output system (BIOS) from ROM. The BIOS provides the computer with instructions on how manipulate storage devices, boot sequence, security, Plug and Play (auto device recognition) devices, monitor resolution and so on.

4. After the BIOS are loaded, the computer loads the operating system (OS) from the hard drive into RAM. ROM-BIOS maintain the operating system in RAM for as long as the computer has power. The OS enhances and the overall performance and functionality of the CPU and ensures a smoothed human interface.

5. After the OS has loaded, the operator interfaces with the computer to retrieve any file store on the hard drive or externally on a communications network.

6. The OS resides in RAM until the operator terminates computer activity. The OS directs the computer's operations, which may entail writing to files, erasing files, sending messages, etc.

There are two basic memory technologies: ROM (read only memory) and RAM (random access memory). RAM is the memory referred to when you purchase a computer (8 gigabytes) from your local electronics store. RAM is main memory.

There are special forms of RAM called virtual RAM. Virtual RAM occurs when the computer's physical memory is insufficient for the task. For example, to accommodate some programs such as Madden Football XV, the operating system resorts to the use of virtual memory. Virtual memory is a special form of RAM borrowed from the hard drive. The operating system designates a portion of the hard drive to extend capacity of RAM. The OS divide virtual ram into pages. A virtual RAM page is a block of contiguous virtual memory addresses between 2 kilobytes and 4 kilobytes in size on the hard drive. The operating system designates as many pages as needed to complete the task. The OS does not manipulate VR one byte or one word at a time. The OS moves the entire virtual ram page between main memory and the hard drive as needed.

If virtual RAM did not exist, computers would have a very limited capacity. In other words, if the fills the capacity of memory, the computer would constantly prompt the user to close one or more other applications before it could complete the present task. Virtual RAM allows the user to operate without limitations.

The remainder of this chapter will provide a more detailed discussion of the various types of ROM and RAM found on a computer. The discussion begins with the explanation of ROM.

ROM

ROM is an acronym for read-only memory also known as firmware. ROM is an integrated circuit programmed with the microcode instruction from the computer manufacturer. ROM contains data that is permanently written to a non-volatile integrated circuit or chip on the chassis of the motherboard of the computer or other electronic device. The basic responsibility of ROM is to guide the computer in booting (starting-up). Since the introduction of the PC, microcode has contained all the instructions necessary for the hardware. Once the computer verifies there is a keyboard, RAM, a monitor, etc.; it loads the ROM BIOS. ROM BIOS is the microcode that contains all the instructions or device drivers of the entire computer system keyboard, floppy speakers, printer, MP3, and modem, etc. (Mueller, 2004, pg. 371).

There are four other kinds of ROM chips: PROM, EPROM, EEPROM, and flash memory. Each form of ROM has its own distinctive qualities. Despite their differences, they all have two commonalities. First, data stored on a ROM is not lost when the power is turned-off. Second, data stored in these chips is either unalterable or require special attention by the operator to initiate a change to code stored on it (Mueller, 2004, pg. 373).

PROM

The letters P-R-O-M is an acronym for Programmable Read-Only Memory. In contrast to ROM, a PROM chip comes from the chipmaker without programming. PROM chips can be programmed to adapt or updated a computer's hardware. PROM chips—because they are cheaper to manufacture than ROM chips—are also used as prototypes for the final version of ROM during the design phase of a computer. A PROM chip can be programmed only once with the desired data. Once data is stored or written to the PROM chip, it is permanent and cannot be erased or altered. Information on a PROM chip is a non-volatile so data is not lost when power is removed. OTP, one time programmable, is another acronym for a PROM chip, (Sinard, 2006, pg. 24).

EPROM

EPROM stands for erasable programmable read-only memory. Like the PROM chip, the EPROM chip is manufactured blank and then programmed with a PROM burner. Manufacturers of EPROM chips often call them RPROM (Reprogrammable Read Only Memory) chips. An EPROM differs from the PROM in that it is has a quartz window on top of the compartment containing the chip. This allows erasure of the information or data stored on the chip. Erasure of the chip is accomplished by removing it from the computer and bombarding it with ultraviolet radiation. Afterward, the irradiated chip is re-inserted in the computer and ready to capture data.

The chip becomes unreliable after a number of rewrites, usually between a 100 and a 1000 depending on the chipmaker. EPROM chips, like PROM chips, are used to prototype the final version of ROM chips (Sinard, 2006, pg. 24) (Abd-El-Barr & El-Rewini, 2005, pg. 157).

EEPROM

EEPROM is an acronym for electronically erasable programmable read-only memory. It is a third type of read-only memory (ROM) chip. The EEPROM chip does not have a quartz window. As its name indicates, it is erased electronically. Removal from the computer or electronic circuit therefore is not necessary when it is being reprogrammed. The EEPROM is more expensive than EPROM but has a greater flexibility, reliability, and ease of use, a greater number erase-write cycles capacity. Normally an EEPROM chip is reliable from 10,000 to a million erase and write cycles. This reliability is dependent on the price the manufacturer paid for the semiconductor circuits (Abd-El-Barr & El-Rewini, 2005, pg. 157) (Sinard, 2006, pg. 25).

Flash Memory

Flash memory is a special EEPROM circuit, which has an almost unlimited life span of erase and write cycles. Flash memory like all ROM chips is non-volatile and retains its data when power is removed from the circuits. Flash memory was developed to address the slow processing speed of EEPROM chips in portable devices.

Flash memory processes data faster than EPROM or EEPROM by changing the way EEPROM reads and erases. Rather than reading data on the chip bit by bit, flash memory reads and writes data at a rate between 512 bytes to 16 kilobytes, based on the chipmaker specifications and the capacity of the chip. By reading and writing data in blocks instead of bit, flash memory behaves in the same manner as a conventional hard drive. Although flash memory is said to have unlimited life span, it is more like EEPROM and has a reliable life span between 10,000 and million erase-write cycles.

Memory cards or USB thumb drives made extensive use of flash memory. Use of flash memory has expanded to general data storage, transfer between computers and MP3 players. The most extensive use of flash memory is now in portable devices such as cell phones, personal digital assistants (PDAs), laptop computers, and digital cameras (Sinard, 2006, pg. 25).

CACHE MEMORY

Cache memory is random access memory (RAM) that a microprocessor accesses much more quickly than other potions of RAM. The purpose of the cache is to place data closer to the CPU. Consequently, when the CPU processes data, it searches the cache memory first, before it searches other potions of RAM. If the CPU does not find the data in the first cache, it searches the second cache and so on until it finds the information needed.

Cache memory has multiple levels or hierarchies. Level one cache—often abbreviated as L1 cache—is located on the microprocessor. L1 cache size ranges from 8 kilobytes to 64 kilobytes. The access speed of L1 cache is between 15-20 Nano seconds.

The level-two cache or L2 cache memory is larger than L1. L2 cache is located on the system motherboard or on a separate chip outside the CPU microprocessor chip. Typical size of the L2 cache has a size between 64KB and 2MB. Data missing from L1 is found in L2, the microprocessor swaps the data in the L1 cache with the data in L2 cache.

Some manufacturers began locating L2 caches at the microprocessor chip to increase processing speed (Docter, Groth, Dulaney, & Skandier, 2006, pg. 21) (Whitaker, 1996, pg. 721) (Sinard, 2006, pg. 29 - 30) (Soper, 2004, 240 - 241)

RAM

RAM is the computer's main memory. RAM is an acronym for random access memory. Other synonyms for RAM are read/write memory, volatile memory, and static memory. Semiconductor RAM like L1 and L2 is volatile memory. In other words, when the electric current stops, the information on the chip is lost.

In addition to cache memory, one can think of semiconductor RAM as cache of memory from the hard disk. That is because once all the consumable data on built in RAM fills, the hard disk becomes available for CPU usage. Once your computer powers up, it loads the operating system from the hard drive into RAM (Sinard, 2006, pg. 23) (Null & Lorbur, 2006, pg. 281).

RAM has two distinct technologies: static and dynamic. Static RAM (SRAM) holds its contents only as long as power is applied to the circuit. SRAM is very fast and relatively expensive. SRAM memory cells consist of four, five, or six transistors the six transistor cells the most popular. SRAM built into the CPU serves as cache memory.

Dynamic RAM (DRAM) unlike SRAM is relatively inexpensive and holds its content for a brief period, usually less than 1 one-hundredth of a second. DRAM memory cells consists of paired transistors that requires continued refreshing or charging else the content contained therein is lost or drained (Sinard, 2006, pg. 24) (Null & Lorbur, 2006, pg. 281).

Engineers and computer designers of a computer main memory prefer DRAM to SRAM for the following reasons:

    a) Denser circuits
    b) Less expensive
    c) Generates less heat
    d) Requires less power

All versions of DRAM utilize the same memory concepts, even though there are several versions of DRAM. Some versions of DRAM are described below:

1. Synchronous DRAM—SDRAM is faster than non-synchronous DRAM because it has the capacity to synchronize its frequency with the frequency of the CPU. SDRAM has 4 to six times the clock speed of EDO and FPM RAM.

2. Multibank DRAM – MDRAM

3. FPM DRAM—Fast page mode dynamic random access memory is an obsolete form of RAM that did not use a clock. Its circuits measured access speeds ranging from 200 – 50 ns. FPM DRAM had to match the speed of the motherboard to achieve maximum effectiveness.

4. EDO DRAM—Extended Data out DRAM provided a slight improvement over the FPM DRAM. EDO DRAM's only advantage, it allowed more data read before refreshing. In other words, it was refreshed less often than FPM DRAM (Meyers & Jernigan, 2003, pg. 120).

5. DDR SDRAM—Double Data Rate SDRAM is a type of RAM that makes two processes per clock cycle. It was popular with AMD computers. It could not be added to a motherboard from Intel (Meyers & Jernigan, 2003 pg. 124).

6. RDRAM—Direct Rambus DRAM is Intel's version of DDR SDRAM. Intel introduced DDR SDRAM with the Pentium IV (Meyers & Jernigan, 2003, pg. 122).

7. Credit card memory developed by a consortium of manufacturers to give the early laptop computers more functionality. The industry dropped the name credit card in favor of Personal Computer Memory Card International Association (PCMCIA) memory card (Docter, Groth, Dulaney, & Skandier, 2006, pg. 156 - 157).

15

African American Pioneers

This chapter like the overall book is divided into two sections. In the first section, I discuss the plight of the 19th century African American inventor and scientist who contributed to either the growth of telecommunications or electric industries. In section two, the discussion concentrates on the achievements of African American engineers and scientist who contributed to electronics or computer science during twentieth century.

In the first section, I focus on the two notable African American inventors Granville T. Woods and Lewis H. Latimer. First, I discuss Woods the inventor of the first commercially successful induction radio. Next I examine the contributions of Lewis H. Latimer, the Edison Pioneer, whose amazing ability as an artist and knowledge of United States patent laws assisted Alexander Graham Bell in the filing the patent for the telephone, improved the manufacturing process of the Edison incandescent lamp, and made General Electric the predominant distributor of electricity.

19TH CENTURY ACHIEVEMENTS

Before I close the study of the early computing devices, it is necessary to examine the contributions of African American inventors no matter how small or insignificant their efforts to the over-all tenor of the conversation. The Gilded Age described two Americas. One America that was incredibly wealthy. The other, the home of the less fortunate, is where one finds the post-Civil War African American. The African Americans—unlike the Asians, Italians, Irish, or Hispanics who came to North America willingly to escape dire circumstances in their homeland—came to the United States as slaves.

Emancipation Proclamation and the 13th and 15th Amendments to the United States Constitution describe the political atmosphere towards the African American after the Civil War. The documents state slavery, shall not exist in the United States, and gives the African American the right to vote, respectively.

After the Civil War, the political attitude of the nation toward the African Americans, at best, was contemptible. The well-meaning politics described for the newly emancipated slave as well as that of the *freedmen of color* soon succumbed to the white supremacy attitude found in both the North and the South. The subsequent Compromise of 1876 and the Supreme Court decision of Plessey versus Ferguson (1896) frame the suppression of African Americans legal reality.

In the first instant, the Compromise of 1876 illustrated a sharp deviation from the government of the people, for the people, and by the people characterized by Lincoln in the Gettysburg Address. Instead of predicating citizenship on the *better angels of our nature*, political decisions became an object of greed and money. The politician during the Compromise of 1876, one of the darkest moments in United States history abandon legal responsibility for gold. It is closest the nation has come—outside of the Civil War and the War of 1812—to disintegrating.

The Compromise of 1876 describes the events surrounding Presidential Election of 1876 between Rutherford B. Hayes the Republican and Samuel l. Tilden, the Democrat. After the election, there was no clear-cut winner of the Electoral College. Tilden held the edge in the popular vote; he did not have the necessary Electoral College votes win the election. In such situations the 12th amendment to the Constitution states:

> "The person having the greatest number of votes for President, shall be the President, if such number be a

majority of the whole number of Electors appointed; if no person has such majority, then from the persons having the highest numbers not exceeding three on the list of those voted for as President, the House of Representatives shall choose immediately, by ballot, the President. But in choosing the President, the votes shall be taken by states, the representation from each state having one vote…"

In the general election, the Tilden won the popular vote by 300,000 over Hayes. Tilden, also, held a 19-vote lead in the Electoral College 184 to 165 over Hayes, one vote shy of a majority.

After the initial vote, four states were still undecided: Oregon, South Carolina, Louisiana, and Florida. Republicans controlled the legislature of Oregon and quickly decided to cast it three electoral votes for Hayes without the benefit of a recount. The electoral votes in the states of South Carolina, Louisiana, and Florida were hotly contested; Tilden held a slight edge in the popular vote in each state. Each political party claimed victory for its candidate and accused the other of voter fraud.

As a consequence of political rigmarole South Carolina, Louisiana, and Florida each sent two Electoral College delegations to the District of Columbia—one delegation casting its votes for Tilden the other delegation casting its votes for Hayes. The laissez faire policy of the 1876 Supreme Court was not to expand the authority of the Federal government and declined to render an opinion.

Without the fear of a Supreme Court invalidation, the Washington power brokers felt no obligation to follow Constitutional protocol in accordance to the 12th Amendment. Congressional power brokers and lobbyist chose to form a so-called impartial election commission of 15-members, eight Republicans and seven Democrats.

Hayes was elected president by a margin of one vote 8 to 7. Many historians say Hayes won the election because he (capitulated to) negotiated the demands of Southern politician's to end the eleven-year Federal policy of Reconstruction. Without Federal troops to force the former Confederates to comply with the 13th, 14th, and 15th amendments to the Constitution, they became inept pieces of paper.

In the second instant, Plessey versus Ferguson sealed the African American's fate as a second-class citizen during the Gilded Age and for the next sixty years. The rendering by the Fuller Supreme Court allowed advocates of intolerance and the "Separate but Equal" policy dominance. Justice Harlan expressed the dissenting opinion.

> "...But I deny that any legislative body or judicial tribunal may have regard to the race of citizens when the civil rights of those citizens are involved. Indeed, such legislation, as that here in question, is inconsistent not only with that equality of rights which pertains to citizenship, National and State..."

GRANVILLE T. WOODS

One question that still haunts the mind of every African American historians is why not credit Granville T. Woods with the invention of the first radiotelegraph instead of Marconi. Historians often overlook Woods's accomplishments in favor of the more emblematic and iconic Marconi. Another reason Woods is overlooked has more to do with the tenor of racial tolerance. During the 19th century, white Americans considered anything associated with African Americans inferior.

The Woods's radio was the Synchronous Multiplex Railway Telegraph. The Synchronous Multiplex Railway Telegraph was an induction radiotelegraph that could receive as well as send messages from a moving train. To state in other terms, the induction radiotelegraph worked by using magnetic fields to transfer signals to telegraph wires that paralleled railways instead of radio waves to transfer energy to an antenna. Albeit a very limited range, the principle of the radio still exists.

The Synchronous Multiplex Railway Telegraph worked because it created a powerful magnetic field around the compartment containing the telegrapher key (the caboose) allowing it to receive from or send messages to the telegraph wires. The same induction principles are described by the experiments of Michael Faraday. The Synchronous

Multiplex Railway Telegraph proved an invaluable tool for the railroad companies. It allowed railroad companies the luxury of coordinating locomotive traffic on railroad routes, avoid scheduling bottlenecks, and minimize collisions. It also made it possible to notify moving locomotives of any unforeseen danger on the route it traveled (the Hole in the Wall Gang) bandits, floods, landslides.

The veracity of much of the information on Woods is questioned upon further research. For example, Thomas Edison had filed a patent for a similar induction radio device; he coined Grasshopper Telegraph, two years earlier. What we do know is that Woods prevailed over Edison in the courts. Edison embarrassed by the defeat to the lowly African American offered to purchase the patent from Woods. Woods rejected the offer. Edison offered to make Woods a partner in the induction telegraph again Woods rejected the Edison offer.

Most historical documents paint Woods as a hero and do not emphasize the importance of his radiotelegraph. The documents also stated Woods earned a fortune from his induction radio. As of this edition, I have yet to find any evidence contrary to the notion of a heroic Granville Woods. Sources used for research on Woods were:

1. Black Inventors in the Age of Segregation: Granville T. Woods, Lewis H. Latimer, and Shelby J. Davidson. Rayvon Fouche. Baltimore, Maryland: The Johns Hopkins University Press, 2003.
2. Granville T. Woods, Massachusetts Institute of Technology
3. Granville T. Woods, IEEE Global History Network.
4. Black Inventor website, Blackinventor.com
5. L. Haber, *Black Pioneers of Science and Invention* . Orlando, FL: Houghton - Mifflin.)

The story of Granville T. Woods begins in Columbus, Ohio in the year 1856. Granville T. Woods, like Thomas Edison, never received the formal education of many of his contemporary rivals in telecommunications and electricity. He never completed grade school because at the age of 10, he had to work to help support his family. Records show he served as an apprentice in a machine shop where learned the machinist and blacksmith trades. In 1872, the family moved to Missouri, there Woods found a job with a railroad company. Woods worked as a railroad fireman and later as an engineer. During his leisure time, he read books.

His knowledge of steam engines allowed him to travel the world. He was able to obtain a job on a British merchant ship where he served as a steam engineer. Later he found similar work with the Danville and Southern Railroads. Finally, in 1881, Woods tired of traveling, settled down in Cincinnati, Ohio. In Cincinnati, Woods opened a manufacturing factory. It was not long before all the years of experience Woods had accumulated aboard ships and trains paid off. He filed for a patent on a unique steam boiler furnace in 1884 (Haber, 1970, p 62).

Woods received a patent (number 373,915) from the U. S. Patent office in 1887 for his induction telegraph (Haber, 1970, p. 65). That is almost nine years before both the Marconi patent in Great Britain or Tesla's patent in the United States. Wood's Synchronous Multiplex Railway Telegraph revolutionized railway communications and saved countless lives. According to the patent records, Woods applied Faraday's Law of Electromagnetic Induction:

1. To create a magnetic field, electric current was passed through an oblong coil suspended beneath the train
2. In turn, a magnetic field developed around the train. That moved when the train moved,
3. The field created around the train induced current in the telegraph wires that ran parallel to the railroad tracks, allowing the sending and receiving of telegraphic messages uninterrupted.

It is unfortunate that a man of Woods's intelligence lived during a period of heighten racial intolerance which, hindered the commercial value of his inventions. Instead of praise, Woods often faced ridicule, harassment, and contempt. There were many legal challenges for patent infringement because white supremacist attitude of America that believed African Americans less than human and possibly the missing link between apes and humans.

Granville Woods's legal problems did not end after the patent trial with Edison. He suffered many other legal injustices. One of the most contemptuous incidents occurred when authorities jailed him for saying a white rivals infringed on his patent. Granville Woods fought many legal battles just because of his color and race. To this fact, his many legal woes drained financial resources, keeping Woods impoverished until his death in 1910.

All told, Woods received more than 45 patents overall and was known as the Black Thomas Edison. Woods received seven patents that directly applied to telephone or telegraph equipment. In the broadest sense created the first telephone with texting capabilities when he received a patent for the Telegraphony in 1885. The Telegraphony combined the features of both the telephone and telegraph allowing operators to send and receive messages quicker than they had previously. Woods' name is also mentioned as a contributor of the third rail innovation on New York subways, eliminating the trolley car (IEEE, 2009). Woods died in 1910, in New York City's Harlem at the age of 53.

LEWIS LATIMER

Fortunately, Lewis Latimer did not have the same attitude as Granville Woods had towards Civil Rights. Instead of following the advice of Frederick Douglass—the preeminent Civil Rights advocate of the 19th century—who advised African Americans to instigate or agitate on matters of Civil Rights. Latimer worked quietly within the system building an impeccable reputation for himself and among industrial icons such as Alexander Graham Bell, Thomas Edison, and the United States Electric Light Company. During his career, Latimer worked for General Electric and Bell Telephone.

Lewis Latimer was born in 1848, the son of two fugitive slaves, George and Rebecca Latimer of Chelsea, Massachusetts. Latimer began his career aboard the USS Massasoit a side-wheeled gunboat in the Union Navy during the Civil War. His vessel fought Confederate naval forces on the James River in Virginia (1861-1865).

Latimer began his civilian career working as an office boy in 1868 at Crosby and Gould, a well-known patent law firm, in Boston. Crosby and Gould specialized in helping inventors protect their intellectual properties from patent infringement. In his spare time, Latimer taught himself the art of mechanical drawing, first by observing other draftsmen employed by Crosby and Gould, then later by reading books on the subject. After several months of study and practice, he requested an opportunity to demonstrate his talent to his employer. Latimer's drawings were described as beautiful works of art. As a consequence, Crosby and Gould promoted Latimer to the position of draftsman with a salary of $20 per week (Haber, 1970, p. 73) (George, 1999).

Latimer's first important client was Alexander Graham Bell. Latimer provided Bell with the technical drawings for the historic telephone Bell submitted to the United States patent office in 1876. (There are always challenges to the veracity of historical African Americans. Some historians maintain Latimer never worked for Bell during the patent race with Gray.) Some historians claimed that Latimer (Massachusetts Institute of Technology, 1996), not Bell, invented the telephone; however, that notion is mere speculation, because Latimer worked as a draftsman for Bell providing him with the blueprints and expertise for submitting patent applications. Because of Latimer's dedication to the task, Bell was able to submit his patent for the telephone a few hours before rival Elisha Gray. (In fact, Bell was not the first to invent the telephone. Antonio Meucci invented the telephone. Bell submitted his patent a year after the Meucci patent caveat expired.) (George, 1999).

In 1880, Latimer worked for Hiram Maxim, an inventor and founder of the United States Electric Lighting Company (since 1888 a subsidiary of Westinghouse Electric) of Brooklyn. After familiarizing himself with the design and fabrication of the light bulb, Latimer made a number of improvements to Maxim's method of manufacturing incandescent bulb filaments. Among them, he initiated a change in the way to attach the carbonized wire filaments that provided light in the bulb (Schneider & Singer, 2005). Latimer along with Maxim received patents for developing a method for connecting the metal wires to the carbon filament inside an incandescent lamp in 1881 (Haber, 1970, p. 75). Latimer's filament helped make electric lighting in homes and businesses a commercial success. Light bulb technology based on Latimer's carbon filament was an industry standard until the 1939, when the tungsten-based filaments replaced it.

In addition to the carbon filament Latimer, also, fostered the threaded socket for the light bulb that allows users to screw the bulb into the socket (Massachusetts Institute of Technology, 1996). Latimer added a new drying agent for the inert gas pumped into the bulb replacing the need for a perfect vacuum in the light bulb (Schneider & Singer, 2005). In 1882, Latimer received an individual patent for creating the first commercially viable long-lasting light bulb based on the carbon filament. Later in 1882, Latimer received a third patent for creating a globe for arch lights (Haber, 1970, p. 77).

Thomas Edison became aware of Latimer's skills as a draftsman and inventor and retained his services and patents for Edison General Electric during 1884. His knowledge of electric lighting and electric patents proved invaluable. Edison at first made him a draftsmen and engineer, and then later made Latimer the company's chief draftsmen and patent expert. In that, position Latimer investigated patent encroachments on Edison General Electric products without permission (Vetter, 2011). When Edison General Electric Company merged with Thomson-Houston in 1892 to formed General Electric, Latimer remained with the legal department.

Before General Electric replaced him as company leader, Edison placed Latimer in charge of the General Electric Library. In this capacity, Latimer gathered information worldwide about rivals and potential infringement of Edison General Electric patents and inventions (Schneider & Singer, 2005). Latimer's thorough knowledge of the light bulb and the Edison General Electric product line made him an instrumental expert witness in cases of patent infringement brought by Edison General Electric in the United States and Europe.

Edison was so appreciative of Latimer's diligence he made Latimer a member of the original Edison Pioneers in 1918. Only now is history beginning to reveal the true story behind the Edison invention of the light bulb or incandescent lamp. While it was Edison who was given credit for inventing the incandescent lamp, Latimer provided the backbone in perfecting a commercially viable long-lasting bulb.

In 1918, Latimer wrote his only book entitled *Electric Lighting: A Practical Description of the Edison System*. All told, Latimer filed seven patents in the field of electricity and assisted with the presentation of several other in electrical engineering before his death in 1928 (George,

1999). The most notable contributions made by Latimer are listed below:

a) Water closet for railroad cars (1874)
b) Improved electric lamp (1881)
c) New and improved manufacturing process for carbon filament for incandescent lamps (1882)
d) Globe support for arc light (1882)
e) Cooling and disinfecting device (1886)
f) Lock for hats, coats, and umbrellas on hanging racks (1895)
g) Lamp fixture (1910)

20TH CENTURY INVENTORS

It would be fitting to state that the accomplishments of Lewis Latimer and Granville Woods in the previous century opened the doors of opportunity for all African Americans in the fields of electrical engineering and telecommunications. However, that is not the case. During the Gilded Age, democracy for the African American citizens was anything but straightforward. As described in the prolog for this section, civil rights for the African American suffered several setbacks as attitude of whites grew from cool to icy towards African American.

Segregation became the law land, established by the Supreme Court decision Plessey versus Ferguson (1896). Intolerance extended its prohibitions beyond the accommodations for interstate travel to encompass every phase of African American life with legalized sequestration. Not only were blacks were forced into second-class citizenship. Many were forced into involuntary servitude via peonage slavery until the end of World War II. Records show as many as 800,000 African American men, women and children were forced into a system of convict slavery in the former Confederate states for such inconsequential offenses as unemployment and vagrancy (Blackmon, 2008).

African Americans not entrapped by convict servitude lived under the suppression of *Jim Crow*. In the former Confederate states, blacks used separate hotels, rooted sports teams, read African American newspapers, served in segregated armed forces units, and attended public schools, and universities. Blacks could not vote nor could they marry outside their race. Punishments for such violation of the *Jim Crow Codes* led to incarceration in the convict labor system or brutality from a lynch mob justice.

Despite of their meritorious service in the armed forces of the United States during both world wars, former African American veterans faced racial barriers and inferior services from the G.I. Bill for education, housing, and health benefits. Segregation did not yield until the combined efforts of a determined activist carried the fight for Civil Rights forward in the press, in the courts, and to the segregationist.

Thurgood Marshall spearheaded the battle for equality when he successfully argued before the United States Supreme Court to strike down the Plessey versus Ferguson 1896. The landmark Brown vs the Board of Education 1956 paved the way for the dismantling of Jim Crow. Simultaneous to Marshall's victory in the Supreme Court came Dr. Martin Luther King's leadership of the campaign of non-violent demonstrations against institutionalized segregation in major Southern cities between 1956 and 1968, Montgomery to Memphis.

Also rooted in the Civil Rights campaign were job opportunities for African Americans in corporate America and government. Immediately they begin to validate the quest for equality. In the fields of education, computer science, electronics, and telecommunication African Americans made an immediate impact. The remainder of Chapter 12 pays tribute to those 20th century pioneers who knocked down the barriers for those seeking a career in engineering, computer science, and telecommunications.

OTIS BOYKIN

Otis Boykin was born in the city of Dallas, Texas on August 29, 1920. His mother was a homemaker, his father a carpenter. He attended both Fisk University and the Illinois Institute of Technology. Historians remember Boykin for his contributions to the field of biotechnology, electronics, and electrical engineering.

In the field of electronics, Boykin received his first patent in electronics for engineering a resistor. The resistor if you remember, Chapter 8: A Brief Course on Electricity is a device that restricts the flow of electricity through an electric circuit. Boykin invented a device called a *wire resistor*. The wire resistor measured precise amounts of electricity flowing through a circuit for a selected task. Two years later, Boykin file a second patent for a second kind of specialized resistor. The second Boykin resistor had the ability to withstand extreme accelerations, violent shocks, and extreme temperature changes without the danger of losing its resilience. An added feature of the second resistor, it was easy to make and inexpensive. Because of the component's resilience, IBM and the United States Department of Defense adapted the resistor for its computers and strategic combat equipment electronic circuitry. Boykin, also, created an electronic capacitor in 1965 and an EMP (electromagnetic pulse) resistant capacitor in 1967, along with a number of EMP resistant electric and electronic elements. (An EMP occurs when a nuclear weapon explodes and creates an electromagnetic firestorm that renders electronic and electrical devices useless. Boykins devices defeated the EMP and were launch ready after a sneak nuclear attack.) Boykin earned name recognition amongst his peers for creating a wide range of innovative consumer products as well. These products included a burglarproof cash register and a chemical air filter.

Another contribution Boykin made was in the specialized field of biotechnology was a heart stimulator. He created and patented the first control unit for the heart stimulator (pacemaker). Ironically, Boykin died for need of a heart pacemaker in 1982. Below is the list of the eleven patents filed at the United States Patent Office and received by Otis Boykins:

1. Patent number 2,891,227, 6/16/1959, Wire type precision resistor.
2. Patent number 2,972,726, 2/21/1961, Electrical Resistor.
3. Patent number 3,191,108, 6/22/1965, Electrical capacitor and method of making same.
4. Patent number 3,271,193, 9/6/1966, Electrical resistance element and method of making the same.
5. Patent number 3,304,199, 2/14/1967, Electrical resistance element.
6. Patent number 3,329,526, 7/4/1967, Electrical resistance element and method of making the same.
7. Patent number 3,348,971, 10/24/1967, Method of making a thin film capacitor.

8. Patent number 3,394,290, 7/23/1968, Thin film capacitor.
9. Patent number 4,267,074, 5/12/1981, Self-supporting electrical resistor composed of glass, refractory materials and noble metal oxide.
10. Patent number 4,418,009, 11/29/1983, Electrical resistor and method of making the same.
11. Patent number 4,561,996, 12/31/1985, Electrical resistor and method of making the same.

MARK E. DEAN

Mark E. Dean was born on April 28, 1957, in Jefferson City, Missouri to James and Barbara Dean. He is famous because of his contributions to computer technology. Historian credit Ted Hoff with the invention of the first microprocessor. Other historians credit Steve Jobs and Steve Wozniak as the creators of the first commercially successful preassembled personal computer, the Apple I (one).

Contemporaries of the Apple II computer was the Tandy TRS–80, the Commodore–64, the Atari 800, and the Texas Instruments' Ti–99. What the three computers had in common was their own unique proprietary architecture. To state in laymen's terms, a word processor written for a Texas Instruments Ti-99 could not run on the Commodore, the same limitation prevented software written for the Commodore–64 and Tandy TRS–80. Another limitation of early personal computers was output. An Atari could read, edit, or save a spreadsheet created on a Zenith Data System, Tandy TRS–80, or a Texas Instruments Ti-99.

In addition to the architecture problems, computer manufacturer used different BIOS (basic input and output system) standards. The differing BIOS compounded the architecture and output issues. Differing BIOS limited the accessories for personal computing keyboards, modems, printers, floppy disk drives, and sound cards to the computer manufacturer. That is to say, a Sony computer could not use a printer built by Commodore.

Mark E. Dean ended the chaos surrounding personal computer ownership with the invention of the Industry Standard Architecture (ISA). ISA established a standard for computer architecture and ROM BIOS. For that accomplishment, Dean was given the moniker *Father of the Modern Personal Computer.* ISA enables computers made by different manufacturers to connect and use multiple devices modems, disc drives, computer mice, and printers, regardless of manufacturer. In addition, eliminating compatibility issues, ISA enabled personal computers to read software designed by a publisher other than the computer manufacturer. A computer manufactured by IBM could read and edit a spreadsheet created by Dell, Acer, or Gateway. (The compatibility problem still exists for the Apple. That is because Apple stubbornly continued its own set of standards for the manufacture of computers.)

Dean along with colleague Dennis L. Moeller received a patent for the invention of the ISA bus system in 1983. Their partnership also led to the development of the IBM PC/AT, the IBM PS/2, the Color Graphics Adapter (CGA), other personal computer subsystems.

All told, Dean holds more than 30 patents including the invention of the first 1-Gigahertz RISC microprocessor. For his accomplishments in the field of computer engineering, Dean was made an IBM Fellow, the only such award ever bestowed upon an African American. Other awards Dean received were 1988 PC Magazine World Class Award, 1997 Black Engineer of the Year President's Award, the Ronald H. Brown American Innovators Awards, National Inventors Hall of Fame in 1997, Distinguished Engineer Award of the National Society of Black Engineers in 1999, and the National Academy of Engineering in 2001 (IEEE, 2009) (Taborn & Thompson, 2006).

Although there are hundreds of citations listing Dean and Moeller's accomplishments, the patent for ISA and the gigahertz (Pentium) microprocessor are withheld because Dean worked at IBM. According to labor laws based upon the UCC (Uniform Commercial Codes), the employer, in this case the IBM, owns any innovations or patents created by its employee. Intel holds the copyright for the popular name for the gigahertz microprocessor, Pentium.

JOHN HENRY THOMPSON

John Henry Thompson is famous in the history of computing because he invented the programming language Lingo and is one of the co-founders of the software company Macromedia. Lingo is the programming platform that created Macromedia Director, Macromedia

Flash, and Macromedia Shockwave programs (Macromedia is now Adobe). Flash and Shockwave are essential components of every web browser Safari, Internet Explorer, Mozilla, and Chrome. The Adobe Shockwave allows the publication of Adobe Director Applications on the Internet. Director software creates games and educational software for private intranets and internet. Adobe Flash is used to add animation, video, and interactivity to web pages.

From 1987 until 2001, Thompson was the chief computer programming engineer at Macromedia. In that position, he developed the first version of Director Video Works. He also developed Video Works Accelerator, VideoWorks II, MediaMaker, Action, Macromedia Flash, and Macromedia Director. He became Principal Software Engineer at Macromedia in 2003. In 2005, Adobe purchased Macromedia for 7.5 billion dollars. John Thompson is now an owner of JHT Consulting, Bala Cynwyd, PA, which provides consulting services for web-based application development (IEEE, 2009).

Thompson is reclusive and does not grant interviews. In researching him, in the twenty-six years since the invention of Lingo and the founding of Macromedia, this author has not been able to retrieve any information about Thompson existence over the Internet except for the information already posted on his web page and an occasional dedication of a charter school he has built. There is sparse information on his website that has already been repeated by websites featuring the accomplishments of African Americans in computer science. In addition to the Internet, I have searched magazine and newspaper archives in the Denver Public Library for articles about Thompson in the leading African American magazines Black Enterprise, Ebony, and Jet. I also performed the similar searches the New York Times and the computer magazine Wired.

PHILIP EMEAGWALI

Dr. Philip Emeagwali is sometimes known by the title of "Father of the Internet" for his groundbreaking theory of 1989 about supercomputing. His theoretical plan for connecting more than 65,000 microprocessors created the world's fastest computer. Emeagwali's revolutionary idea for an international network of computers is said to be the technology that gave birth to the Internet. Since his accomplishments, Emeagwali has received international recognition in the scientific community and beyond. In 1989, he won the Gordon Bell Prize, a prestigious award in the field of supercomputing. (His microprocessor technology was used by Apple to build the PowerPC G4 model). Emeagwali was born on August 23, 1954, in Akure, Nigeria.

JANET EMERSON BASHEN

Janet Emerson Bashen was born Janet Rita Emerson on February 12, 1957, in Mansfield, Ohio to James L. Emerson Sr. and Ola Emerson. Shortly after her birth, the family relocated to Huntsville, Alabama where Ms. Emerson spent her childhood. Janet Emerson Bashen is listed in this text because she is the first African American woman to hold a patent for a computer software invention. Her software, LinkLine, is a web-based application designed for Equal Employment Opportunity Commission (EEOC). The software interface manages claims intake and tracking, document management, and numerous other reports for the cases of the EEOC. Ms. Bashen was issued U.S. Patent number 6,985,922 on January 10 2006, for creating a "Method, Apparatus, and System for Processing Compliance Actions for a Wide Area Network."

Bashen now works for the company she founded Bashen Corporation. It is a human resources consulting firm that pioneered end-to-end EEOC compliance and administration services. In September 1994, Bashen built the business from her home office, which was, like Stibitz before her, no more than her kitchen table, a laptop, no money, one client, and a fervent commitment to succeed. Bashen Corporation is recognized for its achievements in Human Resources management.

CLARENCE ELLIS

Clarence "Skip" Ellis was born May 11, 1943, in Chicago, Illinois. He is listed herein because of his work at the Xerox Research labs in Palo Alto, California (PARC). He helped bring to fruition the seminal notions of Vannevar Bush and Douglas C. Engelbart. He was instrumental in the creation of the PARC icon driven operating system. The PARC operating system was adapted to Apple Computers for the

Macintosh computer. Bill Gates replaced the MS-DOS operating system in favor of a PARC system. The PARC OS became Microsoft Windows.

Clarence Ellis's career as a computer scientist began at age 15 when he took a job as a (would be) night watchman. A job he took to help his family pay expenses. Since computers were a rarity in the 1950s, Clarence found plenty of free time for reading. The only reading material available to him on the job were the computer manuals. He, like many African Americans, became a self-taught computer expert.

This knowledge became useful one day during a company crisis when it ran out of new punch cards. Since their inception in the 1950s, computers have been, for the most part, controlled (programmed) by punch cards and without new cards, many projects routinely rolls to a stop. One day at work when this situation occurred, Clarence, because of his reading material, was the only person who knew how to reuse the old punch cards. He told the project manager how to change the settings on the computer to allow it to accept the old cards and it worked perfectly.

In 1964, Clarence earned a BS degree, double major in math and Physics, from Beloit College. Clarence attended graduate school at the University of Illinois majoring in computer science. He specialized on the hardware, software, and applications of the Illiac 4 Supercomputer. In 1969, Clarence Ellis became the first African American to receive a Ph.D. in Computer Science.

GERALD A. LAWSON

Have you ever wondered who made it possible to play video games? The answer to the question is Gerald A. Lawson. Lawson a self-taught engineer worked for Fairfield Semiconductor of who pioneered electronic video entertainment when he created the first home video game system with interchangeable game cartridges. In 1976, Lawson directed the Fairfield video game division to produce Fairfield's Channel 76. Before Channel 76, a computer user could only play the games built in to the operating system.

KATHERINE COLEMAN GOBLE JOHNSON

Katherine Johnson was born in 1918 in the White Sulphur Springs West Virginia to Joshua and Joylette Coleman. She was the youngest of four children. Always the trailblazer, in 1938, she became the first African American woman to attend and graduate school from West Virginia University. While attending West Virginia, Katherine majored in mathematics.

After graduation, at a family reunion, Katherine was made aware NASA was looking for people with mathematical skills. They were recently open to hiring African American women for their Guidance and Navigation Department. Johnson was offered a job in 1953, and she immediately accepted and became part of the early NASA team.

Katherine used her skills to track and verify trajectories of manned and unmanned NASA space crafts. Her most notable calculations were that of the "Friendship Seven" Mercury spacecraft of John Glenn, in 1962, the first American to orbit the Earth. She was also instrumental in verifying the trajectory of the Apollo 11 moon landing in 1969 (Core, 2016).

16

Networks

"...No man is an island, entire of itself; every man is a piece of the continent, a part of the main; if a clod be washed away by the sea, Europe is the less, as well as if a promontory were, as well as if a manor of thy friend's or of thine own were; any man's death diminishes me, because I am involved in mankind, and therefore never send to know for whom the bell tolls; it tolls for thee. (John Donne, 1624)..."

In the first fifteen chapters, I discussed the precursors of the modern digital computer. I also touched upon the modern network in describing the historic contributions of Granville T. Woods's patent for the Synchronous Multiplex Railway Telegraph (the first commercially successful short-range induction radio telegraph) and the Grasshopper telegraph of Thomas Edison—a short-range induction radiotelegraph. Others subject pertinent to understanding the direction taken by early calculating machines were electricity, electronics, and the contributions of Nikola Tesla and George R. Stibitz.

In this chapter, I discuss the precursors of modern computer networks and the contributors to that technology Marconi, Morse, Meucci, Bell, and Thomas Edison. Another pathfinders was Charles F. Kettering who envisioned OK Charge Phone," the forerunner to the credit card. Kettering also developed the Class 1000 Register Accounting Machine for banks, the earliest Point of Sale calculating device.

Edison's name surfaces again with the introduction of the thermionic discharge the birth of electronics. His understanding of thermionic discharge, the crude vacuum tube he created to counter act the discharge, and the electron was negligible. Edison was self-taught and had little formal education in science or physics. Consequently, Edison is ignored, when contributors to the development of the vacuum tube electronics are listed.

In this chapter, I attempt to explain the nature of the communications network that has cell phone companies competing with satellite companies and cable television companies and traditional landline telephone companies. The computer network is the driving force behind information age economy. The computer and network technology anchor the fabric in the sail the economic revolution banking, education, and entertainment.

Network computing has transformed traditional brick and mortar business models from product provider to information services provider. The computer network—the Internet—expands by more than a million web pages every day. It has made financial information more important than labor or fixed assets. The Internet has made it easier for corporations to make a profit off the global market by manipulating assets and financial paper rather than satisfying domestic needs of its customers. Witness the 2008 real estate meltdown. It was easier to make a profit of differentials (a legal paper insuring real estate) than to sell real estate.

In another example, the United States customer service industry once the exclusive domain of the American workers (sometimes Canadians); is now just as likely to be outsourced overseas. It is more cost effective for United States corporations to use the networking technology Voice over Internet Protocol (VoIP) and foreign workers than hire Americans. VoIP makes it cost effective to do business in

English speaking nations overseas (Singapore, Australia, Bahamas, India, or New Zealand) because labor is cheap and the monetary exchange rate consistently favors the United States. In most, US call centers the company must provide FMLA, Workman's Compensation, health insurance, AD&D insurance, and disability insurance in addition to a salary starting at $15.00 per hour. In Singapore, there is no such thing as fair labor practices. The dollar is equal to Indian 60 Rupees.

What is VoIP? VoIP is a form of telephone communications that works over the internet. It is less expensive that traditional telephone services. Hundreds if not thousands of VoIP telephone calls can be placed over an internet connection for the price of a single broadband connection in the United States, usually $35 and $50. VoIP are similar to home Wi-Fi connections. Since its inception, VoIP, equipment, and software technology has made it possible for traditional residential and commercial telephones to receive and make VoIP without special equipment.

Other traditional brick and mortar businesses that were transformed by the advent of the Internet (computer networking) are banking and postal systems. Prior to the advent of the Internet, people paid their revolving charge accounts, mortgages, utilities, insurance premiums, and automobile loans plan via the United States Post Office. After the introduction of the electronic Bill Pay service over the Internet, it became the standard method of paying bills.

Bill Pay expanded personal banking with the addition of electronic investments into IRA accounts, brokerage accounts and other personal finances. For example, a day-trader living in New York can purchase American stocks in the markets of Hong Kong, Singapore, and Tokyo before the start of the business day in New York. That same person can watch the price of the stock rise or fall before deciding to sell or purchase more stock before the start of the business day begins in New York.

The brick and mortar stores most affected by the Internet commerce are music stores, video stores, retail store, and bookstores. Prior to the advent of the internet, music and motion pictures were distributed by one of three methods in store, over radio or at the cinema, or via record or movie clubs through the postal service. This method of doing business continued until the late 1980s and early 1990s.

Music was the first of the brick and mortar stores to feel the effect of Internet. A phenomenon known as online file sharing communities began on college and university private internets. File sharing on private intranets allowed students to acquire copies of music without purchasing the recording from a vendor such as Columbia House. Online social communities such as Audio Highway, Napster, and Kazaa followed the collegiate model of sharing music. The online communities earned their money through advertisements. As the presence of the online file sharing communities spread, many people found it much easier to obtain a bootleg copy of their favorite music rendition than purchasing a copy at the local shopping mall for $10 or $20.

File sharing communities for motion pictures emerged almost simultaneous to the music communities. The motion picture industry countered the file-sharing pirates by pressuring the Congress and the FCC for strict enforcement of copyright laws. The efforts of renowned motion picture stars as Clint Eastwood and Harrison Ford force the Congress to act swiftly. It expanded the copyright laws and made it easier to prosecute the owners of the file-sharing communities for copyright infringement and piracy. With the new laws, the government moved to shut down the free music and movie file-sharing websites.

The new laws changed forever how music and movies were sold and distributed. If an artist does not have an Internet presence, he, she, or they are not likely to succeed. In response to the new medium, Apple Incorporated created ITunes Online Music Store. ITunes is the largest music vendors in the nation. There are no brick and mortar iTunes stores to act as a central processing place only a file server. The second largest music store is Amazon followed by the brick and mortar stores BestBuy and Wal-Mart.

Similarly, Netflix created an online empire selling motion picture online. The ripple effect of Netflix success led to variation to the distribution of motion picture channel on the major premium cable channels HBO, Starz, and Showtime. Each allows the rental of motion pictures without full subscription services. The entity that has suffered the most from the modification of the movie and music industries is the United States Postal Service. Before file-sharing societies and later online music and movie stores, the postal service delivered music and movies.

Traditional brick and mortar schools have also felt the effects of the Internet. The online school, once scoffed at and considered a pariah, has become a very profitable enterprise. For profit, online schools began making billions of dollars from English speaking students living in Asia, Africa, and Europe as well as the tradition Australia, New Zealand and Great Britain. Students began to enroll in American institutions by the millions just to obtain a degree from an American school of higher education. The influx of students allowed the for profit online school to hire professors with prestigious credentials Harvard, Yale, MIT, Smith, and Stanford to compete with traditional brick and mortar institutions.

Newspapers also feel the effect of the Internet. Newspapers unable to compete with the 24-hour news cycle of the Internet began to go out of business. For example, when I was a very young man, the source of sports information about baseball came the following day from the local newspaper. As the Internet burgeoned, I accessed the box score and story of the games before going to bed. The information provided by the newspaper became stale. The internet provided online interviews of players offering their opinion for winning or losing.

People became reluctant to pay for news when they can get it free. While at work, I knew the moment Barry Bonds broke the Hank Aaron career home run record. Without looking at television or listening to a radio, I knew Charismatic failed to win the Triple Crown. If a big city newspaper wanted to survive, it had to adapt to the new information age. It needed to hire professional bloggers—in sports, entertainment, and politics—that are willing to work for a percentage of the revenue generated from advertising. In turn, the reporter/blogger will have articles, if relevant, printed in the newspaper and news wire.

In certain specialized fields, medical billing clerk, software testing, it is possible to work from home without ever meeting your employer. The Social Security Administration has rehabilitative lists of employers who offered positions to people on disability wanting to return to the work place.

The computer as an isolated entity enhanced the 19th century business model envisioned by Herman Hollerith, John H. Patterson,

William Seward Burroughs who with either the Bankers' and Merchants' Registering Accountant, Hollerith Tabulating Machine, cash register, or the Sholes typewriter. Each entity was required to use a messenger services, postal services, or the telegraph service, Western Union, to relay messages across town or across the nation. The computer linked to a network becomes a business looking for an industry.

OPTICAL TELEGRAPHS

The earliest forms of telecommunication was found in the records of the ancient people of China, Egypt, and Greece who sent messages by smoke signals during day and by beacon fires during the night. Ancient and primitive people sent messages via acoustical telegraphs in the form of drumbeats and ram's horn to extend the range of the human voice. The ancient Greek poet and historian, Polybius states the Greek military and navy use of semaphores (flags) to transmit messages ship to shore and ship to ship.

Perhaps the most famous of the pre-electric telecommunication systems involved the relay messenger. If you recall your ancient history from high school, then you are familiar with the Greek soldier Pheidippides. He collapsed and died after courageously running 26 mile to Athens to deliver the news of the Greek victory over the Persians at the Battle of Marathon. The modern Olympic Games celebrate his triumphant run with the Marathon, the last event of the summer games.

The most successful pre-electric telecommunication was the semaphore or visual telegraphs deployed by the Chappe brothers Ignace and Claude of France in 1791. During the period between the overthrow of the French monarchy and the establishment of first French Republic, Claude Chappe proposed building a visual signaling network to span the distance between Paris and Lille, France. With the approval of the French Revolutionary Legislative Assembly, the two brothers built a series of towers at least 30 feet in height with two adjustable arms (Schlager & Lauer, 2010).

Each tower was equipped with a codebook to interpret the signals created by the tower arms and a telescope directed towards to the next tower and backwards to the preceding tower. Each tower had movable arms mounted at the end of a crossbeam. Each arm of the semaphore could assume seven positions, and the horizontal beam could tilt as much as 45° clockwise or counterclockwise. In this manner, it was possible for a tower to forward as many as 196 possible codes, numbers, and letters of the alphabet. The towers sat between 5 to 10 kilometers (3 to 6 miles) apart.

The Chappe Optical Telegraph lasted for 61 years, until the French government replaced it with the electric telegraph in 1846. The Chappe Optical Telegraph largest optical telegraph ever assembled. The Chappe telegraph, first message, transmitted the French victory at Quesnay in 1794. Supposedly, the last message it transmitted the fall of Sevastopol in 1855 during the Crimean War (Dilhac, 2001).

George Murray of England developed a similar optical telegraph in 1795. The Murray's device relayed messages via shutter and light source (blinking open and closed). Combinations of open and closed shutters represented letters and numbers the tower conveyed. This system quickly became popular in England and the United States. Electric telegraph displaced visual telegraphs by the middle of the 19th century (Mokyr, November 2001).

The Electric Telegraph

Charles Wheatstone and William Cooke of Great Britain invented the first commercially practical telegraph in 1837. The Cooke-Wheatstone Telegraph (Figure 47) was a very complicated instrument. It required six wires and five magnetic needles to create messages even though six letters (C, J, Q, U, X and Z) of the alphabet were omitted. The Cooke-Wheatstone Telegraph created messages using electric current to deflect the needles on its face either left or right to convey messages (Derfler & Freed, 2002) (Hardy, 2008).

Almost simultaneous to the Cooke-Wheatstone Telegraph came the telegraph developed by Samuel F. B. Morse in the United States in 1837. The Morse Telegraph worked decidedly different from its European counterpart. For starters, the Morse telegraph was much simpler than the Cooke-Wheatstone Telegraph. Second, it required only one wire instead of six to transmit messages. Finally, it relied on a series of electric pulses rather than deflecting needles to send messages (Derfler & Freed, 2002). The simplicity of the Morse Telegraph made it the worldwide standard before the end of the century (Calvert, 2000).

Figure 47 Cooke Wheatstone Telegraph

The next major change in telegraphy occurred because of the efforts of French inventor Emile Baudot. First Baudot replace the telegrapher switch (key) with a keyboard. One result of the innovation, Morse code became a standard size five-unit or five-bit Baudot code supplanting the irregular sized dots and dashes of Morse code. Each letter and number in for example in Morse code one dot represented the letter *e*; five dashes represented the number zero. Eventually all major telegraph companies converted to Baudot code, which eliminated the need for a skilled Morse code interpreter (Derfler & Freed, 2002).

In 1901, Donald Murray modified Baudot's code. Murray's motivation came from the development of a typewriter-like keyboard he had invented. The Murray system added another bit to the Baudot code making it a six-bit code. The Murray code used a transitional step, a keyboard perforator not used by Baudot, which allowed an operator to use a paper tape, and a tape transmitter. On the receiving end of the message, a machine reciprocated the originating mechanism and printed the message or perforated paper tape for later translation. The Murray code introduced non-printing characters LF for linefeed, CR for carriage return, and NULL/BLANK for blank spaces.

Baudot's final contribution to telegraphy came seven years earlier in 1894, when he invented a distributor. The distributor allowed his printing telegraph to carry a multiplex signals. Instead of carrying one message per broadcast of code. With the innovation, the telegraph could now broadcast messages from as many as eight telegraphs simultaneously over one telegraph circuit (Britannica Concise Encyclopedia, 2006). The Baudot printing telegraph paved the way for the Teletype and Telex (Derfler & Freed, 2002) (Hardy, 2009).

History of the Telephone

The history of the telephone is not as clear-cut as the popular legend. For instance, everyone is familiar with the story of Alexander Graham Bell's race with fellow inventor Elisha Gray to the United States Patent Office. The true story of the origin of the telephone belongs to neither Gray nor Bell but to a little known Italian American inventor Antonio Meucci. Antonio Meucci invented the telephone in 1861—an invention he called the talking telegraph.

He built a working prototype connecting his two laboratories, one behind the house, one in the basement, and one in his bedroom. This odd configuration grew out of Meucci's desire to be near his ailing wife who suffered from a severe case rheumatoid arthritis that made her bedridden. The invention allowed Meucci to converse with his wife while he worked one of the laboratories. However, as her illness progressed, he chose to work on the telephone at her bedside.

Meucci made several efforts to find financial backing, but met with little enthusiasm from potential investors. In December 1871, he formed a partnership with three others to promote the telephone. They hired a lawyer to file a patent, but the partners could not muster the $250 patent application fee. Instead, the partnership filed a patent caveat that cost only $20. The primary purpose of a caveat was to prevent the issuance of a patent by rivals for the same invention. The lawyer preparing the Meucci caveat did it hastily and did not include any drawings.

The Meucci telephone partnership dissolved shortly after the filing of the caveat: one partner returned to Italy. The other partner died. Meucci renewed the caveat in December 1872, and again in 1873. He did not renew the caveat in 1874 choosing to let it expire. Less than 2 years after the caveat expired in 1874, Alexander Graham Bell filed his patent in 1876. In 2002, the Congress of the United States passed House Resolution 269 recognizing Antonio Meucci's contributions in the development of the telephone (Hardy, 2009) (IEEE Global History Network, 2009) (Library of Congress, 2009).

Radio Telegraph

Several scientists have made the claim of inventing the radio or radiotelegraph. Among them are Nikola Tesla, Alexander Popov, Sir

Oliver Lodge, Reginald Fessenden, Mahlon Loomis, Nathan Stubblefield, and James Clerk Maxwell. Maxwell put Faraday's suppositions about the electromagnetic field into written form when he published his notes and manuscripts entitled *A Treatise on Electricity and Magnetism*. Maxwell made possible for a much better understanding of the phenomena electricity and magnetism. His conclusions led to the theory that electric and magnetic energy traveled in the same transverse waves at the speed of light.

Heinrich Hertz, a German physicist, began the study of electromagnetism in 1886—as a professor at Karlsruhe Polytechnic—to affirm or reject the Maxwell theories conclusions about the attributes of the electromagnetic wave. Hertz demonstrated that electromagnetism, rather than being instantaneous, spread at a finite speed. He, also, was able to measure electromagnetic wavelength, velocity, and explained the nature of their reflection and refraction. Hertz, also, discovered the existence of the radio waves behaved in the same manner as light.

Guglielmo Marconi was able to capitalize on the efforts of Hertz, Maxwell, and Tesla when he built the first radio in 1895. The significance of wireless data transmission is readily apparent when one realizes the proliferation of WLAN (Wireless Local Area Network) and cellphone technology. For his efforts, Marconi won the Nobel Prize in physics in 1909 for the wireless telegraph and the creation of the first radio.

COMMERCIAL RADIO NETWORKS

The thermionic discharge discovery laid the foundation for the invention of a variant light bulb, the vacuum tube, and the radio. The Edison Effect proved insignificant until 1904. That is when a British scientist named John A. Fleming developed a vacuum tube, based on the "Edison effect." The Fleming vacuum tube is better known today as a diode. In turn of the century Great Britain, the diode is known as a "valve," because it forces electric current to travel exclusively in one direction in an electric circuit. Fleming's diodes were no more than modified light bulbs.

The early vacuum tubes consisted of a glass bulb with a filament and a second electrode called an anode. The filament acted as the cathode, emitting large numbers of electrons, while the anode consisted of a small metal plate mounted near the base of the bulb connected to the outside of the bulb by a thin wire. A diode regulated the flow of electric current and acts as a one-way valve turning current on or off. The Fleming vacuum tube was both receiver and transmitter in the radio.

By 1907, Lee Deforest invented the triode vacuum tube or three-element light bulb he named the Audion. With the triode, current is on, off, or any state in between. The triode is created by inserting a tiny wire grid between the cathode and the anode to form a third electrode. The primary use of the triode is as an amplifier of radio waves. Not only could the triode receive Morse code in the form of radio waves, it also received voice and music.

One of the major contributors to the birth of commercial radio broadcasting was Edwin Armstrong. Armstrong invented a regenerative circuit that sent part of the current back to the triode of the Audion. The result of the feedback strengthened the incoming signals. Armstrong could receive distant broadcasts clearly without the need of headphones.

Further experiments with regenerative circuits led Armstrong to invent the super heterodyne circuit. The super heterodyne circuit increased the feedback into the Audion tube, which produced rapid enough oscillations in the tube allowing it to act as a transmitter and a receiver. This work on regenerative circuits became the basis for the continuous wave transmitters. Continuous wave transmitters are the basis of radio and television broadcasting (Lessing, 2008). Armstrong sold his invention to major radio corporations and became a multimillionaire. Armstrong also invented the technology for FM radio.

ORIGIN OF THE LAN

A computer network is a high-speed connection for a group of computers sharing resources and information link together by cable or radio. A computer network is classified by the level of its complexity from simple to complex. As the geographic area of the LAN grows, the complexity of the network grows. Several remote LANs combine to form a metropolitan area networks or (MAN). The most complicated computer network based on geographic size is the WAN. WAN encompass a geographic area larger than a city. The most popular WAN is the Internet. The LAN serves as the basic building block for the two larger networks. A MAN connects distant LANs in a metropolitan area. A WAN does the same for distant MANs. An example of WAN is the

Colorado Public Library system. Another iteration of the WAN comes in the form of a widely dispersed national corporation, Sprint-Nextel for example. Sprint-Nextel has data centers in several American and Canadian cities.

A local area network can be as small as two computers or as large as all the computers of a college campus. A LAN covers a small geographic area ranging in size from a two computers in a home network to as large as a hundreds of computers in a public school computer lab or an accounting department of a large retail franchise. Computer networks covering a larger geographical area are metropolitan area network or MAN. Metropolitan area networks are a combination of several smaller distant LAN networks such as the LANs for each school within a metropolitan school district, the network connecting police precincts, or the computer network connecting a card catalog in a metropolitan library system.

Computer networks that cover geographical areas that are larger than a metropolitan area are WANs. The geographical footprint of a WAN can ranges from several counties in a state, to an entire state, to an entire geographic region, such as the Mountain West or the continental United States. The most famous WAN is the Internet. Examples of wide ranging WANs are AFIS an acronym for Automated Fingerprint Identification System, CODIS an acronym for the Combined DNA Index System, and ERIC an acronym for the Education Resources Information Center.

From the 1970s, forward the computer network, as we know it, was grounded at two non-competing focal points. The first efforts of the United States Defense of Department (DoD) attempts to link its super computer centers. The second focal point rested at the Xerox Palo Alto Research Center (PARC). Each organization set about designing its own standards for computer networking. Prior to 1970, computer network existed as an extension of a business entity, the American Airlines Reservation system (SABRE) for example.

The eventual merger of the Institute of Electrical and Electronics Engineers (IEEE) and the International Organization of Standards (IOS) proved a contributing factor to the standardization of networking technologies. Networking opponents could no longer circumvent the achievements of rivals.

The primary motivating factor bringing about internetwork standardization came as a request from the DoD. It commissioned the development of a network protocol software to connect the assorted computers and accessories contained at its five supercomputing centers.

The networking protocol contractors developed was Transmission Control Protocol/Internet Protocol (TCP/IP). TCP/IP accepted the data transmissions from the varying computer architectures without regard to individual proprietary schemes of manufacturers. The Defense Department's acceptance of TCP/IP led to the creation of Arpanet.

Arpanet was the predecessor to the Internet. The Department of Defense created Arpanet as a guarantee the nation has computing ability in the event of a nuclear attack. Arpanet proved more successful than anticipated. Changes began to manifest after Stanford, IBM, UCLA, UC Santa Barbara, and the University of Utah supercomputer centers began using Arpanet for non-military purposes.

Eventually, the Department of Defense withdrew from Arpanet in favor of creating a fortified computer network. The non-military use of Arpanet continued to multiply culminating with the creation of the National Science Foundation (NFSnet) network. The NSF network included the five supercomputer centers along with connections to the computer networks at every major research center and university across the nation.

In the interim, the DoD efforts to secure its new fortified network, led to the replacement of the circuit switching technology favored by the telephone company with a new technology, packet switching. The DoD believed packet switching technology superior to circuit switching First circuit switching data transmission relied on a dedicated path of leased circuits. Second, Circuit switching was vulnerable to sabotage, general wear and tear, and anonymous discovery. Third Packet switching was less expensive than circuit switching. It did not rely on expensive leased lines or hard circuits to transmit data. Data sent via packet switching technology chose the best available path to and from the aforementioned supercomputer centers. Eventually, as Arpanet grew in size, it adapted the PARC Ethernet (Carrier Sense Multiple Access/Collision Detect) CSMA/CD technology as the transmission protocol for its networks.

The role PARC played in the development of LAN connectivity and the Internet although not as expansive as the role of DoD was as conspicuous. PARC developed Ethernet. Essentially Ethernet defines the wiring and signaling standards for the Physical Layer of the Open System Interconnection (OSI) Reference Model. Ethernet uses carrier sense multiple access with collision detection (CSMA/CD) methods for data transmission to avoid corruption of data transmission.

Robert Metcalfe led the development of Ethernet in 1973 while at Xerox Palo Alto Research Center (PARC). The Ethernet on ALOHAnet inspired Metcalfe's development of the PARC Ethernet. ALOHAnet a packet-switching wireless technology developed by Norman Abramson, Frank Kuo, and Richard Binder at the University of Hawaii-Manoa. ALOHAnet included a number of communication firsts. In addition to Ethernet, it was the first wireless local area network or WLAN and the first packet switching computer network.

NETWORKING BASICS

In a previous section, *History of the LAN*, the initial scope of a computer network referred to the geographical size of a computer network. A computer network has three sizes: LAN, a MAN, or a WAN. This section discusses the attributes of the LAN from a technical viewpoint and a historical viewpoint.

The LAN is the basic building block of the computer network. The MAN and the WAN are a combination of multiple LAN. Size however is not the only way to categorize a LAN. Its administrative purpose, topography, architecture, protocol, and connection media also describe a LAN.

Implementing a computer network is not an easy task. Many challenges exist in the areas of data integrity, system reliability, network management, and scalability. Each a key element to making a network work efficiently and effectively. The integrity of the data on the network is very important. If the data on the network is unreliable, it defeats the business model. Reliability refers to the accuracy of the server to connect each client to the correct location facsimile, printer, or email. Scalability refers to expansion. A poor engineer builds a LAN that cannot be expanded.

The challenge of connecting divergent systems, to equally disparate technologies requires real study. At the local level, a LAN may have clients that have different operating systems, or use different network protocols. For example, the accounting department prefers Netware, which uses IPX/SPX. The graphics department prefers using the Macintosh computer. Apple computers at one time used its proprietary AppleTalk. It did not use TCP/IP until it made the switch to UNIX type operating systems. Members of the marketing department prefer Windows systems 3.1, which uses the archaic Windows networking protocol NetBuei.

Because a company relies heavily on data communication, its internetworks must provide very high levels of reliability and redundancy. Many large internetworks include redundancy to ensure data security and communications. To circumvent conflicting proprietary systems, engineers frame the protocols on the OSI reference model.

OPEN SYSTEMS INTERCONNECTION

The Open Systems Interconnections (OSI) Reference Model is a virtual model of information that defines the internal functions of a network communication system. It provides the ideal model of how software applications on two different computers transfer information. The OSI reference model does not exist. The International Organization for Standardization (ISO) developed the model in 1984.

The OSI Reference Model is the basic network architectural model for teaching internetworking. It is used to explain the intricacies of engineering to beginning network engineers.

The OSI Reference Model divides the task of moving information between networked computers into seven smaller, more manageable layers. Each layer is compartmentalized so that the tasks assigned to that layer implements independently. This enables the solutions offered by one layer to update without affecting the other layers. The following section describes the seven layers of the Open Systems Interconnection (OSI) Reference Model:

1. Layer 7-Application
2. Layer 6-Presentation
3. Layer 5-Session
4. Layer 4-Transport
5. Layer 3-Network
6. Layer 2-Data link
7. Layer 1-Physical

CHARACTERISTICS OF THE OSI LAYERS

As described in the previous section the OSI Reference Model is the primary teaching tool for basic network engineering. The OSI Reference Model has seven logical layers. A layer is a collection of functions that provide services to the layer above it and receives service from the layer below it. For example, a layer that provides error-free communications across a network provides the path needed by applications above it, while it calls the lower layer to send and receive packets that make up the contents of the path. The upper layers of the OSI Reference Model manage application issues and software. The highest layer, Level 1, the Application Layer, interacts with the end user. The term upper layer refers to any layer above the transport layer in the OSI Reference Model.

The lower layers of the OSI Reference Model refer to the network connections below the session layer. The lower levels manage medium and data transport. The lowest layer, the physical layer, is nearest the network medium (the network cabling or transceiver). The physical layer is responsible for placing information on the medium.

OSI REFERENCE MODEL PHYSICAL LAYER

The physical layer defines how the computer attaches to the network medium and functional specifications. The physical layer describes methods used for activating, maintaining, and deactivating the link with the network. The physical layer defines data transmission characteristics such as voltage, timing, physical data rates, maximum distances, and physical connectors. The physical layer implementations are either LAN or WAN specific.

OSI MODEL REFERENCE DATA LINK LAYER

The data link layer provides reliable transit of data across a physical network link. The data link layer defines different network and protocol characteristics, including addressing, network topology, error handling, frame sequencing, and flow control. Network topology consists of the data link layer specifications that often define how devices are connected physically, such as in a bus, star, or ring topology. Error handling notifies upper-layer protocols a transmission error occurred, and reorders transmission of frames out of sequence. Flow control manages data transmission so that the receiving device is not overwhelmed. Physical addressing (as opposed to network addressing) defines how devices are addressed at the data link layer.

The Institute of Electrical and Electronics Engineers (IEEE) divides the data link layer into two sub-layers: the Logical Link Control (LLC) and the Media Access Control (MAC).

The Logical Link Control (LLC) sub-layer of the data link layer manages communications between devices over a single link of a network. LLC is defined in the IEEE 802.2. The specification supports both connectionless and connection-oriented services. The IEEE 802.2 defines the number of fields (sections) in a data link layer frame. The division enables multiple higher-layer protocols to share a single physical data link.

The Media Access Control (MAC) sub layer of the data link layer manages protocol access the physical network medium. The IEEE MAC defines MAC addresses. The MAC is a unique identifier of network interfaces that permits communications on the physical network segment.

OSI MODEL REFERENCE LAYER

The network layer defines the network address. It differs from the MAC address in that it defines logical networks instead of a physical medium. Some network layer implementations, such as the Internet Protocol (IP), define network addresses in a way that route selection can be determined systematically by comparing the source network address with the destination network address. Because the network layer defines the logical network layout, routers can determine how to direct packets to their eventual destination.

OSI MODEL REFERENCE TRANSPORT LAYER

The transport layer receives data from the session layer and prepares it for transport across the network. The transport layer ensures data is delivered error-free and sequenced properly. The transport protocol most commonly used on the Internet is the Transmission Control Protocol (TCP) and the User Datagram Protocol (UDP).

Flow control manages data transmission between devices. It ensures the transmitting device does not overwhelm the receiving device processing ability. TCP is a connection-oriented protocol. It creates a virtual circuit to control data transference. It establishes maintains and terminates data transmissions. Another attribute of TCP is error checking. Error checking involves creating various mechanisms to detect transmission errors and initiates data recovery processes to resolve any errors that occur.

User Datagram Protocol is connectionless protocol. It does not concern itself with delivery of the data. It sends the data and disconnects.

OSI MODEL REFERENCE SESSION LAYER

The next OSI Model layer is the session layer. It connects, manages, and terminates communication sessions. Sessions layer consists of service requests and responses that occur between applications on different network devices. Examples of session-layer implementations include Zone Information Protocol (ZIP). AppleTalk is an example of ZIP protocol.

OSI MODEL REFERENCE PRESENTATION LAYER

The presentation layer provides coding and conversion of functions applied at the application layer data. The presentation layer ensures that information sent from the application layer one computer is readable by the application layer on another compute. Examples of presentation layer input include data representation formats, conversion of character representation, data compression, and data encryption.

Data representation formats permits the exchange of application data between with different operating systems. Conversion schemes exchange information between systems using a variety of text and data standards. EBCDIC and ASCII were early examples of this process. Standard data compression schemes allow compressed data at the source computer to decompress by the destination computer. Data encryption schemes allow data encrypted at the source device decrypt at the destination computer.

OSI MODEL REFERENCE APPLICATION LAYER

The application layer is the OSI layer that interacts with the end user. Examples of application layer protocols are Telnet, File Transfer Protocol (FTP), and Simple Mail Transfer Protocol (SMTP) (Palmer, 2006) (Shinder, 2002).

LAN BASICS

A proper definition of a LAN states it is a high-speed data network that covers a small geographic area and shares resources workstations, printers, servers, files, facsimile machines, and other devices. There are three basic local area network configurations: peer-to-peer, ad-hoc, and client-server networks according to administrative purposes.

In the first instance, peer-to-peer, the LAN does not have a centralized file system or server to monitor access to the network and data services. Typically, in a peer-to-peer network, each member (client) of the network assumes the responsibilities of a server and a central resource monitor. In other words, one member of the network assumes responsibility for sending facsimile messages; another assumes the responsibility for routing email, while another member of the peer-to-peer network is responsible for managing printing.

The efficiency of a peer-to-peer network depends on the presence of all network members. If one of the peers is absent the service, that particular peer provides is lost until the he or she returns. Another disadvantage of the peer-to-peer network is security. In the peer-to-peer network there is no centralized security entity monitoring network security. If one machine becomes infected with a virus, in all likelihood the same virus may infect all the computers on the peer-to-peer network.

Peer-to-peer network are more prevalent in home networks and small office networks. Peer-to-peer networks work for new companies with limited financial resources. Microsoft MSCE manual states peer-to-peer network are networks with ten or fewer computers.

Ad-hoc networks are another form of the peer-to-peer network. The computers on an ad-hoc network share resources without a system server. Unlike the aforementioned peer-to-peer network, ad-hoc networks are always a temporary aggregation of ten or fewer portable computers. Ad-hoc networks are sometimes referred to as wireless peer-to-peer networks. The ad-hoc network does not rely on a preexisting

LAN infrastructure, routers and bridges. Instead, each member of an ad-hoc network assumes the responsibility of forwarding data on the network.

The client-server based network is the business model for all large-scale LAN systems (10 computers or more). The traditional client-server system consists of four elements:

1. User interface – the user interface is where the end user communicates with computer.

2. Business logic – The basic logic of the LAN adheres to the mission of the business and applies to its financial transactions.

3. Data-access – Data access occurs as the computing system retrieves manipulates and updates the business data.

4. Data storage – Data storage is where all the records of transactions, between the business the clients are held.

Client-Server based LANs are sub-divided into two categories thin-client systems and thick-client systems. In the thin-client system, the server like the early days of computing performs the majority of the processing. The client only provided the user interface, the server performed business logic, data-access, and data storage. The earliest LAN systems used thin-client systems.

In the thick-client system, the client computer performs the majority of the data processing. The client computer manipulates the data according to the business logic. In the thick-client system, the server's primary function is to provide data access and data storage (Hardy, 2009).

HISTORY OF THE OPERATING SYSTEM

The early structure of network computing, quite naturally, was based on the centralized computing model. In the centralized computing model, all the processing power belongs to the big iron or mainframe computers. All the first and second-generation computers from the ENIAC to the IBM System 360 featured centralized computer processing. The key component of the historic computer networks are the terminal. The first remote computer terminal was established before computers became electronic. George Robert Stibitz demonstrated that punch cards and physically reconfiguring (reprogramming) the circuitry were not the only means of communication with the mainframes when he connected a teletypewriter sitting in a Dartmouth College classroom in New Hampshire to the Complex Number Calculator in sitting in a New York City office building by means of a telephone line.

The advent of the electronic computer brought about the evolution of the operating system software. Operating systems made the operation of the computer more efficient, less labor intensive and easier to access. At first glance, a discussion of operating systems seems out of place in the discussion of a LAN. However, operating systems permit the expansion of the foundations set forth by Stibitz. The early operating systems were rudimentary programs like the General Motors Batch System. (The Autoexec.bat file in Windows is an example of how a batch program works, sequentially. If you feel brave, locate Autoexec.bat and copy the contents into notepad, then close the file without making any changes to it. Each line of the file loads a procedure Windows is required to perform. In the early days of Windows before the internet, Autoexec.bat and its companion file Config.sys were the primary cause of system problems.)

The General Motors Batch System allowed for the more economical use of the mainframe computers reducing the downtime between processing jobs. As the software evolved in complexity so did the use of the computer terminal. The next step came was the invention of a more sophisticated collaborative schemes for operating systems such as time-sharing programs Compatible Time Sharing System (CTSS) and the Dartmouth Time Sharing System (DTSS). Time-sharing programs allowed multiple users to share the idle time of the mainframe processors with remote terminals. These terminals utilized the cathode ray tubes (CRT) for display of output instead of punch cards.

These were the foundations of the first local area network (LAN). In the first LANs, all the processing was performed by the mainframe, thus the term centralized. The terminals that make the requests for data perform no processing other than that of a receptacle for information transmitted by the mainframe. The computer terminals in mainframe-centralized data processing were dumb terminals. The only command they could issue besides inquiry was print.

The terminals that comprised the early American Airlines seat reservation system were dumb terminals. These terminals were issued for database inquiries with the IBM 7090, IBM System 1401, or its Honeywell clone.

Thus far, this chapter has described two of the six methods of categorizing a LAN—scope and administrative methods. It also introduced a brief history of the network operating system. The remaining sections will describe the other four methods operating system, protocols, topology, and architecture.

OPERATING SYSTEM

The easiest method of classifying a LAN is by the operating system on the primary domain controller or root server. Operating systems on the client computers can and often differ from the domain server. For example, many end-users believe that the Apple Macintosh is better suited for desktop publishing and prefer it to a Windows based computer. Microsoft accommodates the end-user wishes with services for Macintosh. In addition, Microsoft makes it possible for a UNIX client to attach to a Windows network with the client application POSIX. POSIX is built into the Windows server software. To determine the network operating system or NOS, access the server and select administrative tools, about, or system info. The operating system version and distribution will be listed. The most dominant operating system is the Microsoft Windows Operating System. Microsoft Windows claim as much as 91% of the desktops operating system worldwide and 74 % of the world's network operating systems. The first network operating system was UNIX, and that is where I will begin the discussion.

UNIX

UNIX was built in 1969. It was the brainchild of a partnership between General Electric, MIT, and Bell Laboratories. This collaboration aimed to show that a general purpose, multiuser operating system was a viable solution. This conclusion was based on the MIT research of the operating system Compatible Time Sharing System (CTSS). CTTS evolved into MULTICS (Multiplexed Information and Computing Service) which resulted in a wide range of new approaches computing. Bell Lab researchers Ken Thomson and Dennis Ritchie while working on MULTICS adapted many of the ideas developed through MULTICS and applied them to a new operating system they had developed, UNIX (Lohr, 2002).

The creation of UNIX was first of major step in the movement away from the IBM centralized method of computing. The program although inspired by MULTICS, was simpler than MULTICS and easier to use. The UNIX operating system was interactive, while MULTICS was a batch system. The basic tenets of the UNIX operating system were the notion of pipes. Pipes, in laymen's terms, allow an end-user to pass the results from one program as input for another program. This innovation in programming style led to the clustering of several small, targeted, single-function programs to achieve a more complicated goal.

UNIX became the first portable operating system when its creators Dennis Ritchie and Ken Thompson created the programming language C to modify actions of the operating system based on the computing environment and business need. The relative simplicity of the operating system's design turned UNIX into a favorite of the academic world and a fixture on many university computer networks.

The expansion in popularity of the UNIX operating system belongs to the computer science department at the University of California at Berkley. Between 1974 and the Berkley campus made several revisions to the original code and released several versions of BSD UNIX, later renamed BSD 2, 3, and 4 etc.. The different versions of BSD operating system was ported (adapted for use) on PDP 11, VAX, and Bell computers.

UNIX came to the forefront of networking when the original membership of Arpanet and DARPA, discovered that many of the computers linked together across the nation was nearing end of life usefulness. Defense Advanced Research Projects Agency (DARPA) opened discussions to resolve the crisis. Resolution discussed include all members of Arpanet use a single hardware vendor, which was impractical because of the widely varying computing needs of the research groups and the undesirability of depending on a single manufacturer. As a consequence, DARPA planners decided the best solution for the problem was through software. After much discussion, UNIX was chosen as a standard because of its proven portability. DARPA later sent TCP/IP protocols to the

The UNIX operating system consists of three parts: the kernel, the shell, and the programs. The kernel communicates with computer hardware and controls the resources available to programs by allocating processor time and memory for each process. The kernel also controls which programs shall have access to files and networks.

The shell is the interface between the end-user and the kernel. When a user logs on to the computer, the login program verifies the username and password, then starts the shell. The shell is a command line interpreter (CLI). The CLI interprets the user requests to access programs and files (Lohr, 2002).

LINUX

A discussion of Linux at this juncture of the book is historically out of place. Discussions of Linux should follow Windows. However because Linux is a based on UNIX I placed a discussion of it here to compare the two systems. As said previously, Linux is a derivative or subset of the UNIX operating system, a Unix-like operating system designed to provide personal computer users a free or very low-cost alternative to the more expensive UNIX and Windows. There are a number of different versions of Linux listed by the following names: Red Hat, Mandrake, Debian, SuSE, and Slackware. In Linux, there are a number of options in the desktop environment—including a system similar to Microsoft Windows—that allows Linux users to customize to their liking. This kind of selectivity (manipulation) is not available in the Microsoft Windows environment and it is difficult to perform in Macintosh OS X environment.

Linus Torvalds, from the University of Helsinki in Finland, created Linux in 1991. He created the operating system because he was dissatisfied with the operating systems available to him on his personal computer.

Linux provides personal computer users an operating system that is comparable and compatible with the UNIX operating systems. The Linux operating system includes a graphical user interface, an X Window System, and TCP/IP.

X Windows control Linux networking. The X Window System (X-11 or X) is the standard graphical interface for the Unix operating system, Unix-like operating systems, and OpenVMS. It is available for most other modern operating systems. The X window system was originated at MIT in 1984. The current version, X-11, was released in September 1987.

X Windows is an open operating system—that is to say; any programmer can modify it without fear of retribution. X Windows is a cross-platform, client/server system for managing a windowed graphical user interface in a distributed network (Linux Documentation Project, 2008).

NOVELL

NetWare is a network operating system developed by Novell Incorporated based on the Xerox Network Systems stack. It initially used cooperative multitasking to run various services on a personal computer, with the network protocols supporting various proprietary computing equipment. Novell, in 2003, announced it was discontinuing the Netware operating system in favor of a Netware shell on top of a SUSEX Linux operating system.

Novell Netware was once the predominant networking software claiming a market share of 70%. It was introduced in 1983 using the network protocol suite or stack IPX/SPX.

At the time of its introduction IPX/SPX, protocol stack was the most sophisticated networking on the market, more agile than NETBEUI, and more flexible than XNS.

The way IPX listed its addresses ignored TCP/IP dotted decimal addresses. IPX used a combination of the network address and the MAC address. An IPX address is an 80-bit address, represented in hexadecimal. An IPX address is comprised of two parts: the network address and a host address. An example of an IPX address is as follows: 0000000A.0101AE560163AC.

The one disadvantage that occurred with Netware was its implementation of Ethernet. In the original version, Netware implemented a non-standard version of Ethernet on the IEEE 802.3. The other manufacturers used IEEE 802.2.

WINDOWS

The first graphical interface operating system was Windows 1.0, which Microsoft released in 1985. It was a great improvement for users because it eliminated the CLI (command line interface) of DOS. Before, Windows users were required to memorize a couple of dozen DOS commands to make the computer function. Users would type the commands at the prompt similar to the following: C:\>. For instance, if the user typed the command "dir" for directory at the prompt and the computer would display all the programs on drive c. With the Windows interface, the user or operator simply clicked on a program icon and voila, a program opened. The next two versions Windows 2 and 3.1 were slightly improved.

Microsoft added networking support to Windows 3.1 in the form of Windows for Workgroups 3.11 and peer-to-peer networking. Later Microsoft added domain-networking support.

After moderate success with the networking addendum, Microsoft took aim at the Novell Corporation's dominance in computer networking. It introduced the Windows NT (New Technology) operating system, adding adaptations to allow UNIX, Netware, and Apple computers to access the NT network seamlessly.

Microsoft Windows now captures more than 90% of the market for networking software. It succeeded because it recognized the importance of the Internet as the future of computing and built its software to utilize TCP/IP as early as 1983. Consequently, in the 1990s, as other networking companies Novell and Apple were trying to adjust their native software to accept TCP/IP, Microsoft already had the solution.

TOPOGRAPHY

Topology is another method of classifying a client-server LAN. The three basic LAN topologies are bus, star, and token ring. Then there is the combination of the star and the bus, and the multiple star networks. However, the variations of the basic three networks will not be discussed here. The bus topology connects all nodes to a central bus or backbone. Most illustrations display a bus network as a straight line on a single floor for a cluster of offices. This is not always the case. A bus network could circumnavigate through the offices. The star topology connects all devices to single hub. The ring topology conceptually connects all devices to one another in a closed loop. However, in the IEEE 802.5 protocols for the Token Ring, IBM—the creator of the token ring network—connects the clients of the ring to a multi-station access unit (MSAU) in the shape of a star. A MSAU can be a hub, concentrator, bridge, switch, or router. To resolve the issues with interoperability, the International Organization for Standards (ISO) developed the Open System Interconnection (OSI) Reference Model as a guideline for telecommunications software and hardware manufacturers to create interoperable equipment and software. The OSI Reference Model is a theoretical blueprint that divides network communications into a hierarchy of logical outcomes. There are seven logical layers in the OSI model.

To insure that LANs and MANs created by differing groups of contractors, vendors, and manufacturers were compatible the IEEE created the 802.x family of networking standards. This group of standards is numbered from 802.1 through 802.22. The most commonly used of these standards for the LAN are those, which regulate the Data Link layer's two sub-layers in the OSI Reference Model. Standard IEEE 802.2, which describes the Logical Link Control sub-layers Data Link layer. The other commonly used standard is the IEEE 802.3, which describes the Media Access Control sub-layer of the Data Link layer. The IEEE 802.5 standard describes the Media Access Control sub-layer for Token Ring LAN technology was adapted from IBM (Hardy, 2009).

BUS

A bus topology is a linear LAN architecture where transmissions from one network station propagates the length of the medium and is received by all workstations on the network. A linear bus has terminators on each end of the bus to prevent degradation of the signal. Linear bus technology uses CSMA/CD technology.

Graphic diagrams of a bus topology resemble the five-yard markers of a football field. Theoretically, a bus network is just a straight line with differing nodes tapping in to gain access. However, in reality, the bus network may resemble a meandering bus route of the local mass transit company. The single cable connecting the network acts like a backbone supporting all clients, servers, and accessories without the assistance of a MSAU or repeater. The bus configuration is the simplest of the network topologies. It was originally created for ThickNet and ThinNet coaxial cable.

Figure 48 Bus Network

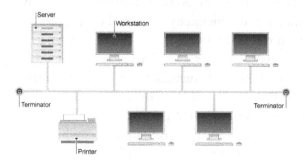

TOKEN RING

When introduced in some textbooks, the term Token Ring implied that all the computers and network resources on the LAN were connected in a continuous loop or ring. Textbooks often picture the token ring network, as a closed circle that portray is incorrect. The IBM token ring network specifications stipulate the LAN topology shall be achieved with the use of a multi-station access unit (MAUS): a hub, switch, or router. All the members of the LAN shall attach at the MAUS making the topology, in reality a star. The IEEE 802.5 does not make such stipulations but does not object to the IBM strategy.

STAR NETWORK

Figure 49 Star

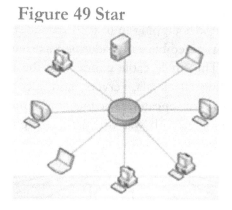

A star network is a network with its center of activity located on a networking hub a concentrator, router, bridge, or switch. Unlike the token ring network, which may use a concentrator, to make the star topology more efficient, the use of intelligent hub a switch, a router, or a bridge is required. Another difference between the Star and the Token Ring topologies is the token. The electronic token of the token ring network gives nodes on the token ring permission to transmit. The star network relies on CSMA/CD or Ethernet. The Star topology dates back to circuit switching ARPANET networks.

Star topologies are often combined with Bus and other Star networks to create complex topologies that require the use of a bridge, switch, or router to break the large network into the smaller more manageable local area networks. Star networks are cable of using unshielded twisted pair copper cables.

ARCHITECTURE

Another way to connect LAN is by architecture. LAN architecture is no more than a set of specifications that consider the physical and logical topologies, the connection media, distance limitations, and access methods. The most popular LAN architectures are Ethernet, Token Ring, ArcNet, and AppleTalk (Shinder, 2002).

ETHERNET

The term Ethernet refers to the family of local-area network protocols describing the IEEE 802.3 standard, which, also, defines the Carrier Sense Multiple Access/Collision Detection (CSMA/CD) protocol. In addition to the standards for the original Ethernet, IEEE has published standards for Ethernet on fiber optic cable and twisted-pair cable:

- 10Base5—this is the original standard Ethernet. It has a top speed of 10 megabytes per second (Mbps). The five refers to the range of the signal over thick coaxial cable 500 meters. It is no longer popular because of the availability of faster Ethernets

- 10BaseT—Ethernet refers to the speed 10 Mbps of Ethernet over twisted pair cable.

- Fast Ethernet—refers to Ethernet software that can support 100 Mbps LAN traffic.

- Gigabit Ethernet—refers to Ethernet on fiber optic cables usually at 1000 Mbps (Hardy, 2009).

There have been two sets of Ethernet standards over the years. The first standard is the original Ethernet protocol, developed by the consortium of Digital Equipment Corporation, Intel, and Xerox. This version of Ethernet became known as DIX Ethernet. The DIX Ethernet standard was first published in 1980 and defined a LAN running at 10 Mbps using RG-8 coaxial cable in a bus topology. This standard is also called thick Ethernet, ThickNet, or 10Base5. The DIX Ethernet II standard, published in 1982, added a second physical layer option to the protocol using RG-58 coaxial cable. This standard is called thin Ethernet, ThinNet, or 10Base2.

In 1980, the IEEE Ethernet group began work on the publication of an IEEE 802.3 standard for Ethernet-like networks. They called the 802.3 standard Ethernet-like because Xerox had trademarked the name Ethernet. However, in 1985, IEEE published the 802.3 Carrier Sense Multiple Access with Collision Detection (CSMA/CD) access method and Physical Layer Specifications. These two documents included specifications for networks using the DIX coaxial cable consortium options. In addition, IEEE added specifications for unshielded twisted pair (UTP) cable options for Ethernet-like networks known as 10Base-T. Additional documents published by the IEEE 802.3 in later years included IEEE 802.3u in 1995, which defines the 100-Mbps Fast Ethernet specifications, and IEEE 802.3z and IEEE 802.3ab, which are the 1000-Mbps Gigabit Ethernet standards (Zacker, 2001).

TOKEN RING

IBM invented the Token Ring LAN technology in the 1970s. It is the second most popular LAN architecture for businesses. The IEEE 802.5 for specification token ring is almost identical to and completely compatible with the IBM token ring network. Coincidently, the IEEE 802.5 specifications were modeled after the IBM token ring, and it continues to shadow IBM's token ring development.

Unlike Ethernet that was originally designed for coax cables, token ring technology was designed for unshielded twisted pairs (UTP).

Top transmission speed of the original token ring technology was four Mbps, which eventually grew to 16 Mbps as the technology improved.

Token ring technology is not deterministic; it does not employ collision detection software found in Ethernet systems. Instead, token ring technology moves a small frame, called a token, around the LAN.

Token Ring and IEEE 802.5 support two basic frame types: tokens and data/command frames. Tokens are 3 bytes in length that consist of a start delimiter which signals the arrival of the token, an access control byte which follows the start delimiter and signals the node it can access the network, and an end delimiter which in summary terminates access to the network and passes the token to the next member.

Possession of the token grants the right to transmit made available periodically to each client of the LAN. The client computer with the token has the privilege to transmit data on the LAN. Clients without the electronic token must wait until it has possession of the token to access network resources. Once the data exchange is complete, the token is passed to the next client in the ring.

Figure 50 Virtual Token Ring

ARCNET

The Datapoint Corporation developed the Attached Resource Computer Network technology (ArcNet) in 1977. An ArcNet is configured either as a star-bus topology or as a bus topology. The specifications for ArcNet are loosely defined in the IEEE 802.4 publication.

The original ArcNet transmission speed was 2.5 Mbps. Improvements to ArcNet called ArcNet-Plus increased data transmission rates up to 20 Mbps. Like Token Ring, ArcNet uses a token-passing method to access network resources and to send data. The token moves from one computer to the next according to the order in which they are connected to the hub, regardless of their physical location. This means that the token moves from computer 1 to computer 2 in that order, even if computer 1 is at the north end of the building and computer 2 is at south end (Microsoft Corporation, 1999).

LOCAL TALK

The AppleTalk is the network architecture developed for the Apple Macintosh. AppleTalk supports three network protocols: Ethernet, Token Ring, and LocalTalk.

LocalTalk by tradition is configured with star topology. It uses shielded twisted pairs (STP) cabling to connect the members of the network. LocalTalk differs from Ethernet in that it uses CSMA/CA rather than CSMA/CD.

The Apple Computer Corporation announced AppleTalk in 1983 as its proprietary network. The built-in networking functions of the Macintosh made managing an AppleTalk network easy. AppleTalk networks have a hierarchical order. There are four basic components to an AppleTalk network: sockets, nodes, networks, and zones.

1. A *socket* An AppleTalk socket is similar to the concept of ports in TCP/IP.

2. An *AppleTalk node* a uniquely identified host on the network includes Macintosh computers, printers, Windows PCs, and routers.

3. An AppleTalk network consists of a single logical cable and multiple attached nodes. The logical cable is either a single physical cable or multiple physical cables attached to bridges or routers. AppleTalk sub-networks are divided into two categories non-extended and extended.

    a. Non-extended networks can have as many as 254 nodes. However, a non-extended network has only a single network number.

    b. An extended network is a group of non-extended networks on the same physical data link, and contains a range of network numbers

4. An AppleTalk zone is similar in concept to a v VLANs; it is used to control broadcast traffic by dividing internetworks into logical groups.

The Apple Computer Corporation abandoned AppleTalk in favor of TCP/IP in 2009.

PROTOCOLS

Network protocols are a set of specifications by which computers are told to communicate. Protocols often come in protocol suites or stacks, which contain multiple rules for communications between like and unlike operating systems and computers. Network protocols are either connection-oriented or connectionless-oriented protocols.

Connection-oriented protocols establish a connection or form a virtual network before transmitting data. When the transfer of data is completed, it disconnects. TCP is an example of a connection-oriented protocol.

A connectionless protocol does not create a virtual circuit before it transmits its data. An example of a connectionless protocol is the User Datagram Protocol (UDP). Listed below are the most widely used protocol suites. TCP/IP has a separate chapter and is not discussed in depth in this chapter.

NETBUEI

IBM developed NetBEUI for small work groups. Since Microsoft was IBM's partner, NetBEUI was automatically installed on Microsoft servers and client software. NetBEUI is not a routable operating system like TCP/IP or IPX/SPX. NetBEUI was appropriate for work groups and peer-to-peer networks.

IPX/SPX

IPX/SPX was the basis for Novell Netware networking protocol suite for until Novell abandoned it for the Linux NOS incorporating TCP/IP. IPX/SPX was ideal for the DOS based operating systems, however it lost favor as first Apple, then Microsoft preferred the GUI interface for their computer operating systems. The biggest shortcoming of IPX/SPX was its incompatibility with TCP/IP and the internet. IPX/SPX is an excellent NOS for home and small office and peer-to-peer networks. IPX/SPX is automatically installed on Windows NOS clients and servers to accommodate servers and clients using Netware software.

TCP/IP

TCP/IP (Transmission Control Protocol/Internet Protocol) is the basic communication language or protocol of the Internet. It can also be used as a communications protocol in a private network (either an intranet or an extranet). When you are set up with direct access to the Internet, your computer is provided with a copy of the TCP/IP program just as every other computer that you may send messages to or get information from also has a copy of TCP/IP.

TCP/IP is a two-layer program. The higher layer, Transmission Control Protocol, manages the assembling of a message or file into smaller packets that are transmitted over the Internet and received by a TCP layer that reassembles the packets into the original message. The lower layer, Internet Protocol, handles the address part of each packet so that it gets to the right destination. Each gateway computer on the network checks this address to see where to forward the message. Even though some packets from the same message are routed independently from others, they will be reassembled in proper sequence at the destination.

17

Network Cables

L ocal area networks are connected by a sundry of wired media The three most popular are discussed in this text:

1. Coaxial Cable
2. Twisted Pairs
3. Fiber Optic

Over the next few pages, I will attempt to enlighten you on the cabling options available to build a LAN.

COAXIAL CABLE:

Figure 51 Coaxial Cable

Coaxial cable comes in two versions ThickNet and ThinNet. Coaxial cable or coax was at one time the most widely used cabling media. Coaxial cable in its simplest form, consist of a core made of solid copper surrounded by insulation and a braided metal shield.

ThickNet is first, it is relatively rigid with a diameter of roughly half an inch. It is referred to as Standard Ethernet. ThickNet coaxial cabling has a single copper conductor at its center. A plastic layer provides insulation between the center conductor and a braided metal shield. The metal shield helps to block any outside interference.

Although coaxial cabling is difficult to install, it is very durable and highly suitable for LAN connections. In addition, it can carry signals—uncorrupted—a greater distance between devices than twisted pair cable. The maximum range a signal can travel on ThickNet before signal deterioration is 1640 or 500 meters. The maximum transmission rate of ThickNet is 10 Mbps.

Chart 1	
ThickNet Coaxial Cable Characteristics	
Bandwidth	10 Mbps
Maximum Cable length	1640 ft.
Connectors	BNC
Diameter	.0.5

Thin coaxial cable is often referred to as ThinNet or CheaperNet. Thin coaxial cable resembles television coaxial cable, but differs in that coax is manufactured more precisely. Network administrators refer to ThinNet as 10Base2 because it has bandwidth of 10 Mbps for approximately two hundred meters. Thin coaxial cable was popular in school networks and e linear bus networks.

Chart 2	
ThinNet Coaxial Cable Characteristics	
Bandwidth	10 Mbps
Maximum Cable length	607 feet
Connectors	BNC
Diameter	.0.25

TWISTED PAIRS

Twisted pair wiring refers to shielded twisted pairs (STP) wires and unshielded twisted pair wires (UTP). An unshielded twisted pair is the most popular and is generally the best option for school networks.

Twisted pair wire has seven categories; the quality of UTP may vary from telephone-grade wire to cables with high-speed capabilities. The cable has four pairs of wires inside the jacket. Each category of twisted pair wires has a different number of twists per inch to improve quality of data transmission. UTP transmission speeds increase with the number of twists per inch, the tighter the twists, the higher the baud rate, the higher the cost per foot (See Chart 3). The EIA/TIA (Electronic Industry Association/Telecommunication Industry Association) has established the standards for the seven categories of UTP. The standard connector for unshielded twisted pairs is the RJ-45 connector, which looks remarkably like telephone jack, only larger.

Chart 3 Unshielded Twisted Pair Categories

Category	Bandwidth	Use
1	1 Mbps	Voice Only (Telephone Wire)
2	4 Mbps	LocalTalk & Telephone (Rarely used)
3	16 Mbps	10BaseT Ethernet
4	20 Mbps	Token Ring (Rarely used)
5	100 Mbps (2 pair)	100BaseT Ethernet
	1000 Mbps (4 pair)	Gigabit Ethernet
5e	1,000 Mbps	Gigabit Ethernet
6	10,000 Mbps	Gigabit Ethernet

FIBER OPTICS

Fiber optic cabling consists of one or more glass or plastic cores surrounded by several layers of protective materials. Fiber optic cabling transmits light (photons) rather than electronic signals (electrons) eliminating the problem of electrical interference. This makes it an ideal medium for environments containing large amounts of electromagnetic radiation. This capability has also made it the standard for connecting networks between buildings, due to its immunity to the effects of moisture and lighting.

Fiber optic cable has the ability to transmit signals over much longer distances than either coaxial cable or twisted pair cable with less impendence. It also has the capability to carry information at vastly greater speeds. This capacity broadens communication possibilities to include services such as video conferencing and interactive services. The cost of fiber optic cabling is comparable to that of copper cabling; however, it is more difficult to install and modify. 10BaseF refers to the specifications for fiber optic cable carrying Ethernet signals.

Figure 53 Unshielded Twisted Pairs

Figure 52 Fiber Optic Cable

18

Network Equipment

The components that direct the data through the cabling to the correct computer or LAN resource is the focus of this chapter. Networking equipment includes routers, bridges, switches, brouters, servers, clients or workstations, network interface cards, and repeaters.

A network interface card (NIC) is a specialized circuit board that allows a computer to connect to a LAN. Back in the day, before manufacturers started placing the circuitry for a NIC inside the motherboard, NIC cards came in three flavors micro-channel, ISA, EISA, and PCI. Micro Channel Architecture (MCA) was a bus design used by IBM for its PS/2 family of computers. MCA was not compatible with ISA, and the availability of MCA peripherals was limited when the PS/2 family was first introduced. MCA cards were very expensive and eventually abandoned by IBM (Habraken, 2003).

IBM adapted Industry Standard Architecture (ISA) for use in its IBM-PC and IBM-XT computers in the early 1980s. ISA supported all 8-bit expansion devices. ISA was upgraded to 16-bits in 1984. However, as technology advanced ISA was abandoned, it lost popularity as preferences for the Peripheral Component Interconnect (PCI) bus gained popularity. PCI bus introduced in 1993, it was a 32-bit expansion card. PCI popularity grew as the microprocessor improved from the 286 to the 386 to the 486, etc. Version 2.1 of the PCI bus supported 64-bit bus expansion, which coincides with the Core 2 processors word size.

Despite the advances of PCI, EISA (Enhanced Industry Standard Architecture) ISA expanded to 16-bit and 32-bit channels in the late 1980s to retain lost patronage. The initial use for ISA bus, sound cards, and NIC are obsolete, because most manufacturers auxiliary basics in the motherboard of microprocessor. The slots in the rear of most personal computers are for the most part PCI expansion ports.

Laptop computers once used a NIC device the size of a credit card. The official name for them was Personal Computer Memory Cards International Association (PCMIA). These devices fit into the side of the laptop or notebook computer. Laptops like their desktop counterparts have LAN connectivity, modems, and sound cards as part of the motherboard making PCMIA cards obsolete (Shinder, 2002).

BRIDGE

A bridge is a LAN hardware device, which separates or partitions large LANs into smaller more manageable segments. Alternatively, one could use inverse logic and declare a bridge joins two smaller LAN segments into one larger LAN. The bridge operates in principal on the Data Link Layer of the OSI Reference Model of computer networking. When a packet is sent from a workstation, the LAN Bridge checks the source and destination address (MAC address) and forwards the packet accordingly. The MAC is a unique identifier assigned to network interfaces for communications on the physical network segment. The Media Access Control sub-layer of the Data Link Layer controls the MAC address.

SWITCH

A switch is another LAN hardware device that filters network traffic and forwards data. A switch uses one of two schemes to forward data on a LAN:

a. Cut-through – Cut-through switching is an asynchronous method of forwarding data where the switch starts sending the packet to its destination, in no particular order, as soon as the destination address is process before receiving the entire packet.

   b. Stored-and-forward switching – In this method of forwarding messages the switch waits until it receives the entire packet from the sender before sending it to the destination.

The switch operates at one of three OSI Model layers: Layer 2, Layer 3, or Layer 4.

   a. Layer 2 switching – Layer 2 switches operate in the same manner as a hub. There is a difference however. A hub is the classical sense is dumb. It forwards packets to all connected nodes. A switch, on the other hand, is an intelligent device that reads the packet destination address and sends the message to the port connected to the matching node address.

   b. Layer 3 switching – Layer 3 switches behave like routers with the added ability to use Layer 2 addresses to forward packets. Layer 3 switches are used because they are less expensive than routers.

   c. Layer 4 switching – Layer 4 switches have the ability to manage load control and balance bandwidth allocation to maintain QoS. A layer 4 router has the enhancements that allow them to use information from TCP and UDP headers to forward data on the LAN. Layer 4 switches are often built into high-end routers.

ROUTER

A router is a network hardware device that operates at the Network Layer in the OSI Reference Model of computer networking. Routers connect separate LANs. Because of this ability, a router is sometimes referred to as a gateway or a firewall. Routers are similar to bridges in that each filters the traffic on a LAN. The router filters traffic on the LAN using the logical address of IP or IPX instead of the MAC address used by the bridge.

BROUTER

A brouter is a hybrid device that is combines the functions of a router and a bridge. A brouter works best in a non-routable network such as NETBEUI.

APPLICATION GATEWAYS

An application gateway is a hardware/software system for connecting two networks together, in order to serve as an interface between different network protocols.

When a remote user contacts the gateway, it examines his/her request; if that request corresponds to the rules that the network administrator has set, the gateway creates a link between the two networks. The information, therefore, is not directly transmitted; rather, it is translated in order to ensure continuity between the two protocols.

Besides an interface between two different kinds of networks, this system offers additional security, as all information is carefully inspected (which may cause a delay) and is sometimes recorded in an event log.

The major drawback of this system is that there must be an application of this kind available for each service (FTP, HTTP, Telnet, etc.).

HUB

A hub is an element of hardware for centralizing network traffic coming from multiple hosts, and to propagate the signal. The hub has a certain number of ports (it has enough ports to link machines to one another, usually 4, 8, 16 or 32). Its only goal is to recover binary data coming into a port and send it to all the other ports. As with a repeater, a hub operates on layer 1 of the OSI model, which is why it is sometimes called a multiport repeater.

- Active hubs: are connected to an electrical power source and are used to refresh the signal being sent to its ports.
- Passive ports: They simply send the signal to all the connected hosts, without amplifying it.

REPEATER

On a transmission line, the signal suffers from distortion, and becomes weaker as the distance is between the two active elements becomes longer. Two local area network nodes are usually no further than a few hundred meters apart; this is why additional equipment is needed to place nodes beyond that distance.

A repeater is a simple device for refreshing a signal between two network nodes, in order to extend the range of a network. The repeater works only on the physical layer (layer 1 of the OSI model), meaning that it only acts on the binary information travelling on the transmission line and cannot interpret the packets.

MSAU

A multistation access unit (MSAU) is a hub, switch, bridge, router, or concentrator. It connects a group of computers or nodes to a token ring, or star local area networks. MSAU are not used on bus networks unless it covers multiple buildings.

ROUTING PROTOCOLS

The program, which guides the hardware in sending the data over the internet, is called a routing protocol. There are three kinds of routing protocols Distance Vector, Link State, and Hybrid. The distance vector protocols measure the distance between sender and receiver by measuring the hops. The Link State routing protocol uses several values such as bandwidth, latency, reliability, and load to route messages. As the name implies, the Hybrid routing protocols incorporates portions of both the Link State protocol and the Distance Vector routing protocol.

RIP

The oldest routing protocol is the Routing Information Protocol (RIP). RIP has been around since in some algorithmic version 1957. RIP is based on a set of algorithms that uses distance vectors to mathematically compare routes and identify the best path to a given destination. RIP is widely used for routing traffic in the global Internet and is an interior gateway protocol (IGP), which means that it performs routing within a single network.

Despite its long standing with network managers, RIP does have shortcomings. For instance, the maximum number of hops RIP can manage is 15. A second drawback of RIP is that it does not read subnets or subnet masks well. This limitation forced network engineers and administrators to make all subnets uniform.

RIP VERSION II

RIP version II was developed in 1993. It was developed to satisfy the limitations of the original version of RIP. It included the ability to read subnet information, and support Classless Inter-Domain Routing (CIDR).

IGRP

Interior Gateway Routing Protocol (IGRP) is a distance vector Interior Gateway Protocol (IGP) developed by Cisco Systems in the 1980s. Cisco's goal in creating IGRP was to provide a sturdy protocol for routing within a network. This was due in part to the limitations presented by RIP. Cisco original implementation of IGRP worked on Internet Protocol (IP) networks.

Later, Cisco Systems ported IGRP to run in OSI Connectionless-Network Protocol (CLNP) networks. Because of it progressive insight, Cisco recognized the durability of RIP and was careful to include the RIP standards and not create a schism between competing standards within the industry. Cisco through IGRP exceeded the RIP protocol standards by adding several a composite metric that is calculate routes by factoring weighted mathematical values for internetwork delay, bandwidth, reliability, and load.

EIGRP

Enhanced Interior Gateway Routing Protocol was implemented because of the limitations of IGRP. Like RIP, IGRP did not support variable-length subnet masks (VLSM). Instead of creating a version 2 of their product, Cisco Systems created EIGRP.

OSPF

Open Shortest Path First (OSPF) is a routing protocol developed for Internet Protocol (IP) by networks working group of the Internet Engineering Task Force (IETF). OSPF was developed from the research efforts of Bolt, Beranek, and Newman's (BBN's) SPF algorithm developed for the ARPANET, in 1978. It is an interior gateway protocol. This incarnation of SPF was developed to address the inefficiencies of RIP in 1989.

OSPF has two primary characteristics. The first is that it is open, which means that its specification are not proprietary but in the public domain. The OSPF specification was published as Request for Comments (RFC) 1247. The second principal characteristic was that OSPF was based on the SPF algorithm.

OPSF is a link state protocol. That is to say, it calls for the sending of link-state advertisements (LSAs) to all other routers within the same network. Information on attached interfaces, metrics used, and other variables are included in the link state advertisements.

The fundamental idea of OSPF is based on the data structure, the link-state database (LSDB). Each router within a LAN maintains a copy of this database, which contains information in the form of a directed graph that describes the current state of the LAN. Each link to a router or LAN (WAN, MAN) is represented by an entry in the database, and each has an associated overhead (or metric). The metric may include many different aspects of route performance, not just a simple hop common to RIP.

The shortest path first routing algorithm is the basis for OSPF functions. When an OSPF router is powered up, it initializes the routing-protocol data structures and waits for notifications from lower-layer protocols that its interfaces are functional. After the router receives notification that its interfaces are functional, it acquires neighbors, which are routers with interfaces on the network.

Examples of link-state routing protocols are listed below:

- Open Shortest Path First (OSPF) for IP
- The ISO's Intermediate System-to-Intermediate System (IS-IS) for CLNS and IP
- DEC's DNA Phase V
- Novell's NetWare Link Services Protocol (NLSP)

HYBRIDS

Hybrid Routing, commonly referred to as balanced-hybrid routing, is a combination of distance-vector routing, which works by sharing its knowledge of the entire network with its neighbors and link-state routing which works by having the routers tell every router on the network about its closest neighbors. EIGRP is an example of a hybrid routing protocol.

RADIA PERLMAN

Radia Perlman is one of the finest computer scientists in the world. She is a renowned computer engineer who specializes in computer networking. Ms. Perlman became prominent in the computing industry with a 1988 Ph.D. thesis while matriculating at MIT entitled *"Routing with Byzantine Robustness."* The paper produced networking theory that was ahead of the rest of the computing networking industry. The theory guaranteed that data communications was possible as long as at least one non-faulty path existed on the network (IEEE Global History Network, 2012).

She is the inventor of the Spanning Tree algorithm used by bridges, and the mechanisms that make modern link state protocols more efficient and robust. All told, Ms. Perlman holds patents on over 70 inventions and has several dozen more patents pending. Ms. Perlman has contributed to network security, credentials download, password protocols, analysis, and redesign of IPsec's IKE protocols, and PKI models. Her Ph.D. revelations have earned her the moniker of "Mother of the Internet."

SPANNING TREE ALGORITHM

The Spanning Tree Algorithm (STP) is a specialized computer networking protocol. STP is a Layer 2 (OSI Reference Model) that provides path redundancy while preventing loops in the network. For a Layer 2 Ethernet network functions. In the Spanning Tree Algorithm, only one active path can exist between any two stations. Spanning-tree operations are transparent to end stations, which cannot determine whether they are connected to a single LAN segment or to a switched LAN with multiple segments.

When a fault-tolerant internetwork is created, it must have loop-free paths between all nodes on the network. The spanning-tree algorithm calculates the best path throughout a switched network. Switches send and receive spanning-tree frames, known as bridge protocol data units (BPDUs), at regular intervals. The switches do not forward BPDU frames and uses the frames to create a loop-free path.

Multiple active paths between end stations create loops in the network. If a loop exists on the network, end stations may receive duplicate messages. When switches learn end-station, MAC addresses on multiple Layer 2 interfaces. It is one of the conditions to create an unstable network.

A Spanning Tree Algorithm defines a tree with a root switch and a loop-free path from the root to all switches on the network and standby paths. Spanning tree forces redundant data paths into a standby (blocked) state. If a network segment in the spanning tree fails and creates a redundant path, the spanning-tree algorithm recalculates the network topology and activates a standby path.

19

Wireless Networking

The IEEE classifies four categories of wireless networks: Wireless Personal Area Network (WPAN), Wireless Local Area Network (WLAN), Wireless Wide Area Networks (WWAN), and Satellite networks.

The IEEE 802.15 describes WPAN standards. The WPAN is a wireless computer network that connects handheld devices, mobile phones, and mobile computers around an individual. The average range of a WPAN is approximately ten meters. WPAN use either Infrared or Bluetooth technology. Bluetooth uses Frequency Hopping Spread Spectrum (FHSS) within the 2.4 to 2.4835 GHz frequency range. Bluetooth technology also uses Time Division Duplexing (TDD). Transmission speeds for Blue are between 57.6 Kbps and 721 Kbps. Infrared uses Diffused infrared technology. It has a bandwidth of two Mbps with a transmission range of nine meters. The IEEE 802.11R describes Infrared LAN standards. Infrared technology is not popular because strong sunlight can interfere with the signal.

WLAN

Historically WLAN systems have acted as adjuncts to wired local area networks (Ohrtman & Roeder, 2003). WLAN networks have frequency of either 2.4 Gigahertz or 5 Gigahertz depending on the standard and technology. Two standards 802.11a and 802.11g operate the higher 5-GHz with a bandwidth of 54-Megabytes per second, while 802.11b uses the lower frequency and lower bandwidth of 11 Mbps.

802.11 STANDARDS

WLAN network protocols based on the OSI Reference Model differ from wired LANs at the Data Link Layer and the Physical Layer. At the Physical Layer, instead of wire, WLAN communications occurs at the unlicensed 2.4-GHz radio communications frequency, the unlicensed industrial, scientific, and medical (ISM) designated bands (Mallick, 2003)—802.11a being the exception occurring at the 5-GHz frequency.

Before starting the discussion of Wireless Fidelity, I will explain IEEE 802.11n. IEEE 802.11n was created in 2009 to correct flaws in the previous standards. Its acronym is 802.11n. 802.11n is a wireless networking standard stipulates the use of multiple antennas to speed data rates. It is an amendment to the 802.11a and g. Its purpose is to improve network throughput of the previous standards—802.11a and 802.11g.

IEEE 802.3 CSMA/CD defines connectivity, Ethernet, for the wired LAN for its Ethernet or by IEEE 802.5 Token Ring whilst the IEEE 802.11 defines Ethernet WLAN is technology. The original 802.11 IEEE document also defined Ethernet. Wireless Ethernet Compatibility Alliance (WECA) defines wireless Ethernet technology. Wireless Ethernet is better known as Wi-Fi or Wireless Fidelity. It employs the CSMA/CA method of access instead of the CSMA/CD.

The 802.11 MAC specifications for Carrier Sense Multiple Access with Collision Avoidance (CSMA/CA) protocol describe WLAN access. If you recall with CSMA/CD, wired Ethernet networks had no methods to prevent two workstation from broadcasting on the network simultaneously, if a packet collision was detected both nodes stopped broadcasting its message.

Wireless Ethernet CSMA/CD cannot be used because of price constraints and distance between access points and computers transmitting. Therefore wireless Ethernet is based on the CSMA/CA protocol, which observes when a node receives a packet to be transmitted, it first listens to ensure no other node is transmitting. If the channel is clear, the node transmits the packet. Otherwise, it chooses a random "back-off number" which determines the amount of time the node waits before it will attempt to transmit the packet again. (When the channel is busy, it does not decrement its back-off number.). If the channel is idle, the transmitting node with shortest back-off time gets priority to broadcast. The Receiver Signal Strength Indicator (RSSI) constantly monitors the node transmission frequency.

There are three standard implementation options, Infrared technology (IrDA), Direct Sequence Spread Spectrum (DSSS), and Frequency Hopping Spread Spectrum (FHSS) with a shared data rate of 2 Megabytes per second (Mbps) at 2.4-GHz (Coyle, 2001).

SPREAD SPECTRUM

The United States Navy developed Spread Spectrum radio techniques during World War II as method to overcome enemy radar jamming on torpedo guidance systems. The essentials of Spread Spectrum technology is as follows: the radio signals, in spread spectrum broadcasting, from sender to receiver, hops from one frequency to another frequency to avoid jamming.

The signals of WLAN broadcast have the same intent as their WWII counterparts. Only instead of guidance instruction to ordinance, it sends data for computer consumption. The signal is superimposed over ever-modulating radio carrier waves, to insure secure radio transmission. Several types of spread spectrum techniques are available. The most prevalent techniques are Direct-sequence Spread Spectrum (DSSS) and Frequency Hopping Spread Spectrum (FHSS) (Mallick, 2003). According to Cisco Systems, there are over 400 wireless communications features. To elaborate all 400 is not the purpose of this book.

A Direct-Sequence Spread Spectrum radio technique spreads a signal across a broadband (several) of radio frequencies simultaneously. A signal at the transmission point data is combined with a higher data-rate sequence—known as a chipping code—which in turn divides the data according to a spreading ratio. The redundancy of the chipping code allows the signal to resist interference and enables the original transmission to be recovered if data is damaged. In 1999, DSSS speed was one (Mbps).

Frequency-Hopping Spread Spectrum (FHSS) transmits data over a narrowband that cycle through the frequencies. The sender and the receiver know the frequency pattern used. The idea is to insure transmission recovery in the event one frequency is block. Top throw put for FHSS is two Mbps. The IEEE addendum 80211b specifies the bandwidth at 11 Mbps. The IEEE addendum 802.11a for ISM broadcast at the 5-GHz increased speed to 54 Mbps (Mallick, 2003).

HEDY LAMARR

The Spread Spectrum radio techniques are the invention of Austrian born Hollywood movie actor Hedy Lamarr. Lamarr once known as the world's most beautiful woman, with the help of composer George Antheil invented the technology. Spread spectrum was communication system created to help the allies defeat the Nazis during World War II. The invention, was patented in 1941, manipulated radio frequencies between sender and receiver. Lamarr developed data transmission method allowed top-secret messages to be sent without interception or jamming. The technology called spread spectrum, now takes on many forms especially in cell phone technology. The spread spectrum technology in use today is directly or indirectly based on the Hedy Lamarr-George Antheil invention.

The idea that Hedy Lamarr conceived of was also a radio control mechanism for torpedoes. This idea of radio-guided torpedoes was not an original in and of itself. The idea of using a frequency hopping radio signals to control the torpedo and avoid jamming was new and never tried before. In fact, it was not until the Cuban Missile Crisis of 1962 that the United States Navy implemented the process. The major drawback to previous attempts at radio-guided torpedoes was a reliable transmission method. Antheil's contribution to the patent was proposing the concept by which the synchronization of frequencies could be achieved. The method he came up with was to use perforated paper rolls similar to those found in player pianos.

INFRARED TECHNOLOGY

Infrared (IrDA) LAN technology uses part of the electromagnetic spectrum just below visible light as a transmission medium. For that reason, IrDA wavelengths possess the same advantages and disadvantages as visible light. Infrared light travels in straight lines; an IrDA receiver not in the line of sight of an IrDA transmitter will not hear (receive) the signal. IrDA signals cannot turn corners, do not bleed into other venues, nor can they penetrate opaque (paper or cardboard) or physical obstructions. Plain glass, sunlight, and shadows greatly affect the effectiveness of an IrDA transmission. On the other hand, IrDA technology is more secure than other LAN technologies. However, because of its drawbacks IrDA technologies are not widely used for WLANs (Bing, 2000). IrDA technology is divided into two categories Directed IrDA or Directed Beam IrDA and Diffused IrDA or Diffused Beam IrDA.

DIRECTED IRDA

In Directed Beam IrDA LAN, transmitters are aimed at each other to achieve a line of site connectivity. The transmitters utilize a narrow IrDA beam. The majority of directed beam IrDA LANs provide connectivity in Token Ring, ArcNet, or Ethernet. Directed Beam IrDA technology is applied to laser beam LANs. The data rate for IrDA technology varies from one to 155 Mbps with a maximum range from one to five kilometers. The data transmission speed for a typical IrDA LAN was between 9600 bps to 4Mbps.

High performances IrDA LANs are primarily used only to augment wired networks. Directed Beam IrDA is not an ideal technology for mobile nodes, because the line-of-sight alignment requirement between the receiver and transmitter (Bing, 2000).

DIFFUSED IRDA

Diffused Beam IrDA LAN systems do not require line-of-sight connectivity. Diffused Beam IrDA transceivers flood the room with reflected infrared light. The IrDA signals bounces off the walls, floors, and ceiling filling the coverage area with infrared energy. A simple description of a typical infrastructure IrDA LAN has the WLAN access points housed in the ceiling and the transceiver (antenna) pointed toward the upward. The advantage of this approach is that an access point can communicate to multiple transceivers without degradation of signal. The disadvantages to this method of data transference are reduced speeds. The maximum range for diffused LAN connectivity is 10 to 20 meters. The maximum data rate for a diffuse LAN is four Mbps. It is not a technology for outdoors (Bing, 2000).

BLUETOOTH

The IEEE 802.15 defines MAC and PHY specifications for a wireless technology that connects devices fixed or portable coexisting with the specifications of IEEE 802.11 at 2.4-GHz. The 802.15 specifications are bases for Bluetooth and the based upon Bluetooth much like the standards for IEEE 802.5 Token Ring coexist with the parameters for ArcNet. More specifically this standardization was developed, because of the existence of Bluetooth technology automatic discovery of devices at short-range (Mallick, 2003).

Bluetooth is another radio technology that operates in the 2.4-GHz frequency ranges specified by the IEEE for 802.11. Bluetooth maximum operates at a range of 10 meters or less. Its optimal throughput is approximately 720-kilobytes per second (Kbps)

Bluetooth is a wireless technology that takes its name from the Viking warrior Harald Bluetooth who unified Denmark and Norway. Like the legendary Bluetooth, Bluetooth technology brings together the varying technologies of the cell phone, Wi-Fi computers, PDAs, printers, and other devices to form a single close-range wireless network.

Figure 54 Basic Piconet

Bluetooth developed by Ericsson in 1994 as a mean of using a cellular telephone headset without wire. In 1998, Ericsson formed a partnership with Nokia, IBM, Intel, and Toshiba to form the Bluetooth special interest group (SIG) (Coyle, 2001).

Unlike IrDA, Bluetooth does not require a line of sight connectivity to be effective. It utilizes a technology known as auto-discovery (Mallick, 2003). Briefly, in auto-discovery, Bluetooth automatically discover other Bluetooth devices. Bluetooth specifications define three modes of auto-discovery: General discoverable mode, Limited discoverable mode, and Non-discoverable mode.

The General Discoverable Mode allows a Bluetooth device to discover any Bluetooth device in close proximity. In The Limited Discoverable Mode, Bluetooth allows only well-defined devices to be able to detect a device. In The Non-discoverable Mode, Bluetooth makes a device invisible to other devices so it cannot be detected (Mallick, 2003).

Bluetooth technology creates a special ad-hoc network called a piconet. Piconets have a size limit of eight devices. Figure 54 illustrates the very basic Bluetooth piconet. A piconet is formed when at least two devices, such as a portable PC and a cellular phone, connect. A piconet can support up to eight devices. When a piconet is formed, one device acts as the master while the others act as slaves for the duration of the piconet connection. Another name for piconet is Personal Area Network (PAN) (Webopedia, 2004).

If more than eight participants want to take part in a Bluetooth session, several piconets are interconnected. This kind of network is called scatternet (Fujitsu Computer Siemens, 2002).

In a scatternet configuration, not all devices are visible to one another. Only devices with the individual piconets can communicate. In Figure 55 there is one scatternet consisting of five piconets. The hands-free mobile telephone is a member of three different piconets. It is able to communicate with the headset, the Bluetooth pen, and the access point, but not with the laptop, printer, or facsimile machine (Mallick, 2003).

Figure 55 Scatternet

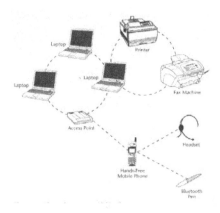

Bluetooth Technology is not a competitor in the market place for wireless LAN. Instead, because of its low speeds and limited range, experts consider Bluetooth a complimentary technology that replaces close range cable technology. Results of Bluetooth testing for IEEE 802.11b standards indicate a degradation of services unless Bluetooth transceivers are within 3 meters of each other (Coyle, 2001).

Bluetooth connections and networks are very popular in automobiles. The driver synchronizes cell phone with automobile stereo system. Once the connection is made, the driver issues voice commands to the stereo speaker system to cell phone. The cell phone then makes or receives telephone calls without the driver using hands or diverting eyes from the road.

WI-FI

Cisco systems advise that there are more than 400 wireless technologies in the United States. Wireless Fidelity (Wi-Fi) is the most popular and easiest technology to implement. Wi-Fi is found in homes, schools, offices, and science. The Wireless Ethernet Compatibility Alliance (WECA) certifies the Wi-Fi industrial standards and equipment (Wi-Fi Consulting, 2004).

Typically, when an employee sits down at a workstation, he or she is stationary. The range of worker mobility is limited to the assigned workstation. Wi-Fi replaces the network wires with low powered two-way radio transceivers (Ohrtman & Roeder, 2003).

The most popular and WLAN implementation is the DSSS radio technology of 802.11b or wireless Ethernet. However, 802.11g standard is gaining ground and soon will replace 802.11b as the Wi-Fi standard in both the corporate office and SOHO (Small office-Home Office). 802.11b has also taken root in home network computing supplanting HomeRF. That is because, SOHO and home networking, technological innovations allow the local telephone company or the local cable company to provide Wi-Fi services at a lower rate than the old HomeRF standard. 802.11g is backwards compatible with both the 2.4-GHz frequency of 802.11b and the Orthogonal Frequency Division Multiplexing (OFDM) technology used in 802.11a transmitting at 5-GHz.

The IEEE 802.11b specifications permit wireless a transmission rate of approximately 11 Mbps of raw data at distances up to 300 hundred feet over the 2.4-GHz ISM radio bands. The distance varies depending on ambient electromagnetic interference and the quality of the equipment (Wi-Fi Consulting, 2004).

The 802.11a standard was designed to operate in the 5-GHz UNII (Unlicensed National Information Infrastructure) band. Unlike 802.11b, which uses spread-spectrum technology, standards for 802.11a use a frequency division-multiplexing scheme that supposed to be friendlier to an office environment?

The 802.11a standard, which supports data, rates of up to 54 Mbps. It is called Fast Ethernet compared to 802.11b, which supports data rates of up to 11 Mbps. Like Ethernet and Fast Ethernet, 802.11b and 802.11a use an identical MAC (Media Access Control) (Conover, 2001).

The IEEE 802.11a implementation has distinct advantages over 802.11b. First, it increases the bandwidth from 11 Mbps to 54 Mbps. Second, the bandwidth that is available 5-GHz range is larger and outside the heavily used ISM 2.4-GHz. Third, the 802.11b 2.4-GHz spectrum is plagued with the saturation by other wireless technologies, IrDA, Bluetooth, and microwave ovens (Conover, 2001).

The disadvantages of the 802.11a at 5-GHz frequencies are a shorter transmission range. Second, it costs more to provide 802.11a than it costs to implement 802.11b. One of the reasons it costs more is the price to maintain the quality of service (QOS). Networks using

802.11a web administrators and technicians must create more access points. A second disadvantage of OFDM technology at 5-GHz is its higher operating frequencies requires more power consumption. Third, increased power rates equate to shorter battery life for mobile users (Mallick, 2003).

Each implementation of Wi-Fi may act—depending on software—as a hub for computer-to-computer communications, an ad-hoc network. However, a more likely scenario for a Wi-Fi enabled computer is in conjunction with a wired network infrastructure network. The access points often includes routing, Dynamic Host Configuration Protocol (DHCP) services, Network Address Translation NAT, and other infrastructure services required to complete the business mission (Wi-Fi Consulting, 2004).

SWAP: THE HOMERF STANDARD

SWAP, Shared Wireless Access Protocol, is a wireless LAN protocol for the home office or small office. The HomeRF Working Group (HRFWG) is a consortium of over 90 companies conforming to the IEEE 802.11 standards for home and small office wireless computing (Coyle, 2001).

SWAP can operate at 10 Mbps on the 2.4-GHz frequency band. The range of a SWAP network is about 50 meters. It incorporates Digital Enhanced Cordless Telephony (DECT) the same technology that creates cordless phone (Mallick, 2003). SWAP as other wireless technologies used CSMA/CA and Time Division Multiple Access (TDMA), which guarantee bandwidth and latency. TDMA is used in the digital 2G cellular systems such as Global System for Mobile Communications (GSM) of Cingular and AT&T, IS-136, Personal Digital Cellular (PDC), and iDEN by Nextel now Sprint.

These are important criteria for real-time voice streaming and media streaming (Coyle, 2001). The major advantage of SWAP over WLAN is price. SWAP access points, routers, and switches are much cheaper than comparable WLAN equipment. The HomeRF consortium disbanded in 2003 making it a defunct standard because of the introduction of Wi-Fi in the SOHO markets (Mallick, 2003).

3G

Three-G technology is not WLAN technology. Although the two technologies may appear redundant, they are entirely different technologies. First WLAN technology is based upon narrow band broadcasting. 3G or Three-G connectivity, on the other hand, is based upon a broadband technology. It is sponsored by the cellular telephone industry: Sprint, T-Mobile, Cingular, and AT&T. WLAN operates under the specifications of the IEEE 802.11 protocol suite and is certified by the Wi-Fi Alliance. Wi-Fi clarifies how computers talk to each other using CSMA/CA using DSSS or OFMD. 3G is also a DSSS technology but it operates at different frequencies, 850-MHz and 1900-MHz. 3G is based on Code division multiple access (CDMA) technology or Global System for Mobile Communications (GSM) technology use of cell phone technology. Three-G performs more like a telephone technology than a computer technology.

Other differences between the two technologies: 3G is an innovation of mobile phone providers who try for global coverage. WLAN is an adjunct of a privately or publicly supported LAN such as the city library system or Colorado University. Another distinction is observed in the access of the services. To obtain 3G service, mobile phone providers charge a monthly subscription fee to each user. Wi-Fi service is free, it is provided by the company one works, by municipalities such as libraries, airports, or courthouses. Private coffee shops, bookstores, and sandwich shops also provide Wi-Fi free of charge.

Although terminology between WLAN and 3G sometimes overlap, the term WiMax for instance, it is strictly purposeful. WiMax, is an alternative acronym for a wireless Metropolitan Area Network (WMAN), it describes how computers connect over a specific geographical area using IEEE 802.16 WLAN technology (Microwave). A WiMax tower is similar to that of a cell phone tower. However, it is a broadband technology.

In cell phone the industry, the same term WiMax is the acronym for the Sprint 4-G philosophy. Sprint has a WiMax covering all of its stores in a large metropolitan area, a cellular WiMax. Investors hoped WiMax has the effect home and office WLAN (Wi-Fi) subscribers that cell phones had on home telephones; that is customer shut down home and cable and DSL services, and subscribe to WiMax. 4G did have that effect on the telephone. However, it was LTE 4G not WiMax.

The promise of WiMax fizzled in 2006 with the effort of the Nokia, Intel, Clearwire, and Sprint partnership. Originally Sprint, Intel, and Nokia (SIN) formed a partnership to make WiMax the worldwide industry standard for 4-G. At the time of this alliance, LTE (3GPP Long Term Evolution) standards were still on the drawing boards. LTE was not released until 2008. The SIN partnership did not produce one WiMax tower until 2008. It did not cover one city until 2010, Baltimore. By 2010, SIN had squandered it technological lead. WiMax the one time worldwide industrial standard is relegated to Russia, Mongolia, Pakistan, and 30 cities in the United States covering a meager 27 million customers.

LTE, by 2009, was building cell towers for its customers by 2010 it had past the crumbling SIN partnership. Cisco dropped out to take advantage of LTE. Nokia followed Cisco soon after. The decisive blow in the 4G battle came when the two largest cell phone providers in the United States Verizon and AT&T decided against WiMax in favor of LTE. Verizon and AT&T together have approximately 200 million customers. Sprint had at the time it initiated WiMax had roughly 60 million customers. WiMax supposedly offered subscribers' speeds of 144 Mbps download and 138 Mbps upload. In laymen's terms, that is about 1 GHz point to point.

LTE on the other hand offered speeds of 326 Mbps with 4 by 4 MIMO (multiple-input and multiple-output) and 172 Mbps with 2 by 2 MIMO in the 20 MHz spectrum. MIMO refers to the antenna at each end of a wireless connection. LTE supports both GSM and CDMA cell phone technology. In laymen's terminology, that is supposed to be about 3-Ghz point to point. The acronyms are Frequency Division Duplexing and Time Division Multiplexing respectfully. The major advantage in LTE is high throughput with low latency. According to most professionals, LTE is the faster technology.

20

Wide area Networks

The acronym WAN is short for Wide Area Network. A WAN connects remote single computers, LAN, and MAN networks. A WAN is not based on wireless or 3G technologies. A WAN is a private network created by corporate entity or government agencies for its employees and customers. The telephone companies were the first source of WAN networks. The most famous WANs discussed in this book were SAGE and SABRE created by IBM. The first WAN connection was circuit-based technology. It provided a point-to-point connection over a leased telephone line.

WAN connections include the plain old telephone service (POTS) connection at 56-Kbs and dedicated high-speed data connections called T – carriers. The smallest of the T-carriers are the T-1 line. T-1 transmits data at 1.544 Mbps. T-1 lines consists of 24 sub channels of service at 64 Kbps. The next level T – carrier is the T-2 line. The T-2 line transmits data at 6.312 Mbps. Dedicated lines are very expensive and most customers choose only to buy a portion of a dedicated line. Some company elects to purchase either one or two sub channels. T-3 lines are the next in sequence in our discussion of T lines. A T-3 line is a high-speed transmission line. T-3 lines transmit data at a rate of 45 Mbps.

OVERVIEW

WAN communications are governed by a set of compatibility protocols. The WAN standards evolved as the technology to connect remote LAN and MAN services. After, the building of the nationwide telephone network, engineers built the Point-to-Point Protocol (PPP). PPP was followed by circuit switching. Shortly thereafter, the first high-speed WAN technology, was born, X.25. Frame Relay followed X.25 and made it obsolete. Frame relay is capable of speeds of 45 Mbps. It is usually offered on T-1 or T-3 dedicated lines. Unlike X.25, which functions on the first three layers of the OSI Reference Model, Frame Relay operates only on the first two layers. Even though both technologies are packet-switching technologies, Frame relay does not have an error-checking component, as does X.25, which limits its speed to 64 kbps.

A third packet-switching technology is ATM or Asynchronous Transfer Mode. ATM has a top bandwidth between 25 Mbps to 155 Mbps. ATM is not a software solution like Frame Relay and X.25. ATM does not establish PVC, private virtual circuit; it uses special equipment to increase transmission speed. WAN technologies operate on the lower three layers of the OSI reference model: the physical layer, the data link layer, and the network layer.

Also discussed in the section are LAPB, HDLC, and ISDN.

Wireless Wide Area Networks communicate by means of radio, satellite, and microwave. WWAN transmissions vary and encompass one or more forms of switching methods to provide multiple data paths.

POINT-TO-POINT PROTOCOL

A Point-to-Point Protocol provides a single, pre-established WAN communications pathway. Point-to-Point Protocol uses a Data Link layer protocol that works at the OSI Reference Model. It is used over either a synchronous serial ISDN or a synchronous dial up connection. The purpose of a Point-to-Point Protocol is to transport Layer 3 packets across the Data Link Layer point-to-point link.

The point-to-point connection maintains for components:

1. EIA/TIA-232 C, V.24, V.35, and ISDN are an OSI Reference Model Physical Layer standard for serial communications.
2. HDLC is a method of encapsulating datagrams over serial links.

3. LCP are methods of connecting configuring, maintaining, and transmitting data over a PPP connection.

4. NCP is a Network layer protocol. It was designed to use simultaneous multiple Network layer protocols.

CIRCUIT SWITCHING

Circuit switching is connection oriented technology WAN switching method based on a dedicated physical circuit. Circuit switching technology provides for two types of transmissions: datagram transmissions and data-stream transmissions. Circuit switching is based on POTS. Consequently, the landline telephone companies provide the circuit switching technology for a WAN. An example of a circuit-switched WAN technology is Integrated Services Digital Network (ISDN). Circuit Switching is similar to making a telephone call because not data is transferred before connection is secured.

X.25

From a historical view, X.25 is the oldest of the WAN technologies. X.25 was invented in the 1960s. It defines how data from the data terminal equipment (DTE) is sent to the data circuit equipment (DCE) or in laymen's terms how an end user connects to a remote network. X.25 is a connection-oriented technology that verifies data connection and data integrity. The International Telecommunication Union-Telecommunication Standardization Sector (ITU-T) maintains standards for X.25 protocols. X.25 standards were established before the OSI Model. X.25 WAN technologies function on the three lower layers of the OSI reference model: physical layer, data link layer, and network layer.

X.25 has three transmission modes: switch virtual circuit (SVC), permanent virtual circuit (PVC), and datagrams. An SVC is a temporary connection for indiscriminate data transfers. Switch virtual circuits require two DTE devices establish, maintain, and terminate a session during each communication session. A permanent virtual circuit (PVC) is a permanent connection and remains so after the completion of the data transmission session. The permanent virtual circuit does not require an electronic transmission handshake before beginning data transmissions. A datagram is a connectionless data technology that does not guarantee delivery of data. Since datagrams are a connectionless technology, packets sent via datagram may arrive out of order, duplicated, or missing.

FRAME RELAY

Frame Relay is a WAN protocol that operates at the lower two levels of the OSI reference model. Frame Relay was originally designed for ISDN communication standards. However, with innovations Frame Relay is capable of accommodating a variety of other WAN communication standards. Frame Relay is an example of a packet-switching technology.

Frame Relay like TCP is a connection-oriented technology. As a connection-oriented protocol, Frame Relay must establish and maintain a virtual circuit before transmitting data. A Frame Relay virtual circuit is identified by a Data-Link Connection Identifier (DLCI). The DLCI values are assigned by the Frame Relay service. A Frame Relay DLCI has local importance because its value is unique for the LAN, but is unimportant to the WAN serviced by Frame Relay.

Frame Relay is sometimes considered a simplified version of X.25, yet more reliable than X.25. Frame Relay WAN technologies originated the 1990s compared to the 1970s X.25 (Lammle, 2004) (Shinder, 2002).

ASYNCHRONOUS TRANSFER MODE

Asynchronous Transfer Mode (ATM) is govern by the International Telecommunication Union - Telecommunications Standards Section (ITU-T). It was designed as a high-speed transfer technology for voice, video, and data over public networks. However as the technology evolved, it was used for a variety of data services that included voice, video, or data.

ATM networks are connection-oriented. ATM is considered a unifying technology because it is now used to transport voice, data, and video (including graphics images) on both local and wide area networks. Before the development of ATM, networks were built based on the bases of the data it transported. An ATM is designed as scalable. It structure allows its 53-byte cell to be transported from LAN to LAN over a WAN connection, as well as for use on public and private wide area networks. On LANs, ATM support is offered at rates between 25 and 155Mbps. WAN-based ATM carrier networks can interface with T1 and T3 (Microsoft Corporation, 1999). ATM operates on the data link layer of the OSI Reference Model.

Some of you my prefer the WAN created by the cell phone companies. That is a matter of taste not a business model. Again, these business models are based on wired technologies connect by satellite transmissions. These WANs are technically hybrid, because the transmissions no longer depend on leased lines. For example, the FBI office in Washington DC no longer depends on fiber optics or T3 lines to connect to its Birmingham or Jackson offices. The radio transmission is sent via satellite then converted back to LAN packet of TCP/IP. The most famous of these networks are AFIS and CoDIS.

LAPB

Link Access Procedure, Balanced is a connection-oriented protocol that works on the Data Link Layer of the OSI Reference Model. It was developed for use with the X.25. LAPD causes transmission overhead in its transmissions because of its rigid timeout and windowing technique.

HDLC

IBM invented HDLC (High-Level Data-Link Control) deriving it from SDLC (Synchronous Data Link Control). It does not have high transmission overhead because it was not designed to carry multiple transmissions. It is unique for data transmission protocols because it does not have identifiers in its head. The originators of HDLC believed every vendor has a proprietary control over data packets.

ISDN

Integrated Services Digital Network is a series services designed to transmit data and voice messages over existing telephone lines. It is a cost efficient solution for rural and remote users needing a high-speed data connection.

21

TCP/IP

Transmission Control Protocol/Internet Protocol was developed by the Department of Defense in the early 1970s to counteract the vulnerabilities and proprietary compatibility issues found in circuit switching data transmission or fixed pathway data transmissions. To circumvent the apparent weaknesses in its computing services DoD commissioned ARPANET. In the early 1970s even though IBM still manufactured 90 percent the world's mainframe computers, only an elite few of the DoD partner universities, corporations, and research centers utilized IBM computers exclusively. Most relied on cloned IBM products and computer systems produced by other companies Digital Equipment Corporation, Honeywell, General Electric, or Data General Computers. To avoid compatibility issues from competing companies with its partners, the DoD commissioned the creation of a universal telecommunications software.

TCP/IP is the brainchild of two of the DoD's premier computer DARPA network engineers, Robert E. Kahn and Vincent Cerf. The two men were intent on overcoming existing connectivity issues between ARAPA ground and satellite transmissions. The implementation of TCP/IP represented a software solution to hardware issue. It replaced the gateway, which used routers to convert signals between the various ground and satellite facilities. TCP/IP also replaced gateway solutions connectivity issues between members of the DoD partnerships. After

ARPANET transmogrified into NSFNET TCP/IP remained the protocol suite of choice for the networking community.

TCP/IP is a dual layered suite of protocols that proliferated outside of its original government-sanctioned mission in the commercial, educational, and scientific communities. The upper layer of the protocol suite TCP or Transmission Control Protocol TCP is a connection-oriented protocol that keeps track of the individual units of data (called packets) sent across the internet.

TCP works at the transport level of the OSI Reference model. It provides reliable delivery of data. IP is the lower layer of protocol suites in the TCP/IP internet protocol suites. IP offers features for addressing, fragmentation and reassembly of data transmissions.

TRANSMISSION CONTROL PROTOCOL

TCP is a connection-oriented protocol. That is to say at the point of origin, sending computer, TCP establishes and maintains a connection with the destination computer. This action creates what is known as a virtual circuit. During the virtual connection or handshake, the two computers establish the size of the document or data that is going to be transferred. Once both computers have established the size of the data transmission, TCP acknowledges the connection integrity and data transmission begins.

TCP provides a reliable, resilient, and accurate delivery of data while monitoring the transmission for accuracy and receipt of the frames by controlling the flow of data between computers or nodes. TCP on the originating computer breaks the information down into segments or frames. Each segment or frame is numbered and sequenced so that the computer at the destination end of the connection can reassemble the data exactly as it appears on the originating computer. The sequence number not only shows in what sequence the frame or segment are sent in the transmission, it also indicates how much data is contained in each frame. Once the destination computer receives a frame, it sends an acknowledgement to the originating computer. When the transmission completes, TCP verifies the document on the destination computer is an exact duplicate of the document on the originating computer. The final step in the verification process is the termination of the session (LAMMLE, 2004) (PALMER, 2006).

Besides TCP and IP there are eight other services listed in the suite:

a. DHCP—Dynamic Host Configuration Protocol allows clients to issued IP address from a poor available. DHCP is a valuable tool building a private LAN. Administrators or engineers automate the protocol to assign the IP address to each computer, printer, and fax machines on the LAN.

b. DNS—Domain Name Service is an Internet standard protocol that translates host names into corresponding IP address.

c. Telnet—is an application protocol that supports terminal emulations. Telnet was developed when client on a network did not have on board processor and depended solely on the mainframe.

d. ARP—is short for Address Resolution Protocol. It enables the sending of a node to obtain the MAC address of the intended recipient.

e. HTTP—Hypertext Transfer Protocol used by browsers on the World Wide Web.

f. FTP—File Transfer Protocol allows the transfer of files between computers.

g. SNMP—Simple Network Management Protocol allows network managers to continuously manage network activity. It was developed in the 1980s as an alternative to CMIP or Common Management Interface Protocol.

h. SMTP—Simple Mail Transfer Protocol is designed to exchange electronic mail between network systems (PALMER, 2006).

The TCP frame contains a header and data payload. The header is a minimum of 20 bytes and contains the port source, destination port, sequence number, Window, flag controls, acknowledgement number, offset length, checksum, options, urgent pointer, and padding.

USER DATAGRAM PROTOCOL

User Datagram Protocol (UDP) is a part of the used when the reliability of a transmission of data in TCP/IP is not an issue. UDP operate on the Transport layer of the OSI Reference model. It is a connectionless protocol. Its sole purpose is the fast data transmission without guarantees of delivery. The header of a UDP frame is much simpler than the header of a TCP frame. The header of a UDP frame consists of the source port, the destination port, the length of the frame and checksum (PALMER, 2006).

INTERNET PROTOCOL

The primary functions of IP are to prove for the transfer of data, packet address, packet routing, fragmentation, and detection of packet errors. Unlike TCP, IP is a connectionless protocol. This due part because the primary purpose of IP is to deliver network – to-network addresses and routing of information. IP can make the delivery of frames, segments, or packets from LAN to WAN as longs as the networks one of the following transport protocols:

    a. Ethernet
    b. Token Ring
    c. X.25
    d. FDDI
    e. ISDN
    f. DSL
    g. Frame Relay
    h. ATM

An IP address distinguishes clients on a network. It assigned each node on a network an IP address. An IP address, in the original IP version 4 (IPv4), was 32-bit number displayed in a dotted decimal format as so: 198.62.22.2. The IP address is divided into four parts known as octets.

IP version six created in the 1980s emerged when engineers realized there was a limited (finite) number of networks possible but there were millions of network users. In response to the increase usage of computer technology the IP Next Generation Initiative started. By 1996, IPv6 was established to provide a pathway for expansion. IPv6 offered several advantages over IPv4. First, the address 32-bit address was changed to a 128-bit address. Second, a single address associated with multiple interfaces, auto configuration, and CIDR (Classless Inter-Domain Routing) address, a 40-byte header instead of a 20-byte header. Classless Inter-Domain Routing is an IP method of addressing that ignores address class and uses a slash at the end of the dotted decimal address to show the total available addresses, similar to subnet masks.

A portion of the IP address is a network address and a portion of the address is the host address. The division between the components depends on the class of the class of the address. The IP address has three classes A, B, and C (Moncur, 1998, pp. 120-125).

Chart 4 IP ADDRESS

IP Address Classess and Ranges			
Class	First Byte Range	Network /Host Octet	Number of Networks	Host per Network
A	1-126	1/3	126	16,777,214
B	128-191	2/2	16,382	65,534
C	192-223	3/1	2,097,150	254

SUBNETS

A subnet or sub netting (short for "sub network") is a special portion of an organization's internal network. It is based upon the IP address issued by the organization InterNIC (Internet's Network Information Center). InterNIC is a registered service mark of the U.S. Department of Commerce. It is licensed to the Internet Corporation for Assigned Names and Numbers (ICANN). The primary reason for learning to create a sub network is that the Internet community is firm about limiting the number available IP address, due to the explosive growth of Internet services. Network administrators will have to improvise with current network limitations while increasing their internet capacity.

One way of increasing the IP address capacity while conserving resources expand the IP address already assigned to current networks. Subnets are one solution to the limited number of IP addresses. Sub nets allow for more IP addresses, increase security, and organize a network into logical groups. Without subnets, an organization must request multiple connections from InterNIC, but this would require an unnecessary use of the resource.

The IPv4 addressing framework allows one to address 16,777,214 unique hosts for a Class A address, 65,534 hosts for a Class B address, but only 254 hosts for a Class C address. Using the IPv4 version of IP, there are no more Class A addresses available. In addition, InterNIC has stopped assigning Class B addresses. Class C addresses are the most numerous, but have a limitation of 254 unique hosts.

The IP address is composed of 32 bits, which consist of two parts: the most significant bits (MSBs) identify a particular network and the remaining bits specify a host on that network. A Class-A network address would have a range of IP address numbers from 1.0.0.0 through 126.0.0.0. This is done by using the 16 high-ordered bits of the host portion for the subnet number and the lower eight bits for the host.

This is where the creation of a sub network becomes tricky. In order to create the sub network a subnet mask is needed to determine the number of bits used for the subnet and host portions of the address. The mask is a 32-bit value that uses one-bits for the network and subnet portions and zero-bits for the host portion.

For example, the Class-B address of 191.70.55.130 is converted to its binary equivalent, which is 1011 1111(191), 1000 0110(70), 0011 0111(55), 1000 0010(130). Then apply the subnet masks. A logical AND operation is performed between the IP address and the subnet mask as shown: 1111 1111   1111 1111   0000 0000   0000 0000. The resulting sub network is 1011 1111   1000 0110   0000 0000   0000 0000. The mask retained the default 16-network and host bits (Cooney, 2011).

HOST.TXT

Long before the Internet became an integral part of everyday life, shortly after the ARPANET—the Internet forerunner—was created. Long before the DHCP and DNS became second nature, the list of ARPANET host sites were kept on a file in an alphabetical list known as HOST.TXT or the DoD Internet Host Table. The Host Table was machine-translatable ASCII text file. It was obtained from of the Stanford Research Institute - Network Information Center (SRI-NIC) host, the list caretaker. As more colleges and research centers saw the advantages of ARPANET, updated list of HOST.TXT were obtained by members of ARPANET using the file transfer protocol of the TCP/IP application protocols. As stated earlier, the problem of maintaining a typed list of names is human error. If errors occurred, the error was multiplied when members downloaded new copies. Corrections only occurred after the HOST.TXT file was updated again.

IPV4

The Internet Corporation for Assigned Names and Numbers (ICANN) is the private sector, non-profit corporation created in 1998 to assume responsibility for assigning internet addresses. It announced on February 11, 2011 that it has assigned its last IPv4 address. The end of the central supply of IPv4 addresses most certainly means that internet service providers have migrated to IPv6. IPv6 is the latest iteration of the internet protocol. It has been available for more than a decade and allows for an almost unlimited number of IP addresses. TCP / IP v6 unlike v4, which was based on a 32-bit IP address, is a 128-bit number, comprised of hexadecimal digits separated by colons. So instead of an IP address looking as 192.158.7.5, the new IPv6 address will have an appearance similar the following list of hexadecimal characters 85ah:16ag :3wfg :324m :63rh :64gd :3sgh :987f (Lawson, 2011).

22

Malware

On January 16, 2011, the United States launched an attack on Iran, not a military attack, but a cyber-attack. According to television and newspaper reports in the United Kingdom and the United States, high echelon experts in the field of protecting American industry and infrastructure from cyber-attacks has told the *Financial Times* that a computer worm launched more than a year ago was a deliberate attempt by the U.S. and Israeli governments to destroy Iran's primary nuclear facility in Dimona.

The Stuxnet worm, which has caused all the trouble with the Iranian computer systems, has been researched for months, but its design is so complex that security experts are still unable to say definitively say who or what created the attack. The Financial Times also reported, the worm exploited gaps in the Windows operating systems (which Microsoft has since patched) and attacked Siemens software used to operate the Iranian centrifuges, which were used to create weapons grade uranium.

Since the beginning of computer technology, the threat of computer espionage and terrorism has loomed like a ticking time bomb ready to explode without warning. Before the Internet, espionage, and corporate spying was the exclusive venue of secret agents accessing files, traitors passing classified documents, or disgruntled employees selling the secret files. After the onset of the Internet, cyber espionage became a sophisticated game of cat and mouse with the security of a nation is computing infrastructure at stake. It is a game, more explosive than any plot found on television or in motion pictures. The outcome has dire circumstances for the losers. Cyber terrorism is not the exclusive playground of nations. It was played by virtually everyone who had access to the Internet. The role of the villain was assigned to those holding a grudge or was without moral integrity. A cyber terrorist ranged from a 13-year-old hacker down the street, to computer savvy member of a crime syndicate, to nations described in the opening paragraph.

Cyber attackers exploit the vulnerabilities of operating systems, web applications, web servers, and various collections of databases called data stores.

This is not a comprehensive compendium on the latest threats to computer security. The thing the reader must keep in mind is the continual ebb and flow between those that would subvert the internet for their own criminal purposes and those that try to protect the millions of people trying promote commerce, education, and science.

For example, in the late 1990s, cyber attackers used classic denial of service attacks (DoS) in the form of Trin00, SYN Flood, Tribe Flood, and Stacheldraht to exploit weaknesses in corporate America. They became notorious by successfully bringing down UNIX and Linux based servers. At one time Nextel, Yahoo, EBay, and CNN all came under cyber-attack, which cost the companies millions of dollars in lost production. The worms and viruses followed with minor successes. There are those who keep an accurate timeline of the malware attacks and can dispute the accuracy of this document, defeating the purpose. I try to remain, as faithful to the timeline as reasonably possible.

THREATS

The threats to a computer network come in three basic forms, internal espionage, external threat, and employee carelessness. Internal espionage is the easiest to find but the most difficult to detect. Confidential corporate information has a habit of leaking into the hands of a competitor. Sometimes employees expecting a promotion become disgruntle and leak information to rivals. At other times long time vendors leak information to competitors if they feel the work they do is receiving a low ball instead of a bid that will allow it to expand and increase sales.   The trick in discovering malcontents within an organization was to maintain accurate records of when leaks were discovered.   To avoid this compromise, it sometimes required the hiring of counter-espionage agents and perform thorough background checks of vendors, employees, and consultants. This includes e-mail auditing as well as workstation auditing of the server.

Assuming the employee was not leaking the information via a MP3 device, smart phone, or thumb drive then network security was compromised.   A thorough software scan of all access points, which included pinging of intranet hardware, visual inspection, comparing architecture with known changes and the list of IP addresses maintained by the network server.   If the access points, employees, vendors, and consultants were not the point of attack then malware compromise was the source of the leaks. The malware discussed herein is listed below:

- Spam
- Phishing
- Worm
- Virus

- Trojan
- Denial of service
- Rootkit
- Spyware

SPAM

One of the first problems encountered when Arpanet was created was spam. Spam is unsolicited email that clutters the inbox of private and business email accounts. Today spam originates when a person decides to purchase music, books, or any other item over the internet and inadvertently creates a tracking cookie. The tracking cookie is a program that attaches itself to the browser of the buyer. It then records or logs the uniform resource locator (URL) the buyer visits and reports that back to the seller usually a corporate entity such as Amazon. The corporate entity then creates emails for your inbox catered to the websites you have recently visited. Problems came about when the vendors sold the list of customers to less than reputable entities. The disreputable characters used the lists to create email forays that solicited people who looked for free items or virtually free items.

303

Spam increased the criminals ability to contact people particularly susceptible to certain types of fraud. Before the use of email, a scammer had to contact each potential victim individually via postal services, magazines, telephone, or through direct personal contact. These methods would often require a significant investment in time and money. To improve the chances of contacting susceptible victims, the scammer might have had to do advance research on the "marks" he or she targeted.

As the internet grew, the chances of contacting people susceptible to the scam artist's game increased as the scam artist overhead decreased. Some the favorite fraudulent activities made over the internet are promises of health and diet, bogus business opportunities, discount software offers, and 419 advanced fee fraud.

1. Health and Diet plans are fraudulent activities that prey on the insecurities some people have about the state of their well-being. These insecurities make some people particularly susceptible to the scams because they have phobias that prevent them from discussing their problems with a physician, or they are not able to afford the standardized medical treatments offered by licensed physicians. Some of the fraudulent diet programs promise miraculous weight loss without regard to exercise or eating habits.

2. Bogus Business Opportunities (BBO) are another criminal activity that puts the scam artist in contact with potential victims. In the BBO, the scam artist promises the victim, he or she will have unbridled moneymaking opportunities with very little effort. BBO are filled with such enticing phrases as "Be your own boss," "Set your own hours," and "Work from home." The BBO messages offering these opportunities have email subject lines that have the name of legitimate internet enterprises such as EBay, Yahoo, or Amazon. Still others offer fantastic business opportunities such as earning a commission cashing checks for foreign companies.

3. The 419 Advanced Fraud Fee schemes are quite elaborate yet preposterous. The goal of the criminal is to entice a fee from the victim. The essential scam elaborates to the victim about a long-lost relative (aunt or uncle) who has left you a large

sum of cash or about the misfortunes of person who wishes to avoid taxes and asks if you would be willing to conspire in scheme that could make you very rich. Many perpetrators of this scheme are Nigerian citizens. The scheme gets its name from the section of the Nigerian penal code that addresses fraud, section 419. 419 scams are recognize by their subject lines, which asks for an urgent response or referral   of personal introduction. They always state a small fee is necessary for processing fees. Do not pay the fee (US-Cert, 2005).

WORMS

A computer worm is a destructive, self-replicating for of computer malware, which uses a computer network, file-sharing system, removable drives, such as USB drives, and email to send copies of it to other computers. Computer Worms wreak havoc by exploiting security loopholes and flaws in Network Operating Systems (NOS) like Window NT or desktop operating systems (DOS) such as Windows 7 or Linux. A worm differ from computer virus in that it does not spread by modifying programs on a single computer system, instead it seeks and implants destructive code onto other systems. Worms replicate rapidly by commandeering an infected computer's resources and then seeking other computers on the network with the same or similar vulnerability. Its penchant for spreading quickly within a corporate or government website can cause catastrophic outcomes (Winferno Software, 2011).

In 1988, Robert Morris unleashed a worm that invaded computers connected to ARPANET. The small program disabled roughly 6,000 computers on the network by flooding their memory banks with copies of it. Morris confessed to creating the worm because of boredom. He is fined $10,000 and sentenced to three years' probation add (Krebs, 2003).

One of the most notorious computer worms were the Melissa and ILOVEYOU email worms or bombs that exploited the macro feature in Microsoft Office documents. A macro is a series of instructions that are intended to simplify repetitive tasks. In the case of the Melissa worm, when it infected a Microsoft Office document, it immediately reproduced itself into other documents, emailed itself to the other computers via the Microsoft Outlook address book. All told before the Melissa virus was contained, it caused $80 million in damages (Winferno Software, 2011)

Another infamous computer worm was the ConfickerB (or Conficker.B). After installing itself, it created a patch to hide the vulnerable port it had exploited so other malware could not derail its intentions or betray its presence. ConfickerB communicated with its creators every day, by using a meaningless string of 250 letters attached to a domain name such as a.com, a.net, a.org, a.info, or a.biz. At the end of each was a series of internet addresses, or URLs. It was a clever disguise and only recognizable when an infected computer made contact with the source for updates.

The ConfickerB worm was a two-stage worm with inner and outer shells of encryption to deter exposure of its definitions or programming. After a few months of decryption by laboratories in Russia, San Diego, and Europe the ConfickerB worm was resolved. However, its creator countered with a new version that spread just as rapidly as the original. More than 3 million vulnerable machines may ultimately have been infected in Russia, Great Britain, France, Germany, and the United States. The Microsoft Corporation offered a $250,000 reward to anyone who knows the identity of ConfickerB authors.

ConfickerB was defeated through a coordinated effort of Internet Corporation for Assigned Names and Numbers (ICANN), Microsoft, and several research laboratories worldwide that were able to isolate the author's intent. Solutions to the ConfickerB worm are on the Microsoft Website. Major antivirus software has the solution to ConfickerB built into its operations (Bowden, 2010)

VIRUSES

A computer virus is a program or a segment of executable code designed to replicate itself in the memory of an unsuspecting host computer. A computer virus spreads by inserting a copy of itself into and becoming part of another program. It propagates from one computer to another, leaving infections as it travels. The malware is labeled virus because it behaves like its genetic counterpart. A computer virus can only replicate itself in the programming of a host. Viruses can range in severity from causing mildly annoying effects to damaging data, corrupting software, or causing conditions that initiate a denial-of-service (DoS) attack (Cisco Systems).

Technically, the concept of a computer virus was suggested in 1949 by computer pioneer John von Neumann when he wrote a monograph entitled "Theory and Organization of Complicated Automata." In this monograph, von Neumann speculated a computer program could be self-replicating—this many computer scientist say predicted today is self-replicating virus programs.

Programmers at Bell Labs brought the theories to life in the 1950s when they developed the "Core Wars." Core Wars was a computer game where two players would release software "organisms" into the mainframe computer, and watch as the competing programs vie for control of the machine—in the same manner as present day computer viruses operate (Miller, 2008).

Viruses exploit computer networks and spread from computer to computer by sending itself as email over the Internet. Both viruses and worms replicate themselves. To distinguish a computer worms from a computer virus one must be mindful that worms activate when the operator activates the host. Viruses, on the other hand require a host program to be effective attacking memory and files while worms are standalone programs that attack the operability of networks of computers (Gilman, Computer Virus, 2004).

In actuality, there is no hard fast rule or academic definition to distinguish a virus from a worm since the authors of the malware are not inclined to follow the protocols set up by colleges or their professors.

TROJAN HORSE

If the virus and the worm are the diseases of the cyber world, then the Trojan horse is the contaminated hypodermic needle used to inject the disease. The Trojan horse is the most sophisticated of the malware programs. A Trojan horse is destructive program that masquerades as a beneficial application such as antispyware. In contrast to the worm or the virus, the Trojan horse does not replicate itself. The primary goal of a Trojan horse is to hide on the victim's computer invisibly carrying out ill will, such as downloading spyware and recruit zombie computers as part of a Denial of Service or Distributed Denial of Service (DDoS) attack. Initially victims continue to operate performing their normal activities. No matter the purpose the Trojan has for infecting the victim, the results are similar to the Trojan horse legend of mythology.

A quick refresher of Greek mythology tells us the Trojan horse originated during the Trojan War. Mythology stated the Greeks after years of laying siege to Troy and capture it by direct assault, decided to try an indirect approach to capture the city. Led by Odysseus, the Greek Army feigned and defeat then withdrew to a point at sea just beyond the horizon and waited. To seduce the Trojans into the trap, the Greeks left behind a giant wooden horse as a tribute to the courage of the defenders of Troy.

The Trojans naively accepted the gift and rolled the giant horse inside the city gates. The Trojans wildly celebrated their supposed victory with a daylong festival of drunkenness. That night while the Trojans slept, the Greek soldiers—hidden inside the horse the belly of the horse —emerged from the horse and opened the city gates for the bulk of Greek forces that had returned to Troy under the cover of darkness.

Trojan horse computer malware, like its mythological counterpart, clandestinely emerges from its hiding place on your computer's motherboard to destroy or steal information. The modern day Trojan horse is classified into five categories. However, one must remember criminals, authors of malware do not conform to the standards set by greater society. A Trojan horse program may be the product of government espionage, criminal enterprise, or criminal mischief. Listed below are the five major Trojan horse categories:

1. Remote Access Trojans
2. Security Disabler
3. Data Sending Trojans
4. Proxy Trojans
5. FTP Trojans

REMOTE ACCESS TROJAN

A Remote Access Trojan Horse program or Backdoor Software is part of a Trojan horse attack. Remote access Trojans are potentially the most damaging. It gives control of your computer to the hacker. If your system is infected, there is virtually no limit to what these programs can do:

    a.   Use your computer to relay spam to other individuals.

    b.   Steal your passwords and other stored information, such as credit card numbers.

    c.   The Remote Access Trojan allows the hacker to turn the victim's computer into a zombie or robot computer as part of a wider denial of service attack.

SECURITY DISABLER

A Security Disabled Trojan is a special remote access Trojan horse that destroys all passwords to a security measures on a network leaving vulnerable to attack. These are special Trojan programs designed to disable anti-virus software, firewalls, etc.

Examples of malware that delivered security disabler Trojans are the Bugbear virus, which installed a Trojan horse on the machines of all employees. The Bugbear Trojan horse was capable of disabling popular anti-virus and firewalls software. The Goner worm delivered another destructive Trojan horse. The Trojan horse in this program deleted anti-virus software from hard drives (GFI Software, 2010).

DATA-SENDING TROJANS

The purpose of these Trojans is to send data to the hacker with information such as passwords, credit card details, email address lists, contact information, etc. The Trojan is designed to look for specific information in specific locations. Data sending Trojans, also, can install a key-logger to send all recorded keystrokes to the hacker.

Examples of data sending Trojan horse programs are BadtransB that installed with an email virus (GFI Software, 2010) and KeyloggerX it may have been installed by Worm: Win32/SogluedaA. Data Captured by the aforementioned programs sent the information back to the hacker (Microsoft Corporation, 2011).

PROXY TROJANS

A Proxy Trojan is a stealth security intrusion. In this kind of attack, the criminal subverts the security system of the victims and installs a Trojan horse to hide his or her identity and location. The unsuspecting victim is held liable for any action taken by the intruder. Often this kind of security intrusion does not result in the loss of the victim personal data by the victim, however, in this kind of attack the victim is often investigates as spammer or as part of a crime syndicate (PCPerformanceTools.com, 2011).

FTP TROJANS

An FTP Trojan attack causes the victims computer to function as an FTP server. The perpetrator subverts a known security vulnerability of the operating system of the victim's computer and then installs a FTP Trojan. Once this occurs, the intruder can download any program or file from the victims computer and likewise the perpetrator can download anything onto the victim's computer. This kind of attack most often leads to identity theft and continual wreaking havoc of a victim's personal life until all malware is removed (PCPerformanceTools.com, 2011).

DENIAL OF SERVICE

The denial of service (DoS) attack is a strategy employed by computer hackers to deny legitimate users access to a commercial, educational, or informational website by exhausting network resources, attacking known software vulnerabilities, or overloading protocols. The attacks begin when a cyber-criminal installs a program onto networked computers to create high volumes of specious requests or messages that result in an interruption of network service.

The DoS attack is intentional and requires premeditation on the part of the cyber-criminal. DoS attacks consist at least of two phases and possibly three. During phase one of the attack, the hacker uses stealth to exploit vulnerability in an operating system and its antivirus/firewall software to install a form of Trojan horse software or worm to hide his location and identity. During phase two, the hacker plans the attack on the intended target and starts building an army of zombie computers or a botnet to attack a known website. Yahoo, Amazon, CNN and EBay fail victim to the denial of service attack by a zombie army in February of 2000.

A zombie computer is one that has been compromised by a cyber-criminal without the owner's knowledge and is used in a denial of service attack.

There are several categories of denial of service attack. The three basic attacks are listed below:

1. Bandwidth
2. Logic Attacks
3. Protocol Attacks

BANDWIDTH ATTACK

The typical bandwidth attack is a forthright attempts to consume as much of the resources of network bandwidth as possible. High volume data attacks can consume available bandwidth between an ISP and client site. The link fills, and traffic slows almost stopping. Built-in timeouts start occurring, exacerbating the problem, generating even more traffic. An attacker can consume bandwidth by transmitting erroneous traffic at all on your network connections that have been compromised by the installation of a Trojan horse, which makes node members zombie computers. (If zombie computers are involved then the DoS becomes a DDoS.) The basic Bandwidth Attack typically sends either a UDP or ICMP packets to consume all available network bandwidth.

A simple bandwidth-consumption attack can exploit the throughput limits of servers or network equipment by focusing on high packet rates—sending large numbers of small packets. High-packet-rate attacks typically overwhelm network equipment before the traffic reaches the limit of available bandwidth. Routers, servers, and firewalls all have constraints on input-output processing, interrupt processing, CPU, and memory resources. Network equipment that reads packet headers to properly route traffic becomes stressed handling the high packet rate not the volume of the data (Mbps). In practice, denial of service is often accomplished with high packet rates, not by sheer traffic volume.

LOGIC ATTACKS

There are two major reasons making DoS attacks attractive for attackers. The first reason is that there are effective automatic tools available for attacking any victim, i.e., expertise is not necessarily required. The second reason is that it is usually impossible to locate an attacker without extensive human interaction or without new features in most routers of the Internet. The objective of logic DoS attacks is to build a small number of packets exploiting specific vulnerabilities, which cause the victim to perform abnormal routines. The packets are normally sent directly to a victim, because special knowledge about vulnerability is required. There is a wide variety of logic attacks. Typically, an attack is based on more than one of the following issues:

- Exploitation of bugs
- Exploitation of syntax errors
- Exploitation of semantic errors
- Exploitation of missing authentication requirements

PROTOCOL ATTACK

The typical protocol attack is the DoS attack that makes the headlines. These attacks caused EBay and Yahoo to shutdown briefly. The basic flood attack can be further refined to take advantage of the inherent design of common network protocols. These attacks do not directly exploit weaknesses in TCP/IP stacks or network applications but, instead, use the expected behavior of protocols such as TCP, UDP, and ICMP to the attacker's advantage. Examples of protocol attacks include the following:

a) Smurf attack – during a Smurf attack involves a common network tool known as a ping. Ordinarily a ping is used to verify a node or host on a network is receiving signals from router or server. The ping allows the administrator and technician avoid physical inspection of LAN cables or WLAN access points. When used maliciously a ping packet broadcasts to an infinite number of hosts within network. The packet uses a request from another site, the intended target of the denial of service attack. The spoofed host ping request will exponentially increase the normal ping traffic flooding the services.

b) SYN Flood attacks – Normally when a computer wants to connect to a network TCP sends a SYN signal to the server, which will respond with an ACK (acknowledgement) response. During the SYN Flood attack, the attacker sends SYN request with a spoofed IP address or email address. The result is the same whether the address is spoofed or legitimate. If the computer at the address was not expecting an ACK, it will ignore the request. The server is then left awaiting a response. If the address is spoofed, the server is left waiting for a response. In either scenario, the line is idle until the request is completed.

c) Buffer overflow—the buffer overflow is the most common denial of service attack. The object of this form of DoS is to send more traffic to a network address than expected for the size of buffer. A few of the better known attacks based on the buffer characteristics of a network include the following (Mosla, 2005):

    i. Send an e-mail messages that have attachments with 256 character file names.

    ii. Sending oversized Internet Control Message Protocol (ICMP) packets to check for error. Sending oversized packets allows the packet to be sent to all the IP addresses on the network creating an overflow of traffic. IPv4 routers can fragment oversized messages, while IPv6 routers cannot

    iii. The opposite of the first attack listed in this section is to end an e-mail address longer than 256 characters.

The thing to remember about the denial of service attack is there are two kinds. The first occurs when just one computer is coordinating the attack. The is called a denial of service. If there is more than one computer coordinating the attack with a squadron of zombie computers (botnet) creating the attack it is called a distributed denial of service attack. Each of the zombie computers although following the orders of the master control, the hacker, has the same effect of a single attacker on the targeted website.

EMAIL BOMB

In addition to being a nuisances, spam is a carrier of more virulent diseases called an email bomb? An email bomb besides looking like spam entices like a Trojan horse. An email unleashed the Melissa Virus and some versions of the ConfickerB worm. An email bomb is a device used by hackers to render a network's mail servers useless and unavailable. This is accomplished by flooding the email server with large amounts of e-mail has buffer overflow characteristics or some other means of exhausting resources. Some of the e-mail bomb techniques that have been developed include chain bombs, covert distribution, error message bombs and mail exploder exploitation. No matter what the method of attack used by the email bomber, the outcome is the same. In the best scenario, the email bomb will exploit a known weakness of an operating system, copy the contact list information, and email itself to your friends, business associates, and subscriptions. In the worst scenario, the email bomb will hide the vulnerability so as not to attract attention, subvert the operating system, and create a zombie computer for a planned attack on a major corporate or government entity. The accepted wisdom by malware experts state that an email bomb is no more than the reconnoiter and bivouac for a denial of service attack.

ROOTKITS

The term Rootkit refers to malware that employs cloaking techniques and methods when combined with a Trojan horse, allows attackers compromise and exploit operating systems vulnerabilities and security to gain remote administrative access of a computer making it extremely difficult to detect by a system's administrator. The concealment strategies include modifying system code and processes in such a manner that would prevent detection or prevention of remote access. Rootkits alter basic system functions to disguise the cyber-criminal's unauthorized activity.

A rootkit differs from a computer virus in that it concentrates on maintaining control of an operating system, rather than spreading itself and infectious code to other systems. However, it is similar to traditional viruses because each modifies the core software components of an operating system to hide its presence. Once a rootkit has control of a computer, it is difficult to detect or repair. In such cases, the operating system needs to be cleaned and reinstalled.

CRIMEWARE

Crimeware is defined as any computer program or set of programs that are designed for the facilitation of illegal activity online. Consequently, Trojans, key loggers, root kits, adware, and spyware are considered crimeware. What they each have in common is the ability to 'steal' your confidential information – such as passwords and PINs – and send it back to the criminal. With this information in hand, the cybercriminal is able to steal your identity and your money.

Crimeware is a new term used to describe the cybercriminal more interested in obtaining wealth rather than voicing a complaint against a large corporation or hold it hostage for ransom. This type of criminal would rather steal money from lightly protected systems such as rural school districts. For example, Sanford Colorado had $117,000 dollars withdrawn from its checking account by a cybercriminal. The criminal withdrew the money in lots of $9000 so as to avoid the bank's built in banks' anti-money laundering reporting requirements (Krebs, Cyber Crooks Target Public & Private Schools, 2009) to the IRS, FDIC, and FBI.

Unless you think cybercrime is isolated to only lonely individual trying to prove their worthiness to society, the reality, and the depth of criminal activity on the internet will shock you. It is a multilayered, multinational conglomerate just as agile as any legitimate business. At the very lowest level of the organization is the cracker. The cracker is the person that exploits the known vulnerability of the operating system. Immediately above the cracker is the bot herder. A bot in crimeware terminology is a compromised machine or zombie machine similar to the one described in the denial of service section. The bot herders assemble botnets of compromised machines and sell them to the fraudsters. The fraudsters use a remote access Trojan or similar malware to steal the identities of customers, employee data, intellectual property, or other valuable. On the street, the term used for marketing the stolen material, the exploits of a cracker or a botnet can be sold for as little as $200 and as much as $50,000.

SPYWARE

The definition of spyware states that it is software that is surreptitiously installed on a person's hard drive. Second spyware relays encoded information about the user's identity and Internet use through the user's Internet connection. The presence of spyware is hidden and difficult to detect. Corporations typically install spyware on employee computers to monitor their actions. A special kind of spyware (key logger) is sometimes installed on an employee's computer to make sure no technical secrets are compromised.

Spyware is very similar to a virus but technically different in that it behaves more like a Trojan horse. Spyware is also similar to adware but different in that adware displays advertisements. Typically, adware gathers information about an internet user's browsing habits and displays targeted or contextual ads that entice the user into an impulse purchase. Spyware is installed on a computer stealthily, in the background while the end user is installing another program. Spyware does not replicate itself; after it is installed, its job is to spy on your activities and browsing habits. It is built not to spread itself to other computers on your network (Miller, 2008).

23

Network Security

The problem with computer security over a network began the moment Arpanet came to live in October 29, 1969. The first messages were contained within the contained system made it easy for distant nodes to communicate. Three years later, telephone systems are invaded by phreakers who devise the infamous "Captain Crunch," a program that enable people to make long distance calls free.

In 1972, Arpanet introduces a commercial version of itself, known as Telnet. Five years later, Engineers at Xerox Palo Alto Research Center develop the first computer worm. Its purpose was to provide an efficient use by detecting idle computers on a network. The program is the basis for developing all future worms that wreak havoc over the internet. By 1983, hackers begin to appear on the government networks. The most infamous is the 414 group (Krebs, 2003).

The first virus on the Arpanet was the Creeper Virus. It was not a very harmful. On infected machines, it displayed the message "I am the Creeper." The Brain virus (Miller, 2008) followed the Creeper.

As each successive generation of malware grows more sophisticated, it becomes incumbent that the software industry remains vigilant to guard against encroachment by the perpetrators of malware.

The fight against The British standard for the information system BS 7799 was put into effect in 1995 by leading economic organizations so that an effective tool to evaluate the information safety management systems ("ISMS") had originated, which had quickly spread all over the world and in now available in more than eleven languages. In 1998, the standard was adjusted to the requirements of new trends, such as the e-commerce or teleworking, and in 2000, it was promoted to the "rank" of an ISO standard. In 2005 the recent standard has come into force, which included the latest knowledge from the area of the comprehensive information safety, namely, ISO 27001, built on the basis of BS 7799/ISO 17799 Standard.

As the battle continued to rage between those that would shut down the Internet or hold it hostage and those who want an open Internet with free commerce, security came to the forefront of the war. To ward off the wrongdoers, software providers, soft, computer security providers, and government software assurance agencies have combined efforts and shared information about vulnerabilities in software and security. The Internet providers provide anti-malware software in the form of antispyware, antivirus, anti-spam, and internet security software to all users, large and small, corporations, and individuals. The government has funded two projects to increase protection against malware and those that want utilize their skills for illicit gains and criminal activity: US CERT and CERT. Microsoft the worldwide leader providing computer operating system has its own set of experts updating each release of its Windows operating system. The same is true for the other software providers Oracle, Apple, and Linux. In the private market, there are a number of computer security providers. They are ranked by their popularity with the corporate world and individual computer users: McAfee, Norton, Trend Micro, Eset, BitDefender, Kapersky, Webroot, and Avast in no particular order.

US CERT

US CERT is the operational arm of the National Cyber Security Division (NCSD) at the United States Department of Homeland Security (DHS). US CERT was established in 2003 to protect the Internet infrastructure of the United States. It is a public-private partnership. It coordinates defenses against and responses to cyber-attacks across the nation.

The name US CERT is an acronym for United States Computer Emergency Response Team. US-Cert is located in the District of Columbia. US CERT primary mission is to provide response, support, and defense for the Federal Civil Executive Branch against cyber-attacks and information sharing and collaboration with state and local governments as well as with industrial and international partners.

US CERT also provides a way for citizens, businesses, and other institutions to communicate and coordinate directly with the United States government about cyber security.

CERT

The CERT® Program is part of the Software Engineering Institute (SEI), a federally funded research and development center at Carnegie Mellon University in Pittsburgh, Pennsylvania. CERT was established in 1988 after the intrusion of the Morris Worm. The Defense Advanced Research Projects Agency (DARPA) tasked the SEI with coordinating communication among experts during network security emergencies to help prevent future incidents. The program was renamed the CERT Coordination Center. CERT/CC has expanded its role since the Morris Worm because of the steady evolution of the Internet, the program instead on identifying and addressing existing and potential threats, notifying system administrators and other technical personnel takes an active role a diversity of areas:

A. Software Assurance
1. Secure Systems
2. Organizational Security
3. Coordinated Response
4. Education and Training

B. Information Dissemination
1. Publications and Presentations
2. Media Relations

C. Community Involvement
1. Participation in Organizations
2. National Efforts

PRIVATE INDUSTRY

The efforts of private industry have focused mostly on software solutions for the malware. Private companies like Microsoft, Trend Micro, Norton, McAfee, etc. all employ former operating system hackers to exploit known weaknesses in the Windows Operating System. Once the company has identified a weakness, it develops a fix or a patch for the weakness with the help of the operating system manufacturer.

Besides exploiting the weaknesses in an operating system, the companies periodically, develop software that is capable of identifying malware, defeating it, and eradicating or blocking its presence in the operating system.

Private companies sell suites of software protection that includes antispyware, antivirus software, email with spam protection, and personal firewall protection. (A firewall is a protection system is based upon a set of software rules designed to permit or deny which network traffic.)

During the Blaster Worm attack, Microsoft and the three largest of the security organization collaborated to provide a software solution for companies within 3 hours. I know because I was indirectly a part of the Blaster Worm attack while working for Nextel (now Sprint).

24

The Future of Computing

I
t has been almost a 130 years since Herman Hollerith laid the groundwork for modern computing. Unlike Babbage, whose dream it was to create a machine that could print actuarial, nautical, and mathematical functions without error; Hollerith created the modern form of information technology. Hitherto, with the exception of the calculating engines, the business model for office machinery was static centralized machines incapable of storing information except in written form. Hollerith allows the storage of data albeit in the form punch cards without written records. In doing so, he created the rudiments of the modern database.

Hollerith in a six-week period made obsolete all the efforts to build a mechanical calculator or calculating engine. It was not until the mid-1930s when the likes of Aiken, Stibitz, and later Atanasoff started combining the four electric miracles of the previous century—telephone, the telegraph, the light bulb, and the electric tabulator—into elaborate electromechanical devices.

John Atanasoff and Clifford Berry completed the evolution from the Hollerith electromechanical tabulator to computer when they turned on the switch and powered up the ABC digital computer. This seven hundred pound wunderkind worked at an eye popping calculating speed of one calculation every fifteen seconds (Bellis, The Atanasoff-Berry Computer the First Electronic Computer-John Atanasoff and Clifford Berry, 2010). The ABC, invented in 1939, was a first-generation big iron or mainframe computer that used the vacuum tube. It was the scientific marvel of its day and attracted the admiration of scientist the likes of John William Mauchly from the University of Pennsylvania's Moore School of Engineering (Aspray & Campbell-Kelly, Computer: A History of the Information Machine, 1996, pg.).

Since that historic moment, the computer has undergone several transformations. The current iteration of the computer is the fourth-generation even though the direction and shape of the fourth-generation is not complete. Each new iteration of the CPU creates new benchmarks for the technology.

For example, the second-generation computer began when the transistor replaced the vacuum tube, marking the beginning of solid-state technology. Solid-state computer technology guided the United States manned-space program through the lunar landing in 1969. The computer that controlled the Apollo 11 spacecraft weighed 45 pounds.

The third-generation of computers began with the integrated circuit, which combined transistors, capacitors, diodes and the like to make a miniature computer on a silicon wafer. The fourth- generation of computer saw the merger of the von Neumann architecture CPU, Control Unit, and cache memory into one unit on an integrated circuit called a microprocessor. The fourth-generation computer, also, ended the classical von Neumann architecture design with the dual microprocessors on one chip.

Over the last twenty years, the advent of the networked computers has moved to the forefront of economic life in modern society. The computer blended into every aspect of our economy from the point of sale cash registers at the local sandwich shop to smart phone in your pocket or purse. One no longer needs a degree in engineering to understand the operations of a computer.

FUTURE CPU DESIGNS

As awesome as the fourth generation computer might seem, the fourth generation computer is still evolving. The fourth-generation of computing blurs the traditional boundaries of intelligent appliances. Presently, the cell phone is assuming many of the characteristics once relegated solely to the laptop or notebook computer. Cell phones with touch screen technology allow access and manipulation of data once the exclusive domain of the computer.

The mold created by IBM in the 19th and 20th centuries for information technology has been reshaped. The computer is no longer the status symbol of powerful or the wealthy. It belongs to everyone and to no one. Over the past 20 years, computers have extended their power to the entertainment industry, medicine, and industry. They play pivotal roles delivering audio and video to the home, creating virtual worlds for medicine, and controlling the actions of robots.

When coupled with the imagination of cinematographers, computers play an expanded role in the training physicians and scientist through elaborate simulations of the universe and the human body. Besides medical and scientific application, manufacturers now bring the university to the living room. Soon computers will bring in the lecture on bioengineering and nanotechnology from Stanford, Harvard, or Oxford to the den or basement.

Even with the expansion of capabilities, the present is a repetition of history. For example, the Cooke-Whetstone telegraph proved messages could be sent by electricity. Bell proved that electromagnetism was a good conduit of sound. Edison reiterated Bell creating the forerunner of the floppy disk in the form of the phonograph. Then Hollerith provided a hands free control corralling the electromagnetic pulse in a manner entirely different from the telegraph. Bush, Aiken, Stibitz, and Zuse combined those aforementioned efforts into smaller venues, sending messages between different machine components instead of cities, counting in addition to tabulating; proving Babbage was correct a mathematical table could be produced error free. Then Atanasoff, Berry, Mauchly, and Eckert swapped the relays for the vacuum tubes. When the efforts of the behemoths began to show diminishing returns Shockley, Bardeen, and Brattain create the transistor. All of the sudden the miles of wire required to emulate intelligence—and its telegraph forefather—was reduced to a few feet. The computer like all other electronic appliances in the 1950s and 1960s was undergoing a miniaturization process not unlike the transformation of the difference engines of Babbage and Scheutz underwent at the hands of Wiberg and Grant.

Then Jack Kilby invents the first integrated circuit that further reduces the size of a computer, as well as it costs. The integrated circuit creates a prophetic irony: the machine that once cost a million dollars to solve problems becomes a solution looking for million-dollar problem, as its processing size shrinks from cubic feet to a few centimeters.

At present, engineers are able to create an electronic circuit about 65 nanometers in size. To guarantee the fulfillment of the Moore prophesies engineers contemplate shrinking the electronic circuit to 45 nanometers and later to 32 nanometers. To give you an ideal about the sizes being discussed, the shaft of human hair, on average, is about 40 microns or 1000 times as large of the electronic circuits. The remainder of this chapter will discuss the three options currently available for the future design of computing: parallel computing, quantum computing, and DNA computing.

Parallel Computing

Parallel processor linking was born on the breathe of the super computers of the 1970s, for example the Cray super computer, and continued to expand when distributed computing replaced centralized computing. A super computer was no more than a string of processors linked in parallel—similar to the design of the electric parallel circuits. Parallel computing in its simplest form is complicated. The simplest definition of parallel computing implies three distinct functions: First, parallel computing is the simultaneous use of multiple resources on a single computer to solve computational problem; second, parallel computing runs multiple central processing units; third, parallel computing divides problems into discrete parts that are solved concurrently. Then each discrete part is further broken down to a series of instructions (Barney, 2009).

Many national communications corporations such as Sprint-Nextel Communications have utilized parallel databases of services for clients. For instance, customer information is held in a Toronto database, while billing information is located on a computer in San Diego, while a database in Kansas City records the employee working. Until 2002, parallel computing was accomplished with two distinct processors or more on the same motherboard inside the same computer. The technology to create two processor cores on the same silicon wafer did not exist as a practical business appliance.

In advance to the introduction of multicore microprocessor parallel computing had several definitions or inferences that included bit-level parallelism, instruction-level parallelism, data parallelism, and task parallelism

1. Bit-level parallelism was based on increasing processor word size. It emerged as a solution during an early stage of microprocessor development, the advent of very-large-scale integration (VLSI) computer chip. It was conceived that by increasing the word size reduces the number of cycles the processor executes to perform an operation.

2. Instruction-level parallelism (ILP)—there are two forms of ILP. The first is the pipelining, which allows the fetch-decode-execute cycles to process several instructions simultaneously. The second form of ILP has multiple execution units within the CPU, for instance duplicate arithmetic-logic circuits.

3. Data parallelism is a form of parallelism that involves multiple processors.

4. Task is merely performing two tasks simultaneously.

An interesting corollary arises with parallel computing by definition it resembles network computing in that it connects several processors for a common business goal. Researchers at MIT have created a computer with as many as sixteen tiles or processor cores. Now we have the beginnings of the supercomputer in miniature one chip or in parallel with innate processors representing London, another New York. It is Marconi's breakthrough again.

Philip Emeagwali, a Nigerian born computer scientist, in 1989 created a super computer and set a world record when he linked more than 65,000 discrete processors together at the national science facility in Los Alamos New Mexico. His initial project studied the honeycombs of the American honeybee. Colleagues have adapted his project to predict global warming and weather around the world. For his efforts, Emeagwali earn the moniker as the "father of the modern internet," in the scientific community.

The University of Michigan challenged Emeagwali findings and his Doctorate was not awarded. Since his initial computing claim, his record has been eclipsed many times over. The current record is more than 90,000 microprocessors linked together in parallel by a Chinese engineering team.

Quantum Computing

Another possibility for the design of the microprocessor is quantum computing. Quantum computing originated from the branch of physics that examines the infinitesimal, Quantum Mechanics. Quantum mechanics (structure) explains the discrete, indivisible units of energy called quanta as described by the Quantum Theory.

Quantum theory is the theoretical basis for all of classical physics. It explains the behavior of matter and energy at the atomic and subatomic level. Quantum theory was born in the mind of physicist Max Planck in 1900 when he presented his theory to the German Physical Society. Planck's theory evolved after he tried to reason why radiation from a glowing entity changed in color from red, to orange, and, finally, to blue as it grew hotter.

The crucial nexus between quantum mechanics and microprocessor construction began prior to the invention of the present day multicore processor. Computer manufacturers for years had adapted the philosophy to make a processor faster it had to be bigger. By bigger, manufacturers packed an ever-increasing number of transistor-based circuits (integrated circuits) into each new generation of microprocessors. Take, for instance, the Intel Corporation for years followed the bigger is faster philosophy. Every year or two in accordance with Moore's law, Intel introduced the next microprocessor benchmark.

For example, Intel's first commercially successful microprocessor was the Intel 286. In 1982, the 286 was a 16-bit microprocessor that had a capacity of 134,000 transistor-based circuits and a maximum clock speed of 16 megahertz (MHz). The 286 was more than 50-times faster than the original Intel microprocessor, the Intel 4004 that had a mere 2,300 transistor based circuits.

As Intel tried to stay ahead of the competitors Motorola, Cyrix, and Advanced Micro Devices (AMD), it followed the 286 with the 386 microprocessor. The 386 microchip more than doubled the number of transistors of the Intel 286 with an astonishing 275,000 circuits. The 386 was a 32-bit microprocessor with a clock speed between 16 and 33 megahertz (MHz). Intel continued to follow the bigger is faster path until the introduction of the Pentium IV microprocessor. With each progression in size microprocessor, the competition kept pace by producing chips that were the equivalent to the Intel standard.

The Pentium IV had a clock speed of 2.9 Gigahertz or faster that contained 42,000,000 circuits 180 nanometers wide. It was at this time that Intel decided building chips with higher and higher concentrations of transistor-based electronic circuits would eventually lead it away from classical physics and into quantum physics (Agarwal, 2007) (Warner, 2004) (Wikipedia, 2010). This statement may seem like a contradiction, at first glance, because first-generation Intel multicore units had as many as 291,000,000 circuits seven times the number of circuits on the

Pentium IV. This paradox exists because there is more than one processing core on the silicon wafer.

In a nutshell, quantum computing challenges the established wisdom of silicon-based, binary computers. First, because, silicon-based binary computers encode information in two states computers as either on or off, one or zero, true or false. The quantum computer, in contrast, encodes its information in form of quantum bits, or qubits. A qubit has four states instead of two commonplace states with current technology. Consequently, a qubit state exists as either a one or a zero, as both one and zero simultaneously, or at some point between one, and zero. The nature and states existing for the qubit forms the basis of quantum computing.

Richard Feynman first dreamed of building a quantum computer, in 1959. To exploit the power of qubit 'superposition' was indirectly proposed by Nobel laureate Niels Bohr in the text the Copenhagen Interpretation (Faye, 2008). Isaac Chuang, Neil Gershenfeld, and Mark Kubinec built the world's first quantum computer in the 1998. The quantum computer was a mind-boggling two qubits in size, which then loaded data and outputted a solution. It remained coherent, that is stable, for only a few nanoseconds (Encyclopedia Britannica, 2010).

Several barriers exist that prevent the ready exploitation of quantum physics in the computer. The first barrier that prevents the building of a quantum computer is memory or rather execution of programming and the output of data. Until now, the process of information and execution of data has been performed physically using punch cards, or as electromagnetic pulses stored in vacuum tubes, magnetic tape, optical disks, or silicon substrates. To exploit the power of the atom, quantum computing changes this concept and uses the atomic particle to process information. There is no way to predict the behavior of the atomic or subatomic particle—no error correction.

Another key barrier that prevents the building of a functional quantum computer is quantum coherence. Simply put, quantum coherence describes how scientists plan to suspend an atom in a magnetic field to exploit its processing power. This is not an easy task because the Earth is constantly bombarded with cosmic radiation—the Aurora Borealis is an example of visible cosmic radiation bombardment. Shielding of the qubit from radiation is imperative, because if any ambient electron radiation creases the magnetic field—no matter how insignificant. The cohesion of the quantum computer to disintegrates.

Still another barrier to building a practical quantum computer is interface. Currently, humans do not have the ability to interface with a quantum computer. Only binary computers can interface with quantum computers.

The three most relevant aspects of quantum physics are the principles of interference, superposition, and entanglement (Fuss, 2009).

a) Quantum superposition is a phenomenon, which allows an atomic particle or subatomic particle to have multiple states of reality simultaneously (Hoyle B., 2008).

b) Quantum entanglement refers to the fact that each qubit is part of a co-generated pair. Quantum entanglement allows qubits (photons) to reflect changes made to the unattended mate, no matter the distant (Clegg, 2007).

c) Interference refers to the disintegration cohesion of the containment field holding quantum computer allowing it to reads the results of its computations of qubits (Fuss, 2009).

Quantum computing remains in its infancy, it is highly unlikely there will be a technology breakthrough in the immediate future that will revolutionize computing in the near future. However, quantum computing, like photon computing (where are the circuits for the human interface?), does not seem possible in the near future.

Molecular Computing

Another medium possibility for the next generation computer or microprocessor is molecular material. The term molecular as used in this text does not include the discussion in the previous section about quantum computing. Instead, this section discusses computing based on organic material such as DNA and bio-molecular technology. Since the early 1990s, researchers have speculated on how to increase computing power without increasing the need for electrical power.

DNA is a nucleic acid that contains the instructions to develop all known living organisms. DNA has four basic nucleotides—adenine, thymine, guanine, and cytosine—which form the patterns of all genetic material. In 1994 Leonard Adelman, a mathematician at the University of Southern California, demonstrated the potential of a DNA computer by having it solve a problem that is difficult for silicon-based computers—the Hamiltonian Path Problem, also known as the

Traveling Salesman Problem (Lieber, 2007 p. 68). The goal of the Traveling Salesman Problem is to find the shortest route between a given numbers of cities, going through each city only once.

Silicon-based computers solve the problem by listing the possible routes and comparing them. However if the number of nodes increases, the number of possible routes grow exponentially overwhelming even the fastest computer. While silicon-based computers are obliged to performing calculations serially, Adelman realized that he could take advantage of DNA molecules to perform parallel calculation.

To realize the solution, Alderman encoded each city with a DNA nucleotides sequence. In the end, he came up with trillions of solutions. It took him a week to sort out the incorrect routes. Although, DNA computing has its advantages, there are definite drawbacks, no error correction.

Perhaps DNA computers are suited better for biotechnical and biochemical applications, which diagnose and fight disease. Already, scientists at Toyama University in Japan have created synthetic DNA for this purpose (Mallya, 2008).

Israeli scientists have devised a DNA computer with a clock speed of 330 trillion operations per second or 330 THz that is a 100,000 times faster than any PC. As of now, the DNA computer can only perform rudimentary functions; we cannot program the DNA to solve for Pi or any abstract functions (Lovgren, 2003). Then again, DNA circuitry requires no electricity, a worthy trade off considering the server farms prevalent at Amazon, Google, and Microsoft. DNA computers may mark the beginning of a computing 'Green Age.'

BIOTECHNOLOGY

This section of the conclusion is decidedly different from the other two sections.in that it is not concerned with how the microprocessor will evolve. Instead, this section tasks the microprocessor with a new mission interface with the human body. It differs from molecular computing technology searching for a new medium for microprocessor technology. In this section the term biotechnology, focus on the interface between human and machine.

Biotechnology is as ancient as the first humans planting of grains for food. Biotechnology is still in its infancy in much the same manner as the Analytical Engine of Charles Babbage is to the modern personal computer. There have been some minor breakthroughs in recent history. Humans have cured the plagues of Medieval Europe, influenza, polio, small pox and bubonic plague. Much of the work done with the computer however is mundane. It remains contained by the parameters set by Stibitz and to Boykin.

George Stibitz inventor of the Model K electromechanical computer pioneered the use of digital technology to monitor circulatory systems in 1964. Otis Boykin, creator of the electromagnetic pulse resistant transistor, developed the pacemaker. However, most proponents of biotechnology still view it as science fiction. They envision millions of flotillas of tiny robots—similar to that of the Nano-bots found in the bloodstream of the fictional cybernetic creatures the Borg from the television series Star Trek: the Next Generation. These tiny biomechanical robots once injected into the bloodstream go on a seek and destroy missions, like tiny soldiers, hunting for the biochemical signature of a malevolent viruses or tumors then repair the damage tissue of its patient-host. Not as ambition but just as effective many have the Richard Feynman (inventor of the quantum processor theory) vision of creating miniature factories creating nano-machines to build complex medicines.

Over the last ten years, there have been tremendous advancements in the science of cybernetics a division of biotechnology. Although it has yet to create an artificial limb with the same dexterity as an arm or leg depicted in the George Lucas Films Star Wars, scientist have created artificial ears to restore hearing. Other triumphs include using the computer to create artificial life and restore partial vision. Yet these artificial limbs and prosthetics do not replace the missing appendage. They add effectiveness to the remaining portion of the missing limb.

The most promising breakthrough in biotechnology occurred at the J. Craig Venter Institute, in 2010, where scientist successfully replaced the natural DNA of a virus with a completely artificial DNA generated by a computer. Venter documented this watershed event and broadcast it to the world on the Science Television Network in the summer. In the broadcast, Venter stated the breakthrough was the solutions for myriad of problems and issues challenging humanity among them food, the exhaustion of natural resources, converting carbon dioxide to oxygen, terra-forming, organic pollution-clean-up systems, and medicine.

Computers have partially restored vision to previously a blind individual is not as new as the Venter project. In 2007 surgeons—Doheny Eye Institute at the University of Southern California—have installed an artificial retina partially restoring sight to 18 people (Randerson, 2007).

The bionic eye worked by converting images from a tiny camera mounted on a pair of eyeglasses into a grid of 16 electrical signals transmitted directly to the nerve endings of the retina. People who have received the implants are able to distinguish objects such as a cup, a plate, and a knife. They can also tell in which direction an object is moving (Randerson, 2007).

The camera in the glasses transmits a signal to a blackberry size device in the recipient's pocket, which processed the images, in real-time, into a four by four grid of electrical signals. After processing, the grid was then transmitted to the eye implants, which converts the signals into electrical impulses the retina understands. Doctors hope to replace the 16-pixel artificial retina with a 60-pixel retina by 2011. The first retina took 16 years to develop (Randerson, 2007).

FUTURE OF COMPUTER NETWORKS

Cloud computing is the next logical step in distributed network computing providing the tools that extend the capability of client computers with an assortment of exotic services—ranging from increased processor power to extended infrastructure services, to software application, and personal collaboration—delivered wherever and whenever needed albeit laptop computer, tablet computer, or cell phone. In essence, cloud computing makes data more flexible and easier to access.

The first known inadvertent incidents of cloud computing occurred with email applications. Large technology based companies such as Microsoft with its Hotmail and Google with its G-Mail provided space on servers for customer to store indispensable documents in email files without fee.

The term cloud, relative to computing, has dual purposes. First, it is a metaphor for interface with the Internet. Second, it refers to computers and applications accessed remotely or independently of the traditional client's computing model. An example of remote access are the games on Facebook. These games exist on the Internet only. One does not bother with saving the game results to one's hard drive. Allowing the client access to remote resources held by a third, party vendor (Microsoft, Google, Amazon, and Facebook) or resources not physically attached to the company data center or company intranet. In cloud computing, virtual machines in large data centers and replace the traditional client and server model.

One might ask the question, what is a virtual machine? The simplest answer I can offer that is comprehensible is say a virtual machine is a completely isolated operating system within your normal operating system, not dual booting. For example in the late 1980's and early 1990's Apple Computers—when it used the Motorola microprocessor—built virtual machines inside their operating systems to run Windows software to entice new customers. Microsoft never reciprocated with virtual machines inside Windows software to run the then Macintosh System 7 software. Apple was miserly—in the spirit of Rene Grillet—and did not license clones. If it had, there would be a wider variety of computers and computing benchmarks. In the late 1980s and early 1990s, Apple was convinced it was the better computer for education and had several school districts under contract to use the Apple IIe or Macintosh computers. However, Microsoft caught and surpassed Apple by using the same tactic it used to dethrone the Netscape—which cost $29.95—with the Internet Explorer during the browser wars. It started giving away free its flagship NOS product the Microsoft Windows NT 4.0 server and operating system to colleges and school districts just before the launching of Windows 2000. There is no price better than free.

Many experts have declared that cloud computing is in the formative stage. According to IBM, there are three basic cloud configurations Public Private and Hybrid. A public clouds or external clouds deliver carefully selected sets of provisioned, standardized business processes, applications and infrastructure services and resources by way of Internet-based technologies based on flexible, variable payment and self-service needs.

Public clouds are owned and managed by an offsite, third-party providers; the billing is provided on an individualized computing based utility and accessed by subscription. Examples of public clouds are Google Apps, Windows Live, and Amazon's Elastic Compute Cloud.

Typically, private clouds or internal clouds provide security-conscious companies with on demand access to business process, application and infrastructure services, and resources, within the organization's management and data structures. For example, private clouds delivered through a data center or an intranet provide seamless layer of new technologies—virtualization management, cloud infrastructure, self-service portals, chargeback systems, and more—to existing data center infrastructure.

Hybrid clouds as one would suspect is a combinations of the two previously identified cloud types (IBM Global Services, 2009). Typically, cloud computing provides six services to customers:

1. Software as a service (SaaS)—SaaS has the capability to deliver software applications through a browser to thousands of customers using multitenant architecture.

2. Utility cloud services—is not new to the industry. Amazon, IBM, and the like have provided space on their server farms to third party companies for years.

3. Web services in the cloud—is a service related to SaaS, however, it only delivers the API that software engineers and programmers exploit instead of developing complete applications.

4. Platform services deliver the operating environment desired to the clients on the network.

5. Internet integration—talks about the integration of multiple devices computer, cell phone, etc.

6. Management services—these are the programs used to protect the clients from malware (Gruman, 2008).

Entertainment and science is where cloud computing is predicted to accelerate. For example, people with computers a generation or so old, might elect to subscribe to a newer version of their operating system and accessories through cloud computing instead of spending three to five hundred dollars for new computer hardware. In one scenario a customer with older personal computers and limited processor speed, may elect to subscribe to cloud service, connect remotely on a virtual computer, and use the latest version of Microsoft Office or map a genome of disease or virus.

In scenario two, a person with a new computer elects not to bother with the continued hassle of storing music and videos locally and elects to store in a cloud. Presently, Microsoft, Amazon, and Google are permitting the storage of personal music online. Qwest provides a similar service for digital photographs.

The one drawback that is preventing mass appeal is tradition and cost. The individual and the corporation alike are wary of large remote data stores, which are vulnerable to cyber-attack. Consequently, they believe in their own ability to isolate and contain malware directed at their personal and valuable data.

FINAL NOTES

Now we have travelled full circle. Where once humans created rudimentary computing devices with bags of stones, notches on a war club, or knots on a rope, machines, computer (microprocessors) now attempt to create humankind. The efforts in nanotechnology and biotechnology have created an artificial life—albeit not human—in a virus cell. Scientists have already perfected the ear in the form of the cochlear implant to restore hearing, now a similar devices attempt to restore vision. Artificial limbs are moved by impulses from the brain. Prosthetic devices allow people to walk, run, or grasp objects. How long before they are capable of typing or other fine movements.

Is our initial understanding of a computer defined as, one who computes, still valid? I would say yes, biology and technology have merged and formed the new science of biotechnology. Technology applications have come a long way in the years since George Stibitz initiated the use of digital devices to monitor heart, blood, and lung functions.

Are these not analog computers? Yes and no, they are digital computers functioning as analog computers, only in a compassionate manner. A behavior the Tide Analyzer of Lord Kelvin could never understand.

Biotechnology is not the terminator of digital computing. What I did not elaborate on in the earlier text was the advances in parallel computing. Researchers at MIT have created a computer with as many as sixteen tiles (processor cores). Their goal is to place sixty-four tiles (cores) on a wafer. In addition, MIT researchers have breached the 45-nano minimum feature size with a 32-nano minimum feature size. It is quite possible scientists and researchers might squeeze in 128 processor cores or tile onto 1 wafer before worrying about quantum effects.

Will humanity ever tap into the power of the atom and master quantum computing? That is a difficult answer question to answer. Two enormous engineering obstacles block the fate of quantum computing. The first is quantum cohesion. If the atom can be stabilized in radiation free environment—even the radiation from a television set can disrupt its stability—then the first barrier has been eliminated. The costs of doing so however are prohibitive. Remember when we began our journey through time, computers, or calculators—as some like to refer—were built as part of an entrepreneurial enterprise. For example, Pascal, the children of Hahn, and Thomas de Colmar all had financial gain in mind.

Engineers must lower the temperature atom to absolute zero—a feat not easily accomplished in a science lab, let alone in a den or an office cubicle. Alternatively, scientists can build a lead lined coffin in which it shields the atom in a magnetic field that prevents any external radiation disruptions. Both scenarios for the quantum computer make costs of a mass produced commercial adventure extremely remote.

There is the problem that there exists no quantum computer to human interface. Humans must rely on the interface between a binary (ordinary personal computer) computer and the quantum computer to interpret data yielded by the quantum computer. When these two enormous barriers are transverse, tapping the atom as a source of information could be feasible.

Finally, the question arises, what is the fate of computing if not powered by the atom, synthesized by DNA? The answer is just around the corner. Seventy-one years ago, Atanasoff and Berry invented a machine, approximately ten years later Eckert and Mauchly improved upon that ideal. Ten years after that, the transistor made its debut. It took ten years and a moon landing before science adapted the integrated circuit. It has been roughly 20 years since the appearance of the microprocessor. It has been only seven years since the first multicore processor.

History often repeats itself; one just has to be patient enough to enjoy the change. For example, compare the years since the appearance of the microprocessor with the years between the advent of Edison and the coming of age of Tesla. Technology does not just fall from the sky. Here are two more examples compare the span of time between the Cooke-Wheatstone Telegraph and the Morse Telegraph was roughly ten years. Then compare the span of time between the widespread use of the Morse telegraph and the invention of the telephone by Meucci. All major advances in science especially applying the principles of physics to a mode of communication require thought and careful planning.

EPILOGUE

The invention of the computer and later computer networking individuals clearly was the greatest mechanical and technological event of the 20th century and thus far in the 21st century. The computer has led to the plethora of new discoveries. At my disposal are cell phones that not only transmit voice messages but also scan the internet, play games, and monitor financial transactions.

I only wished the discoveries were made when I was young. Oh, but the evilest words in the human language are "what might I have been." Therefore, I am content to grow old and know that my bills are paid, television programs I missed are still available, and thanks to Facebook, I can talk to old friends from high school and college without having to remember their telephone numbers or addresses.

Still the computer can never replace the old-fashioned way of going to class reunions, or holding a newborn baby against your chest, still damp with birth fluids, or having it grab your finger as a way to say hello, I love you too.

Some things the computer has made better, and I do not begrudge it. For example, I no longer have to remember who delivered the pitch to Henry Aaron that allowed him to break Babe Ruth career home run record. Nor do I find myself thumbing through the almanac to remember whom Mr. October is or how many bases Maury Wills stole to set the major league record? I know now without a doubt the Broncos despite beating both Detroit and Minnesota in the pre-season lost the 1968 season opener to the hated Oakland Raiders 51-0. I am filled with unutterable loathing...

4 And they shall turn away their ears from the truth, and shall be turned unto fables. 5 But watch thou in all things, endure afflictions, do the work of an evangelist, make full proof of thy ministry. 6 For I am

now ready to be offered, and the time of my departure is at hand. **7** I have fought a good fight, I have finished my course, I have kept the faith: **8** Henceforth there is laid up for me a crown of righteousness, which the Lord, the righteous judge, shall give me at that day: and not to me only, but unto all them also that love his appearing. **9** Do thy diligence to come shortly unto me: (2 Timothy 4 – 9)

      PS. My beloved Denver Broncos lost Super Bowl XLVIII to the Seattle Seahawks (the gospel bird of the old AFC West) 43 to 8. Agony ohhh agony.

      I dedicate this edition to all those odious foul smelling fools at the University of Colorado Denver, who screamed and yelled at me for trying to date Alice Owens the guidance counselor of the Black Education Program, "She's white!"

      The same cantankerous old farts who believed Martin Luther King was a communist subversive, who'd write racial epithets on the tech department's official webpage because they thought the study of African American history was a dubious academic effort.

Works Cited

Soylent Communications. (2009). *Gottfried Leibniz*. Retrieved October 10, 2009, from NNBDD: http://www.nndb.com/people/666/000087405/

Abbott, S. (1981). *Benjamin Franklin*. Retrieved May 5, 2009, from Smithsonian Institution: History Wired: http://historywired.si.edu/detail.cfm?ID=394

ABC - CLIO. (2003). *Benjamin Franklin*. (W. Burns, Editor, & ABC - CLIO) Retrieved from In Science in the Enlightenment: An Encyclopedia: http://www.credoreference.com/entry/abcscienl/franklin_benjamin

Abd-El-Barr, M., & El-Rewini, H. (2005). *Fundamentals of computer organization and architecture*. Hoboken, NJ: John Wiley and Sons.

Agarwal, A. (2007, April 18). *Future of Computing*. Retrieved January 12, 2010, from MIT Distributed Intelligence: http://mitworld.mit.edu/video/671

AncestoryInc.com. (2009). *U.S. Federal 1850 Census Records*. Retrieved 11 2, 2009, from FamilyHistory.Com: http://www.familyhistory.com/censusyear.asp?y=1850

Anderson, A. J. (1994). *Foundations of computer technology*. London: Chapman & Hall.

Ashenden, P. J., Patterson, A. D., & Hennessy, J. L. (2004). *Computer Organization and Design*. San Franciso, CA: Morgan A. Kaufman.

Aspray, W. (Ed.). (1990). *Computers Before Computing*. Ames, IA: Iowa State University Press.

Aspray, W., & Campbell-Kelly, M. (1996). *Computer: A History of the Information Machine* (2nd ed.). New York: BasicBooks.

Aul, W. R. (1972, November). Herman Hollerith: Data Processing Pioneer. *Think*, pp. 22-24.

Babbage, C. (1864). *Passages from the life of a philosopher.* Public Domain.

Barney, B. (2009, Jan 10). *Introduction to Parallel Computing.* Retrieved Jan 12, 2010, from Lawrence Livermore National Laboratory : https://computing.llnl.gov/tutorials/parallel_comp/#Whatis

Bellis, M. (2009). *History of Lighting and Lamps: Pre - Electrical.* Retrieved September 15, 2009, from About.com: http://inventors.about.com/od/lstartinventions/a/lighting.ht m

Bellis, M. (2010). *The Atanasoff-Berry Computer the First Electronic Computer - John Atanasoff and Clifford Berry.* Retrieved from About.com: Inventor: http://inventors.about.com/library/weekly/aa050898.htm

Blackmon, D. A. (2008). *Slavery By Any Other Name.* New York: Random House.

Bowden, M. (2010). The Enemy Within. *The Atlantic Monthly*, 72-83.

Bromley, A. G. (1982). Charles Babbage's Analytical Engine, 1838. *Annals of the History of Computing*, 192-217.

Bromley, A. G. (1990). Difference and Analytical Engines. In W. Aspray (Ed.), *Computing Before Computers* (pp. 88 - 89). Ames, IA: Iowa State University Press.

Bromley, A. G. (1990). The Analog Computers. In W. Aspray (Ed.), *Computers Before Computing* (pp. 156-199). Ames , Iowa: Iowa State University Press.

Bromley, A. G. (2003). *Analytical Engine.* Retrieved October 23, 2009, from Credo: http://www.credoreference.com/entry/encyccs/analytical_eng ine

Bromley, A. G. (2003). *Difference Engine.* Retrieved 10 21, 2009, from In Encyclopedia of Computer Science: http://www.credoreference.com/entry/encyccs/difference_engine

Calvert, J. B. (2000, April 7). *The Electromagnetic Telegraph.* Retrieved February 5, 2007, from The Electromagnetic Telegraph: http://www.du.edu/~jcalvert/tel/morse/morse.htm#C

Campbell - Kelly, M. (1990). Punch - Card Machinery. In W. Aspray (Ed.), *Computing Before Computers* (pp. 122 - 156). Ames, IA: Iowa State University Press.

Carano, M., & Fjelstad, J. (2004). Printed Circuit Board Fabrication. In C. A. Harper (Ed.), *Electronic materials and processes handbook.* New York: McGraw - Hill.

Ceruzzi, P. E. (1990). Relay Calculators. In W. Aspray (Ed.), *Computing Before Computers* (pp. 207 - 213). Ames, IA: Iowa State University Press.

Ceruzzi, P. E. (1999). *A History of Modern Computing.* Cambridge, MA: 1999.

Charles F. Kettering. (2003). In L. B. Tyle (Ed.), *UXL ENCYCLOPEDIA OF WORLD BIOGRAPHY* (Vol. 6, pp. 1078-1080). Detroit, Michigan: Gale.

Chase, G. C. (1980). H STORY OF MECHANICAL COMPUTING MACHINERY. *IEEE Annals of the History of Computing,* 198-226.

Cheney, M. (1981). *Tesla: man out of time.* New York: Simon & Schuster.

Cheney, M., Uth, R., & Glenn, J. (1999). *Tesla, master of lightning.* China: Barnes & Noble.

Cisco Systems. (n.d.). *What Is the Difference: Viruses, Worms, Trojans, and Bots?* Retrieved March 13, 2011, from Cisco Systems:

http://www.cisco.com/web/about/security/intelligence/virus-worm-diffs.html

Clegg, B. (2007, March 30). *The Strange World of Quantum Entanglement*. Retrieved Jan 27, 2010, from California Literary Review: http://calitreview.com/51

Computer History Museum. (2008). *Georg Scheutz - The Babbage Engine*. Retrieved June 10, 2008, from Computer History Museum: http://www.computerhistory.org/babbage/georgedvardscheutz/

Computer Museum of America. (2006). *Baldwin Machine*. Retrieved July 25, 2008, from Computer Museum of America: http://www.computer-museum.org/main/slide/058.shtml

Computer Museum of America. (2008). *Dionysius Lardner - The Babbage Engine*. Retrieved May 9, 2010, from The Computer Museum of America: http://www.computerhistory.org/babbage/dionysiuslardner/

Conover, J. (2004). *802.11a: Making Space for Speed* . Retrieved 12 2, 2010, from Network Computing for IT by IT: http://www.networkcomputing.com/1201/1201ws1.html

Cooney, R. (2011). *Subnet Addressing*. Retrieved 1 9, 2011, from Network Computing: http://www.networkcomputing.com/unixworld/tutorial/001.html

Cornford, F. M. (1935). *Plato's Theory of Knowledge*. London: Routledge and Kegan Paul Ltd.

Dilhac, J. M. (2001). THE TELEGRAPH OF CLAUDE CHAPPE - AN OPTICAL TELECOMMUNICATION NETWORK FOR THE XVIIITH CENTURY. *2001 IEEE Conference on the History of Telecommunications*, 1-8.

Docter, Q., Groth, D., Dulaney, E., & Skandier, T. (2006). *CompTIA A+ Complete Study Guide* . Danvers, MA: Published by John Wiley and Sons.

Encyclopaedia Britannica. (2008). *Computer.* Chicago: Encyclopaedia Britannica.

Encyclopædia Britannica. (2008). *Frank Stephen Baldwin.* Chicago: Encyclopædia Britannica.

Encyclopædia Britannica. Ultimate Reference Suite. (2008). *Loom.* Chicago: Encyblopaedia Britannica.

Encyclopedia Britannica. (2010). quantum computer. Chicago, IL, USA.

Fara, P. (2002). *An entertainment for angels: electricity in the Enlightenment* . New York: Columbia University Press.

Faye, J. (2008). *Copenhagen Interpretation of Quantum Mechanics.* Retrieved from Stanford University Encylopedia of Philosophy: http://plato.stanford.edu/entries/qm-copenhagen/

Fiell, C., & Fiell, P. (2005). *1000 Lights: 1878-1959.* Koln, Germany: Taschen.

Flegg, G. (1983). *Numbers: Their History and Meaning.* Mineola, New York: Dover Publications.

Freud, S. (1961). *Civilization and Its Discontents.* London: W.W. Norton.

Fuss, A. (2009, September). Advantage. *The Quantum*, pp. 19-20.

Gale Virtual Library. (2008). Herman Hollerith. In E. o. Biography, *Encyclopedia of World Biography vol. 19, 2nd ed.* (pp. 151-152). Detroit: Gale Inc.

Gale Virtual References. (2005). Jacob Leupold. In N. S. Lauer (Ed.), *Science in Its Time* (Vols. 4, 1700 - 1799, p. 3846). Detroit: Gale.

General Electric. (2009). *Thomas Edison and GE*. Retrieved Apr 22, 2009, from General Electric: http://www.ge.com/company/history/edison.html

George, L. (1999). *Lewis Latimer*. Retrieved August 5, 2009, from Innovative Lives: http://invention.smithsonian.org/centerpieces/ilives/latimer/latimer.html

GFI Software. (2010). *The corporate threat posed by email trojans*. Retrieved 2011, from GFI: http://www.gfi.com/whitepapers/network-protection-against-trojans.pdf

Giles, J. (2009). The Enemy Within. *The New Scientist*, 36-39.

Gilman, L. (2004). Computer Virus. *GALE ENCYCLOPEDIA OF SCIENCE 3*, 998-1000.

Gilman, L. (2009). Computer Science: Microchip Technology. In K. L. Lerner, & B. Lerner (Eds.). Detroit: Gale.

Golden, F. (1983, Jan 3). Big Dimwits and Little Geniuses. *Time*, pp. 30-32.

Griffin, S. (2006). *Vannevar Bush*. Retrieved 2011, from Internet Pioneers: http://www.ibiblio.org/pioneers/bush.html

Gruman, E. K. (2008, April 7). *What is Cloud Computing?* Retrieved June 8, 2011, from InfoWorld: http://www.infoworld.com/d/cloud-computing/what-cloud-computing-really-means-031?page=0,0

Haber, L. (1970). *Black Pioneers of Science and Invention* . Orlando, FL: Houghton - Mifflin.

Habraken, J. (2003). *Absolute Beginner's Guide to Networking, Fourth Edition*. Indianapolis : Que Publishing.

Hally, M. (2005). *Electronic brains: stories from the dawn of the computer age* . Washington, DC: National Academy Press.

Hancock, M. (1988, January). *Burroughs Adding Machine Company*. Retrieved August 5, 2008, from Xnumber World of Calculators: http://www.xnumber.com/xnumber/hancock7.htm

Hannibal. (2004). *RISC vs. CISC: the Post-RISC Era*. Retrieved 10 21, 2011, from Ars Technica: http://arstechnica.com/cpu/4q99/risc-cisc/rvc-1.html

Hardy, L. H. (2009). History of Computer Networking. In M. Pagani, *Encyclopedia of Multimedia Technology and Networking* (pp. 613-617). New York: Information Science References.

Hayes, F. (2003, March 17). The Story So Far: Operating Systems. *ComputerWorld*, p. 30.

Heathcote, P. M. (1991). *'A' Level Computing*. London: Gutenberg Press.

Heide, L. (1997). Shaping a Technology: Amercian Punched Card Systems 1880 - 1914. *IEEE Annals of the History of Computing*, 28-41.

Hennessy, ,. J., Patterson, D. A., & Goldberg, D. (2003). *Computer architecture: a quantitative approach*. San Francisco: Morgan Kaufman Publishers.

Hermida, A. (2001, November 5). *Mouse inventor strives for more*. Retrieved 12 6, 2011, from BBC World News Edition: http://news.bbc.co.uk/2/hi/science/nature/1633972.stm

Hook, D. H., Norman, J. M., & Williams, M. R. (2001). *Origins of Cyberspace: A Library on the History of Computing, Networking and Telecommunications*. Novato, CA: HistoryofScience.com.

Hooks, D. H., Norman, J. M., & Williams, M. R. (2002). *Origins of Cyberspace: A Library on the History of Computing and Computer-Related Telecommunications (Limited Edition)*. Navato, CA: Norman Publishing.

Hoyle, B. (2008). Quantum computing. *GALE ENCYCLOPEDIA OF SCIENCE*, 3562 - 3563 .

Hoyle, M. (2004). *The First Mechanical Calculator.* Retrieved May 25, 2008, from The History of Computing Science: http://www.eingang.org/Lecture/pascaline.html

Hutchinson Encyclopedia. (2009, May 5). *Benjamin Franklin.* Retrieved May 5, 2009, from The Free Dictionary: http://encyclopedia.farlex.com/Benjamin+Franklin

Huurdeman, A. A. (2003). *The worldwide history of telecommunications.* New York, New York, United States: J. W. Wiley & Sons, Inc.

IBM. (1990, October 10). *Leupold Calculator.* Retrieved October 10, 2009, from http://www-03.ibm.com/ibm/history/exhibits/attic/attic_177.html

IBM. (1994). *Baldwin Calculating Machine.* Retrieved July 25, 2008, from IBM Archives Exhibit: http://www-03.ibm.com/ibm/history/exhibits/attic3/attic3_063.html

IBM. (2008). *Hahn Calculator.* Retrieved August 6, 2008, from IBM Archives: Hahn Calculator: http://www-03.ibm.com/ibm/history/exhibits/attic/attic_137.html

IBM Archives. (1964). *Tube, Transistor, chip.* Retrieved 11 16, 2009, from IBM Archives: http://www-03.ibm.com/ibm/history/exhibits/vintage/vintage_4506VV21 24.html

IBM Archives. (2009). *Hill Arithmometer.* Retrieved 10 27, 2009, from IBM Archives: http://www-03.ibm.com/ibm/history/exhibits/attic/attic_082.html

IBM Archives. (2009). *IBM 701.* Retrieved 12 1, 2009, from IBM Archives: http://www-03.ibm.com/ibm/history/exhibits/701/701_intro.html

IBM Archives. (2009). *TIM Calculator*. Retrieved October 19, 2009, from IBM Corporate Archives: http://www-03.ibm.com/ibm/history/exhibits/attic/attic_090.html

IBM Global Services. (2009). *Cloud Computing Demystified*. Armonk, New York: IBM.

IEEE . (2008). *John Patterson*. Retrieved 11 1, 2009, from IEEE Global History Network: http://www.ieeeghn.org/wiki/index.php/John_Patterson

IEEE. (2009, September 24). *Charles F. Kettering*. Retrieved from IEEE Global History Network: http://www.ieeeghn.org/wiki/index.php/Charles_F._Kettering

IEEE. (2009). *Granville T. Woods, 1856 - 1910*. Retrieved August 10, 2009, from IEEE History Center: http://www.ieee.org/web/aboutus/history_center/biography/woods.html

IEEE. (2009, 10 14). *John Thompson*. Retrieved 10 25, 2011, from IEEE Global History Network: http://www.ieeeghn.org/wiki/index.php/John_Thompson

IEEE. (2009). *Mark E. Dean*. Retrieved 10 25, 10, from IEEE Global History Network: http://www.ieeeghn.org/wiki/index.php/Mark_E._Dean

IEEE Computer Society. (2009). *George Robert Stibitz*. Retrieved 11 24, 2011, from IEEE Computer Society Awards: http://www.computer.org/portal/web/awards/stibitz

IEEE Global History Network. (2009, July 29). *Antonio Meucci*. Retrieved August 30, 2009, from IEEE Global History Network: http://www.ieeeghn.org/wiki/index.php/Antonio_Meucii

IEEE History Center. (2009). *IEEE History Center: Phillip Emeagwali*. Retrieved July 16, 2009, from IEEE :

http://www.ieee.org/web/aboutus/history_center/biography/emeagwali.html

Ifrah, G. (2001). *The Universal History of Computing: From the Abacus to the Quantum Computer.* New York: J. W. Wiley.

Ikenson, B. (2004). *Patents: ingenious inventions : how they work and how they came to be.* New York: Black Dog & Leventhal Publishers, Inc.

Intel. (2011). *RISC, CISC, VLIW and EPIC Architectures.* Retrieved 10 21, 2011, from Intel-Scientific: www.intel.com/intelpress/chapter-scientific.pdf

International Business Machines Corporation. (1961). *BRL Report 1961.* Retrieved January 12, 2009, from IBM 1401: http://ed-thelen.org/comp-hist/BRL61-ibm1401.html

Jefferson Labs. (2007, June). *How do I make a model of an atom?* Retrieved Feb 2, 2010, from Thomas Jefferson National Accelerator Facility: http://education.jlab.org/qa/atom_model.html

Jonnes, J. (2003). *Empire of Lights: Edison, Tesla, Westinghouse.* New York: Random House.

Kaplan, E. (2004). *The Controversial Replica of Leonardo da Vinci's Adding Machine.* Retrieved August 6, 2008, from Calculating Machines: http://192.220.96.166/leonardo/leonardo.html

Karam, P. A. (2005). Use of Electric Power Becomes Widespread. In N. Schlager, & J. Lauer (Eds.), *Science and its Times* (Vol. Vol. 5: 1800 to 1899, pp. p556-558). Detroit, MI: Gale Group.

Karwatka, D. (2004, November). Blaise Pascal and the First Calculator. *Tech Directions*, p. 10.

Keithley, J. F. (1999). *The Story of Electrical and Magnetic Measurements: From 500 BC to the 1940s .* New York: Wiley-IEEE Press .

Kidwell, P. A. (2001). Yours for Improvement—The Adding Machines of Chicago, 1884–1930. *IEEE Annals of the History of Computing*, 3- 21.

Kidwell, P. A. (2000). The Adding Machine Fraternity at St. Louis: Creating a Center of Invention, 1880-1920. *IEEE Annals of the History of Computing*, 4-21.

Kidwell, P. A., & Ceruzzi, P. E. (2009, 2009). *Landmarks in Digital Computing*. Retrieved 12 12, 2009, from Smithsonian Institution National Air and Space Museum: http://www.nasm.si.edu/research/dsh/LDC/publicit.html

Kidwell, P. A., & Williams, M. R. (1992). *The Calculating Machines: Their History and Development*. Cambridge, MA: Massachusetts Institute of Technology Publishers.

Knipple, D. T. (1998). *John H. Patterson*. Retrieved May 2010, from NCR: http://home.paonline.com/knippd/whoisncr/Patterson.htm

Krebs, B. (2003, Feb 14). *A Short History of Computer Viruses and Attacks*. Retrieved March 12, 2011, from Washington Post: http://www.washingtonpost.com/wp-dyn/articles/A50636-2002Jun26.html

Krebs, B. (2009, September 14). *Cyber Crooks Target Public & Private Schools*. Retrieved April 1, 2011, from Washington Post: http://voices.washingtonpost.com/securityfix/2009/09/cyber_mob_targets_public_priva.html

Lammle, T. (2004). *CCNA: Cisco Certified Network Associate*. San Francisco: Sybex Inc.

Larner, R. A. (2014, March 9). *FMS: The IBM FORTRAN Monitor System*. Retrieved from Computer History Museum: http://www.computer.org/csdl/proceedings/afips/1987/5094/00/50940815.pdf

Lawson, S. (2011, Feb 3). *Update: ICANN assigns its last IPv4 addresses.* Retrieved Mar 23, 2011, from ComputerWorld: http://www.computerworld.com/s/article/9207961/Update_I CANN_assigns_its_last_IPv4_addresses

Lees, J. (1980). *The World in Your Own Notebook (Alan Kay's Dynabook project at Xerox PARC).* Retrieved 9 7, 2011, from AtariArchives.Org: http://www.atariarchives.org/bcc3/showpage.php?page=5

Lessing, L. (2008). Edwin H. Armstrong. In E. Brittanica, *Ultimate Reference Suite.* Chicago: Encyclopedia Brittanica.

Library of Congress. (2009). *Benjamin Franklin and Electricity.* Retrieved May 6, 2009, from America's Story: http://www.americaslibrary.gov/cgi-bin/page.cgi/aa/leaders/franklinb/electric_4

Library of Congress. (2009, February 12). *Who is credited as inventing the telephone?* Retrieved August 30, 2009, from Everyday Mysteries: http://www.loc.gov/rr/scitech/mysteries/telephone.html

Lieber, C. M. (2007, September). DNA Computing. *Scientific American*, p. 68.

Linux Documentation Project. (2008). *What is Linux.* Retrieved 2010, from Linux Online: http://www.linux.org/info/

Linux Documentation Project. (2008). *What is Linux.* Retrieved 2010, from Linux online: http://www.linux.org/info/

Lohr, S. (2002). *Go To: The Story of the Math Majors, Bridge Players, Engineers, Chess Wizards, Maverick Scientists and Iconoclasts--The Programmers Who Created the Software Revolution.* New York: The Perseus Books Group.

Lovgren, S. (2003, February 24). *Computer Made from DNA and Enzymes.* Retrieved   from http://news.nationalgeographic.com/news/2003/02/0224_03 0224_DNAcomputer.html

M.I.T. Libraries. (2009, July). *Project Whirlwind*. Retrieved January 3, 2011, from The Records of Project Whirlwind: http://dome.mit.edu/handle/1721.3/37456

Mackintosh, A. R. (1987, March). The First Digital Computer. *Physics Today*, pp. 25 - 32.

Mallick, M. (2003). *Mobile and Wireless Design Essentials*. Indianapolis: J. W. Wiley.

Mallya, R. (2008, July 22). *DNA offeres radical computing rethink*. Retrieved February 1, 2010, from Computer Weekly: http://www.computerweekly.com/Articles/2008/07/22/2315 91/dna-offers-radical-computer-rethink.htm

Manor College of Technology. (2005). *Blaise Pascal*. Retrieved May 25, 2008, from Learning Center: http://www.manorcollege.org.uk/LearningCentre/blaise%20p ascal.htm

Massachusetts Institute of Technology. (1996, 11). *Lewis T. Latimer*. Retrieved 11 1, 2009, from Inventor of the Week Archives: http://web.mit.edu/invent/iow/latimer.html

Massachusetts Institute of Technology. (2000, January). *Charles F. Kettering*. Retrieved from Inventor of the Week Archive: http://web.mit.edu/invent/iow/kettering.html

Massachusetts Institute of Technology. (2002). *James Ritty*. Retrieved 11 1, 2009, from Inventor of the Week Archives: http://web.mit.edu/invent/iow/ritty.html

Massachusetts Institute of Technology. (2002, 3). *William Seward Burroughs*. Retrieved 11 1, 2009, from Inventor of the Week Archives: http://web.mit.edu/invent/iow/burroughs.html

Massachusetts Institute of Technology. (2009). *Thomas Alva Edison (1847-1931)*. Retrieved November 11, 2009, from Inventor of the Week Archive: http://web.mit.edu/invent/iow/edison.html

McGillem, C. D. (2009). *Telegraph*. (Encyclopedia Brittanica) Retrieved March 22, 2010, from History.com: http://www.history.com/topics/telegraph

Merzbach, U. C. (1977). Georg Scheutz and the First Printing Calculator. *SMITHSONIAN INSTITUTION PRESS*, 1 - 73.

Merzbach, U. C. (2007, September 27). *Smithsonian Digital Depository*. Retrieved July 20, 2008, from Smithsonian Institution: http://si-pddr.si.edu/dspace/handle/10088/2435?mode=full&submit_simple=Show+full+item+record

Meyer, P. (2002). *Precision journalism: a reporter's introduction to social science methods*. Lanham, MD: Rowman & Littlefield Publishers, Inc.

Meyers, M., & Jernigan, S. (2003). *Mike Meyers' A+ Guide to Managing and Troubleshooting PCs*. New York: McGraw-Hill Professional.

Microsoft . (2008, December). *Computer*. Retrieved December 22, 2008, from Encarta Online Encyclopedia: http://encarta.msn.com

Microsoft Encarta Online Encyclopedia 2008. (2008). *Loom*. Retrieved June 1, 2008, from Encarta: http://encarta.msn.com

Microsoft. (2009, September 15). *Lamps*. Retrieved Feb 2008, from Encarta: www.encarta.com

Microsoft. (2010, January 12). *integrated circuit*. Retrieved January 12, 2010, from Bing: http://www.bing.com/Dictionary/search?q=define+integrated+circuit&FORM=DTPDIA

Microsoft. (2010, January 12). *Microprocessor*. Retrieved January 12, 2010, from Bing: http://www.bing.com/Dictionary/search?q=define+microprocessor&FORM=DTPDIA

Microsoft Corporation. (1999). *MCSE Training Kit: Networking Essentials Plus.* Retrieved November 20, 2010, from Microsoft: http://www.microsoft.com/mspress/books/sampchap/1956e. aspx

Microsoft Corporation. (2011). *Malware Encyclopedia* . Retrieved 2011, from Malware Protection Center: http://www.microsoft.com/security/portal/Threat/Encyclope dia/Search.aspx?query=Key-logger

Miller, M. (2008). *Is it Safe: Protecting Your Computer, Your Business, and Yourself Online.* Indianapolis: Que.

Milo. (2009). *History of operating systems.* Retrieved 2 12, 2010, from OSdata: http://www.osdata.com/kind/general.htm

Mokyr, J. (November 2001). *WHY WAS THE INDUSTRIAL REVOLUTION A EUROPEAN PHENOMENON?* Chicago: Supreme Court Economic Review .

Moncur, M. (1998). *MCSE: The Core Exams.* Sebastropol, CA: O'Reilly.

Montgomery County Historical Society. (2010). *Ritty Cash Registers.* Retrieved May 2010, from Ohio History: http://omp.ohiolink.edu/OMP/NewDetails?oid=888984&fiel dname=collection&results=10&sort=title&searchstatus=1&hit s=4&searchmark=1&searchstring=National+Cash+Register+ Archive&searchtype=kw&format=list&count=3

Morgan Reynolds Inc. (2005). *Chapter Three: Edison.* Retrieved April 9, 2009, from Nikola Tesla Taming of Electricity: http://ezproxy.denverlibrary.org:2048login?url=http://search. ebschohost.com/longin.aspx?direct=true&db=khh&AN=2298 3015&site=ehost-live&scope=site

Morrison, P., & Morrison, P. (1999, December). A Century of Physics. *Scientific American*, pp. 146-147.

Mosla, J. (2005). Mitigating denial of service attacks: A tutorial. *Journal of Computer Security*, 807-837.

Mueller, S. (2004). *Upgrading and Repairing PCs, 15th Anniversary Edition*. Indianapolis, IN: Que.

Myrdal, G. (1944). *An American Dilemma: The Negro Problem and Modern Democracy*. New York: Harper & Brothers.

NCR. (2008). *NCR: Card Random Access Memory*. Retrieved October 21, 2008, from Computer History Museum: http://www.computerhistory.org/collections/accession/10264 6240

NCR History Timeline. (2009). Retrieved 11 1, 2009, from NCR History: http://www.ncr.com/about_ncr/company_overview/history.js p

Nebeker, F. (2004, December). *IEEE-USA Today's Engineer*. Retrieved August 24, 2008, from Engineer Online: http://www.todaysengineer.org/2004/Dec/history.asp

New York Times. (1892, Feb 21). Mr. Edison is Satisfied. *New York Times*.

Nguyen, ,. H., Johnson, B., & Hackett, M. (2005). *Testing Applications on the Web*. Hoboken, NJ: J. W. Wiley & Sons, Inc.

Novell. (2010). *Novell History*. Retrieved 2011, from Novell: http://www.novell.com/news/press/pressroom/history.html

Null, L., & Lorbur, J. (2006). *The Essentials of Computer Organization and Architecture*. Sudbury, MA: Jones and Bartlett Publishers.

Ohrtman, F., & Roeder, K. (2003). *Wi-Fi Handbook*. New York: McGraw-Hill.

Palmer, M. (2006). *Hands-On: Networking Fundamentals*. Boston: Thomson

PBS. (2000). *Thomas Alva Edison.* Retrieved April 29, 2007, from The American Experience | The Telephone | People & Events : http://www.pbs.org/wgbh/amex/telephone/peopleevents/pande03.html

PBS. (2004). *Tesla Life and Legacy - Coming to America.* Retrieved 11 13, 2009, from Master of Lighting: http://www.pbs.org/tesla/ll/ll_america.html

PBS. (2004, April). *Who invented Radio?* Retrieved August 5, 2009, from Tesla Master of Lighting: http://www.pbs.org/tesla/ll/ll_whoradio.html

PC Mag.com. (2011, December). *Microcode.* Retrieved December 3, 2011, from PC Mag.com: http://www.pcmag.com/encyclopedia_term/0,2542,t=microinstruction&i=46940,00.asp

PCPerformanceTools.com. (2011). *Beware of PC Trojans.* Retrieved from PCPerformanceTools.com: http://pcperformancetools.com/harmful-trojans.htm

Poe, E. A. (2007, December 14). *THE CASK OF AMONTILLADO.* Retrieved 4 2008, November, from The Edgar Allan Poe Society of Baltimore: http://www.eapoe.org/works/tales/caska.htm

Poole, I. (2010). *History of the vacuum tube.* Retrieved October 2010, from Radio-Electronics.Com: http://www.radio-electronics.com/info/radio_history/valve/hov.php

Price, D. d. (1959). An ancient Greek computer. *Scientific American,* 60-67.

Pugh, E. W. (1984). *Memories that Shaped an Industry Decisions Leading to IBM System-360.* Cambridge, MA: MIT Press.

Randerson, J. (2007, February 17). Six blind people regain partial sight thanks to 'Bionic eye' implant. *The Guardian,* p. 11.

Redin, J. (2007, Nov 22). *A Brief History of Calculators Part I: The Age of the Polymaths*. Retrieved June 30, 2008, from History of Mechanical Calculators: http://www.xnumber.com/xnumber/mechanical1.htm

Redshaw, K. (1996). *Vannevar Bush*. Retrieved 2011, from Pioneers: http://www.kerryr.net/pioneers/bush.htm

Rees, P. K. (1965). *Principles of Mathematics*. Englewood Cliff, NJ: Prentice - Hall Inc.

Rice, R. S. (1995). *The Antikythera Mechanism: Physical and Intellectual Salvage from the 1st Century*. Retrieved 11 9, 2010, from USNA Eleventh Naval History Symposium: http://ccat.sas.upenn.edu/rrice/usna_pap.html

Riddle, L. (1995). *Grace Murray Hopper*. Retrieved September 10, 2011, from Biographies of Women Mathmaticians: http://www.agnesscott.edu/lriddle/women/hopper.htm

Robertson, J. S. (2004). Nits make Lice. In S. D. Houston (Ed.), *The first writing: script invention as history and process* (pp. 16-38). Cambridge, United Kingdom: Cambridge University Press.

Roegel, D. (2008). An Early (1844) Key-Driven Adding Machine. *IEEE Annals of the History of Computing*, 59 - 65.

Romano, M. J. (2003). *CliffAP European History*. Hoboken, New Jersey: Wiley Publications.

Russo, M. (2008). *Jacquard Loom*. Retrieved May 30, 2008, from Herman Hollerith: The World's First Statistical Engineer: http://www.history.rochester.edu/steam/hollerith/loom.htm

San Diego Supercomputer Center . (1997). *Grace Hopper: Pioneer Computer Scientist*. Retrieved January 1, 2011, from Women In Science: http://www.sdsc.edu/ScienceWomen/hopper.html

Schlager, N., & Lauer, J. (Eds.). (2010). Claude Chappe. *Gale Virtual Reference Library, 4*, 1700 to 1799. Gale.

Schneider, J., & Singer, B. (2005, 11 21). *Blueprint for Change: The Life and Times of Lewis H. Latimer.* Retrieved October 3, 2010, from Blueprint for Change: The Life and Times of Lewis H. Latimer: URL: http://edison.rutgers.edu/latimer/catalog.htm

Seifer, M. J. (1998). *Wizard: the life and times of Nikola Tesla : biography of a genius.* New York: Citadel Press.

Shinder, D. L. (2002). *Computer Networking Essentials.* Indianapolis, IN: Cisco Press.

Sinard, J. H. (2006). *Practical Pathology Informatics: Demystifying informatics for the practicing anatomic pathologist .* New Haven, CT: Springer.

Slater, R. (1992). *Portraits in silicon.* Cambridge, MA: MIT Press.

Smart Computing. (2010). *Augusta Ada (Byron) King.* Retrieved from Smart Computing Encyclopedia: http://www.smartcomputing.com/editorial/dictionary/detail.asp?guid=&searchtype=1&DicID=16449&RefType=Encyclopedia

Smith, A. (1776). *An Inquiry into the Nature and Causes of the Wealth of Nations.* London: T. Nelson and Sons, Paternoster Row.

Smithsonian Institution. (2002). *Origin of Electrical Power.* Retrieved August 31, 2009, from Powering a Generation: Power History #1: http://americanhistory.si.edu/powering/backpast.htm

Smithsonian Institution. (2008). *Lighting a Revolutions.* Retrieved January 22, 2009, from Preconditions to 20th Century Lamps: http://americanhistory.si.edu/lighting/20thcent/prec20.htm

Smithsonian Institution Libraries. (2001, August 24). *Physics.* Retrieved Feb 12, 2009, from Science and the Artist's Book: http://www.sil.si.edu/Exhibitions/Science-and-the-Artists-Book/phys.htm#09

Soper, M. E. (2004). *Absolute Beginner's Guide to A+ Certification*. London: QUE.

SRI International. (2011). *Englehart and the Dawn of Interactive Computing*. Retrieved 12 6, 2011, from SRI International: http://www.sri.com/engelbart-event.html

Stein, D. (1985). *Ada: A Life and a Legacy*. Cambridge, MA: MIT Press.

Stross, R. E. (2007). *The Wizard of Menlo Park: How Thomas Alva Edison Invented the Modern World*. New York: Random House.

Swaine, P. F. (2000). *Fire in the Valley*. New York: McGraw-Hill.

Swedin, E. G., & Ferro, D. L. (2007). *Computers: The Life Story of a Technology*. Baltimore: Greenwood Press.

Szucs, L. D. (1998). Research in Census Records. In L. D. Szucs, & S. H. Luebking (Eds.), *The Source: A Guidebook of American Genealogy* (revised edition ed., p. 114). Salt Lake City, UT.

Taborn, T. D. (2002, February). High Tech's Invisible Man. *USBE & Information Technology*, p. 14.

Taborn, T., & Thompson, G. (2006). *20 YEARS AT THE TOP: A Generation of Black Engineers of the Year*. Raliegh, NC: Lulu.

Tannenbaum, A. S. (2002, Jan 12). *A History of Operating Systems*. Retrieved 2 12, 2010, from Informit: http://www.informit.com/articles/article.aspx?p=24972

Tarawneh, Z. (2001, March 22). *A Biography of Herman Hollerith*. Retrieved October 1, 2008, from Computing History Museum Organization: http://www.computinghistorymuseum.org/teaching/papers/biography/hollerith.PDF

Teare, D. (2006). *Internetworking Technology Handbook*. Retrieved February 18, 2006, from Cisco:

ttp://www.cisco.com/univercd/cc/td/doc/cisintwk/ito_doc/intrint.htm

The Free Dictionary. (2010, January). *Microchip*. Retrieved January 12, 2010, from TheFreeDictionary.com: http://www.thefreedictionary.com/microchip

The Gale Encyclopeidia of Science. (2004, Dec 5). *Electric Circuit*. (K. L. Lerner, & B. W. Lerner, Eds.) Retrieved March 10, 2009, from Denver Public Library: http://go.galegroup.com.ezproxy.denverlibrary.org:2048/ps/start?p=GVRL&u=denver

Thomson Corporation. (2005). *Dorr Eugene Felt* . Retrieved August 19, 2008, from World of Computer Science: http://www.bookrags.com/biography/dorr-eugene-felt-wcs/

Thomson Gale. (2005). *Dorr Eugene Felt Biography*. Retrieved August 10, 2008, from Dorr Eugene Felt | World of Computer Science: http://www.bookrags.com/biography/dorr-eugene-felt-wcs/

Turck, J. (1921). *Origin of Modern Calculating Machines: A Chronicle of the Evolution of the Principles that Form the Generic Make-Up of the Modern Calculating Machine*. Chicago: Western Society of Engineers.

U. S. Census Bureau. (2008, September 8). *The Hollerith Machine*. Retrieved 7 2008, October, from U.S. Census Bureau: http://www.census.gov/history/www/technology/012446.html

ULtimate Reference Suite. (2008). *Aiken, Howard Hathaway*. Chicago: Encyclopedia Britannica.

Ultimate Reference Suite. (2008). Lightning. Chicago, IL, USA.

United States Center For Disease Control. (2010). *HIV among African Americans*. Retrieved 2010, from Department of Health and Human Services: http://www.cdc.gov/hiv/topics/aa/

United States Department of Health and Human Services. (2010). *Minority Women's Health: African-Americans*. Retrieved 2010, from Women's Health.Gov: http://www.womenshealth.gov/minority/africanamerican/hiv.cfm

University of Saint Andrews Scotland School of Mathematics and Statistics. (2009). *Frank Stephen Baldwin*. Retrieved October 9, 2009, from The MacTutor History of Mathematics archive: http://www-history.mcs.st-andrews.ac.uk/Biographies/Baldwin.html

US-Cert. (2005). *Recognizing and Avoiding Email Scams*. Retrieved March 11, 2011, from US-CERT: The United States Computer Emergency Response Team: http://www.us-cert.gov/reading_room/emailscams_0905.pdf

Vegter, W. (2005). *Leonardo da Vinci*. Retrieved August 6, 2008, from Prominent People: http://www.prominentpeople.co.za/da-vinci-leonardo.aspx

Vernet, J. (2008). Complete Dictionary of Scientific Biography. Detroit, MI: Charles Scribner's Sons. Retrieved 11 3, 2009, from Torres Quevedo, Leonardo: http://go.galegroup.com.ezproxy.denverlibrary.org:2048/ps/start.do?p=GVRL&u=denver

Vetter, H. F. (2011). *Lewis Howard Latimer*. Retrieved February 2011, from Notable American Unitarians: http://www.harvardsquarelibrary.org/uu_addenda/Lewis-Howard-Latimer.php

Virtual Museum of Old Electric, Electronic and Electrochemical Instruments. (2009). *Leyden Jars*. Retrieved 02 12, 2009, from Famous Scientest: http://chem.ch.huji.ac.il/instruments/archaic/leyden_jars.htm

Voigt, D. (2010). *Recent Work*. Retrieved 2010, from Daniel Eugene Voigt: http://www.danielvoigt.com/index.html

Waldman, D. E. (1998). Rise and Fall of IBM. In D. I. Rosenbaum (Ed.), *Market Dominance: How Firms Gain, Hold, or Lose It and the Impact on Economic Performance* (pp. 131 - 152). London, United Kingdom: Greenwood Publishing Group.

Wallace, P. R. (1991). *Physics: Imagination and Reality.* London: World Scientific Publishing Co. Ltd.

Walters, E. G. (2001). *The Essential Guide to Computing, the Story of Information Technology.* Upper Saddle River, NJ: Prentice-Hall.

Warner, W. (2004). *Great moments in microprocessor history.* Retrieved 2010, from IBM: http://www.ibm.com/developerworks/library/pa-microhist.html?ca=dgr-mw08MicroHistory

Weems, C. C. (2007). *Architecture (computer science).* Retrieved April 22, 2008, from Encarta : http://encarta.msn.com/encyclopedia_761572372_2/Architecture_(computer_science).html

Weiss, S. (2010). Difference Engines in the 20th Century. *IM 2010 Proceedings - Historical Calculating Instruments* (pp. 157-164). Munich: Google.

WGBH/PBS. (2000). *The American Experience.* Retrieved January 22, 2009, from Edison's Miracle of Light: http://www.pbs.org/wgbh/amex/edison/

What is Microcode? (2003). Retrieved 10 18, 2011, from WiseGeek: http://www.wisegeek.com/what-is-microcode.htm

Whitaker, J. C. (1996). *The Electronics Handbook.* Salem, MA: CRC Press.

White, R. (2004). *How Computers Work.* Indianapolis, IN: Que.

Wikipedia. (2009). *Cyrix.* Retrieved 1 3, 2010, from Wikipedia.org: http://en.wikipedia.org/wiki/Cyrix

Wikipedia. (2009, 12 31). *Mac OS X.* Retrieved 1 3, 2010, from Wikpedia.Org: http://en.wikipedia.org/wiki/Mac_OS_X

Wikipedia. (2009, December). *Microcode*. Retrieved December 27, 2009, from Wikipedia: http://en.wikipedia.org/wiki/Microcode

Wikipedia. (2010). *Transistor count*. Retrieved 2010, from Wikipedia.org: http://en.wikipedia.org/wiki/Transistor_count

Wikipedia.org. (2009). *von Neumann Architecture*. Retrieved Sept 2011, from   Wikipedia: http://en.wikipedia.org/wiki/Von_Neumann_architecture

Wikipedia.Org. (2010). *William Austin Burt*. Retrieved March 23, 2010, from   Wikipedia.org: http://en.wikipedia.org/wiki/William_Austin_Burt

Wilkes, M. V. (2003). *Charles Babbage*. (L. John Wiley & Sons, Producer, & Credo) Retrieved 10 21, 09, from In Encyclopedia of Computer   Science: http://www.credoreference.com/entry/encyccs/babbage_char les

Williams, J. (Ed.). (1997). *Money History*. New York: St. Martin's Press.

Williams, M. (1990). Early Calculation. In W. Aspray (Ed.), *Computing Before Computers* (pp. 3 - 59). Ames, IA: Iowa University Press.

Williams, M. R. (1979). The Difference Engines. *The Computer Journal*, 82-89.

Williams, M. R. (1990). Punch - Card Machinery. In W. Aspray (Ed.), *Computers Before Computing* (pp. 122-155). Ames, IA: Iowa State University Press.

Williams, M. R. (2000). On the First Generation of Computers. In R. Rojas, & U. Hashagen (Eds.), *The First Computers: History and Architectures*. Cambridge: MIT Press.

Winferno Software. (2011). *Computer Worms*. Retrieved from Winferno Software.

Winston, B. (1998). *Media technology and society: a history : from the telegraph to the Internet.* London: Routledge.

WiseGeek. (2003). *What is Microcode?* Retrieved 10 18, 2011, from WiseGeek.com: http://www.wisegeek.com/what-is-microcode.htm

Wolf, M. J. (2000). *Abstracting reality: art, communication, and cognition in the digital age* . Lanham: University Press of America.

Wolff, J. (2007, May). *Brunsviga Calculators.* Retrieved August 9, 2008, from John Wolff's Web Museum: http://home.vicnet.net.au/~wolff/calculators/Brunsviga/Brunsviga.htm

Woodside, M. (2007). *Thomas Edison: The Man Who Lit Up the World* . New York: Sterling Publishing Company.

WordiQ.com. (2010). *Procedural Programming.* Retrieved 12 6, 2011, from WordiQ.com: http://www.wordiq.com/definition/Procedural_programming

World - Information Organization. (2007). *Thomas Arithmometer.* Retrieved August 7, 2008, from World - Information.Org: http://world-information.org/wio/program/objects/1037128687/103712871 4/?pl=yu

World - Information.Org. (2007). *Timeline of Communication Systems 1700 - 1800.* Retrieved March 23, 2010, from World - Information.Org: http://world-information.org/wio/infostructure/100437611796/100438659 771/?ic=100446325087

Zacker, C. (2001). *Network+ Certification Training Kit, Second Edition* . Retrieved November 20, 2010, from Microsoft: http://www.microsoft.com/mspress/books/toc/5507.aspx#TableOfContents

Index

10Base2, 263
10Base5, 256
10BaseT, 256
3G, 162
701 computer, 131
abacus, 14
ABC, 91, 119, 120, 144, 319
AC
    alternating current, 96, 99, 106, 109, 138
Ada Lovelace King, 193
Addograph Manufacturing Company, 62
adenine, 327
Alessandro Volta
    voltaic, 111
Altair 8800, 153
Alternating current, 104, 105, 109, 112
ALU
    arithmetic-logic unit, 166, 167, 169, 171, 176, 181

American Arithmometer Company. *See* William Seward Burroughs
AN/FSQ-7, 133
Analog computers, 137
ancient Greece, 93
Andre Marie-Ampere, 111
anode, 238
Antikythera device, 137
Apple Computers, 172
ASCC
    Automatic Sequence Controlled Calculator, 123
ASCII
    American Standard Code for Information Interchange, 83
ASYNCHRONOUS TRANSFER MODE, 288, 290
AT&T
    American Telephone and Telegraph, 73

Atanasoff – Berry Computer ABC, 127
Atanasoff-Berry Computer, 119, 320
Audion, 238
Babbage
  Charles Babbage, 41, 42, 46
Babylonian, 12
Baldwin Calculator. See Baldwin Pinwheel Calculator
Baldwin Computing Engine. *See* Baldwin Pinwheel Calculator
Baldwin Pinwheel Calculator, ix, 55
BASIC, 155
Beginner's All-purpose Symbolic Instruction Code. *BASIC*
Benjamin Franklin, 90
Bit-level parallelism, 323
BLAISE PASCAL, 21
Boolean math, 125
Boykin, 221
bridge, 256, 267, 268, 270
brouter, 268
brouters, 266
Brunsviga, 52, 53
Burroughs 5000 Master Control Program, 186
Burroughs Adding and Registering Machine Limited. *See* American Arithmometer
Burroughs Adding Machine Company, 58
Burroughs Corporation, 59
Burt Typographer, 83
bus, 181
bus topology, 253, 254
Calculating Clock, 142
capacitors, 90
Carlos Glidden, 83
Carrier Sense Multiple Access/Collision Detect, 240
cathode, 238
Census Bureau, 74, 76, 77, 78, 80
census of 1880, 74
Chappe brothers, 233
Charles A. Coffin, 98, 107, 108
Charles Babbage, xiv, 2, 34, 37, 38, 41, 44, 46, 193, 328
Charles F. Pidgin, 77
Charles Ranlegh Flint, 82, 130
Charles Seaton, 76

CheaperNet, 263
CIDR. *See* Classless Inter-Domain Routing
Circuit switching, 240, 289
Cisco Systems, 271
Clarence Ellis, 226
Class 2000 Accounting Machine, 72
Class 29 Post-Tronic Computer, 72
Classless Inter-Domain Routing, 270
Claude Chappe, 233
Clifford Berry, 119, 319
coax. *See* coaxial cable
coaxial cable, 256, 257, 263
Colossus, 125, 144
compiler, 200
Compiler, 200
Complex Number Calculator, 121, 122, 125
Compris Technologies, 74
computer virus, 303, 304, 305, 312
Computing Scale Company, 82
conductor, 110, 111, 112
control unit, 166, 167, 168, 169, 170
Core 2, 171
CP/M, 188
  Control Program for Microcomputers, 155
CPU
  CENTRAL PROCESSING UNIT, 165, 166, 167, 168, 170, 173, 174, 175, 176, 181, 205, 208, 209, 210, 320
CRAM, 73
Crédit Mobilier, 77
Crimeware, 313
CSMA/CA, 259, 276, 277, 284, 285
CSMA/CD, 240, 241, 254, 256, 257, 259, 276
CTRC
  Computing Tabulating Recording Corporation, 130
CTSS, 187
current electricity, 99
Current electricity, 99
Cut-through, 267
Cyrix, 171
cytosine, 327
Dalton Adding Machine, ix
  James L. Dalton, 63, 64
DARPA, 190

Data Link Layer, 267, 276
Data parallelism, 323
datagram, 289
data-link connection identifier, 290
Data-sending trojans, 307
DC
   direct current, 99, 102, 106
decode, 176
denial of service, 300, 307, 308, 309, 310,
   311, 312, 313
Dennis L. Moeller, 224
Difference Engine, 33, 34, 35, 36, 37, 39,
   40, 41, 42, 43, 45, 140, 193
Differential Analyzer, 138
Diffused Beam IrDA, 279
direct current, 99, 100, 101, 103, 105, 107,
   109, 110, 111, 112
Direct current, 100, 104, 112
Directed Beam IrDA, 279
Distance Vector, 270
DIX Ethernet, 257
DIX Ethernet II, 257
DNA, 322, 327
DNA circuitry, 327
DNA computer, 327
DOMAIN NAME SERVICE, 294
Dorr E. Felt, ix, 49
   Felt Comtometer, 49
DOS, 188
DSSS, 277, 278, 283
DTSS, 187
DYNAMIC HOST CONFIGURATION
   PROTOCOL, 294
E. Remington and Sons, 84
EBCDIC
   Extended Binary Coded Decimal
   Interchange Code, 83
Edison General Electric, 97, 98, 107, 108
EDVAC, 144
Edvard Scheutz. *See* Edvard Scheutz
Edwin Armstrong, 238
Egyptian, 12, 93
electric circuit, 109, 111
electric current, 112
electricity, 68, 88, 89, 90, 91, 92, 95, 96, 97,
   99, 100, 101, 102, 104, 105, 109, 110,
   111, 112
Elisha Gray, 236
email bomb, 312

Emeagwali, xiv, 225, 323
Enhanced Industry Standard Architecture,
   267
ENIAC, 82, 113, 119, 120, 127, 135, 142,
   144, 146, 166, 167, 168, 184, 204
Entanglement, 326
Ewald Georg von Kleist, 89
execute, 176
Fast Ethernet, 256
Felt and Tarrant Manufacturing Company,
   52
fetch, 176
FHSS, 275, 277, 278
file server, 143, 161
firewall, 268
FORmula TRANslation, 194, *FORTRAN*
FORTRAN, 132, 184, 193, 194, 195
Frame Relay, 288, 290, 295
Francis Hauksbee, 89
Frank Stephen Baldwin, 53
Frederick de Moleyn, 94
FTP, 294
FTP Trojan, 308
Gary Kildall, 155
gateway, 268
Gaulard – Gibbs transformer, 105, 106
General Electric, 98, 101, 107, 121
General Motors Batch System, 185
Georg Matthias Bose, 89
Georg Scheutz, 40
Georg Simon Ohm, 110, 111
George Antheil, 278
George Grant, 34, 44
George Robert Stibitz
   Stibitz, 121
George Westinghouse
   Westinghouse, 98, 105, 106, 131
Gigabit Ethernet, 257
Gilded Age, 65
GIS
   Global Information Solutions, 73
Gottfried Wilhelm von Leibniz, 23
Granville Woods, 217
graphical user interface, 189
GRID Compass, 157
Grimme, Natalis & Company. *See*
   Brunsviga
guanine, 327
Guglielmo Marconi, 237

Gustav Robert Kirchhoff, 110
Hamiltonian path problem, 327
Harvard Mark I, 123, 125
Hebrew, 12
Hedy Lamarr, 278
Henry Davy, 94
Henry Mill, 83
Henry Swan, 93
Herman Hollerith, 77, 81, 129, 130
Hippolyte Pixii, 92
Hollerith, ix, xiv, xvi, 4, 36, 48, 49, 56, 74,
    77, 78, 79, 80, 81, 82, 87, 147, 150, 193,
    194, 204, 232, 319, 321
Hollerith punch card, 79
Hollerith Tabulating Machine
    Herman Hollerith, 77, 79, 80
HomeRF, 283, 284
HomeRF Working Group, 284
Howard Aiken
    Aiken, 119, 122, 130
HTTP, 269, 294
Hubert Hopkins, 60
IBM, ix, 27, 113, 123, 129, 130, 131, 132,
    133, 134, 145, 146, 151, 168, 172, 175,
    178, 186, 187, 188, 189, 222, 224, 240,
    249, 253, 254, 255, 257, 260, 266, 281,
    292, 321
IGRP. *See* Interior Gateway Routing
    Protocol
incandescent lamp, 94
Industry Standard Architecture, 266
input, 123, 146, 153, 154, 156, 167, 176,
    180, 181, 205
Instruction-level parallelism, 323
insulator, 112
integrated circuit, 112, 113, 144, 145, 168,
    206, 320
integrated Services Digital Network, 289
Intel, 155, 171, 172, 210
interior gateway protocol, 270
International Business Machines
    IBM, 82, 129, 146
International Organization for Standards,
    253
International Time Recording Company,
    82
INTERNET CORPORATION FOR
    ASSIGNED NAMES AND
    NUMBERS, 296, 298, 304

Internet Engineering Task Force, 271
Internet Protocol, 295
INTERNIC, 296, 297
Interpreters, 201
IrDA, 277, 279, 281, 283
ISA. *Industry Standard Architecture*
ISO 17799, 316
J. Pierpont Morgan
    J. P. Morgan, 103
Jacob Leupold, 26
Jacquard, 36, 38, 78, 81, 193, 194
Jacquard Loom, 193
James Clerk Maxwell, 237
James Densmore, 84
James L. Dalton, 62
James Legrand Powers, 80
James Patterson, 130
James Ritty, 69
Janet Emerson Bashen, 226
JAVA, 198
Job Control Language, 186
John Atanasoff, 319
    Atanasoff, 119
John Patterson, 49, 131, 150
John Ritty, 68
John William Mauchly
    Mauchly, 320
Joseph Marie Jacquard, 81
Kirchhoff's Law, 110
Konrad Zuse, 120
LAN, 156, 161, 162, 239, 241, 246
laptop, 156
Leibniz, 26
Leonardo Torres y Quevedo, 45
Lewis Latimer, 107
Leyden jar, 89, 90
Link State, 270
Logical Link Control, 254
Lord Kelvin, 333
Lucent, 73
macaroni box. *See* Dorr E. Felt
Malware, 299
Mark E. Dean, 223
markup language, 199
Martin Wiberg, 34, 43
MCA. *Micro Channel Architecture*
Media Access Control, 254, 267, 283
Meucci
    Antonio Meucci, 236

Michael Faraday, 92

Micro Channel Architecture, 266

microchip
  microprocessor, 168

Microcode, 174

microprocessor
  central processing unit, 155, 168, 170, 171, 172, 174, 175, 176, 177, 181, 208, 209

MITS
  Micro Instrumentation and Telemetry Systems, 153

Model K, 121

Monroe Calculating Machine Company, 56

Moon – Hopkins Billing Machine Company
  Moon – Hopkins Manufacturing Company, 64

Moon – Hopkins Manufacturing Company, 64

Morse code, 96, 169

Motorola, 171

Multics, 187, 188

MULTICS, 187, 188

multistation access unit, 270

Multitasking, 188

Mylar, 73

NCR
  National Cash Register, 57, 59, 70, 72, 73, 74, 130

NETBEUI, 252, 268

NIC, 266, 267

Niels Bohr, 325

Nikola Tesla
  Tesla, 102

Nine's Complement, 50

Novell, 150, 189, 191, 252, 253, 261, 272

Object Oriented Programming, 198

Ohms, 111

Open Shortest Path First, 271

Open System Interconnection, 241, 253

Osborne, 157

OSI Reference Model, 254

OSPF. *See* Open Shortest Path First, *See* Open Shortest Path First

Otis Boykin, 221

Otto von Guericke, 88

parallel circuit, 110, 112

Parallel computing, 322

PARC, 190

PC
  Personal computers, 151

PCI. *Peripheral Component Interconnect*

PCMIA, 267

PDA, 162

peer-to-peer, 246

Peripheral Component Interconnect, 267

permanent virtual circuit, 289

Philipp Matthäus Hahn, 26

Pieter van Musschenbroek, 89

PL/M, 155

Polyphase, 112

polyphase transformers, 107

POTS, 240

Powers Accounting Machine Company, 80

procedural programming, 195, 196, 197, 198

Project MAC, 187

Project Whirlwind, 142, 188

Proxy Trojan, 308

PVC. *permanent virtual circuit*

Quantum computing, 324, 325, 326

qubits, 325

radiotelegraph, 236

RAM
  Random Access Memory, 153, 167, 181, 205, 206, 208, 209, 210

Receiver Signal Strength Indicator, 277

register, 68, 69, 71, 72, 181

Remington Rand, 63, 72, 80

Remote Access Trojan Horse, 306

Richard Feynman, 325

RIP. *See* Routing Information Protocol

Ritty's Incorruptible Cashier, 69

Robert Tarrant, 51

ROM
  Read Only Memory, 166, 174, 175, 180, 205, 206, 207, 208

ROM - BIOS, 175

Romans, 93

Rootkit, 301, 312

router, 255, 268

Routing Information Protocol, 270

routing protocol, 270

SABRE, 134
  Semi-Automatic Business Environment Research, 133, 134

SAGE, 133, 134, 180, 188

Semi-Automatic Ground Environment, 132, 133, 142, 204
Scheutz Calculator
Scheutz Difference Engine, 42
Scheutz Difference Engine, 42
Georg Scheutz, 41
Schickard, 19
scripting language, 198
Security Disabled Trojan, 307
series circuit, 109, 112
SMTP, 294
SNMP, 294
Spam, 301
Sperry Corporation, 59
spread spectrum, 277
spyware, 305, 313, 314
SSEC
Selective Sequence Electronic Calculator, 130, 131
Standard Adding Machine Company, 61
star topology, 253
static electricity, 99
Step Reckoner, 41
stepped drum, 26, 49
Steve Jobs, xiv, 159, 223
Stored-and-forward switching, 268
SUBNET, 296, 297
Sundstrand Adding Machine Company, 63
supercomputer, 162
Superposition, 326
switch, 121, 255, 267, 268, 319
Tabulating Machine Company, 80, 81, 82, 129, 130, 147, 194
TCP, 189, 240, 250, 251, 252, 253, 259, 260, 261, 268, 290, 292, 293, 294, 295, 297, 310, 311
TCP/IP, 240, 252, 253, 292, 293, 294, 297, 310
Ted Hoff, 223
Tesla Coil, 103
Tesla Electric Company, 103
Tesla Light and Manufacturing Company, 103
the Bankers' and Merchants' Registering Accountant, 233
the Gilded Age, 56, 59, 65
ThickNet, 257, 262, 263
ThinNet, 257, 262, 263
Thomas Arithmometer, ix, 26, 54

Thomas Edison, 95, 100, 101, 105
Edison, 93, 94, 95, 100, 105
Thomas J. Watson, 130, 131, 133
Thomas J. Watson Jr, 131
Thomas J. Watson, Sr, 131
Thomson-Houston, 105
Thomson-Houston Electric Company, 107
thymine, 327
Time-sharing, 187
TMC
Tabulating Machine Company, 80, 81, 130
Token Ring, 253, 254
Torres y Quevedo, 46
Transformer, 112
transistor, 7, 54, 56, 67, 112, 113, 114, 115, 116, 118, 131, 144, 145, 149, 161, 162, 168, 205, 209, 320, 321, 324, 325, 328, 333
Transmission Control Protocol, 240
triode, 238
Trojan horse, 305, 306, 307, 308, 309, 312, 314
UNIVAC, 72, 129, 144, 145, 186
UNIX, 172, 188, 189, 249, 250
US CERT, 316
USER DATAGRAM PROTOCOL, 260, 294
vacuum tube, 94, 95, 113, 131, 144, 180, 204, 320
Vannevar Bush, 139, 189
Victor Comptometer Corporation
Felt and Tarrant Manufacturing Company, 52
Voice over Internet Protocol, 229
VoIP, 229
von Neumann architecture, 146, 156, 167, 168, 176
Wallace Eckert, 130
WAN, 162, 238, 241, 287
Warren De la Rue, 94
Westinghouse Electric, 105
Wiberg Difference Engine, 43
Wide Area Network, 287
Wi-fi, 285
Wi-Fi, 156, 162
Wilhelm Schickard, 142
Willgodt Theophil Odhner, 52
William Burt, 83

William C. Hunt, 77, 78
William Gilbert, 88
William H. Hopkins, 59
William Seward Burroughs, 56, 57, 59, 233
William Sturgeon, 92
WiMax, 285
Wireless Local Area Network, 237, 275
Wireless Wide Area Networks, 275, 288
WLAN, 162, 237, 241, 275, 276, 277, 279, 283, 284, 285

worm, 299, 303, 304, 305, 307, 308, 312, 315
write-back, 176
X.25, 288, 289, 290, 295
Xerox, 190
Xerox Network Systems, 252
Xerox Star, 190
XHTML, 199
XML, 200
Zilog, 157

Index of Graphics

Figure 1 Abaci Chinese and Roman 14
Figure 2 Antikythera Device 17
Figure 3 The Calculating Clock 20
Figure 4 the Pascaline 21
Figure 5 The Step Reckoner 23
Figure 6 Hahn Calculator 26
Figure 7 Leupold Calculator 26
Figure 8 Thomas Arithmometer 27
Figure 9 Schilt Calculator 29
Figure 10 Hill Arithmometer 30
Figure 11 Leonardo's Calculator 32
Figure 12 Babbage Difference Engine .... Error! Bookmark not defined.
Figure 13 Scheutz Difference Engine 40
Figure 14 Wiberg Difference Engine 43
Figure 15 Grant Difference Engine 44
Figure 16 pinwheel patent drawings .... Error! Bookmark not defined.
Figure 17 Step Drum Mechanism 49
Figure 18 Felt Comptometer (1890) 50
Figure 19 Macaroni Box 51
Figure 20 Brunsviga Mini .... Error! Bookmark not defined.
Figure 21 Baldwin Pinwheel Calculator 54
Figure 22 Burroughs' Accountant 58

Figure 23 The Standard *61*
Figure 24 The Dalton *63*
Figure 25 Moon-Hopkins Billing Machine *65*
Figure 26 Ritty's Incorruptible *71*
Figure 27 Hollerith Card *80*
Figure 28 Hollerith Tabulator *82*
Figure 29 Typewriter circa 1878 .... *83*
Figure 30 Volta Battery *91*
Figure 31 Edison Light Bulb *95*
Figure 32 series circuit *109*
Figure 33 Parallel Circuit *110*
Figure 34 Vacuum Tubes, Transistors Microchips *113*
Figure 35 Early Microprocessor *118*
Figure 36 Von Neumann architecture *135*
Figure 37 inside ENIAC *144*
Figure 38 IBM 1401 Computer *145*
Figure 39 IBM PC2 .... *151*
Figure 40 The Altair 8800 .... *153*
Figure 41 Apple IIe with disk drives *154*
Figure 42 Laptop *156*
Figure 43 Osborne *157*
Figure 44 Grid Compass *158*
Figure 45 Microsoft Surface Tablet Computer *160*
Figure 46 Handmade Transistor board *168*
Figure 47 Cooke-Whetstone Telegraph *236*
Figure 48 Bus Network *256*
Figure 49 Star Network *256*
Figure 50 Virtual Token Ring *259*
Figure 51 Coaxial Cable *264*
Figure 52 Fiber Optic Cable *267*
Figure 53 Unshielded Twisted Pairs *267*
Figure 54 Basic Piconet *282*
Figure 55 Scatternet *284*